Learning Disabilities in Home, School, and Community

Learning Disabilities
in Home, School,
and Community

WILLIAM M. CRUICKSHANK

 SYRACUSE UNIVERSITY PRESS   1977

LC
4580
.C78
1977

Library of Congress Cataloging in Publication Data

Cruickshank, William M
  Learning disabilities in home, school, and community.

  First ed. published in 1967 under title: The brain-injured child in home, school, and community.
  Includes bibliographies and index.
  1. Brain-damaged children—Education.
2. Learning disabilities.   I. Title.
LC4580.C78   1977   371.9'16   77-473
ISBN 0-8156-2179-5

To DOROTHY WAGER CRUICKSHANK

William M. Cruickshank, Ph.D., is the well-known author of dozens of articles and books. He is Professor of Maternal and Child Health, School of Public Health; Professor of Psychology, College of Arts and Sciences; and Professor of Education, School of Education, University of Michigan, Ann Arbor. He is also Director of the Institute for Mental Retardation and Related Disabilities, University of Michigan.

Contents

List of Figures

List of Tables

Preface

This book, originally published as *The Brain-Injured Child in Home, School, and Community* in 1967, is for parents, teachers, and others who work on a day-to-day basis with learning disabled children. It has been requested by parents and teachers in Birmingham, Alabama, in Milwaukee, Philadelphia, Toronto, and in many other cities where professional activities have carried me. This is a book I wanted to prepare for a long time, for parents and teachers are faced with monumental challenges in their learning disabled children.

Over the years we had three exceedingly normal children born to us, and in addition we have been fortunate enough to have had five children born to other parents loaned to us for long periods of time. These have been normal children, yet as parents we know how much we have needed help, guidance, and counsel in rearing them to take their places in their societies. These have been young people with no special needs reflecting unusual mental or physical deviations. These were children who in themselves were capable of meeting the challenge of their family and their world head-on without major external assistance. These were children whose parents were educated, indeed with extensive backgrounds in the profession of child development. Yet these parents needed help, and undoubtedly they could have used more than they sought.

How much more do parents need assistance if a child with major differences is born into the family circle—a child with learning disabilities in this instance? How much more do parents without backgrounds in child development need to have assistance with the complicated problems that learning disability brings to their children? What of the parents of limited education? How do they meet these complicated and highly technical problems of child rearing or learn of the professional resources available in their community?

Teachers, too, are faced with problems in learning disabled children which most of them are unprepared to handle. These children will be in their classes, however, and these children must be served.

This book is intended to provide parents, teachers, pediatricians, and others who work with children with some insights into the growth problems and the education and homelife problems of learning disabled children. It is not a book pertaining to normal children except coincidentally. It is not inclusive, although we have tried to write about those things which many parents have told us they hoped would be included in such a book as this. There will be unintended omissions that future revisions may fill in as they become apparent. It is a book intended to provide parents and teachers of learning disabled children with information which may make their lives and those of their children more satisfying and less a terrifying struggle.

This volume is not intended to be a detailed reference work. It is obvious from its length and the number of topics which have been covered that it will be more extensive than intensive. No attempts have been made to develop full statements regarding the teaching of reading, number concepts, or motor training, for example. These topics are covered fully in other places. The intent of this volume is to give parents and teachers an overview to the issues germane to the adjustment of their learning disabled children. If the volume provides a basis for further exploration and study, it will have accomplished its purpose.

It must be pointed out, too, that this volume represents but one point of view concerning the education of learning disabled children—the author's. There is general agreement within the professions concerning the point of view represented here, but there are, of course, differences. The volume is not intended to be a survey of all possible approaches to the education of learning disabled children. It is a statement of the approach I have found helpful in understanding the problem, and I have found effective in meeting the needs of learning disabled children with whom I have worked.

In preparing this revision of the 1967 edition, I have not attempted to rewrite the entire volume. Rather, I have attempted to bring the book's contents up to date in terms of vocabulary and terminology, a matter to be discussed more fully in Chapter 1, and to expand and re-emphasize my points of view regarding the nature of learning disabilities in children and youth.

Also addressed briefly here is parental concern for the use of medications to control the behavior of children. I have invited Maria J. Paluszny,

M.D., a long-time colleague and Assistant Director and Chief of Clinical Services in the Institute for the Study of Mental Retardation and Related Disabilities at the University of Michigan, to write Chapter 12. Dr. Paluszny has had extensive experience with children, public schools, and community child guidance clinics. As a medical person she also understands and appreciates the role of neuropsychiatric problems of children in the educational process.

Finally, I have addressed the problem of learning disabilities in adolescents in Chapter 10, a topic regarding which few professionals have much experience, but one which must be given a full measure of concern in the immediate future. Children with learning disabilities do grow up, and in so doing they do not always lose their disabilities.

William M. Cruickshank

Ann Arbor, Michigan
Fall 1976

Acknowledgments

I am very much indebted to many learning disabled children who over the years have permitted me to study and to work with them in order to better understand how their needs and those of others who would follow them could be met. In particular Jeffrey, John, Keith, Gregory, George, David, Stephen, Mark, and Kertin have unknowingly made themselves available to our study for long periods of time, and from their friendship I have learned much about how they learn, perceive, laugh, cry, and grow.

During the period 1962–67, the National Institute of Mental Health sponsored a program in cooperation with Syracuse University for the preparation of teachers of what was then called hyperactive emotionally disturbed and brain-injured children. The full discussion of that project has been reported elsewhere. The experience of the author and his associates in that project indicated the importance of more fully involving parents and teachers of learning disabled children in the educational process. Previous staff colleagues and graduate students who were associated with the project and who must be recognized as having contributed in many ways both to my thinking and to the project include: Miss Ruth Cheves, lecturer, and Dr. Peter Knoblock, professor of special education, Syracuse University; Dr. Gene L. Cary, then at State University of New York College of Medicine in Syracuse, consultant psychiatrist; Mrs. Pauline Stanley, demonstration teacher; Dr. John B. Junkala, now of Boston College; Dr. Andrew Shotick, now at the University of Georgia; Dr. David Lema, now at Ohio State University; Dr. Eleanore Westhead, now at the University of Virginia; Dr. James L. Paul, presently at the University of North Carolina; and Dr. John Garrett, currently at the University of Louisville. These persons all held appointments in some relation to the project at Syracuse University during the period 1962–67. Chapters 7, 8, and 9, about teaching materials and the educational program, were partially but specifically developed, as indicated, by project personnel for the program.

The author is also indebted to Dr. E. Harris Nober, now professor at the University of Massachusetts, and Mr. Frank Dudziak, then of the Photography Laboratory at Syracuse University, who have likewise been most helpful in the preparation of some of the illustrative materials.

I am also indebted to Dr. Jeannie Johns, program associate in special education, and to Lawrence J. Lewandowski, research assistant, both of the Institute for the Study of Mental Retardation and Related Disabilities at the University of Michigan, for their careful reading of the first edition and their suggestions for the revision. Mr. Jessie W. Barr, head, and Ms. Pat Helland, a member of the staff of the Instructional Technology Unit, Institute for the Study of Mental Retardation and Related Disabilities, have assisted me in the preparation of some photographic materials for this edition. Likewise, Ms. M. Frances Ingram and Ms. Nancy Scarbro, my secretaries, and secretarial personnel of the Institute's Word Processing Center, have been most helpful in preparing drafts of the manuscript before publication.

W.M.C.

Learning Disabilities in Home, School, and Community

"Whenever the school has tried to go it alone, it has ended up with a program which, even if exemplary, is yet isolated and has low long-term gain. We should begin to recognize that the child grows up in a total milieu, and it is this total milieu which is the remedial environment."

William C. Morse

An Introduction to the Learning Disabled Child

O F ALL TYPES of exceptional children, the learning disabled child is one of the most complex. Good teaching or programming for learning disabled children as well as good home planning require the services and skills of people from many professions. In all of the needed professions there is a shortage of persons who are interested in the learning disabled child and who have the requisite preparation and practical experience to work with him. This personnel shortage is a very real problem, as most parents of learning disabled children can testify, and is accounted for in part by the brief history of this entire field. This shortage is recognized as a serious factor throughout these pages as the needs and characteristics of learning disabled children are considered.

Interest in the learning disabled child has developed relatively recently. In the United States initial research in the psychological and educational characteristics and needs of learning disabled children began in Michigan with Drs. Heinz Werner and Alfred A. Strauss about 1940. These two researchers, one a comparative psychologist, the other a neuropsychiatrist, were gifts to America from Nazi Germany. Together they did pioneer research for more than a decade, seeking to learn more about the ways in which learning disabled children comprehend—how they see, hear, feel, and understand their world. While the studies of these two important researchers centered around learning disabled children who were also mentally retarded, their findings have stimulated others to continue studies with children of higher intellectual levels. Indeed, much of what Werner and Strauss learned about retardates has been shown by others to apply equally to other classifications of neurologically handicapped children.

In the decades since the Werner-Strauss studies, relatively little professional sophistication has developed. While there are some highly skilled persons in all of the professions dealing with learning disabled children, these persons are too few to serve the needs nationally, and they are too scattered to provide any uniform pattern of quality service. For many years some parents will have to travel great distances to bring their children to qualified diagnostic personnel, and they will have to search even farther for the technical educational services required. The situation here described is, quite frankly, discouraging, but it is improving. In the years since 1940, and particularly since 1960, tremendous strides have been taken to educate parents and to provide services, skilled professional personnel, and research personnel so that today there is greater potential than ever before for learning disabled children. The heroic efforts being made by professionals in this field, however, have not yet met the need, and much remains to be done.

WHAT DO WE CALL HIM?

In this book we have chosen to speak of learning disabled children. We did not always do so, as those who know the first edition of this book will quickly recognize. When the volume was first published it was titled *The Brain-Injured Child in Home, School and Community.* The term "brain-injured" was utilized for two purposes: first, it represented to the author a more exact orientation to the problem than other terms of reference which appeared in the literature, and, second, this book, under that title, formed a link in a series of publications relating to the concept of brain-injury in children. In the climate of a decade later, the term "brain injury" long used in my writings has given way to the more generally accepted term of "learning disabilities," in just the same way as "perceptual handicap" employed by Kephart, "language disturbance" employed by Kirk and his colleagues, and "minimal cerebral dysfunction" and other terms have also fallen before the general usage to the term "learning disability." This does not mean that the term "learning disabilities" is more accurate than the others which it has supplanted. It means it is more acceptable to the parents of the children who are so characterized. The use of a new term does not mean that clarity of the problem has been achieved. Rather greater confusion has often been the result.

Recently a reviewer noted that this author had changed a chapter title from his long-standing term "brain-injured" to "learning disabilities." The comment of the reviewer was that the chapter title should have remained as it formerly was, because the writing was more in terms of the brain-injured child than of learning disabilities! The two terms, practically and functionally, are synonymous from this author's point of view. The latter grew out of the first. If the learning disability chapter sounded like writing on brain injury, the reviewer is insightful, for the term "learning disability," as shall be discussed later, is defined as learning problems resulting from perceptual processing deficits which in turn are based in the function or dysfunction of some portion of the central nervous system. The two concepts are one and the same. The Wepman Committee definition of learning disabilities to be noted later emphasizes the perceptual-neurological relationship of learning disabilities. It is in large part the failure of many persons to recognize and understand accurately diagnosed learning disabilities which leads to much of the confusion apparent in the several disciplines at the present time.

We do not wish to belabor the problem of terminology. Yet it is unfortunate that vocabulary is permitted to confuse issues. Instead of providing a basis of accuracy as words and their usage should do, the concept of learning disability, begun with a specific problem in mind, has had appended to it concepts and problems of child growth and development which were never a part of the original definition. Children with problems of learning are not the same as learning disabled children if the latter are understood for what they really are and are adequately defined. We shall consider this matter later in this chapter.

In attempting to study the available literature, parents and teachers can easily become confused. More than forty terms appear in the professional literature, each slightly different from the others, all pertaining essentially to the same group of children. It is thus not difficult to understand how confusion develops. As one investigates the literature pertaining to learning disabled children, the list of terms quickly becomes a lengthy one. Among those most frequently encountered are the following:

Brain-injured child (sometimes with the adjective *minimal*)
Brain-damaged child
Minimal neurological handicap
Hyperkinetic child
Hyperactive child
"Organic" child
Child with perceptual disability or the perceptually handicapped child

Dysfunctioning child
Child with special learning problems (often *special* is dropped and the word *specific* is used)
Child with developmental imbalances or developmental insufficiencies
Child with language disorders
Child with cognitive defects
Child with dyslexia
Maturational lag
Minimal brain dysfunction
Neurophysiological immaturity
Central nervous system (CNS) dysfunction
Chronic brain syndrome

Why parents should be confused becomes quite apparent when one examines even this incomplete list of professional terms. If the child happens to live in the state of Michigan, some educators refer to him as a "perceptually disabled child." If the child is a resident of California, his education may be provided if he is classified as an "educationally handicapped" or "neurologically handicapped" child. In Bucks County, Pennsylvania, he will be placed in a class for children with "language disorders." If he moves from California to New York State, he may change from an "educationally handicapped child" to a "brain-injured child." On the other hand, if he moves from Michigan to Montgomery County, Maryland, he will stop being a "perceptually disabled child" and become a "child with specific learning disabilities." If by chance his parents move to Russia, he will be classified as one with "temporarily retarded psychological development!"

Fortunately, the child stays the same, and his needs remain relatively static, changing only in terms of his growth and chronological age. The banner under which he flies his course is what changes. His needs, problems, and adjustment potential in home, school, and community are not altered; they must be met despite the battle of words and regardless of the community in which he lives. Parents, however, will have to adjust quickly to the terminology of the field and be patient with those who may find it more convenient for one reason or another to use different terminology.

In this book the term "learning disabled child" will be utilized throughout. It is clear to this writer and to others that the adjectives "learning disabled" are not entirely satisfactory. At this point it is sufficient to recognize the inadequacies of the term while at the same time recognizing that every other term is equally deficient.

Even when it is not possible to diagnose a child definitively, it may be possible to state that he "functions like a learning disabled child." It may not be possible to diagnose a lesion, for example, but it is possible to state that the child's characteristics are identical, or at least similar, to those of children known to have injury. Many children with similar characteristics will in fact be found to have definite neurological injuries, and when diagnostic procedures are improved or new ones are developed these children may be correctly classified. While proper diagnosis is important, the symptomology—the characteristics of the child—is more important, because it is the latter with which educators, psychologists, and others who are involved in habilitative programs and therapy must deal. The diagnosis of specific brain injury is not unimportant, but it is less important than developing a careful description of the child—how he behaves, what his learning characteristics are, and what his potential level of function is.

The term "learning disabled child" contains the germ of an idea and has gained sufficient although confused acceptance so that meanings are translated from one speaker to another, from one profession to another. No terminology will be completely satisfactory. The situation is similar to the terminological problems revolving around the use of the word *blind* or the term "hard of hearing." The legal definition of *blindness* is broad enough to include many individuals who have usable vision. When an individual is reported to be blind, the professional persons who are to implement the diagnosis must immediately ask for a definition of blindness in terms of the usable vision which is possessed. Similarly, the term "hard of hearing" provides only a frame of reference within which physicians, educators, psychologists, and others may work. Always this term must be carefully defined so that it is known what the concept of "hard of hearing" really means.

So, too, definition will be required with the term "learning disabled" This term connotes quite fully a type of problem, a constellation of characteristics, an aspect of child growth and disability which immediately makes possible a meeting of the minds among professionals. As such the term is serviceable and functional. The term is undoubtedly more realistic and representative of the child's actual problems than some of the terms placing an undue emphasis on only one phase of child development (e.g., language disorder), or which in reality gloss over a problem to make it what it is not (e.g., maturational lag), or which tend to apologize for the total matter (e.g., minimal brain dysfunction). It is important to this writer to call a spade a spade, to put the problem in the center of the diagnostic dimension in which realistically it probably is. We shall see that learning disability has a direct relationship to both perception and the neurological status of the child. As such a title which carries the concept of brain injury may be more accurate than one which does not. The issue appears to me more a matter of taste than of inaccuracy. There is nothing final about brain injury; much can be done to help the child grow and adjust. No one need be ashamed of this disability area or feel that all is hopeless. Much can be done, and use of the correct term is a good springboard for action programs.

The term "minimal brain dysfunction" appears frequently in the literature. Derivatives of this term are also often seen. As has been indicated in the preceding paragraph, the use of the word *minimal* frequently serves to minimize the problem in the minds of parents or to place it on a level of less seriousness than it deserves. In reality, these children present the most complicated of all learning and adjustment problems; their problems are as great as those of any other class of handicapped children. There is nothing minimal about any brain dysfunction. If the human organism has experienced any kind of neurological injury, serious physical manifestations or perceptual and learning problems may result. The brain, while having some localization of function, is essentially a unitary organ. A lesion in one portion of the brain may impair function in all aspects of cerebral activity. The term "minimal" has often been used professionally to differentiate children who have gross-motor problems such as cerebral palsy from those neurologically impaired children whose handicaps take the form of perceptual adjustment or learning dysfunction. One type of problem, however, is just as serious from the individual's point of view as is another. Indeed, from some points of view the child with the latter types of problems may have much more difficulty adjusting than the child with the former. One child may have both gross-motor and perceptual problems. This book, however, is essentially concerned with the child who is not characterized by cerebral palsy or by serious gross-motor disabilities, although what we say is appropriate to many children with cerebral palsy and other clinical types of neurological disabilities. Someone has said that the usage of the term "minimal brain dysfunction" is just about as inappropriate as referring to a woman as being a little bit pregnant, and indeed the analogy is apt. It is pretty much an all-or-none situation from the point of view of the functional impact of the brain lesion on learning, adjustment, and personality integrity.

THE PROBLEM DEFINED

Just as professional people and parents moan about the inadequacies of terminology, so do they state that the problem cannot be defined. The seeming lack of definition is echoed in the halls of Congress as well as in the offices of local superintendents of schools. The problem is not the lack of a definition, but the presence of too many definitions. The problem is not one of being unable to comprehend the issue of learning disabilities, but is in large measure a reflection of the superficiality of understanding brought to this phase of child development by a large and ever-growing number of inadequately prepared professional people. It is a commentary on the level of academic preparation in colleges and universities which purport to produce qualified persons in this field. There are a number of published definitions which have been in the literature for some time. In many ways these are more than adequate, and the poor or innacurate statements could easily be ignored. More attention has been given to disagreeing with minutiae in these definitional statements than to the matter of reaching a logical consensus on what the problem really is. Concern over definition has become an exercise in futility and is reminiscent of the medieval arguments of theologians who were concerned with the population of angels who could at one time occupy the space on the head of a pin.

Of course the problem can be defined. Those who repeatedly state that it cannot be defined draw the famous red herring across the face of the problem and use this argument to support a desire to do nothing about it. The problem can be defined as easily as can any other human problem, and those who wring their hands saying it cannot must be ignored, for they have held up progress and services to children and youth for too long a time.

Learning disability is the result of something. In the perspective of this author learning disability is the direct result of a *perceptual processing deficit* (PPD). Perception and perceptual processing are neurologically based. Hence, if there is a perceptual processing deficit, there has to be a neurological deficit, dysfunction, or other term, whether or not the present state of neurological diagnosis permits a definitive identification of the problem. If a perceptual processing deficit can be identified psychologically or educationally (or, in the case of auditory processing deficits, by speech pathology or audiology), then an educational and social program can be developed. It is not necessary to have a specific neurological diagnosis. Such would be helpful, particularly if controlled research is a goal, but it is not an absolute necessity. Much can be done for children who never see a neurologist, and most of the children with learning disabilities will not.

We have stated that there are several definitions of the problem of learning disabilities. One criticism which can be leveled at a number of these statements is that the definition is essentially one of exclusion. It is perhaps easier to state what the problem is not than to define the problem by inclusion. We choose to consider the essence of the problem and to seek a definition which is inclusive and provides a basis for educational planning. Such a definition has been developed, and it is stated here in full. Later in this book we shall discuss elements of this definition in order to provide clarity to the problem.

The definition we select to discuss is that presented by Nicholas Hobbs who, as editor of a set of significant volumes relating to issues in classification of children, organized a series of nationally based committees to examine definitional problems in many aspects of exceptionality in children and youth. One of the committees was charged with the definition of learning disabilities. The committee was composed of Joseph Wepman, Ph.D., Chairman, University of Chicago; William Cruickshank, Ph.D., University of Michigan; Cynthia Deutsch, Ph.D., New York University; Ann Morency, Ph.D., University of Chicago; and Charles Strother, Ph.D., University of Washington. These people over a two-year period examined the problem and the existing definitions, some of which were quite adequate in parts, and then developed a statement which received rigorous critique from others. Since the problem presented by children with learning disabilities is essentially an educational one (in terms of the great amount of time such children spend in an educational setting during their formative years), the authors defined the problem in relation to its psychoeducational reality. A distinction was made between those children who have problems of learning and learning disabled children. The former may be related to poor initial teaching, problems of mother-child separation at kindergarten years, broken homes, emotional tension, or a myriad of other socioemotional factors. Learning disabilities, however, have a neurophysiological base which is specific to perceptual processing deficits.

These are children who can see. There is no visual acuity problem or problems related to visual muscle imbalance, for example. These are children who find it difficult to translate what they see into an appropriate motor function, i.e., a visual perceptual processing problem. These are children who can hear, but who cannot appropriately translate auditory stimuli into socially expected communication systems, i.e., an auditory perceptual processing problem. So with the other sensory modalities. The key work is *processing*. The deficiencies become apparent and basic to the educational situation when it is observed that children are unable to make a one-to-one connection between sensory stimuli and socially expected responses. Learning disabilities result. To emphasize the problem, the Wepman Committee speaks of "specific learning disability"—an attempt to relate the perceptual processing deficit to a specific sensory system and thus to a specific educational outcome or maladjustment. These then "are children or youth of any age who demonstrate a substantial deficiency in a particular aspect of academic achievement because of perceptual or perceptual-motor handicaps, regardless of etiology or other contributing factors. The term 'perceptual' as used here relates to those mental (neurological) processes through which the child acquires his basic alphabets of sounds and form. The term 'perceptual handicap' refers to inadequate ability in such areas as the following: recognizing fine differences between auditory and visual discriminating features underlying the sounds used in speech and the orthographic forms used in reading; retaining and recalling those discriminated sounds and forms in both short and long-term memory; ordering the sounds and forms sequentially, both in sensory and motor acts (Wepman 1968); distinguishing figure-ground relationships (Frostig et al. 1961); recognizing spatial and temporal orientations; obtaining closure (Kirk and Bateman 1962); integrating intersensory information (Birch and Lefford 1964); relating what is perceived to specific motor functions (Kephart 1963). Impairment of the processes involved in perception may result from accident, disease, or injury; from lags in development; or from environmental shortcomings. Impairment of perception may distort or disturb the cellular system and/or the normal function of one or more sensory systems."

In later chapters and sections of this book we will be discussing some of the aspects of this definition in greater detail, and we will add some elements to the definition which are related to but not specifically mentioned in it. The definition to which we subscribe and which has been stated above is a definition by inclusion: it tells us what learning disabilities are. Learning disabilities are revealed in a child who has difficulty in discrimination, in long- and short-term memory, in intersensory organization, and in other basic neurologically based functions which result in perceptual processing deficits and which in turn result in learning disabilities. The positive features of this definition are important, for they not only tell us what the problem is, but they contain the elements necessary in a basic program of teacher education, of psychological training and development, and day-to-day educational planning.

HOW, WHEN, AND WHERE DID IT HAPPEN?

Parents are often stunned when they learn that their child is brain injured or are informed that their child's learning disability is or may be related to a possible neurological dysfunction. Their initial shock is understandable; their problem is real, and they may rightly be stunned. The notion of brain injury, neurological problem, perceptual handicap, or learning disability summons up threatening historical concepts to many people. Parents may know of a relative or the friend of a friend who was reported to be brain injured and has serious problems of motor control, locomotion, or communication. Imaginary pictures of these same problems being invested in their own child quickly come to mind for concerned parents.

Other parents seek to divest themselves of responsibility and quickly recall that "my mother-in-law" was a most unusual person. Joey's problem "must have been transmitted through my wife's side." One mother informed the writer when we were discussing the diagnostic information about her child:

> I married beneath my family, at least everyone reminded me of this when I was married. Many times my parents reported to me things in my husband's family which then sounded like little things, but which I now see are important. There was an uncle of his who was an alcoholic. There was an aunt or a cousin, I believe, who had epilepsy. Somebody else had all sorts of trouble and had several miscarriages. All of these are things which caused Bobby's problem.

While there may indeed have been some relationship between the brain injury and one or two of these incidents, the likelihood is that there is no causal relationship whatsoever between any of them and the production of Bobby and his perceptual or learning problems. Efforts to place blame help no one and generally only cause more tension within the home.

Few data regarding the causes of these neurophysiological problems are available to give direction to professional people or comfort to parents of learning disabled children. Neurological injuries can be experienced while the child is still in the uterus (prenatally); during the birth process (perinatally); or as a result of many types of accidents or illnesses which children may experience in their early years of living (postnatally). While scientists understand much of what may happen to the embryo or fetus as it develops within the mother, they do not yet know how to prevent many things from happening to the developing organism or how to insure that all infants will be delivered as normal functioning human beings. Sometimes a spontaneous developmental arrest is experienced by the fetus (the developing baby) which will result in a neurological injury. Accidents or diseases sometimes may affect the maturing fetus despite nature's having provided a unique protective device for it during the nine months of fetal development. German measles (rubella), a devastating producer of disabilities if contracted by the mother during the early months of pregnancy, should, with the perfection of new vaccines, be a matter of history.

Unfortunately it is not yet. At present, this disease accounts for many types of disability in children and is an important agent in the production of brain-injured children.

The exact role of genetics in the production of brain injury remains vague. Certain evidence does seem to indicate some hereditary causes of injury, but conclusive information is not yet available. Considerable interest has resulted in some initial efforts in studying both the genetic and familial aspects of learning disabilities, but definitive data are lacking. At any rate, parents as yet have no control over these elements, and while they cannot divorce themselves of responsibility for the welfare of the child and his future, they should not blame themselves for the problem or allow guilt feelings to prevent the establishment of effective action programs. A learning disabled child has been produced by whatever cause. Time is too precious, too short; the issue is too great for parents to allow their energies to be siphoned off into useless guilt feelings and emotionalism. The problem must be faced squarely and action programs initiated in order to help the child make the most of a poor situation and to bring him to the limits of his adjustment and learning capacities at the earliest possible moment.

Oftentimes parents and others place blame for the child's condition upon careless physicians or nurses. The medical and allied professions readily admit that errors do occur, but carelessness on the part of physicians or others who work with newborn infants is by no means as frequent as some would like to believe. In itself, carelessness is an exceedingly minor factor, indeed rare, in the production of a learning disabled child. The relationship between birth injury and neurological impairment is generally known. Contrary to some statements, however, birth injury does not account for the majority of neurologically handicapped children. In a study done in New Jersey, the causative factors or etiology of approximately 35 percent of more than fourteen hundred reported cerebral palsy children could be traced to birth-process–related factors. While this is a large percentage, it by no means represents a majority. It is not known what percentage of learning disabilities, as considered in this book, are caused by injuries during birth. It is felt, however, that the incidence from this factor is certainly no greater than in the case of cerebral palsy, and the percentage perhaps is less.

A larger than average fetus, the inability of the ligaments of the pelvic arch to extend sufficiently, a too-small pelvic arch, the unnatural position of the fetus during delivery, the inability to start breathing immediately, and other similar physical factors singly or in combination may account for neurological injuries which will later cause learning and adjustment problems.

Once again, these are matters over which parents have little or no control. These are not things for which a parent can feel a personal responsibility, about which a father or mother should feel guilty. They are not happenings for which one parent should blame the other. Again, these facts must be faced realistically. Instead of internalizing the problem, the energies of both parties should be directed toward assisting the child and providing for him completely and positively. Parents will need one another too much during the life development of the learning disabled child to do anything that will cause barriers to exist between them.

It is not our intention to absolve parents of responsibility for caring for their child and helping him with his problems. We are concerned, however, that parents often are so distraught by their feelings of responsibility for their child's problems that they are unable to focus on more important issues. In some instances parental carelessness may have been a factor in causing the injury, but this too is a rarity. Even if such carelessness is involved, it is anything but an intentional situation. Guilt feelings, destroyers of effective action, are often at the base of serious difficulties between husband and wife; and they are the unseen factors which cause unhappiness in the individual and disharmony in what should be a strong parental team. Parents whose lives are being seriously distorted by feelings of guilt induced by their real or imagined role in the production of a learning disabled child are well advised to seek professional assistance from competent psychiatrists or psychologists. By reducing the force of their guilt feelings through therapy, they will be more able to direct all emotional and intellectual energies toward effective and realistic planning for the child.

A learning disabled child needs every stable external support possible to assist him in developing a strong ego. The emphasis must be on stability, however. An unstable child will not be assisted by unstable parents or by parents whose energies are dissipated by guilt.

In the postnatal period, or after the delivery of the baby, numerous causative factors may be related to perceptual processing deficits. In young children these are most commonly accidents resulting from normal childhood activities. Obviously, many children experience injuries during play, from falls, or on other occasions from illnesses accompanied by high or prolonged fevers. Brain injury and its subsequent impact on learning could, under certain circumstances, be related to practically any childhood illness. Fortunately, most illnesses are not of sufficient severity or duration as to be significant. Mumps, measles, whooping cough, scarlet fever, meningitis, and others may be important in this relationship. The mere occurrence of one of them, however, should not be regarded as the causative factor in the production of a specific neurological injury. Most of the time, children recover from these diseases with no subsequent effects whatsoever.

In recent years a professional debate has arisen regarding the relationship between artificial food coloring as additives and the creation of hyperactivity and learning disabilities. It has likewise been suggested that the total ecological situation has to be considered in relation to the developing child organism. Is air pollution a factor in the maldevelopment of the infant brain? What about the biochemical imbalances noted in some children? Do these factors alone or in combination have a relationship to learning disabilities? What about medications taken in the normal course of a pregnancy? Is it possible that these have effects on the developing fetal nervous system which have not been assumed to happen? The fact of addicted infants born of hard-drug addicted mothers opens up questions as to whether or not the placenta is in reality a screen to protect the fetus from all drugs—any medications taken by the mother during a normal pregnancy. While we do not have answers to these questions, they nevertheless are issues to which scientists must address themselves in an effort to understand the etiology not only of learning disabilities, but of a wide variety of neurological problems relating to both childhood and aging.

It is clear that the question of what causes learning disabilities is an exceedingly complex one, defying easy answers. The point here is that the best medical and psychological counsel does not support any thesis of causality over which parents typically have control. The hope of this writer is that the question "What can be done?" will replace ultimately defeating and almost always misguided concerns with "What have I done?"

HOW DID IT ALL START?

The manner in which perceptual processing deficits affect the child's learning, adjustment, and adult potential is much more important than the nature of the neurological dysfunction itself. Certainly this is true from the standpoint of the parents. It is helpful, however, to try to relate the latter to the problem of learning and to project what might have happened and what may be basic to the learning patterns in the child. No two children are the same in terms of the nature of neurological development or in terms of the way it may manifest itself in home or school adjustment. Hence, what follows may not be applicable to all learning disabled children but will serve as an example of what may have taken place in some children and can serve as a basis for understanding the behavior of the learning disabled children we will discuss later.

In the paragraphs which follow in this example it will be assumed that the child experienced a neurological impairment during prenatal life, i.e., before birth. It has been known for a long time that much learning takes place before birth. Although such learning is primitive in nature, it does take place at this early stage of child development. The arm and leg movements which are so obvious to the mother in the last months before birth are indicative of learning that has already occurred. More important from the point of view of our discussion is the fact that sucking movements of the lips are usually learned before birth too. X-rays of the fetus have indicated that the thumb or fingers are in the mouth and that actual sucking may be taking place. Movements of the fetus within the uterus and the position of the fetus have indicated that the lips are often stimulated and that those movements which are important in the sucking activity are actually "practiced" for several weeks before delivery. Thus, in the normal child the sucking movement is usually established prior to or by the time he is expected to nurse from the breast or from the bottle. If it is not established, it can be learned in a very short time—often in just a few moments.

Let us move from this primitive type of learning to a more subtle and complex aspect of the situation. The mother-child relationship is known to be a most significant one. Nursing an infant is an act with much emotional and social significance. Women awaiting delivery often express the hope that they will be able to breast-feed their babies. Still more often, feelings of warmth, excitement, and anticipation are expressed by expectant mothers concerning the act of feeding a baby. The situation is surrounded with feeling, expectations, and social demands, and the mother is aware of her need for actual physical relief.

Nursing an infant has often been anticipated earlier than the actual pregnancy. It is a social act which is imitated with dolls by girl children, and often by boy children, in their play beginning at a very early age. Toys, parental attitudes, stories, and childhood social situations often contribute to and stimulate "playing house" and "feeding the baby." Oftentimes older children are rewarded by their parents by being permitted to feed the new baby. Our culture provides a long orientation to the individual regarding the importance of the relationship between mother and child which is centered in feeding. The experience is endowed with much more than the mere matter of physical relief or nutrition. It is indeed a most basic emotional experience, for here the mother's total life experience is utilized to give her infant the security it needs. Oftentimes fathers assist in the preparation of formulas and in preparing bottles. The responsibilities they assume in the actual feeding are close, emotionally and socially, to those of the mother. In many families the act of nursing or feeding the baby becomes for several months the hub around which the total family experience revolves, and this has been anticipated for many months previously and indeed for many years as a result of childhood play and experiences.

The normal child can fulfill his mother's physical and emotional needs. When the infant is brought to the mother in the hospital room and is able to take the mother's nipple with no major problem, the experience is satisfying for both. The mother's anxiety that she might be unable to fulfill the requirement of motherhood is immediately lessened; the infant is physically satisfied and falls asleep in the security of his mother's arms. For both, the act of feeding soon becomes symbolic of their investment in one another. The mother delights that she had been able to nurse her child, and mothers often discuss this experience with their friends with much evidence of satisfaction. The feelings of self-confidence which are engendered through this experience form the hub around which positive but more complex mother-child relationships will later develop. The infant's success with nursing and the physical satisfaction which it has experienced by being close to his mother or to one who receives him warmly also form the basic relationship out of which other, more complicated, child-adult relationships will grow. Satisfying experiences in nursing lead to equally satisfying physical and emotional experiences of bathing, dressing, and being "changed," talked to, and played with. Infant learnings are rewarded by mother's kisses, caresses, and love. The positive learnings of the child, the fleeting smile, are welcomed and praised by parents, grandparents, and friends. The child soon learns that "*I* am one who can accomplish; that *I* can through *my* behavior have a close relationship with parents; that on the basis of the things *I* have learned *I* can manipulate any social situation so that everyone in it experiences pleasure." The elements of strong ego development for the child are inherent in these relationships; the elements for the expansion of ego concepts in the parents are closely linked to the child's positive reaction to his father and mother.

The child who has experienced a developmental injury during the prenatal period may not fare so well. Let us suppose that the injury suffered by the fetus results in a disturbance in the ability to perform fine-motor movements. Now, instead of learning the sucking movements which are basic to nursing, the child is born without this conditioning having taken place. The mother is just as concerned about being able to nurse her infant as the mother of a normal baby. Her needs are the same, and she is unaware of what has happened to her infant. Indeed, at this point no

Figure 1. A hungry baby rejects the bottle. The continual rejection of the nipple either with breast feeding or the bottle may be related to the fact that sucking movements have not been learned because of neurological impairment. Failure to establish a happy mother-child relationship during feeding is often the basis for parent-child tensions and maladjustments. The inability to suck properly is one significant and early cue which should alert parents to request a complete and continuous evaluation of the infant.

one is aware, for from outward appearances a perfect baby has been delivered. The infant is brought to the mother for feeding, but now instead of responding to the mother's nipple, the infant, although hungry, cannot suck and refuses it. The child is frustrated, the mother even more so. The mother tries again and again to force the infant to take the nipple; the infant, time after time, repels the nipple and ultimately falls asleep exhausted from the physical effort. Over and over this experience is repeated. The mother becomes tense, because she can neither satisfy her baby nor bring physical relief to herself. Feeding becomes a psychological and often a real battleground rather than a center for the development of close and harmonious relationships. Many mothers of learning disabled children have expressed their outright feelings of fear when after a few dismal failures at nursing the child was brought to them for one more attempt before being transferred to a bottle. The transfer to the bottle does not solve the problem either, for the same fine-motor movements of the lips which could not be coordinated for sucking the nipple cannot be easier developed for a bottle. Feeding may take place, however, because now the mother in her battle with the infant has two hands which can be used to place the nipple in the mouth and keep it there. The drooling and gagging which often occur, however, together with the tension of the infant and of the mother, make feeding a most unpleasant experience. "Just wait until you try strained peaches and beets," grandmother warns.

Out of this experience the mother (and frequently the father as well) have a feeling of failure in being unable to establish what was expected to be a warm relationship. They feel defeated in their inability as adults to meet this tiny organism on their terms. They feel threatened, for other adults are reminding them of the wonderful and easy times they had. The parents of the learning disabled infant, as well as the infant, quickly begin to develop the feeling of "I am one who cannot." Since they do not yet know the reason for the problem which they face daily, misconceptions are bound to arise, and these in turn form the basis of unsatisfactory attitudes toward the infant. As the infant's lack of motor skills begins to manifest itself in other areas of learning—walking, sitting up, talking, and eating—these early memories of failure in nursing form the unspoken basis of tensions within the family. The *agony of learning,* as someone has termed it, begins early.

There will come a day when the child does begin to walk, talk, sit, and eat. Then, in his delight at having learned those things which his parents have been urging him to do for many months and indeed for years, he overcompensates to the dismay of his mother and father, who are unable to understand the seemingly endless hyperactivity of their child. We will discuss the problem of hyperactivity somewhat later. It is sufficient now only to note it and to be reminded how some of the feelings between parents and the learning disabled child develop, how neurological impairments for which there is no conclusive routine diagnosis at this very early age form the base of distortions in parent-child relationships, and how the failure experience in nursing may serve as the cornerstone for reinforcing hundreds of other failure experiences in the child as he grows older and begins to compare his behavior against the attitudes and demands of the society in which he lives.

The importance of the failure experience cannot be minimized. Many

Figure 2. What differentiates this child from the group as one who is hyperactive and with a possible neurological impairment? This is a child for whom the community must mobilize its resources to make good adjustment possible.

studies done by psychologists in human learning indicate the importance of success as a reinforcer in learning and as a stimulator to more learning. "Success breeds success" is a trite but nevertheless true saying. Failure, on the other hand, probably because of the facial expressions, comments, attitudes, or oftentimes the pain which accompanies it, does not serve as an equal motivator to learning. Children want the warm reaction of their parents to their actions. Children are also very resilient. One failure experience is insufficient to deter a child's attempts to gain parental attention, but continued failure plays a unique role. Although the learning disabled child's coordination is poor and his attention span is short, his need for parental love still exists, and he tries over and over again to do things which will bring him positive attention. His immaturity and physical incapacity are more than he can cope with, however, and most of his attempts end in failure. Failure often brings him attention of a negative type, but even this attention helps fulfill ego needs. Failure brings contact with adults, and even though the contacts are unpleasant they are better than none at all. Hence, the child's trial-and-error efforts to please sometimes propel him into orgies of behavior which at least bring the desired contact with his father and mother, teacher, or other adults. By this time an emotional overlay of defense of the ego usually makes it appear that the child is unreachable by the adults who would like to help him. Parents by this time have often almost given up.

The course of events, then, is somewhat as follows: For some reason the fetus has experienced a neurological impairment which, in the case of our example, has affected fine-motor movement abilities; nursing and feeding are difficult to establish; threats to parental egos occur; the infant is tense instead of relaxed in the parental contact; failure experience has taken place. The elements inherent in this physically simple but culturally complex experience are quickly translated to all social situations and learning.

The Composite of a Learning Disabled Child

Some time ago, and for an entirely different purpose, a colleague of this writer prepared what was called a "composite of a child" (Cruickshank et al. 1961). This composite is reproduced here in order to provide a further basis for mutual understanding between the writer and whomever else may use this book. This is not the case study of a specific child but a collection of bits and pieces of many children we have known over the years. From them there may appear a picture familiar to parents and teachers who live and work constantly with these children:

> Keeping in mind that no such child or family as that described in the composite exists in reality, some aspects of the composite behavior response pattern which are familiar to parents will be seen as an entirely different behavior pattern to teachers, and *vice versa*. Psychiatrists, neurologists, and pediatricians will recognize herein some of their most difficult, distracting, and likeable patients. Thus it is entirely possible that if such a child did exist, he might, under various circumstances, be classified as brain-injured, or as one who demonstrates evidence of organicity or minimal brain injury. He might be viewed as emotionally disturbed; as having a home problem; as a psychopathological personality; as having a weak ego or lack of ego integration; as lacking inner controls and requiring a rigid, controlled, and highly structured environment; or as needing an environment which is warmly permissive. He could be regarded as needing immediate long-term residential treatment, or as not being amenable to psychiatric treatment. In some situations such a child might be classified as being a "real boy" whose discipline problems are ones he will outgrow.

The child is usually a boy. His parents are of no specific ethnic or racial background. They may believe in the Catholic, Protestant, or Jewish religion, but do not necessarily attend the church of their faith. The father, a rather quiet man in his late thirties or forties, may be a truck driver, physicist, manager of a chain store, biochemist, or theoretical mathematician, but no matter what his profession, he performs his chosen occupation with outstanding efficiency, dependability, and intelligence. During the week he works long hours, frequently leaving the house before his son is up and returning after he is asleep.

On weekends, if he is not working, he tries very hard to spend some of his time with his son and to find things to do together; but when he succeeds in initiating some joint enterprise, his son for no apparent reason wrecks the afternoon by carelessly thrusting the hammer into the power saw while it is going at high speed, kicking over a bucket of freshly mixed paint, or sticking his finger into a light socket and then exploding into yelling fury when he is jerked to safety. The father, unable to comprehend the violence of the explosion or to control his son's behavior, more often than not retreats to the bastions of his work, remarking to his wife as he does so that she is too easy on the child, that he needs more discipline.

His wife is an attractive, outgoing, intelligent woman who, up to the time of her son's birth, thoroughly enjoyed her job as a secretary, nurse, teacher, economist, or mother of the two previous children. Before children were born to her, she was active in civic affairs and frequently participated in various types of adult study groups. She enjoys a good fight, although she has learned for the most part to control her aggressive drives in the interest of maintaining harmony in the family and neighborhood.

At this point, her relationships with her son are at an all-time low because he demands constant attention and rebels fiercely when he gets it. He refuses to share his toys with his little sister and knocks her down when she asks to play with his truck collection. He fights with the neighbor children, except those much younger than himself with whom he spends more time than a boy of his age should. Although he is constantly hungry, especially for sweets, during the family dinner hour—to which he is customarily late—he fiddles with his food until, under threat of maternal violence, he gulps it down, frequently eating with his hands instead of the silverware which he throws to the floor upon being reprimanded for bad manners. Although he is an alert, attractive lad, he is failing in school and may have been retained a year, or even excluded from school, because he refused to "settle down and get to work."

At their wits' ends, the parents finally take their boy to his pediatrician who more often than not finds him physically healthy, somewhat hyperactive, of normal or superior intelligence and, most comforting of all, a child who will probably "outgrow" his current behavior problems. It is to be noted, however, that during this conference and the many others that follow with teachers, principals, school psychologists, counselors, and therapists, the parents' conversation is apt to have a curiously detached quality, almost as though they were helping the professional to understand the problem of a close friend's child for whom they feel a great deal of warmth and a very deep personal concern but no real responsibility.

The boy established his reputation as a classroom discipline problem between the ages of 6 and 9, He may have had a trial period in a nursery school or a kindergarten group around 5 years of age, but after a very hectic week or so, he was probably sent home as being too immature and not ready for group experience.

In the third grade, if he has not already been excluded from school, he is frequently disruptively aggressive. He talks out of turn, forgetting or neglecting to raise his hand. He appears unable to sit still and is constantly wiggling, fidgeting, twisting, and jouncing up and down in his seat. He runs in the halls, no matter who is watching or how often he is reprimanded. His shoelaces, zippers, and buttons, once undone, remain untied, unzipped, and unbuttoned, until standards of decency and orderliness are finally re-established by weary adults. His pockets bulge with miniature trucks, cars, and playing cards with which he plays all day, frequently humming, making odd noises, or talking to himself as he does so.

He is physically attractive, well-built, and appears to have good motor coordination. Even though he is frequently awkward and clumsy on the play-ground and in the classroom, it is assumed that he does not take time to look where he is going.

In the classroom during work periods, he is unable or refuses to follow directions. If pictures, for example, are to be pasted at the top of the page, he pastes his at the bottom and frequently on the wrong side of the paper. If his teacher takes time to give him the directions again, he loses the thread of what she is saying before she has finished the first sentence. If he manages to complete any work at all, it is indescribably sloppy and carelessly executed. He agrees with everything the teacher says and on occasion treats her with great respect. The next minute he denies he took from her desk the pencil which is sticking out of his pocket. His books are torn and dirty.

He shrieks and cries like a frightened two-year-old if he cuts his finger. However, when the basketball lands on the roof of the school, he climbs the side of the building (with no visible means of support), retrieves the ball, which he refuses to throw to the waiting players, and shinnys down the drain pipe, kicking at someone's head as he jumps the last five feet to the ground.

No matter what he scores in terms of a functioning IQ (intelligence quotient), the school psychologist reports that the test results are characterized by an unusual spread. He fails, for example, in some tasks at a level four years below his chronological age. In general, his greatest strengths are in the verbal concepts and greatest weaknesses in the perfor-mance level. The examiner frequently concludes his report with a statement that he does not feel the final score is a valid estimate of the child's potential.

The boy may not be able to read at all, and he may test at the same readiness level for three consecutive years. Or he may read with great fluency two years above his chronological age, but be so lacking in comprehension that, if he is asked to repeat the story in his own words, he will be unable to think of a single thing to say that is relevant.

He is somewhat better at arithmetic; but his worksheets, which he twists about or turns at an odd angle as he works, are usually in shreds by the time he should have completed the assignment. His spelling and handwriting, if they are at all comprehensible, are atrociously inaccurate and carelessly executed. In his everyday speech, as well as in his reading, writing, spelling, and arithmetic papers, one notes reversals, substitutions, and omissions of words. He dislikes art class, refuses to participate in finger painting, and frequently loathes clay, which he throws at the other students. He likes fans, motors, small trucks, and pets, which he mistreats.

He rarely has friends, although he frequently has accomplices both at home and at school. In playground activities, he is something of a bully. He refuses to participate in organized group games, but then harries his classmates from the sidelines. He appears to be completely devoid of even a rudimentary sense of fair play or of the existence of rules. In general, he gets along better with adults than with children. Adults are often attracted by his graceful charm, but are apt to have the feeling that they are unable to reach him.

On occasions he explodes into temper tantrums or apparently unprovoked rage reactions of such violence that he may constitute a danger to himself or others. At times it appears that his only regret after such episodes is that he did not kill or demolish the offending object.

He loves ritual, marching, and making up elaborate rules. He would give his immortal soul to be a member of the school patrols, but even if he is able to read and understand the patrol pledge, he forgets it two days later, as he does the rules and regulations. He loses his patrol badge, coat, belt, and hat, and has a difficult time giving directions at the intersection because he apparently does not remember the difference between left and right.

And finally, in the neighborhood he may be, or he may only be suspected of being, a thief, a fire setter, or both. On the other hand, he may be the idol of the neighborhood mothers and his teachers, because in both deportment and dress he is always the perfect gentleman. But no matter how he appears to others, after the long day's frustrations and failure to get along with others, at night he wants closeness and warmth more than almost anything else in the world, even when he twists his body sharply out of the very arms which would give him what he needs and wants most.

Whether the boy just described is learning disabled, emotionally disturbed, or both, he is certainly a child who needs understanding and help in order to achieve community acceptance. The composite raises many questions about these children, most of which will be examined carefully in the following pages.

Out of failures during nursing comes a boy with problems. He has arrived where he is by routes which are not always fully clear or understood.

This child is known to many parents and to school teachers, playground supervisors, YMCA swimming pool managers, den mothers, and summer camp counselors. He is a child whose name when mentioned brings lifted eyebrows of recognition. "He's an awfully nice-looking boy, and he has charming parents, but . . ." His reputation goes before him so often that failure experiences are his almost before he has a chance actually to fail. A vicious circle makes many revolutions during the child's waking day. How this circle can be broken to provide relief for parents, for the child, and for his social group is the matter of concern in this book. Parents must have relief. The learning disabled child must have relief. Parents must see their child succeed. The child must experience his own success.

THE COMPLEX NATURE OF THE PROBLEM
OF LEARNING DISABILITIES

While learning disabilities in children and youth can be defined as a specific entity or set of entities, this is an oversimplified concept at best. Figure 3 illustrates the complex interrelationships between and among a variety of variables having an impact on the child.

In Figure 3 one will note that the neurophysiological development or maldevelopment of the embryo, fetus, or child is one factor—a significant factor—in the creation of the learning disability in the child. It is perhaps the initial and central factor. Depicted by arrows, the impact of neurophysiological maldevelopment is seen on perceptual processing, on intellectual level, and on sensory or motor and conceptualization problems. These issues have an impact on parental behavior and attitudes toward the child. Likewise they have a major part in the capacity of the child to respond to the social demands and attitudes of the neighborhood or larger community. When the child cannot quickly respond to these social requisites, negative attitudes are developed toward him—attitudes he does not have the internal resources with which to cope. The internal locus of control is unwillingly transferred to an external locus of control, i.e., in parents or in the community.

Tensions result from the inability of the child to respond to the demands of the home, school, and community. The emotional maldevelopment noted in Figure 3 as an impinging factor on the child likewise tempers perceptual processing, hyperactivity, conceptualization, and many of the other factors noted in the figure as being relatively discrete. The discreteness is, however, an artifact of an illustration; in reality there is close interrelationship among all the elements noted as well as those not specifically included. Such factors as poor auditory acuity and visual

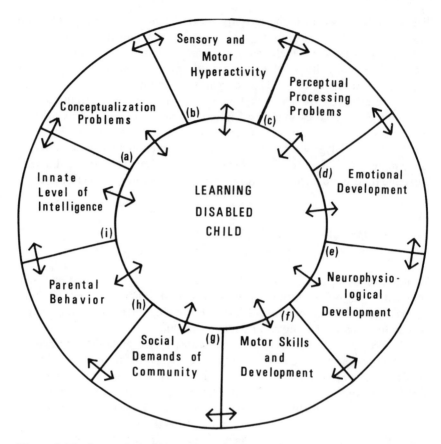

Figure 3. The interrelationships of some of the dynamic factors which impinge on the learning disabled child. Interrelationships noted by letters *(a)*, *(b)*, *(c)*, etc., may each and all relate to some or all others, such as *(a)* to or with *(b)*, *(c)*, *(d)*.

acuity, separate from perceptual processing, may be significant. Learning disability is a conglomerate of many things, each and all impinging on the normative development of the child.

HOW MANY LEARNING DISABLED CHILDREN ARE THERE?

In the composite, references were made throughout to a boy child. There is a greater number of boys than girls who are counted in schools as learning disabled children. As stated earlier, no accurate census exists of the number of learning disabled children, nor is the percentage which they represent in the general childhood population known. Percentages varying from 1 to 80 are heard, but the fact stands that as of now no accurate count is available. However, all reports indicate a higher percentage of boys than girls—and the sex difference is apparently a great one. In a study done by this author some years ago, it was impossible out of a large population of school children to find a fourth girl at the elementary age to match with three other girls. On the other hand, forty boys who were to be included in the same study could be selected easily out of several hundred screened and referred by elementary school teachers. In another public school system, the ratio of learning disabled boys to girls was approximately 25 to 1; in still another system, 15 to 1. Male learning disabled children, then, apparently are in much greater abundance in the childhood population.

Some of the many reasons for this discrepancy are easily understood, but others are not so obvious. The larger size of the male fetus may be a factor, for example, in making the male more liable to injury during the birth process itself. Less understood is the fact that the male organism is more delicate than the female, more susceptible to disease and injury,

Figure 4. Learning disabled children, often handsome and appealing, are only rarely characterized by visible physical stigmata.

more likely to be defective, and more easily responsive to emotional stress. Almost every study concerned with incidence of any type of physical, mental, or emotional disorder shows the percentage of males affected to be greater than females. This is particularly true with learning disabled children. In a demonstration project with which this author was associated for a four-year period, girls between the ages of six and ten were sought for inclusion in a class of learning disabled children. In this period of time no girls were referred, although the school population included nearly twenty thousand pupils at the elementary levels. This is not to say that girls with perceptual processing deficits did not exist in this community, but at least teachers were not threatened by girl children to the point where any were referred for study and for transfer to a special program for this type of childhood problem.

This writer feels, however, that at the elementary school level the learning and behavior problems of learning disabled girls are much more severe than those of boys of comparable ages. This does not mean that girls always experience more severe degrees of learning disabilities; it may be that the normal cultural environment for girls is more nearly comparable to the therapeutic and educational environment which learning disabled children need than is that for boys. Boys are in fact stimulated to be active and aggressive. One needs only to note the kind of gifts fathers bring home for their sons in order to understand the physical role of the male child in our culture. Baseball bats, footballs, boxing gloves, wild West outfits, pistols, and other toys which involve action are basic to the equipment of most boys. There is indeed little in the cultural situation which prompts boys to a quiet and delicate life. Parents, grandparents, and neighbors condone much untoward behavior from a boy because he is just that—a boy. It is not until the boy enters school and fails to read, to write properly, or to adjust to the expectancies of a group in a long school day that parents and teachers begin to ask whether his behavior and development are normal. Only then do most parents begin to seek the help of specialists.

Cultural expectations for girls are different. The traits often expected of little girls in our society are delicateness, social perfection and grace. If a girl child steps outside of this social perspective, learning disabled or not, forces which surround her go into immediate action. Mother constantly reminds her that "little girls do not act that way." Grandmother insists on certain standards of behavior. Even fathers emphasize decorum and are concerned if girls engage in what appears to be inappropriate or uncontrolled behavior. Toys for little girls emphasize the cultural expectancy for them. Thus, spontaneously the girl child is surrounded by a high degree of structure, and fixed limits are placed on her behavior. This is what is appropriate in a learning situation for learning disabled children. She has been subjected to an appropriate learning situation early and spontaneously by parents, and she has been provided with those definite guidelines to her behavior which are apparently needed by all learning disabled children. Thus, if her problems are so great that they remain unresolved when she reaches the second or third grade of elementary school, she undoubtedly will have more difficulty adjusting than a boy of comparable age and mental capacity. Much of what we have just written is conjecture, for indeed no studies are available to support these statements. Observation over a number of years of many learning disabled children, however, has led this writer to these conclusions.

For reasons not at all clear, there does appear to be a greater incidence of intellectually normal learning disabled children in the upper socioeconomic groups. There is nevertheless also a considerable proportion of intellectually normal learning disabled children among lower socioeconomic groups, and in this latter population the incidence of mental retardation in conjuction with learning disablility appears to be higher than in other segments of the population in the United States and Canada. What is known is that the problem exists throughout the world—at least in more recently developed countries. In Belgium, the Netherlands, France, Germany, England, Russia, Japan, and many other countries a few research studies have dealt with the discovery, treatment, and prevention of learning disabilities in children. It is a widespread problem with serious social, educational, and emotional ramifications for the learning disabled individual himself and certainly for his family. While some socioeconomic and cultural groups may include more of these children than other groups, the problem is nevertheless one of all groups in any community. So common is the problem, this writer more than once has stated that it is a problem of every elementary school in every American community and is undoubtedly to be found in almost every elementary classroom in every school. It would appear that if all learning disabled children were adequately screened and diagnosed, the magnitude of the problem would be closely similar to that of the familial type of mental retardation. This statement is made recognizing that the psychological and learning problems to be discussed in Chapter 2 are typical of children in numerous medical classifications as well as in learning disabled children as they are being discussed here. The issue of incidence and prevalence of learning disability in children and youth surprisingly still is an unsolved problem. Demographic studies are likewise totally lacking.

SELECTED REFERENCES OF SPECIAL INTERESTS TO PARENTS

Anderson, C.M., and Plymate, H.B. "Management of the Brain-Damaged Adolescent." *American Journal of Orthopsychiatry* 32 (1962):492–500.

Barsch, R. "Explanations Offered by Parents and Siblings of Brain-Damaged Children." *Exceptional Children* 27 (1961):286–91.

Clements, S.E. *Some Aspects of the Characteristics, Management, and Education of the Child with Minimal Brain Dysfunction.* Glen Ellyn, Ill.: West Suburban Association for the Other Child, c. 1965, pp. 1–3.

Ilg, F.L., and Ames, L.B. *Child Behavior.* Glen Ellyn, Ill.: West Suburban Association for the Other Child, 1955, pp. 1–4.

Johnson, D.J., and Myklebust, H.R. *Learning Disabilities: Educational Principles and Practices.* New York: Grune and Stratton, 1967.

Hallahan, D.P., and Kauffman, J.M. *Introduction to Learning Disabilities: A Psychobehavioral Approach.* Englewood Cliffs, N.J.: Prentice-Hall, 1976.

Kauffman, J.M., and Hallahan, D.P. *Teaching Children with Learning Disabilities: Personal Perspectives.* Columbus: Merrill, 1976.

Laufer, M.W. *Problems of Cerebral Dysfunctions.* New York: New York Association for Brain-Injured Children, c. 1965.

Lewis, R.S. *The Brain-Injured Child.* Chicago: Crippled Children and Adults, 1963, pp. 1–4.

————; Strauss, A.A.; and Lehtinen, Laura E. *The Other Child.* 2d ed. New York: Grune and Stratton, 1960, pp. 1–12.

Siegal, E. *Helping the Brain-Injured Child.* New York: New York Association for Brain-Injured Children, 1962.

SELECTED REFERENCES OF SPECIAL INTEREST TO TEACHERS

Benton, A.L. "Behavioral Indices of Brain Injury in School Children." *Child Development* 33 (March 1962): 199–208.

Cruickshank, W.M. "An Introductory Overview." In *The Teacher of Brain-Injured Children,* edited by W.M. Cruickshank. Syracuse: Syracuse University Press, 1966, pp. 3–19.

————. "The Education of the Child with Specific Learning Disabilities." In *The Education of Exceptional Children and Youth,* edited by W.M. Cruickshank and G.O. Johnson. 3rd ed. Englewood Cliffs, N.J.: Prentice-Hall, 1975, pp. 242–91.

————; Bentzen, F.A.; Ratzeburg, F.H.; and Tannhauser M. *A Teaching Method for Brain-Injured and Hyperactive Children.* Syracuse: Syracuse University Press, 1961, pp. 3–9, 130–33.

Gallagher, J.J. "Children with Developmental Imbalances: A Psychoeducational Definition." In *The Teacher of Brain-Injured Children,* edited by W.M. Cruickshank. Syracuse: Syracuse University Press, 1966, pp. 23–43.

Hellmuth, J., ed. *Learning Disorders*. Seattle: Special Child Publications, 1965.

Kephart, N.C. *The Slow Learner in the Classroom*. 2nd ed. Columbus, Ohio: 1971.

Myklebust, H.R., ed. *Progress in Learning Disabilities*, New York: Grune and Stratton, 1968.

Strauss, A.A., and Lehtinen, L.E. *Psychopatholog and Education of the Brain-Injured Child*. New York: Grune and Stratton, 1947, pp. 7–97.

Strauss A.A., and Kephart, N.C. *Psychopathology and Education of the Brain-Injured Child*. New York: Grune and Stratton, 1955, pp. 11–143.

2

Psychological and Learning Problems

C HILDREN in several different medical classifications may demonstrate psychological and learning problems similar to those of learning disabled children. As will be pointed out in this chapter, research investigations have quite conclusively illustrated this statement.

Some children with *cerebral palsy,* particularly of the spastic and athetoid types, will function psychologically much like learning disabled children discussed here. Some children with a diagnosis of *aphasia* have the same learning problems as learning disabled children. Some children with *epilepsy* also perform as do the children we write about here. These three groups, of course, all represent types of children with neurological impairments, and it might be expected that they would function similarly. We have come to realize, however, that many children with a diagnosis of *hyperactive emotional disturbance* without a specific diagnosis of neurological impairment also demonstrate the same characteristics as do learning disabled children, and furthermore they frequently respond to the same type of educational and psychological treatment programs. It is this group of children to which the writer referred earlier in suggesting that, as diagnostic instrumentation in neurology and psychology is perfected, some of these children may be shown indeed to have suffered neurological disturbances. These problems are still too vaguely understood to be a matter of record at this time. One prominent authority has stated his belief that the great majority of *reading problems* in elementary school children will ultimately be traced to neurological deficit. His belief is not farfetched because visuomotor problems of learning disabled children are basic to poor learning habits in reading, number concepts, writing, and spelling. The exact role of neurological impairment will be more fully understood in the future when instrumentation is

30

further refined. Many serious professional persons are troubled concerning the large number of so-called *culturally deprived children* and the learning characteristics which they appear to have in common with learning disabled children. Certainly not all culturally deprived children are learning disabled. However, if a child has experienced severe environmental deprivation during his early life, some neurological insult may also have been experienced which will have significant impact on the child's ability to learn when the environment improves educationally and psychologically. The research and writing of Joaquin Cravioto illustrate well the relationship between both environmental and nutritional deprivation and the problems of perceptual processing and learning disabilities about which we write here. Some of the old professional arguments of the 1930s of nurture *vs.* nature are related to this problem. Certainly the longitudinal studies of Drs. Marie Skodak and Harold Skeels support the significance of environmental deprivation in relationship to lowered intellectual function if not indeed to learning disability. Finally, for many years, as noted in Chapter 1, there has been recognized a large population of mentally retarded children who functioned as we will be describing the performance of learning disabled children. This group has professionally been called one of *exogenous mental retardation.* It was this group that Drs. Werner and Strauss originally studied, and it is their studies out of which our current concepts of the learning disabled child of all intellectual levels have developed.

It is thus possible to see that some children from many different clinical groups may function similarly. One problem frequently experienced by special education teachers results from the fact that children in special schools are grouped on the basis of medical classification instead of on the basis of psychological characteristics. In a group of cerebral palsied children, for example, there may be some quite capable of learning in a classroom with normal children. Others in the same group with quite different learning problems may learn and perceive in the same manner as learning disabled children. Having children with both types of problems in the same classroom produces serious teaching difficulties. Likewise, in a class of mentally retarded children, there may be familial or hereditary-type retarded children as well as learning disabled *mentally retarded* children. Teachers frequently have complained that they are unable to meet the needs of both groups in a single classroom. What is done for one type of child may be inappropriate for another. The children with different problems are in the same classroom only because educators continue to group children according to the medical or legal classification of mental retardation instead of on the basis of their learning needs. It is for the same reason that the learning disabled child with normal intelligence is unable to learn satisfactorily in a regular classroom. Children requiring two kinds of teaching face the teacher: the normal children, who are the majority in the class, and the learning disabled child, whose needs are quite different from those of the other children.

It is important here to consider once again the definition of children with specific learning disabilities which was discussed in Chapter 1. The Wepman Committee pointed out quite accurately that this problem is a respecter of no one intellectual level, but may be found in some children and youth of any and all intellectual levels. This concept runs counter to a generally accepted statement that learning disabilities are characteristic of children of IQs of 80 or above. Such a statement, promulgated by many parent groups and actually integrated into the definitions of numerous states and local boards of education, is made without one iota of research as a basis, and in reality it ignores the research base of the total field. The initial research done in this area was completed with the cooperation of mentally retarded boys at the educable level. A state director of special education, in a fury of defensiveness, once told this writer that the states could define the problem in any way they choose. One cannot deny the bureaucracy that questionable privilege, but to define an educational problem in an incorrect way so that a large percentage of children is deprived of educational opportunities is both incorrect, professionally questionable, and subject to legal examination. There *is* such a thing as a mentally retarded learning disabled child, perhaps more of them than there are those of intellectual normal range of intelligence! Educators must face this fact as must the parents who initially advocated the arbitrary intellectual cutoff point.

In summary, learning disabled children, as they are being considered in this book, are (a) those with a definite diagnosis of a specific or diffuse neurological injury and who are also characterized by a series of significant psychological problems; (b) those with no positive diagnosis of neurological injury (although such may be suspected by the neurologist), but whose psychological and behavioral characteristics are identical with those children for whom a diagnosis can be definite; or (c) some children in specific clinical groups such as cerebral palsy, epilepsy, aphasia, mental retardation, cultural deprivation, emotional disturbance, and others whose members show the common psychological characteristics of brain injury and where it is either definitely known or logically suspected that some neurological deficit is present. Furthermore, the matter of level of intelligence is unimportant in describing the perimeters of the problem. These children may be of any intellectual level whatsoever. Insofar as IQ is concerned, there are gifted learning disabled children, intellectually normal learning disabled children, as well as slow-learning and mentally retarded learning disabled children. The problem is almost always complicated by an emotional overlay in the child which oftentimes causes the initial diagnosis to be one of emotional disturbance rather than what in reality it probably is. The issue is a complicated one with many dimensions—physical, intellectual, and emotional.

Dr. James Gallagher of the University of North Carolina has written that these are "children with developmental imbalances . . . who reveal a developmental disparity in psychological processes related to education of such a degree (often four years or more) as to require the instructional programming of developmental tasks to the nature and level of the deviant developmental process." While there are other considerations to be given to a definition of a learning disabled child, this statement provides the basis for a discussion of the psychological characteristics of the child. Dr. Gallagher speaks of a "developmental disparity in psychological processes." What is the nature of this disparity, and what are the psychological processes which are involved? They are many, and the problem is central to the total adjustment of the learning disabled child. Hence, although the problem admittedly is somewhat technical, considerable time will be spent on it.

The normal child, as described in Chapter 1, comes into the world with his nervous system intact. Thus he is able to learn and relate positively to his parents and others in his expanding world. When he begins school at the age of five or six, the physical structure of his eyes will have almost reached the maturity necessary for reading. His auditory mechanisms will have matured to the point where sounds may be both perceived and understood. The child is ready to learn, or as educators say, he has reached the "readiness stage." Given normal intellectual abilities and a secure family situation, this child will grow and achieve in school as his parents and the community expect him to.

We have already spoken several times to the fact that learning disabilities are the result of perceptual processing deficits. In reality it would be more accurate to speak of these children as perceptual-processing-deficit children (PPD children). Except for the fact that terminology is such a maze of confusion in this field, we would be prone to do so, for perceptual processing deficit is so much more accurate. From time to time we may refer here to the PPD child, recognizing full well that the term will not be employed widely, but to emphasize the accuracy of what the term learning disabilities is. If the focus of educators, and others who attempt to deal with learning disabilities, were on the perceptual processing aspect of the problem, much of the confusion observed in the field would be reduced. To recognize the role of perceptual processing immediately belies the attempts of many to place remedial reading, learning problems in childhood, and other essentially disrelated issues into this nomenclature. The issues are often quite different.

We have already traced the initial unhappy learning experience of an infant who has in some manner received a neurological impairment. The factors basic to his inability to nurse, as we outlined the problem, contribute to faulty learning in many aspects of the child's life and development, that is, to eating, dressing, running, climbing, and other childhood activities. In large measure these learning problems are due to the child's possession of several very important related psychological characteristics which in effect minimize his possibility of learning, at least as society would like him to learn.

HE IS ALWAYS ON THE QUI VIVE!

The first barrier to good adjustment, and perhaps the most significant, is the characteristic of *hyperactivity*. Hyperactivity takes on two related forms. The first form, which is most significant to school achievement, is *sensory hyperactivity;* the second form, which often creates management problems in the home and the school, is *motor hyperactivity.*

Sensory hyperactivity may cause the child to respond to unessential or irrelevant stimuli. This behavior characteristic may be due to cortical brain damage, but it may also be a learned type of behavior, employed by the child in the hope of somehow or somewhere finding a point which will provide him with a cordial relationship with others. Perhaps both cortical or other central nervous system damage and learned behavior are involved.

Sensory hyperactive children, because of some neurological impairment, are unable to refrain from reacting to stimuli, irrespective of whether the stimulus is significant or insignificant to their immediate activity. Any movement, color, or sound, any smell or unusual experience in the child's immediate presence may distract him. That the sound or color is unrelated to the task at hand is of little consequence. The child is drawn to the stimulus itself and may indeed "forget" what he was originally doing until he is returned to the task by the parent or teacher. Oftentimes the term "hyperactivity" is replaced by the term "distractibility" in psychological literature, for indeed the child is constantly distracted from one situation to another by stimuli. These stimuli distractors, apparently, can involve any sense—sight, smell, hearing, taste, or touch—and can be either external or internal to the child. Hence, as we

Figure 5. Hyperactive children can at times be relaxed. They become more re-laxed as the educational setting becomes more appropriate to their complex ad-justment and learning needs.

will note again later a tight belt or a fly buzzing in the room may be as much of a distractor as an epigastric sensation or a hunger pain.

It is suggested that the reader put down this book a moment and look around the room in which he is sitting. Notice the tremendous number of things which are in the room right now, things which you have "ignored" while you have been reading. If you are sitting in the living room of your home, there will be pictures, designed curtains, lamps, *objets d'art*, books, furniture, rugs, perhaps a stereo-recorder playing. If you stop to notice, you will quickly perceive dozens, perhaps even hundreds, of things in the room to which you have paid no attention: colors, shadows, angles, home noises, movements of people, and other similar things. They have been there all the time you have been reading, but they have been unessential to you insofar as your adjustment to your reading has been concerned. Since they are unessential to your activity, you have ignored them. You negatively adapted to them, as psychologists sometimes say. This ability to ignore, to block out, or negatively to adapt to the unessential is a significant characteristic of normal human beings. Advertisers recognize this capacity in people, and they try to overcome it by constant repetition or by unusual presentations which force their product momentarily into the individual's conscious experience. This ability to ignore and negatively to adapt accounts for the capacity of many normal teenagers to memorize French irregular verbs or algebraic formulas successfully while radios are blaring on their desks. When the harried parent, who after a while is unable to ignore the musical beats, begs for relief, the young person is surprised. "I didn't even know it was on," says he, amazed at the adult's frustration. This child had negatively adapted to what for the moment was an unessential stimulus. Fortunately, most people are able to do this, and as a result they are able to deal with the demands which face them in the normal course of their daily lives.

On the other hand, the learning disabled child, perhaps because of a cortical injury, does not have this capacity to ignore or negatively to adapt. Every stimulus coming within his purview is something to which he must react. Thus at the dinner table his attention is distracted away from the meat he is attempting to get on his fork by the polished surface of the knife as it lies next to his plate, by the milk in the glass, by the candle flickering in the center of the table, by the movement of the person sitting next to him, by the shapes of dishes, by the colors of food, by the scratching of someone's knife against a plate, by passing dishes, or by a hundred and one other stimuli which are at that point in time unessential to his eating. As a result the meat never gets onto the fork, for the child has long since "forgotten" what he was going to do. He has to be constantly reminded to "eat your dinner."

In the classroom the same problem is experienced. Bobby, in the second grade, is asked by the teacher to do some practice exercises in penmanship. "Start here," the teacher says to the child as she points her finger at the top line on the page and at the same time notes that Bobby is looking in the direction of the paper. "Write your name here, first." With a pat on his shoulder she moves to another child, but before she has taken three steps Bobby has dropped his pencil, since he was distracted by a book falling somewhere in the room. Before the teacher can return to Bobby a few seconds later, he has reacted to the grinding of the pencil sharpener, to the colors of dozens of shirts and dresses which surround him, to the movement of the child next to him across the aisle, to an announcement on the intercommunication system, to the leaves on the tree blowing in the wind outside the room, to the movement of the goldfish in the aquarium, to another child who just sneezed, to the teacher's whispers to yet a third child, to the footsteps of a group of children walking past his room in the hall, to the crack at the top of his desk into which his pencil point will just fit, to the flag hanging in the front of the room, to the Thanksgiving Day decorations on the walls, to dozens and dozens of other unessential things in the room which prevent him from writing his name on the top line! It isn't that he refuses to cooperate with the teacher's request to "start here." It is that he simply cannot refrain from reacting to the unessential stimuli in his environment. This is, we think, the result of a neurological impairment. The difficulty he experiences in carrying out the simple request of the teacher occurs again and again each day as one learning opportunity after another is presented to him. The other children in the room get along very well because these unessential stimuli for them remain just that—unessential. They are ignored. Bobby would perhaps like to ignore them, but he is unable to do so.

There is a great amount of individual difference among learning disabled children. Some children show characteristics of sensory hyperactivity only; others are characterized by both sensory and motor hyperactivity. Motor hyperactivity is often referred to in professional literature under the name *motor disinhibition,* which is defined as the child's inability to refrain from reacting to stimuli which produce or prompt a motor response. Thus, anything within the child's visual field or arm's reach that can be touched, pulled, twisted, bent, pushed, or turned becomes a stimulus to which some learning disabled children must respond. This behavior is so significant that it is also often called *hyperkinetic.* These are the children who are described by Sheldon Rappaport as being up by 5:05 A.M., into the kitchen by 5:08 A.M., having the pans out of the cupboard by 5:09 A.M., mixing the flour and sugar on the floor by 5:11 A.M., walking through it in bare feet by 5:15 A.M., turning attention to the living room drapes by 5:18 A.M., and inadvertently knocking over a table lamp at 5:20 A.M. This wakens all members of the family who individually and collectively descend on the first-floor scene, and thus begins another day of tension, discipline, and frustration.

The author has frequently had a learning disabled child in his office who, while parents try to converse, shortly has made a full cycle, touching everything on the desk top, removing books from shelves, opening and shutting drawers, constantly building up to greater heights of motor activity until father or mother firmly, definitely, and finally puts a stop to further chaos.

It is easy to understand why parents often say, "My child is always on the *qui vive.*" These are children who seem to be constantly alert. They are always triggered to respond. They wiggle, squirm, and seem never at rest or relaxed. In school, paper clips, pencils, paper, books—all things which may be required in the learning experience—cease to be aids to learning and become motor distractors to learning. These are children who, when exposed to a sharp noise or unexpected situation, appear to fall apart. They experience what psychologists call a *catastrophic reaction* in which the total body may react to the situation in quite an uncontrolled manner. The child may not always react physically but may appear confused and unsure of himself; he does not respond rationally. The behavior of such children may then become immature, and they may become aggressive, verbally or physically.

Motor disinhibition, motor hyperactivity, hyperkinetic behavior—or whatever it may be called—presents a most serious situation for both parents and the school. Certain behavioral patterns may be predicted for both home and school situations. Children who cannot control their physical behavior are quickly termed behavior or management problems by school people. Regardless of what the child's problem is called, his hyperactivity is not easy to live with. The child soon develops a reputation, and he is isolated from other children in the neighborhood, in boys' clubs, and on the school playground. Other children simply do not understand his behavior, and while children are usually flexible and can take a great deal of the unusual, these children often exceed even these liberal childhood norms.

It is also easy to understand how the motor hyperactivity of which we speak will in itself serve as a deterrent to learning fine-motor skills. A child who is unable to control his motor activity will have a difficult time attending to such sedentary activities as writing, tying his shoes, cutting his food, or eating. The motor activity involved in these seemingly simple skills stimulates the child to additional and increased movement. The fine-motor movement required by the task at hand becomes psychologically lost to the gross-motor activity that is stimulated by the task. Practice in brushing teeth, for example, may be interfered with by the greater response possibilities of the running water and the many things which can be done with water! Trying to stand on one leg while attempting to tie a shoe may be a more challenging physical feat than are the more mundane movements of manipulating the fingers around the shoelace. A child begins appropriately enough to cut a piece of meatloaf on his plate at dinner with a knife and fork. The movement of the utensils and their clicking against one another serve as stimuli for waving the knife, stabbing with the fork, and ultimately falling out of the chair in a fancy matador lunge.

Thousands of degrees of hyperactivity exist. It is important to remind ourselves that not all learning disabled children are hyperactive. As a matter of fact some having developed extraordinary psychological controls may actually appear hyperactive or withdrawn. Other learning disabled children are able to function on a motor basis well within normal behavioral expectancies while still others function as we have described them in the preceding paragraphs. These different degrees of hyperactivity are the essence of the concept of individual differences. Some children, as we have already said, are visually or auditorily hyperactive to extraneous stimuli. They show little or none of the motor symptoms we have just discussed. Other children in varying degrees of severity show motor disinhibition, often to the point where parents seek the assistance of their physician to have medication prescribed which may hopefully make life more livable for all members of the family. Hyperactivity in all forms and degrees is one of the most significant hurdles to adjustment in the home and in the school. It is perhaps the single most debilitating characteristic of learning disability in children. In the chapter on psychological diagnosis of learning disabled children is a discussion of some of the ways in which the relative importance of hyperactivity as a part of the child's total problem is determined.

HE SEES THE TREES BUT NEVER THE FOREST

One very important characteristic of learning disabled children is that of *dissociation*. Dissociation is the inability to see things as a whole, as a totality, or as a *gestalt,* to use a psychological term. The child sees parts of things but oftentimes does not comprehend the total mosaic. As one parent reported, "He sees the trees but never the forest." Dissociation is relatively easy to detect in the psychologist's examination. It is closely related to sensory hyperactivity of a visual nature. As a matter of fact, it is likely that dissociation may often be caused by visual or auditory hyperactivity. Dissociation, not mentioned specifically in the definition discussed in Chapter 1, is closely related to the inability of the child to obtain closure, a concept which is included in the definition. Let us examine what is involved.

Figure 6 depicts a marbleboard, one of the psychologist's tools used to obtain important understandings of learning disabled children. On the board a design is constructed using black marbles, and this design is to be reproduced by the child on a second board which he is given for his use. Examine the board for a moment and analyze it. At first glance it looks like a Chinese checkerboard except that it is not in color. As you look at it

Figure 6. *a.* Original marbleboard design. *b.* and *c.* productions, which both tend toward the incoherent, of two intellectually normal learning disabled children.

you see the design constructed there, and by now you may even have counted the number of marbles which you will need to construct the design or you may have decided upon a plan of attack as you start to reproduce the object. You see the design as a total entity, as a figure, as a whole. This is not the case for many learning disabled children.

On the marbleboard, if you count them, you will find one hundred holes arranged in rows of ten. Each of these holes is a stimulus. Hence there are one hundred stimuli on that board to begin with. The angles created by the holes in relationship to one another, the shadows, and the marbles themselves constitute other stimuli. In studies with various clinical groups of neurologically handicapped children, it has been observed frequently that, in contrast to normal children, learning disabled children perform this task in a manner approaching incoherence. If they are motor disinhibited as well as sensory hyperactive, they may distract themselves further by putting their fingers in the holes to the extent that they have to be reminded of the task. Some children make a good start but end up with a nearly unrecognizable production. Others simply place marbles at random on the board. Normal children are able to disregard the unessential holes in the board and deal solely with the figure to be copied. They envision a meaningful entity with which they are able to deal. The learning disabled child cannot function as the normal child does, because the tremendous number of stimuli which exists for him causes him to react to things in isolation, not as parts of a meaningful unit.

Another manifestation of dissociation can be observed through the psychologist's use of the Bender-Gestalt test. This seemingly very simple instrument provides professional people with much insight about the behavior and learning problems of the learning disabled child. Figure 7 illustrates one of the nine designs from this test. The test is printed on a small card which is given to the child with the request that he reproduce it on the piece of paper. Figure 7 shows what two learning disabled children did in this situation. The children were not being purposely uncooperative. The relationships between the children and the examiner were excellent. They were friends after many visits. After numerous attempts these children were simply unable to reproduce with their hands what they saw with their eyes. A child trying hard to please the adult may occasionally offer an acute self-diagnosis when he asks, "Why can't my hand do what my eye sees?" The child sees what is to be done, understands the task at hand, but is unable to interpret what he sees into an appropriate motor action. In addition to disturbance as the result of background stimuli here, the child is also characterized by a visuomotor problem involving interpretation. This is the perceptual processing problem mentioned in Chapter 1.

At this point parents may appropriately ask, "What is the meaning of all this for my child's school achievement?" The relationship between the psychologist's findings and the program which should be set up by the teacher is a close one. Consider, for example, the matter of handwriting. In elementary schools it is customary for teachers to begin teaching writing by use of what is called a manuscript method, a type of printing. The results are quite similar to the print utilized in this book. Suppose the child is to form the letter *m*. What is involved here? The *m* is formed by bringing together three distinct lines and arranging them appropriately, as noted in the example:

Obviously the child does not make the three separate lines that we have

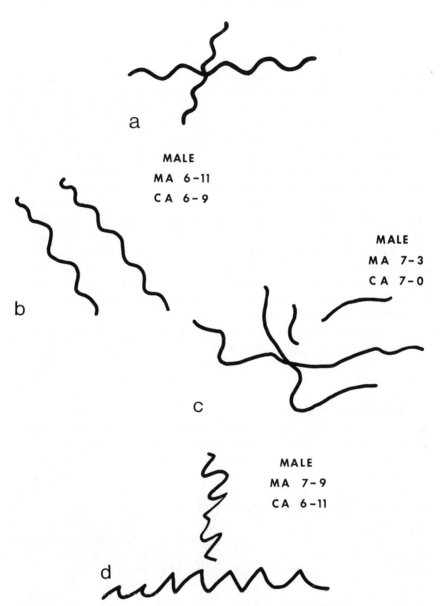

Figure 7. Bender-Gestalt Test Drawings. *a* One of the stimulus cards from the test; *b, c,* and *d* are reproductions of this model made by three learning disabled children illustrating the problem of dissociation. *a* is reproduced here by permission of the American Orthopsychiatric Association, Inc.

shown, but these three lines are necessary for him to understand and to make in order to achieve the proper outcome. For a child characterized by dissociation, this is initially almost an impossibility. Dissociation is the inability to conceptualize separate things into a meaningful unity. The three separate lines of the letter *m* will be conceptualized as such, but to bring them together into something recognizable is oftentimes beyond the ability of the child to accomplish. Dissociation is a great handicap when a child is trying to learn to write, read, and spell, for the same principle applies when the child tries to conceptualize a word or on still a larger basis, a line of print. We have found that these children are assisted significantly when handwriting is taught initially by use of the cursive method, a method which significantly reduces the necessity of putting parts together into new wholes and minimizes the number of times a child has to lift the pencil from the paper and begin a new segment of the letter. As a matter of fact the Palmer Method of teaching handwriting so popular in schools in the decades following 1920 contains most of the elements recommended in good visual perceptual-motor processing recommended here. It contains those elements which reduce the dissociative tendencies in children with learning disabilities.

At a more primitive level, information which psychologists gather regarding dissociation will tell teachers about potential problems and failures children with learning disabilities are likely to have in performing satisfactorily on pegboards, puzzles, and other assembling tasks. As we will mention again later, much practice must be provided the learning disabled child by his teacher so he may develop conceptual skills, and this involves daily activities with pegboards, block designs, and puzzles. There are many of these materials published commercially which parents can purchase for their children as both play toys and as practice experiences. The advice of a teacher or other knowledgeable person should be sought in order to be sure that the materials purchased are appropriate to the chronological age and mental ability of the child.

REVERSING THE FIELD

Another characteristic of learning disabled children, which is a significant one in their inability to learn easily, is what is referred to professionally as *figure-background reversal,* an integral part of the definition of learning disabilities mentioned in Chapter 1. Once again as you read, put down your book. Look around you in the room where you sit and you may perhaps notice a vase or other object resting on a table near you. Now

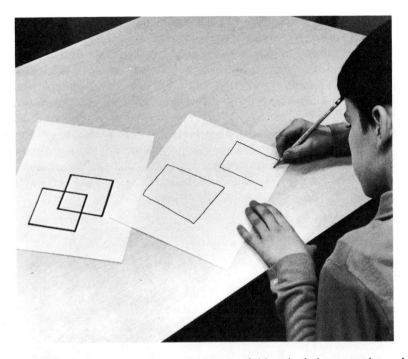

Figure 8. Children who are unable to see parts of things in their appropriate relationship to the whole are said to be dissociating. This boy will have much trouble learning to write letters and numerals because dissociation is still an active problem for him.

analyze the setting in which the object is placed. As you examine the situation more closely you become aware that behind the table on which the vase is placed there is a chair, and behind that the wall of the room on which perhaps a picture hangs. However, we asked you to direct your attention to the vase, and this you initially did. The background of the table, the chair, the wall, the picture, or whatever else may be in your view was not particularly important as you examined the vase visually. You kept the figure (the vase) and the background in their proper relationship one to the other. Now look back again to your book and put your finger on the first word of the first line of the second paragraph on this page. Begin reading here orally. You can do this, because you have the ability to differentiate the figure (the first word on the line) from the background (in this instance all the other words on the page).

The learning disabled child does not have this ability. He is often asked by his teacher to begin reading at such and such a place on the page. The teacher knows that the child knows the word or words. However, in this instance the child in question is characterized by *reversal of field,* a situation wherein the background stimuli take precedence over the foreground stimulus. Thus in the situation of reading at the teacher's request, the child, although he may know the word, may be unable to read upon command because of the greater stimulus value of the background in comparison to the relatively low stimulus value of the word (the figure) to which the teacher has called his attention. This is a confusing situation to both the teacher and the child, for the teacher knows that often in a flash-card drill the child has responded appropriately, but now he apparently cannot do so. The child becomes confused in not being able to discriminate the desired word from the others on the page. (See Figure 9.)

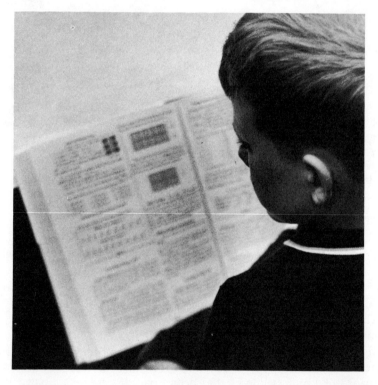

Figure 9. What does the child who is characterized by dissociation, figure-background reversal, and hyperactivity actually see when he looks at a school book? Learning becomes a meaningless experience to him because he is unable to relate appropriately to his learning environment. His books become blurs—enemies instead of friends.

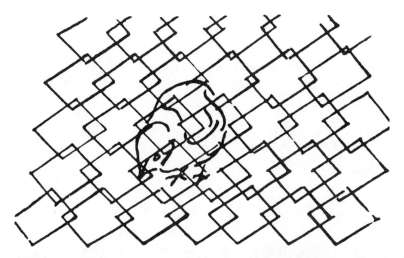

Figure 10. One of nine cards presented to perceptually handicapped and learning disabled children for the purpose of determining figure-background relationship. By permission of the publishers from Strauss and Lehtinen 1947.

Shortly he is given another failure experience when the teacher says, "I guess Billy can't read today. I am sure that Suzy can read it well. You begin, Suzy." Suzy, unfortunately for Billy, starts off reading like a house afire.

Figure-background reversal is observed in many different clinical types of neurologically handicapped children. Figure 10 illustrates one way in which psychologists and educators may test for this. This slide, one in a series of nine developed originally by Strauss and Werner, is exposed in a projector for a brief period of time, just long enough for perception normally to be experienced. Table 1 records the scores achieved by a group of cerebral palsy children between the chronological ages of 6 and 16. Note that the 30 children in the experimental group (cerebral palsy) produced 24 responses which involved figure only (see comparisons 1 plus 2). In contradistinction, the normal children produced 130 figure responses. This discrepancy is statistically significant. The neurologically handicapped children also produced many more (94) "background only" responses in comparison to the normal children. The 27 background responses produced by the normal children were the responses of the youngest children in that group. Comparisons 1, 2, 4, and 5 in Table 1 all indicate statistically significant differences.

Another large group of cerebral palsy children, again 6 to 16 years of age, also performed quite differently when compared with normal

TABLE 1
COMPARISON OF FREQUENCY SCORE OF CEREBRAL PALSY AND NORMAL CHILDREN ON
A FIGURE-BACKGROUND TEST

Type of Response	Cerebral Palsy Frequency Scores	Normal Children Frequency Scores
1. Correct figure	16	74
2. Incorrect figure	8	56
3. Background with correct figure	55	53
4. Background with incorrect figure	97	60
5. Background only	94	27

Figure 11. One of the test items used with perceptually handicapped children in determining figure-background relationship. A three-dimensional presentation, this item is one of sixteen in the total test. It is reproduced by permission of the publisher from Cruickshank *et al.* 1966.

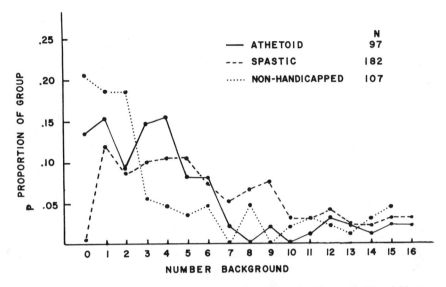

Figure 12. Number of background responses made to the Syracuse Visual Figure-Background Test by three groups of children: normal, athetoid, and spastic types of cerebral palsy. Reproduced by permission of the publisher from Cruickshank *et al.* 1966.

children. Figure 11 illustrates one of the items in a test involving sixteen different slides. The slides this time were produced to stimulate a three-dimensional situation. These slides had different kinds of back-grounds—some difficult, others easy; some meaningful, others nonsense. The slides were carefully evaluated from the point of view of difficulty level. Figure 12 illustrates the different types of responses which three groups of children made in this test. (Spastic and athetoid groups are two types of cerebral palsy.)

It will be noted in Figure 12 that approximately 20 percent of the 107 normal children made no background responses whatsoever, approximately another 20 percent made only one such response, and a like percentage made only two background responses. Approximately 60 percent of the normal children thus produced very few or no background responses whatsoever. Almost all the spastic children, on the other hand, produced one or more background responses. The great difference in the responses of these two groups of children is significant statistically and indicates psychological differences.

Cerebral palsy children are, of course, much more severely affected motoricly than perceptually handicapped or learning disabled children.

The latter children, however, perform similarly to the other groups of children with neurological disabilities on tests of figure-background relationship. Mentally retarded brain-injured (learning disabled) children were shown by Strauss and Werner to do likewise. The types of learning problems caused by figure-background reversal are not related to the severity of the motor problem. They are apparently associated with the perceptual processing problems related to neurological dysfunction and the resultant learning disabilities.

Not too much data appear in the professional literature regarding the implications of figure-background reversal in learning disabled children insofar as general environment is concerned. This writer is of the opinion that the impact of this psychological disability may extend over a broader perceptual area than simply that involved in the immediate visual field—for example, the things on the desk in front of the child in the form of a puzzle or book or arithmetic assignment. Oftentimes, for example, teachers have asked us, "Are these children more sexually motivated than normal children?" When asked the reason for their question, the teacher states, "They are always touching me. They are always pawing me and feeling me. Some of them constantly run their hands over me, and it concerns me." The answer is that they are not to our knowledge more sexually curious than other children. However, because they may be dissociating as well as experiencing figure-background reversal, they may not actually know where the adult is all the time. Indeed, they may not be seeing the teacher as an entity. The child may be getting the teacher confused with the other things in the background of the classroom. These children need the security of knowing that the adult is present, that he is real. They touch him and feel him in order to assure themselves that he is there and in an effort to get some idea of what he is really like. The teacher may minimize the child's need to approach him physically by taking the initiative himself. Always teach within arm's reach of the child. Touch him; put your arm around his shoulder. Pat him on the head as you pass him. Give him reminders that you as a person do really exist. Help the child in this way to form a visual impression of you which is distinct from the background stimuli of the room or place in which you work.

From the preceding discussion it may be seen why some children have difficulty with school learning as well as with adjustment at home, on the playground, and in other social situations. The reader may perhaps feel that we have been speaking of extremes. We do not think so. Many parents will recognize their children in the brief descriptions we have included in this characterization. On the other hand, it must be pointed out that there are learning disabled children who fortunately do not have any of the psychological or learning characteristics of the group described here. In some instances brain injury may exist without observable manifestations of the injury. For some reason or another the neurological impairment has not in any way affected perception or other aspects of learning or motor development. These children and their families are fortunate indeed.

Furthermore, as we have already mentioned, there are other perceptually handicapped children who do not show motor hyperactivity. These children, as a matter of fact, may be extremely quiet and withdrawn. They are so "good" that oftentimes their difficulties in learning are overlooked by teachers and parents. These sweet, quiet, respectful children may be using the technique of withdrawal and retreat into seeming shyness as their method of control. They escape in this way from the confusions of their perceptual problems. Whereas, because of visuo-motor problems, one child may strike out against his world in an uncontrolled and random fashion, another may find security from the confusion of a misunderstood childhood by retreat, withdrawal, and quiet. Such children present very difficult diagnostic problems. In our experience, many of these children when evaluated by skilled personnel have been found to demonstrate many, if not all, of the psychological characteristics of hyperactive learning disabled children.

The important lesson to learn from this is that learning disabled children do not all fit into the same mold. The significant point is that all children who show deviations from what is generally considered to be normative childhood growth and behavior should be referred for competent professional evaluation and diagnosis as early as possible. No criticism will ever be brought against parents who try to find out more about their child and who seek early help in the hope that discovery may mean prevention of more serious problems later. No stigma is ever attached to a parent or child because of being referred to psychological or psychiatric clinics for evaluations which can become the basis for advice and counsel to parents. While there are still not sufficient professional personnel available in most parts of the country who understand the nature and needs of learning disabled children, parents should make an effort to seek out professional advice and assistance. School officials and parents will be censured only for failing to try to understand the child in their charge.

Thus far we have examined briefly the role played by hyperactivity, dissociation, and figure-background reversals in the adjustment of learning disabled children. Still further characteristics of PPD children should be mentioned which have significance to home and school achievement.

THE MUSIC GOES ROUND AND ROUND

A fourth characteristic affecting the learning process of learning disabled children is what psychologists and psychiatrists refer to as *perseveration*. This characteristic is found in many different clinical groups and is typical of other than learning disabled children. In the perceptually handicapped, however, perseveration has a somewhat different relationship and is exhibited differently than when it is observed in the familial type of mental retardation or in schizophrenia, for example.

Perseveration may be defined as the inability of the individual to shift with ease from one mental activity to another. A seeming inertia in the organism makes it impossible for the individual to move quickly from one idea to another, from one set of mental activities to another. While this is the accepted definition of perseveration in mental retardation and in certain types of mental illness, it is not a completely satisfactory definition of perseveration as it is manifested in learning disabled children. With these children perseveration appears to be the prolonged after-affect of a stimulus on subsequent activities in which the child may be engaged. Why one child is affected and not another is unknown. What causes perseveration to characterize a child's adjustment one day and not another is equally as mystifying. When perseveration does occur, it is difficult to interrupt spontaneously by the child or externally by the teacher.

Perseveration has been experienced by most adults from time to time. It may be illustrated by the experience most of us have had in becoming aware that we have been humming a tune for some time, and that we are repeating it over and over again. We make a mental note not to hum it again, only to find seconds later that we are in fact doing just that. At this point we may speak about it to someone near us, relating the problem, and stating, "I'm not going to sing that again." But later we may find ourselves singing the tune again. An hour or so later we may abruptly recall that we have not hummed the tune for a long while, and indeed we may not be able to remember what tune it was that was on our mind. This variety of perseveration is harmless in itself. However, some learning disabled children may have the experience time after time in the course of a school day, and it will have a detrimental effect on their learning.

For example, let us consider handwriting. The teacher has asked the child to do some drill work and to practice writing certain letters. In this case the child is asked to write a row of letters alternately using *"m"* and *"p."* The child understands and agrees. When the teacher returns to the child a moment or so later, he finds that the child has written an entire row of "*m*'s" one after another. He has thoroughly understood the original task. He has not ignored the teacher's request but has simply been so involved with the stimulus "*m*" that he has been unable to shift from one concept to another and thus produce an "*m*" followed by a "*p*," followed by an "*m*," et cetera. On another occasion the child's perseverative tendency may result not in the letter "*m*" at all, but something that looks like this:

Perseveration manifests itself in other than written expressions. Parents and teachers will frequently overhear a child repeating a phrase or sentence again and again. Recently the author was watching a learning disabled child begin to solve some arithmetic problems. The first problem was a two-digit addition: 3 plus 2. The child read the problem to himself, and then, although he has written the answer correctly, he continued to say aloud "Three plus two is five. Three plus two is five. Three plus two is five." This verbalization continued as he attempted to deal with the second problem and, of course, the second problem was incorrectly computed. Perseveration was the cause of the child's error, not his unfamiliarity with the number fact or the technique of problem solution.

There are numerous items from several psychological tests which can be utilized by competent diagnosticians to determine the presence of perseveration, among other characteristics in children and youth with learning disabilities. Figure 13 illustrates one such technique. Here the child has been asked to group a set of forms in any way he wishes. Each form is painted one of four colors. In this set of forms the colors used were brown, yellow, orange, and purple (not shown in illustration). The Goldstein-Scheerer Color-Form Sorting Test (Psychological Corporation) is similar; the colors used in this test are red, yellow, green, and blue. In Figure 13 the child has grouped the blocks according to commonalities in form. He is asked to group them in another way (color). Although the child's movements cannot be ascertained from the illustration, he has been unable to shift from form to color after several requests by the examiner. He illustrates perseveration and the inability to shift from one concept to another.

The Kohs Block Design Test frequently utilized in standardized intelligence tests (Grace Arthur Performance Scale, Wechsler Intelligence Scale for Children) can also be utilized in the same manner as described

Figure 13. A qualitative testing situation in which the child can be observed to perseverate if that characteristic is a dynamic one in his perceptual processing behavior. By permission of Psychological Corporation.

in the preceding paragraph. Obviously, when used in this manner, the subtest is not time-limited. It is utilized in a qualitative rather than quantitative manner.

Figure 14 illustrates another technique which may be utilized in considering both the characteristics of perseveration and concept formation. Shown here is the boy's attempt to organize the blocks of the Vigotsky Test (often also called the Hanfmann-Kasanin Test) into four groups with one common characteristic. The inability to shift often shows itself in this situation, one which is appropriate for older youth and adults. If the subject is able to group the blocks adequately, then he is asked for the generalization which applies to his grouping efforts. Capacity to shift from one approach to another and the ability to generalize into an appropriate concept can be observed.

Perseveration shows itself in numerous other forms. Sometimes a child continues coloring long after the picture has been completed. He may continue to bounce a ball for many minutes after it is appropriate for him to stop. Sometimes these children find it very difficult to stop laughing once they have started. If he tells the teacher a joke, he may want to continue telling it over and over again to everyone around him. If he plays

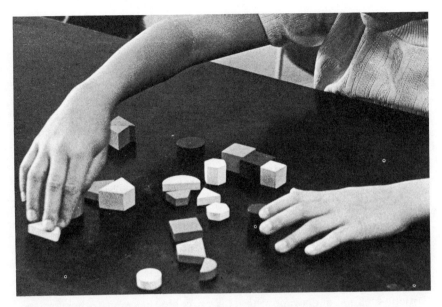

Figure 14. A youth with perceptual processing deficits attempting to perform on the Vigotsky (Hanfmann-Kasanin) Test. Blocks illustrated by permission of Stoetling Company.

with blocks, instead of building a house or building, he may place his blocks in one long continuous chain. If he sharpens a pencil, he may grind it down completely rather than stopping when the lead is sharp. The motor activity in all these cases has been perpetuated—perseverated.

Perseveration is indeed a significant problem for a child to handle. It is not always obvious to the adult that the child is in fact experiencing perseveration. When it is obvious, it is a difficult psychological manifestation to dispel. What the teacher can do to minimize perseveration in learning disabled children will be discussed in a subsequent chapter.

MOTOR SKILLS AND MOTOR DEVELOPMENT

Poor motor skill, another aspect of the development of learning disabled children, is not in reality a psychological characteristic and is thus somewhat out of place in this chapter. Since poor motor skill is usually demonstrated by learning disabled children and is closely related to still another characteristic of psychological development which will be discussed in this chapter, the next few paragraphs are devoted to a discussion of the motor problems of the learning disabled child.

The professional literature contains no extensive studies comparing the motor development of learning disabled children with that of normal children. Therefore, we do not have group data to discuss. But faulty motor ability is so much a part of the picture of the learning disabled child that teachers and clinicians have come to expect it as a typical part of the total syndrome. Faulty motor ability is not the same as motor disinhibition, discussed earlier in this chapter.

In prenatal life the nervous system develops in a very orderly sequence or pattern. The neural tissue in the brain and upper portions of the fetal body develop first. If for some reason at this time or later the fetus experiences an injury, even though it may be slight, specific, or diffuse, motor disability of some degree may result. In the case of learning disabled or perceptually handicapped children, in contrast to cerebral palsied children, the motor disturbance may not be obvious except upon careful and long-term observation. We have already seen how a neurological impairment may affect the fine-motor movements involved in lip motion, sucking, and swallowing. It is probable that many other fine-motor activities will be likewise impaired, and indeed gross-motor activities may also be affected. In the case of the latter the injury would not be sufficient to produce an athetoid or spastic-type movement as in cerebral palsy, but it might very well be sufficient to produce what on first glance appears as a clumsy or uncoordinated child.

In the clinic, for example, it is observed that when walking up the stairs to the examining room, Stephen habitually snags the toe of his shoe on the stair riser. This happens too frequently to be called accidental. The boy appears able to mount the stairs satisfactorily, but he catches his shoe on the stair riser three or four times each time he goes up. Using this behavior as a clue, the examiner later may ask Stephen to perform numerous gross- and fine-motor movement tasks.

Stephen is asked to get down on his hands and knees and to crawl across a gym mat to where the examiner stands. Stephen, aged nine, confesses that he cannot do this. The examiner encourages him and helps him into a crawling position. Stephen makes one or two thrusts forward on the mat but ends up sprawling as a week-old puppy might do. Stephen has little reciprocal-action ability. His arms and legs do not automatically move in a good relationship to one another.

We try again. This time Stephen is asked to swing a baseball bat and hit a large plastic ball which is resting on top of a four-foot pedestal standing in front of him. Stephen takes the bat in his hand, swings it, but misses. A second attempt results in his hitting the pedestal, not the ball.

A third attempt achieves a glancing blow to the ball, but it is sufficient to knock the ball off the pedestal. Once again, it is observed that, although Stephen has good arm movement, he is inaccurate and uncoordinated. He really is what his father calls "a terribly clumsy boy."

A thorough neurological examination gives no definitive clues concerning the cause of his motor uncoordination. The neurologist, however, independently reports the same observations. A careful examination of Stephen's motor skills by the neurologist, psychologist, and his teacher shows that at the age of nine he is unable to tie his shoes, has difficulty in buttoning shirt and coat buttons regardless of their size, often trips when he runs, cannot hop on either foot, and cannot perform satisfactorily on a walking rail. His handwriting is infantile and almost unrecognizable; he has major difficulty in getting the two parts of a zipper connected and then in operating the zipper. In many other aspects of motor development he functions as would a much younger child. For example, instead of picking up a sandwich with two or three fingers, Stephen grasps the sandwich with his whole hand the way three-year-old children generally do.

Later Stephen is asked to do some other things for the examiners. He is asked to lie down on a mat on his back. "Now raise your right leg." Both legs are moved. "Raise only your right leg." Again both legs are moved, and he starts to sit up. "Stephen, this is your right leg. Now raise your right leg." He does so correctly. "Now raise your left leg." Both legs come up off the floor. "Stephen, raise your right arm." The left one moves. "Roll over on your left side." He does not move at all.

Stephen is unaware of body parts, has little orientation to himself, and is not well oriented in space. He fails to comprehend direction and has little or no notion which is his right foot, his left hand or arm, or what to do when asked to move both his right foot and his right arm. His body to him is a relatively meaningless thing. It is there, all right, but it is unorganized and unnamed. People have names for his body parts, but he has not yet related these names, right-left, right arm, left foot, to their appropriate parts. Stephen has really no notion of what his body is like or of how it functions.

Two aspects of motor development then are typically defective in learning disabled children, namely, motor incoordination based on what is believed to be a neurological impairment, and a psychological orientation to self. In this latter connection some further elaboration might well include reference to studies which have been reported by several investigators dealing with finger localization in learning disabled children. Dr. Arthur Benton, of the State University of Iowa, has supplied normative data on this problem and has made the greatest contribution to understanding in this area. Several others who have investigated finger localization abilities in learning disabled children have observed that they are less skilled in this ability than are comparable groups of normal children. Others have observed that there is a positive relationship between skill in finger localization and written arithmetic. While most of these studies have been carried out with children in the range of mental retardation, and too little research is available on the subject at best, it is believed that this aspect of poor conceptualization of the body, its parts, and their functions is interrelated with at least some aspects of school learning and achievement in learning disabled children.

Stephen is an intellectually normal boy with all the classical signs of neurological impairment. He is a learning disabled hyperactive child. He is not unlike the great majority of learning disabled children we have observed over the years. It is not so much the fact that there is a specific physical disability present, a disability which can be classified within a medical category, as there is a tendency for the child to function motoricly as would a much younger child. As Gallagher is quoted earlier in this chapter as saying, there may be a difference of as much as four or more years between his motor-skills level and his chronological age. These children have difficulty riding bicycles, and indeed they may have difficulty in pedaling a tricycle. Steering the latter through a series of obstacles may prove to be very difficult to him, although he may be able to handle it quite well on an open sidewalk where there are no interferences. In swimming pools these children ar generally insecure and uncoordinated. Learning to swim often is accomplished only with difficulty.

SUMMARY OF CHARACTERISTICS

We have mentioned five significant characteristic deficiencies of learning disabled or PPD children, the presence of any one of which may result in serious problems of learning and adjustment: *sensory* and *motor hyperactivity, dissociation, figure-background reversals, perseveration,* and *motor immaturity* or *incoordination.* It must be pointed out again that children will differ markedly one from the other in each of these manifestations of brain injury. Furthermore, these deficiencies may not exist in every child at the same time or in the same degree if they are all present. It is not to be inferred that one can measure degrees of perseveration or dissociation, for example. But one can get an understanding of the relative significance which the problems may have for learning and adjustment in the child. Dr. Gallagher has spoken of the fact that in these children there is a "developmental disparity" between psychological characteristics. This disparity does exist, and it is one of the most interesting as well as one of the most complicating aspects of perceptual processing disabilities which lead to learning disabilities. Psychologists sometimes plot on a graph the performance levels of the child in the several aspects of psychological growth and adjustment which have been measured. On such a graph one expects to see, if the child is learning disabled, a very wide range between the lowest and highest scores achieved. Indeed the range may be considerably more than the four years which Dr. Gallagher mentions. From the point of view of parents, however, and indeed from the point of view of teachers too, the normal picture of a learning disabled child is one of inconsistency and unevenness of performance. If it is the adult's intention to provide the most secure life experience possible for the learning disabled child, then it is necessary for them to come to expect great variation in his abilities and in his characteristics, at least during the early years following the discovery of the problem and the beginning of appropriate education and home training. The external world will have to provide the consistency for him which he cannot provide for himself.

MEMORY AND ATTENTION

One of the most frequently heard complaints from parents and teachers regarding the learning disabled child has to do with the child's inability to remember anything for any length of time. Psychological literature contains reports of much research dealing with memory and remembering. It is generally recognized that memory functions are closely related to emotional tension. Under stress one of the first psychological processes to fail the individual is that of memory or recall.

In Chapter 1, in discussing the definition of learning disabled children, the issue of memory was included. It was then stressed that these children demonstrated an inability to recall, both in terms of long- and short-memory items. This deficiency is increased under conditions of emotional stress and when pressure for rapid recall is required. A teacher in haste to get on to the next child or topic may ask the child a question for which a quick response is expected and is usually produced by normal children. Under the pressure of knowing that an answer is expected, that the teacher or other adult is waiting for a response, that classmates already know the answer and in a variety of ways are straining to catch the teacher's attention to give the answer—under these pressures the child becomes tense, forgetting things which under circumstances of less environmental stimuli he might recall. Regardless of the stress factors in the immediate situation, long- and short-term memory will be affected also by the presence of environmental stimuli which are unessential or not specific to the situation in which the child finds himself.

Numerous examples of this situation could be stated. An eleven-year-old boy, for example, during the annual performance for the Parent-Teachers Association is unable to recall a word of the poem he had memorized perfectly a day or so previously. The tension of the situation has rendered his recall completely ineffective.

"Yesterday," says the teacher to her class, "we learned some number facts. Let's see if we can remember them all today. John, what is the sum of 3 and 2?" Although every other child in the class knows this, John does not. The teacher sighs, and John is embarrassed again.

As we have stated, children with learning disabilities are under almost constant tension and emotional stress. Hence as a group they have exceedingly poor memories. This means that initially parents and teachers must be prepared for much repetitive teaching. What was taught and seemingly learned one day may have to be retaught and relearned the next. A child with poor recall needs much more patience from adults than do normal children, although all children need more patience extended to them than is the usual measure.

Closely associated with the matter of memory is that of attention and attention span. We have already commented upon the fact that the learning disabled child is easily distracted by external and internal stimuli—unessential and irrelevant stimuli. When a child is distracted by something his attention span is interrupted for the task assigned to him or immediately at hand. When one considers how frequently in the course of a short time the learning disabled child is distracted to things in his environment, it is easy to understand that the attention span for the child may indeed be exceedingly short. It is only during this attention span that the teacher or parent may reach the child. It is during periods of attending that rational learning takes place.

The attention span can be measured. The attention spans of learning disabled children have been measured in terms of seconds. Stephen, previously mentioned, when first seen had an attention span of approximately ninety seconds to two minutes under good conditions. Let us assume for a moment that Stephen is in the third grade in his neighborhood school where a good teacher has developed a reading program around a twenty-minute reading lesson. With Stephen's possible two-minute attention span, the likelihood is that the last eighteen minutes will develop into a disciplinary tussle between Stephen and his teacher. Stephen is not being purposely inattentive or disrespectful of his teacher. Indeed, he may love her a great deal, for he knows that she is concerned for and about him. He does not, however, have sufficient understanding of himself or sufficient control to refrain from reacting to the unessential stimuli which are so much a part of this environment. His attention span, then, is short. As the teacher speaks to him and cautions him to "pay attention," tension increases. His ability to remember what has just been said to him is reduced, hyperactivity increases, attention span shortens, and so the vicious circle develops until, as can be expected by the parent or the teacher, things can go no further and an explosion results. A failure experience has again been registered for the child.

WHAT MANNER OF MAN AM I?

In the literature of psychology and psychiatry one reads much about the *self-concept*. The importance of the self-concept cannot be underestimated either in considering normative development or the growth of the learning disabled child.

Let us return for a moment to our discussion of the initial feeding experience which the infant has had either at his mother's breast or by means of a bottle given the baby by his mother. The normal child is responsive to the mother's need to be nursed, and at the same time the mother is responsive to the child's need to be free from hunger. Feeding becomes a truly happy experience. It is an experience filled with warmth, emotional security, low-pitched conversation, and indeed with generally pleasant overtones throughout. The basic physical needs of the child are met, and the child has the elemental structure out of which strong ego concepts will develop. Having properly nursed, and having received a warm response from his parents because of this, he can fall asleep to be awakened later by the same loving people who now play with him and bathe and dress him. Positive responses are given and taken by both sides. Positive emotions fill this situation, leaving the child with a strong feeling of "I am one who can."

As walking and talking begin to develop, the child receives more and more encouragement. His accomplishments are daily reported by telephone from mother to grandmother, from father to office colleagues. As an infant and young child he is told he excels in growth, that he talks and walks well, but soon the child begins to seek praise because of accomplishments in other areas. He learns to read, to ride a bicycle, to swim, to drive a car; he graduates from high school; he earns a scholarship to a university. Obviously there are points of failure in the developmental se-

Figure 15. The young perceptually handicapped child frequently has a mutilated self-concept and body image. She sees herself as one who cannot achieve, and she indeed is a puzzle to herself, her family, and the community. Until the child achieves a wholesome self-concept and becomes aware that her body can work appropriately as a unity, little learning or school achievement will take place. This photograph reproduced with the permission of the Montgomery County Public Schools, Rockville, Maryland.

quence in any child. But for most children, fortunately, successes outnumber failures, and out of successes come strong egos and strong self-concepts. As one deals with groups of children and adolescents, one is often amused at, but always admires, the self-assurance which they have about many matters. It is only when one of them may be embarrassed before the others that assurance gives way to overaggression or withdrawal. Normally, these young people look to the future with no qualms and little hesitation. "My son is never afraid to try anything. I wish I had at my age the nerve he has at his." "They're ready for anything. They never give up." These are statements heard daily by parents who greatly admire their children, but who at the same time are a little awed by them. There is a normal course of development which, with variations, all children experience as they grow from day-old infants to take their place in a teen-age world. With a secure background, reasonably loving and understanding parents, and opportunities for experimentation they develop into well-adjusted young people. Throughout

Figure 16. How does the perceptually handicapped child see himself? A healthy self-concept is essential to positive adjustment of all children. With an appropriate educational program and with supportive services to parents and to the child, he can learn to see himself as a child who can achieve. He learns that his body works for him in a coordinated and appropriate way to accomplish the things which society expects of him.

this period of growth the emerging self-concept has been a controlling factor, for the manner in which the child perceives himself in one situation will have a significant impact on how he conceives himself in many other situations. If he looks upon himself as a "naughty boy," he will tend to behave as he thinks a naughty boy should behave. If he considers himself a failure, he will function as he thinks failures are supposed to function. If he is constantly reminded that he is "not as good as George," he will function in a subordinate role not only to what his friend may do but to what all of his peers may do. The self-concept is a powerful and dynamic force in the development of strong ego characteristics in children.

The author once took a group of four boys to a swimming pool for an afternoon swim. Three of them were high school seniors; the fourth was the thirteen-year-old brother of one of the older boys. The younger boy played the trombone in his school orchestra and was a reasonably accomplished player for his age. At the pool the boys were challenged by a high-diving board. The three older ones vied with each other to demonstrate their prowess, but the younger one held back. He was a little afraid to dive from such a height, yet he felt he must keep up with the others. The adult, sensing what was in the boy's mind, said, "John, you're a remarkable trombone player. I suspect you're just as good a diver too, aren't you?" With this he dived off the tower, and as he came to the surface of the water to be met with applause from the older boys, he commented, "If you can do one thing good, you ought to be able to do two things." Two forces were operative here. First, there was a subtle recognition of the boy's feelings and an acceptance of that feeling by the adult, and the boy knew it. Secondly, there was the reminder that the boy had already succeeded at something for which he was justifiably proud and that on the basis of that success he could probably achieve another feeling of success even in something quite unrelated. Out of a feeling of accomplishment from which ego strength comes there develops a self-concept of one who can succeed. Out of subsequent success came proof for this boy that even in the task which was "scary," as he put it, more success could come. The self-concept was again strengthened. This is the story of ego development in most normal children.

Ego development and the formation of positive self-concepts in normal children are related also to their recognition of a well-conceived *body-image.* The human organism is a source of interest and mystery to human beings. There is little need to remind ourselves of the pride people take in their bodies. This pride supports national industries worth billions any day on the market. Most young people have a good feeling about their bodies. They know how the body works. They can trust it. They know how the fingers work in relation to the hand, the hand to the arm. They know that under certain circumstances their legs will permit their bodies to run. They know that with other coordinations they can dance, skate, ski, swim, and climb. They have a feeling of oneness with their bodies. They conceptualize it as a smoothly operating machine. It is a source of pride to them.

Out of a good and positive body-image comes a good and positive self-concept. Out of warm psychological settings and success also comes a positive self-concept. Out of positive self-concepts come the strong ego forces which make it possible for human beings to adjust well in the complex society in which we live. This is the story of the normal child; it is the story we would wish for all children.

The development of the self-concept of a learning disabled or PPD child is quite another matter. The dynamics of whatever may have developed is similar to that of the normal child, but the hurdles encountered by the child as he grows and develops are quite another story. From the first frustrating moments when feeding does not bring satisfaction to either the child or his mother there develops an endless series of events that emphasizes to the child, "I am one who cannot." Although his father wants to be a pal to him, he as a learning disabled child fails to bring to the father the satisfactions which are needed to cement the relationship. The problems in establishing this relationship remind us again of the composite in Chapter 1. Motor coordination is faulty so that athletic skills cannot be or are not spontaneously achieved. Frustrations which occur when efforts are made to accomplish those things for which the body is not ready to guarantee success bring emotional outbursts which discourage everyone within the sound of the child's screamings. When the nine-year-old sucks from the straw in a bottle, milk drools from his mouth. Classmates call him a "baby." "You need a bib," they say. His younger brother is given a bicycle, although the older child has not been trusted with one because of his poor coordination. He cannot be trusted to go to the grocery store and return without fear of becoming distracted by something along the way or because he may knock bottles off the shelf if he does get there. He is the excuse which he overheard mother give a friend on the telephone for not inviting guests for dinner with the family. He is the one who cannot read, although everyone says that he has plenty of ability. And so, on and on the series continues and builds up over the years to remind him, "I cannot, I cannot, I cannot."

Fingers will not do what they are supposed to do, and apparently do for others. Hands and feet do not perform for him the way he sees them performing for his friends, even though they are younger than he. Arms, legs, and his whole body simply frustrate him instead of helping him.

Another factor which militates against the development of positive self-concepts and of a positive body-image in learning disabled children is the series of psychological characteristics which has been described in this chapter. Just as dissociation interferes with the child's perception of a word or number concept, so it may interfere with his perception of himself or of other human beings. Just as figure-background reversal may confuse the child as he attempts to perceive things written on a blackboard or in his book, so it may confuse him as he attempts to understand the human form against the environmental background. Because hyperactivity tends to reduce their attention span and to give them only fleeting and highly inaccurate perceptions, these children appear never to have had an opportunity to study the human form for a long enough time

Figure 17. Draw-a-Person test productions of four children with visual perceptual processing deficits resulting in motor inadequacies. This is a common characteristic in children with learning disabilities: *a.* male C.A. 9-9; M.A. 9-0 (courtesy Dr. Harry V. Bice); *b.* male C.A. 9-1; M.A. 8-9; *c.* male C.A. 8-6; M.A. 8-8; *d.* male C.A. 7-1; M.A. 7-4.

to get a reasonable impression of what it is like. Just as pieces in a puzzle remain in the hands of a learning disabled child quite separate elements and are fitted into the whole concept only with much difficulty, so the pieces of the human form which the child has perceived come to be a part of his understanding of how the whole body works much later than with most children and sometimes even then in a confused and inaccurate manner.

As a result of these children's long experience with failure, and as a result of the perceptual problems which they have, their body-images become very distorted. Figure 17 illustrates the body-images of several learning disabled children who were asked by the psychologist to draw a picture of a person. Note Figure 17a. This is a drawing by a nine-year-old boy of good mentality. The small lines at the right of the body are fingers. When asked why he didn't put the fingers on the arm which is attached to the body, he responded, "My fingers never do anything for me. Why should I put them on my hand?" Note the immature body-images which the other three drawings depict. There are many elements in these drawings which give important personality clues to trained psychologists, but for now we shall be concerned only with the general body-image concepts which are involved. The boys who drew these pictures are all nearly seven years of age or older. Do you recall what a normal child in the second grade can do when asked to draw a human figure? The results are much more perfect and accurate. In drawing some of the figures depicted here, the learning disabled children seem hardly to have had a concept of what the human body is like.

It is indeed impossible for the child to develop a positive self-concept when it is based on the distorted body-image he holds of himself. With a self-concept which is based on the distorted body-image, he will behave ineffectually in society. With a body-image which is imperfect and unclear to the child, there is little chance for strong ego concepts to develop. When all reminds him that he is not what he should be, how can he develop the internal strengths which will permit him to meet the daily challenges of both his own society and that of the adults with whom he lives? Because he does not possess the internal security by which to measure and direct his life, he frequently must operate in an unthinking, trial-and-error fashion. The demands of society are pressing in on him, constantly requiring him to do things; yet at the same time his past experiences remind him that he cannot do anything sufficiently well to satisfy anyone. To protect what ego there is, the child then may react aggressively, by striking, by displaying emotion, by screaming, by withdrawing and refusing to talk, by too much sweetness, by infantilism, or by other means which serve his purpose but which are usually inappropriate to the situation. As with the normal child, the self-concept is a significant and controlling force in the behavior and adjustment of the child. If the learning disabled child conceives of himself as a failure, he will act in terms of his concept of a failure. If he conceives of himself as one who is always at the mercy of adults over whom he has no control, he will act, if he is to survive psychologically at all, in a way which convinces him he is protected. These are not easy points of view to live with if one happens to be the parent of such a child. These are realities, however, which must be faced. Fortunately, they are reversible if an attempt to do so is initiated early enough by competent professional personnel and if the professional attention is continued long enough.

CONTROLS AND SOCIAL RELATIONSHIPS

The perceptual processing deficits together with the resultant problems of attention and memory separately and together have a great influence on the child's adjustment in social situations. The manner in which the social situation and the child react on one another, the techniques which the child employs to adjust, and the interrelations of these variables with some or all of the psychological characteristics which have been described here—all combine to provide a total description of the child in society. Each is important in and of itself, but parents, teachers, and others must also be prepared to deal with the total constellation of factors.

Learning disabled children characterized by perceptual processing deficits essentially are controlled and control themselves in terms of external stimuli and situations. The lives of these children and youth are essentially spent in *reacting to* the external world and all it contains. The goal is to assist the child to control his world from within rather than reacting to his world—often in desperate and thoughtless ways. If, for example, the child for whatsoever reason is unable to refrain from reacting to the external stimuli of his environment, his controls will essentially be in terms of the multiplicity or strength of those stimuli, whether sensory stimuli or those eliciting a motor response. Even internal stimuli can be considered in this same perspective: a gastric disturbance, genital discomfort, intestinal flatulence, or skin irritations. The stimuli of whatsoever source distract. The child reacts to the stimulus in a manner to reduce the value of the stimulus or to protect the self and control the stimulus. It is the *environmental* situation which is causing the child's reaction. It is not the *development* of insight, the thoughtful analysis of cause and effect, or the intellectual desire to modify a situation which prompts action. It is a cause-and-effect reaction without the imposition of intellectual controls from within. As we shall note in later pages, this random reaction to a situation usually results in a failure experience.

When the same factors as we have described in the preceding paragraph are operative in social situations—responses without thoughtful analysis—the child finds himself in ever more stressful situations. Now, not only is failure a factor, but the self-concepts of parents, teachers, or other adults who have a vested interest in the child and a feeling of responsibility for what he does serve to create an added level of tension. The author and his wife were on one occasion invited to dinner in the home of a family where there was among three children one with severe and specific learning disabilities. At the dinner table, around which seven persons sat, the child in question was faced with a social situation of great proportions. He had already spilled his gingerale "cocktail" on the living room floor and had upset a dish of peanuts when he was asked to pass them to guests. At the dinner table he was confronted with a highly stimulating visual situation. One can easily envision the appearance of the table set for guests. His father placed a dinner plate (the plate itself decorated) in front of the boy on which there were mashed potatoes and gravy, a large helping of green peas, and a slice of roast beef. This plate was surrounded by a salad plate, eating utensils, a glass of milk and another of water. As the father placed the plate in front of the boy he said, "OK, Jimmy, now cut your meat and eat it. Show us what a young man you are." He was nine years old.

The father's tone of voice indicated expectancy. The boy was still concerned over his earlier poor behavior in the living room. Six pairs of eyes were on him to see if he carried out his father's commands. The table top was covered with visual stimuli. There was movement of the diners which caused further distraction. The child over-reacted to the stimuli in the situation, grabbing his knife and a spoon, bumping the glass of milk in the process and overturning it, and pulled back quickly from the table to avoid getting wet. In the process of temporary escape he hit his mother's arm which bumped against the glass of water and overturned it as well. The family as a unit descended on Jimmy with cries of exclamation and concern. Here is a situation, not uncommon in the daily life of these children, where Jimmy's reaction to a situation without analysis and thought, without inner controls, resulted in havoc. A failure experience was superimposed on a childhood history of failure—with more to come.

As we shall see in the chapters which follow, the educational goals, whether in school, the home, or in the community at large, are to substitute failure with success experiences, to substitute spontaneous physical reactions with intellectual analysis before action, and to provide the child with an internal locus of control rather than to further his agony in responding to the external controls inherent in the stimuli which constantly surround him. To accomplish this is difficult and painstaking, but it is not impossible.

There is one further comment which should be made with respect to the impact of perceptual processing deficits on adjustment. The sum total of all which has been said in this chapter is an often-observed characteristic of inadequate social perception in children with learning disabilities. This is not merely a matter of misperceiving in social situations those things which are related to faulty development of eye-hand coordination or auditory-motor incoordination, but is the end result of all the factors here discussed as they impinge on the total adjustment of the child in a given social situation. Sometimes the behavior being considered here is viewed as exaggeration, "story telling," boasting, or bragging. In part some of the behavior may be related to these terms, for, if anything, the learning disabled child needs experiences which bring him ego enhancement. However, there is also a failure to perceive socially appropriate responses to a given situation. This failure comes from a lack of appropriate success experiences which both the child and his peers or adult friends can accept. A child reports that his father just bought the family a new motor boat. "Boy, my Dad got us eleven of those," said Mark, a child with severe perceptual and learning problems, "and one of them is twenty-three feet long with two inboard motors."

On another occasion, Joey, who was always seeking much-needed attention, arrived at school with the announcement, "Mrs. Stanley, do you know what I saw walking to school on the other side of the street? A lion!" "Oh, Joey," responded the teacher, "lions aren't out walking along the sidewalks, at least in this town." "Yes, they are," was the rejoinder, "and he came over and licked my hand, too. I petted him." Often socially inappropriate statements such as these are made in a situation where they cannot with certainty be challenged. There might be a lion! The inability to perceive and report situations with social accuracy is a combination of the emotional tensions experienced by the learning disabled child as well as of his need for success experiences. These, coupled with a long series of perceptual processing deficits, combine to produce a child who has marked difficulty in making appropriate social perceptions.

SUMMARY

In general this is the way learning disabled children are. We have taken time in this chapter and in Chapter 1 to examine briefly from whence the learning disabled child has come, how he got the way he is, and what he is like psychologically. The learning disabled child is a complex creature, not yet completely understood by those who work with him. He is an educational and psychological challenge to professionals and frequently an enigma to parents. It is rather obvious from even the brief description which we have included in this chapter that this child has problems which make it difficult for him to be included in the regular grade group of his neighborhood school.

He is not a child who should always be placed permanently in a residential school, although some such schools are outstanding and are needed for many children. He is a child who can profit from specialized educational and psychological services which should be established in his own school district. If the services are sufficiently comprehensive, if the educators are qualified, if they have appropriate administrative supports, if they have the full and requisite parent cooperation, much should be accomplished for the child in a reasonable period of time to make it possible for him to return to the neighborhood school and to live a healthier life in his own home.

SELECTED REFERENCES OF SPECIAL INTEREST TO PARENTS

Bakwin, H., and Bakwin, R. M. *Behavior Disorders in Children.* 4th ed. Philadelphia: Saunders, 1972.

Bateman, B. "Three Approaches to Diagnosis and Educational Planning for Children with Learning Disabilities." *Academic Therapy Quarterly* 11 (1967): 215–22.

Beck, H. "Detecting Psychological Symptoms of Brain Injury." *Exceptional Children* 27 (1961): 59–63.

Clements, S. D. *Some Aspects of the Characteristics, Management, and Education of the Child with Minimal Brain Dysfunction.* Glen Ellyn, Ill.: West Suburban Association for the Other Child, c. 1965, pp. 1–4.

Gordon, S. *The Brain-Injured Adolescent.* New York: New York Association for Brain-Injured Children, March, 1964.

Ilg, Frances L., and Ames, Louise B. *Child Behavior.* Glen Ellyn, Ill.: West Suburban Association for the Other Child, 1955, pp. 1–4.

Madsen, C. K., and Madsen, C. H. *Parents/Children/Discipline.* Boston: Allyn and Bacon, 1972.

Laufer, M. W. *Problems of Cerebral Dysfunctions.* New York: New York Association for Brain-Injured Children, c. 1965.

Lewis, R. S. *The Brain Injured Child.* Chicago: National Society for Crippled Children and Adults, 1963, pp. 1–14.

Lewis, R. S.; Strauss, A. A.; and Lehtinen, L. E. *The Other Child.* 2d ed. New York: Grune & Stratton, 1960, pp. 4–12.

Strother, C. R. *Discovering, Evaluating, Programming for the Neurologically Handicapped Child.* Chicago: National Society for Crippled Children and Adults, 1963, pp. 1–10.

SELECTED REFERENCES OF SPECIAL INTEREST TO TEACHERS

Ayres, A. J. "Patterns of Perceptual-Motor Dysfunction in Children: A Factor Analytic Study." *Perceptual and Motor Skills* 20 (June 1965): 335–68.

Bateman, Barbara. "Learning Disabilities—Yesterday, Today, and Tomorrow." *Exceptional Children* 31 (December 1964): 167–78.

Bannatyne, A. *Language, Reading and Learning Disabilities; Psychology, Neuropsychology, Diagnosis, and Remediation.* Springfield, Ill.: Thomas, 1971.

Cohn, R. "The Neurological Study of Children with Learning Disabilities." *Exceptional Children* 31 (December 1964): 179–86.

Cruse, D. B. "The Effects of Distraction upon the Performance of Brain-Injured and Familial Retarded Children." In *Readings on the Exceptional Child,* edited by E. P. Trapp and P. Himelstein. New York: Appleton-Century-Crofts, 1962, pp. 492–500.

Fouracre, M. "Learning Characteristics of Brain-Injured Children." *Exceptional Children* 24 (January 1958): 210–12, 223.

Frostig, Marianne. "Visual Perception in the Brain-Damaged Child." *American Journal of Orthopsychiatry* 32 (March 1962): 279–80.

Hewett, F. "A Hierarchy of Educational Tasks for Children with Learning Disorders." *Exceptional Children* 31 (December 1964): 207–14.

Kephart, N. C. "Perceptual Motor Aspects of Learning Disabilities." *Exceptional Children* 31 (December 1964): 201–206.

Paine, R. S. "Organic Neurological Factors Related to Learning Disabilities." In *Learning Disorders,* edited by J. Hellmuth. Seattle, Wash.: Special Child Publications, 1965, pp. 1–29.

Strauss, A. A., and Lehtinen, L. *Psychopathology and Education of the Brain-Injured Child.* New York: Grune & Stratton, 1947.

3

Finding Out About the Child or Youth: Diagnosis

In order to deal with a problem one should first determine what the problem is. This is true for a scientist whether he is working in the field of metallurgy or with a human being. Understanding the problem is considerably easier sometimes when working with inanimate objects, but efforts must be made to understand the human with a similar degree of exactness. At present such an understanding is not possible, for the diagnostic tools available to professional people in studying human beings have limitations. Also, the human being varies from day to day and from week to week and will tolerate only so much disturbance, discomfort, or pain while under study. Both the subject being studied and the tools which may be used to study him, while good, could often be much better. This is particularly true with children and especially with learning disabled children and youth.

However, it is essential that teachers and other professional persons who are going to work with the learning disabled child have an opportunity to understand him as completely as possible before education or therapy is initiated. If a teacher does not have access to the vast amount of compiled data concerning a particulat learning disabled child, much time will be wasted while the teacher, over the school year, gradually learns what diagnosticians should have told him initially. Often because of lack of information about a child the teacher is confused and stumbles along until gaining the insight weeks later which he should have already had; valuable time is wasted. While we use the teacher as an example here, the same is true of the speech therapist, the psychologist, the psychiatrist, or any other professional person who will work with the child on a long-term basis. Furthermore, out of complete studies can come accurate parent counseling and guidance. The more imcomplete the data, the more does advice, guidance, and programming for the child have to rest upon conjecture.

Parents are often concerned when professional people apologize for their data with such statements as, "We just don't have ways of finding out." "At this time we cannot be certain." "The instruments are too crude." Why, say parents, do these things need to be said in a century when mechanization and scientific instruments can send a man to the moon? It does seem perplexing. Yet the human organism does not lend itself to study or perform according to the fine mathematical formulas that rockets do.

While there are newer professions, the professions which must deal with the learning disabled or perceptually handicapped child are essentially in their infancy. Psychology as a profession really came into its own during World War II, and clinical psychology as a professional field was not accepted by the American Psychological Association until after that. Psychiatry is one of the newest specialities within the medical profession and, like psychology, even today is often not accorded equality with other branches of medicine by all medical persons. It is gradually receiving more acceptance, but still has a long way to go. Neurology, too, is youthful in the medical profession, particularly pediatric neurology, the speciality needed with learning disabled children. Well-prepared educators of learning disabled children, as parents of many learning disabled children have become aware, are still very scarce. Furthermore, whereas millions and millions of dollars have been spent in developing the scientific tools and instruments for the jet age, the diagnostic tools which the professions of medicine, psychology, and education use have mostly been developed with comparatively few dollars—frequently dollars which an interested teacher or psychologist himself has invested.

Society still has much to do in understanding human beings and making it possible for all children to grow and to develop to the maximum of their potential. These statements are made not by way of excuse or rationalization but to remind parents that there are valid if not good and just reasons why it may not always be possible to provide an exact blueprint of their learning disabled child, why it may not always be possible to determine that the child is indeed learning disabled, a P.P.D. child, or why the professional person hesitates when parents ask for a prediction concerning the future adjustment of the child. It is often impossible to obtain the facts needed to render an accurate diagnosis or prognosis.

THE EDUCATOR'S ROLE IN DIAGNOSIS

It has generally been assumed that the psychoeducational diagnostic responsibility is one reserved to clinical or school psychologist. The failure to provide such personnel within the public school systems in a number sufficient to provide necessary information to educators has prompted many who work with children with learning disabilities to encourage teachers themselves to assume this role. In many ways this is a very appropriate decision, but its success depends entirely on the quality of the teacher and the clinical adequacy of the teacher education program.

This author is unimpressed with the teacher-education program nationally in the area of learning disability. The "instant specialist" in both universities and public schools is an unfortunate phenomenon, and there appears to be no rational move to correct this situation. However, if there is a quality teacher-preparation program and a careful selection of teacher personnel for the learning disabled, it is relatively easy to turn the teacher of the perceptually handicapped child into a teacher-diagnostician. As will be discussed in later pages, the relationship between perceptual processing deficits and educational programming is a close and intimate one. It requires a clinical teacher in order to be able to make responses to the child's specific learning (perceptual processing) needs. Because the child's needs change rapidly, if the educational program is a good one and is responsive to learning needs, there is a demand for constant updating of psychoeducational diagnostic information.

The educational program will quickly get out of joint insofar as the child's development is concerned, if the teacher does not have continuous status information regarding the child's attention span, figure-ground development, dissociative tendencies, body-image concept, and other characteristics basic to growth and development. Over the years, in working with teachers, we have provided them with extensive training in the application and interpretation of both qualitative and quantitative measures of these factors and others which are inherent in the definition of learning disabilities discussed in Chapter 1. If the educator has up-to-date information about the learning needs of each child, it is possible to achieve on a constantly progressive basis what Newell Kephart referred to as the *perceptual-motor match* and which I have referred to as the *psychoeducational match*. With respect to the former, Kephart recognized an intimate relationship between the perceptual processing deficits of a child and that child's motor development. Kephart, like A. Jean Ayres and others, recognized that intellectual development is essentially a response to a perceived stimulus. In the case of the psychoeducational match, it is felt that there is a direct relationship between the perceptual processing deficit in learning disabled children and the type or nature of the learning task prepared by the educator for the child. Within this concept, if the educator does not know the status of the perceptual processing deficits in a child at a particular time, it is not possible to meet that child's needs with appropriate educational materials in an appropriate setting. The child's progress is retarded significantly.

THE NATURE AND SCOPE OF DIAGNOSIS

The learning and adjustment problems, of perceptually handicapped or learning disabled children are among the most complicated of any found in childhood. Their nature is such that an *interdisciplinary diagnostic team* is required for the diagnosis of such a child. It is this writer's feeling that parents should be aware of the type of information which teachers and others must have about their child in order to serve him well; parents who have this awareness will want to refer their child to diagnostic centers where such information can be obtained. The necessary diagnosis may be expensive. Many highly specialized individuals may be utilized in trying to find out what the child is like both so as to be able to advise parents and to provide meaningful information to the persons who will carry on the long-term treatment and training.

Parents may have difficulty in finding appropriate diagnostic services, and school authorities will be able to make helpful suggestions. Medical centers related to universities frequently have outpatient clinics which perform these services. Speech and hearing centers sometimes have multidisciplinary staffs with interests in the field of learning disability. Larger cities may have medical centers, psychological centers, and child guidance clinics with appropriate diagnostic staffs. Pediatricians frequently will know of local services which have proved helpful to them in other situations and may again in this instance be appropriate. When going to a psychological services center or to a child guidance clinic, parents should not simply follow the yellow pages of a telephone book. Listings there insofar as the professions are concerned often leave much to be desired. Seldom, if ever, is professional screening employed in accepting advertisments. One should always make certain before utilizing an unfamiliar service or individual that the agency or individual is recognized by the examining board of the profession involved. Even this does not insure that all services will be of the highest nature, but it certainly helps. The first responsibility of the parent, however, is to seek out and utilize the best diagnostic services which can be found near where the child lives.

That the services be located near the child's home is important. As will be discussed later, there will be a need to utilize some of these services at intervals for a long period of time; hence, the closer the services to the child's home, the greater the convenience to all concerned. If the child can be seen by the same professional personnel from time to time, or a least by personnel within the same clinic, comparative data regarding his progress is at hand; this is particularly helpful to the educators.

We have already stated that interdisciplinary diagnosis will be required. This means that persons representing several different professions will need to examine the child. If not all professions required are available in the same center, one individual—perhaps the pediatrician or the psychologist—can see the child first then refer him to other specialists for additional information. The information will then be routed back to the first member of the diagnostic team. It is better if a broadly based clinic or medical center can be utilized for this purpose, because then there is also the possibility of interdisciplinary staffing and consensus before final decisions regarding the learning disabled child are reached.

The following examinations will have much to contribute to the parents' and teachers' understanding of the child. Their separate pieces of information together will form the picture educators need which makes it possible for parents better to deal with the child while he is home. These are not listed in the order of their importance, for each is important in some way.

1. Educational evaluation
2. General pediatric examination
3. Opthalmological and optometric examination
4. Pediatric clinical psychological examination
5. Pediatric neurological examination
6. Pediatric psychiatric examination
7. Social history questionnaire
8. Speech and hearing examination
9. Psychological evaluation

This is rather a staggering list of tests for a young child, but each has a purpose, and each is important for the welfare of the learning disabled child. Cantwell has edited a volume which we highly recommend as one which contains excellent information regarding diagnosis. Although he and his contributing authors speak of "hyperactive children," they are referring essentially to the same child discussed here.

The remainder of this chapter will be devoted to brief discussions of each examination; an attempt also wll be made to indicate the kind of information needed by the school to plan its program. Attention at this point is focused on information needed by the school rather than on that needed by other professional groups or by parents. Educators will have responsibility for the child for more hours each day, for more days each week, and for more weeks and years in the life of the learning disabled child than will the members of all the other professions combined. This is in keeping with the definition of learning disabilities presented in Chapter 1. Only the parents themselves will have more continuous contact with the child than will educators. Much of the diagnostic data prepared for school use in curriculum planning will be appropriate also for parent counseling and assistance.

Following the discussion of each type of examination is the case data of a learning disabled child so the reader may see what sort of information is considered important and is made available on a confidential basis to the professional people who will work with the child. We stress the confidential nature of these examinations. Parents must trust professionals that the information gathered will be utilized only for the benefit of their child and for a better understanding of him. Information received in this situation of trust must be treated confidentially by all professionals. Never should anyone not directly involved in assisting the child be given information without parental knowledge and consent. Parents, on the other hand, must not feel that those who ask questions are doing so from any point of view but that of concern for the child.

The development of a diagnosis and complete case history is a time-consuming and laborious task. Parents, therefore, should approach the many tests and interviews with patience, not expecting immediate notification of results. The speed with which the process is completed depends on the availability of the specialists and upon how many tests the child can tolerate. Several visits may be required in order to complete the psychological evaluations alone.

Social Work Responsibility

The first person with whom the family will have contact in a large medical or child guidance center is likely to be either a medical or psychiatric social worker. This is an individual with much professional preparation and experience who will receive from the parents the initial family data. He will present the information he collects to the examining personnel, and he may go with the child to some of the examinations or at least see that appointments are appropriately made and kept. This person will participate in all staff conferences regarding the child, and he may be the person through whom all specialist reports are routed. The social worker may then be asked to integrate the information received and interpret it to the family or send it to the school or agency which may originally have referred the child or who will work with the child. At other times the social worker may also engage in parent counseling or maintain a therapeutic relationship with the child for many months or years.

The social-work interview included below was with the parents of a perceptually handicapped boy who when he was first seen was slightly more than eight years old. The reader will note that this case material includes information from more than one examination. This child was reevaluated, and that later material has been integrated into the picture being presented here. When first seen, the parents had been told by the school authorities that their child had a problem which could not be handled in a regular grade, and a recommendation had been made for special class placement. The parents were not at all certain that they wanted their boy in a special class for children with learning disability, but they knew they had a child with problems and they had initiated the total evaluation. As the reader examines carefully the case data presented, he should keep in mind the characteristics of learning disabled children which were discussed in Chapters 1 and 2. Note also that this particular child is not looked upon as extreme in his behavior. There are many aspects of his development which are little different from that of other children. It will be apparent, however, that the child does show characteristics which prevent him from making full use of the learning situation in his neighborhood school and which produce problems for him and others in his home.

PROBLEM

Tom's difficulties apparently started off with speech. He received speech therapy and was making progress. Then he had some difficulty reading (which his father said he had supposed would be the case). Last year there was a question of discipline in school as well. Because of the discipline problem and the speech and reading difficulties, he was placed in Special Education (at the end of his first year in school).

He seems to get excited when something new occurs and this difficulty became more apparent when he entered the second grade. At home apparently he is not much of a discipline problem, although he is said to be quite strong-willed. His reading difficulty seems to center around a reversal problem with his b's and p's, his s's, w's and m's. This was noticed by the parents. He has had a neurological examination, including an EEG which apparently was normal. At the clinic where this was done, no reason could be found for some of his difficulties and at that time the suggestion was made that a psychological test should be done and Special Education might be helpful. Last year, when in Special Education, he seemed to do well. He presently is receiving remedial reading instruction from a neighbor who apparently does this work quite well. There was no apparent retardation in appearance of speech; it is just that it was always unclear and immature. His speech has markedly improved, although there are one or two sounds which he still does not get right. His dislike for school might have stemmed from the difficulty with some of his playmates who were making his life rather miserable because of his inability to function on their level. He tends to get excited easily in groups and is certainly easier to handle in a smaller group setting or when alone. He is said to "open up" more with other people than he will at home with his parents.

FAMILY HISTORY

1. Maternal grandmother living and well.
2. Maternal grandfather living and well. The grandparents are separated.
3. Paternal grandmother died when father was 2 years of age in an epidemic of influenza.
4. Paternal grandfather died of cancer.
5. Mother has one brother who is living and well.
6. Father has one brother and one sister, both of whom are living and well. The sister has two girls who apparently are also having reading difficulty.

FAMILY BACKGROUND

Father: (age 41). He is in good health, wears glasses for myopia, and has retenitis pigmentosa. He is a research assistant at a physics lab, has a master's degree in electrical engineering. Interests: reading, community discussion groups. Problems: he was raised by an aunt, but traveled about quite a bit, from one relative to another, until he was 7 years of age, at which time he and his aunt went to live with his father. He was always small for his age and therefore had difficulty defending himself. Personality: quiet, retiring individual who is said not to be an extrovert. Attitude toward patient's difficulties: he tried to be very understanding and patient and he said that he might be a little more strict than other parents in the neighborhood.

Mother: (age 38). She is in good health. Finished high school and used to do clerical work. Interests: Handiwork and photography. Personality: quiet, calm and cheerful. Attitude: not nearly as concerned as other people seem to be with some of the difficulties of Tom.

Marriage: The parents have been married fourteen years. It is the first marriage for both. The marriage is said to be compatible.

Siblings: None. (Tom has a cat and more recently has acquired a rabbit.)

MOTHER'S MEDICAL HISTORY DURING PREGNANCY WITH CHILD

The mother has had three miscarriages—one at six weeks, one at four weeks (then Tom was born), and the third one (after Tom's birth) at four weeks. Apparently no explanation for these miscarriages has been attempted. During her pregnancy with Tom she received hormonal therapy. Apparently there was an indication of her losing Tom, due to bleeding, and so she was put to bed where whe remained for about six months of the pregnancy and received Stilbestrol. She was 30 years of age at the time of his birth. Tom was born in a local hospital. The bag of water was ruptured six or eight hours prior to delivery. The delivery itself was uneventful except that Tom apparently was born a month earlier than the due date. His birth weight was 5 pounds 7 ounces. He was seen within the first twelve hours. He was placed on formula feeding and was slow in eating and sucking. Apparently he tired easily, although there was no difficulty in the actual nursing or in swallowing.

PAST MEDICAL HISTORY OF PATIENT

DPT and smallpox vaccination during first year of life. He has had his polio immunizations. He had chickenpox at the age of 5, measles at the age of 7, mumps at the age of 6. At 3 years of age, on the way back from a trip, he was hospitalized. Apparently he had a type of breathing difficulty which was described as asthma, and at that time, during his hospitalization, an anemia was discovered and he was transfused. Since then he has been on medication for the anemia and apparently at present is back to normal. He has never had any convulsions and currently is on no other medication.

DEVELOPMENTAL HISTORY

Tom was always a slow feeder, he was slow in sitting up, standing, walking, teething, and speaking. He seemed to be a happy baby though. His bottle was propped. There was no sleeping difficulty. He started counting when he went to kindergarten and was able to understand and perform instructions and commands. There was apparently no visual or audiotory difficulty. He likes to be outside playing a great deal and will sit and watch TV only if he is really interested. Does not like to sit through Sunday School. His toilet-training was uneventful, being accomplished by 3 years of age with no history of enuresis. He is said to be right-handed and at one time there was a question of whether he might not have been ambidextrous. He is said to be able to dress himself and does better with one other playmate, rather than a large group. He is said to be able to ride a two-wheeler bicycle and to roller-skate, and is said to be active in general. At the table he used to fidget quite a bit, but is much better now. He does not suck his thumb, bang his head, or rock. Personality: logical, loves to argue. He is not particularly friendly. Punishment: he is either spanked or put in his room. He will argue at first and then sort of respond. Fighting: he is able to fight and will fight. Frustration: he gets and throws things but does not have actual temper tantrums.

The reader can see that in the case of this child the social worker has elicited considerable information which will quickly provide a background of understanding for each of the examining specialists. Parents will not have to give this recital each time a new person sees their child. A careful reader will have already noted several things the parents have told the social worker which in turn begin to form a picture for the diagnosticians of possible neurological problem learning disorder: speech distortions, "excited easily," "making life miserable," history of miscarriages and other positive prenatal signs, breathing difficulty, anemia, transfusion, and the question whether the child was to be left or right handed. There are also many things in the social case history which are, of course, typical of all children. The reader may wish to compare the child in this diagnostic summary with the "composite of a child," presented in Chapter 1.

PEDIATRIC EXAMINATION

This writer prefers to have children seen next by a well-prepared pediatrician. The pediatric examination will give to the other members of the interdisciplinary team a clear picture of the general health history of the child, for the pediatrician knows both the medical problems of young children and the relationship of these to normative child development. The pediatrician in his professional preparation has also had sufficient background in pediatric neurology, pediatric ophthalmology, pediatric cardiology, and in other pediatric specialities so as to be able to recognize problems requiring the attention of another specialist.

PHYSICAL EXAMINATION

General appearance. Tom was a pleasant boy who came along without difficulty and who was noted to talk in a rather babyish, immature way. When we walked into the examining room he recognized the pipe on the table and immediately put into his mouth, saying that he smokes and asked me to light the pipe for him. He wanted to know what I was going to do, adding, "You are not goint to put me to sleep and cut me open—I'm tough—I could knock your brains out." He kept jabbering away about this and was somewhat hyperactive.

His three wishes included (1) jet bomber, (2) helicopter, (3) horse. He said he didn't know about a good mommy or a bad mommy. To the ambulance story he said, "A man who was driving it was killed with a twelve-gauge shotgun." He recognized a penny, nickel, dime, and quarter, and knew their value. In counting, he said "thorty" for thirty and "thorteen" for thirteen. Of note is the fact also that he kept saying, "I don't know," rather than risking an answer which he was unsure of. However, when reassured, he frequently did give a proper answer. Tom was able to hop equally well on both feet and could skip. He was able to walk on both heels and toes.

The remainder of the physical examination, including the neurological exam, was negative. When approached for an examination of his genitalia he made a movement to protect them. He was able to dress himself rather well, including the tying of his shoelaces.

This pediatrician has some interest in child psychiatry as well as pediatrics, and he made some attempts to understand the child from the point of view of concept formation. His observations can serve as a point of departure for the psychologist or psychiatrist. There are also references to hyperactivity, speech substitutions, and the motor hyperactivity displayed by the boy when he took the physician's pipe and placed it in his mouth.

NEUROLOGICAL EXAMINATION

The neurological examination of learning disabled children should be completed by a pediatric neurologist. One who has had extensive experience and professional pediatric preparation is more skilled in understanding the problems of learning disabled children than is one who has spent his life working with adults. Children are different from adults neurologically as well as psychologically. The purpose of the pediatric neurological examination is to discover if there are areas of actual

Figure 18, *a, b.* Testing the ability of the child to identify body parts is an important aspect of the diagnostic program. Following diagnosis, those children who need it are given daily activities to aid them in recognizing body parts and understanding the coordinate function of their bodies. An understanding of the fact that the body can and must work as a unity is an important element in the development of a positive self-concept in perceptually handicapped and learning disabled children.

damage and to determine which areas of neurological functioning appear to be intact. On this information educators and others can base much of their educational programs.

Normally as a part of the total neurological examination of learning disabled children, the physician will request an electroencephalogram (often referred to as an EEG or popularly as a brain wave test). Some school systems require this as a routine measure. This writer disagrees with this latter policy. There is little need for requiring such a time-consuming and expensive undertaking as an EEG as a part of a routine admissions program for every child. The electroencephalogram may provide important information to the neurologist regarding the brain's activity, but at other times it is not particularly helpful. There is no danger to the child in having this test completed, however, nor is there any discomfort or pain. Since the test may be helpful, it is certainly wise to have it administered if it is recommended by the physician. This examination is usually administered in a hospital setting.

Frequently the physician may feel also that the child should have a pneumoencephalogram. When this is requested, overnight admission to the hospital is customary, and there may be some temporary discomfort to the child. However, the findings of this test may often help the physician to pinpoint the injury or to substantiate what otherwise would be conjecture.

NEUROLOGICAL EXAMINATION

Cranial nerves: First cranial nerve was not tested. Second cranial nerve: visual fields were normal; fundi normal. Third, fourth, and sixth cranial nerves: pupils were equal and round and reacted to light and accommodation. Extra-ocular movements are intact. No nystagmus is seen. Fifth cranial nerve: normal for motor and sensory function. Seventh cranial nerve: normal for motor function. Taste was not tested. Eighth cranial nerve: Tom was able to hear the tuning fork on both sides without difficulty. Air conduction is greater than bone conduction. There is no lateralization. Ninth and tenth cranial nerves: gag reflexes normal. The boy was able to swallow without difficulty. The uvula went up to the midline. Eleventh cranial nerve: the boy was able to shrug his shoulders without difficulty. Twelfth cranial nerve: the tongue protrudes in the midline. Sensory: Normal for pinprick, touch, vibratory, position, and stereognosis. Two-point discrimination and other modalities involving the cortex are also normal. No extinction is seen in this boy. Reflexes: Reflexes are equal and active throughout. No pathological reflexes were present. Motor: Motor system is normal. There is good strength throughout. Cerebellar: Finger-to-nose and heel-to-shin tests were well performed. He was able to spin the jack well with his right hand, but not so well with his left hand. Station and gait: The boy was able to walk on his heels and on his toes without difficulty. His gait is normal. Comment: There is some slurring of speech when he talks. The boy is right-eyed and right-handed.

ELECTROENCEPHALOGRAM

Attitude and condition of patient: alert and cooperative. Fundamental frequency: ranges between 8.5 and 9 waves per second. Slow waves: occasional short volleys of approximately 5 per second waves are observed in the frontal derivations (bilateral). With the onset of sleep this activity became more prominent. With sleep the normal frontal and parietal slow activity became dominant. Fast waves: are not prominent, but short runs of bifrontal 18 per second activity is observed. Amplitude characteristics: average to high voltage (100 microvolts); irregular modulation. Hyperventilation: accentuates the prominence of the bioccipital slow output. Impression: moderate generalized abnormal EEG.

It will be noted that although the gross neurological examination indicates a relatively normal child, the EEG finding is the first positive statement that there may be some neurological impairment in this boy, "moderate generalized abnormal EEG." The neurologist also confirms the slight speech problem reported previously by the pediatrician and the social worker.

Speech, Language, and Hearing Evaluation

The evaluation of a child's hearing and speech is often completed by persons from two different professions, namely, a speech and language pathologist and an audiologist. In Tom's case, one fully qualified person was able to de all examinations. The examiner is concerned to find out the exact status of the child's speech and language usage. Where must the therapist begin? What does the therapist have to work with? What must be developed or retrained? We are interested not only in knowing whether or not the child has normal or abnormal hearing acuity, but whether or not he understands and can interpret what he actually hears. Is there a perceptual problem involving sound stimuli which is involved in this child's poor adjustment to school and home? While the information which the speech pathologist gathered about Tom's speech and hearing is significant in itself, note also the several references to distractibility, hyperactivity, and short attention span. It is also important to obtain a complete understanding of the language usage of the child. It will be recalled that the definition of learning disabilities included an inadequate ability to handle the symbols used in sounds in speech, in ordering, sequencing, and in otherwise conceptualizing appropriate communication. Communication is the normal outcome of good auditory-motor function (auditory perceptual processing and its resultant motor responses).

GENERAL APPEARANCE

His early difficulties centered around his speech and he has been having difficulties with reading. The general developmental picture suggests considerable retardation. Tom sat up at 10 months and walked at 30 months, with no following difficulties in locomotion reported. Mother reported that he babbled a lot as a young infant, but there was evidently a long period of pre-speech jargon. Around the age of 3 he began to talk in phrases, rather than in words. Speech was then very unclear. The summer before he entered kindergarten the child was taken to the Speech Clinic where they worked with him for about two years. In first grade he received his speech therapy in school. His speech has been described as follows: " . . . shows a marked dyslalia, with many details of infantile articulation carried over. There is a fairly severe lateral lisp and distortion of all the alveolar sounds as they occur in the sound blends. The blends are generally poor, as is his connected discourse." Mother reports that he has not been having speech therapy for the past year. Improvement has been gradually occurring. Mother feels that he still has some occasional errors.

BEHAVIORAL OBSERVATIONS

Tom came willingly with the examiner. He is a well-dressed, clean-looking youngster. At first his manner was very tentative and all his gestures were in "slow motion." This is in line with his speech which is quite prolonged. He would engage in some of the test procedures, but would immediately return to those objects in room that had attracted his attention. He was not uncooperative, but determinedly willful.

ORAL EXAMINATION

There is a marked overbite. Teeth are widely spaced and there is a high palatal arch. Tongue and palatal mobility are good, as is pharyngeal stricture. He has good control of his tongue and lips.

ARTICULATION

This child's speech has improved. The *s* and *s* blends are still unstable. *J* is pronounced as *ch* and there is still distortion of the alveolar sounds as they occur in sound blends. There are many vowel distortions, particularly on the diphthong, but these are not consistent.

VOICE

Voice is unprojected and prolonged.

PROPOSITIONAL SPEECH

The content of this child's connected discourse is good. We started talking about airplanes and he indicated that he was goint to be a pilot. He then got into a discussion on the differences between a propeller and a jet plane. When he is talking freely about a topic in which he is interested, he is using complex sentences and a good vocabulary. His vocal utterance stands out because of the prolongation rather than the articulation errors. He knew all the animals and gave a sentence about each one. He was quite scornful about the idea of telling the story about the picture. He started to tell about the picture of shopping at the A & P: "They went shopping too," and then he broke in with a loud, "No." He then grabbed the picture about the family and muttered scornfully, "They kissing and all that crazy junk, peuh!" The ejaculation was said with real feeling. He looked over the one about fishing and commented, "They already caught some fish—they are just beside some boats. " He was finally induced to tell the story of the Three Bears, which he did in quite some detail, but interspersed with giggles and playing with cigarette tobacco which he took from a pack lying on the desk.

HEARING

This child's hearing is well within normal range. He gave the following pure-tone audiogram:

Right	15	20	10	0	−10	5
	125	250	500	1000	2000	4000
Left	10	15	10	0	−10	0

He repeated the spondee words quickly and accurately. He missed three of the PBK words. It was felt that this was more the lack of attention than inability to hear.

INITIAL IMPRESSION

While this child's speech has improved, it is still conspicuous in its prologation and vowel and alveolar distortion.

The auditory evaluation can be criticized, for there is not evidence in the report that auditory perceptual processing was evaluated. While this is often more difficult to accomplish than visual perceptual processing, it nevertheless should be evaluated carefully. Auditory figure-ground problems, auditory sequencing, closure and dissociation are very important issues in the learning process.

Pediatric Psychiatric Examination

The psychiatric examination has several purposes. It is important to obtain an understanding of the child's awareness of reality, of his relationship to his environment, and to himself. Efforts will be made to assess the child's concept of himself, his rational thinking, and his skills at concept formation.

PSYCHIATRIC EVALUATION

Tom is a friendly youngster whose speech defect was quite noticeable today, but everything he wished to say was understood without difficulty. He was quite mischievous during the hour and attempted to tell jokes and play jokes on the examiner. In testing a bullet from the cork gun, he lined up a good target and fired, but discovered that the bullet went a few inches and dropped down without having any projectile force. At this point he said, "Oh, that's not much of a gun."

He joined the fence sections quite easily, building up a little fantasy around the fence and the ranch house, having one side of the house on the edge of a 200-foot cliff. He arranged it so that when the button was pressed, the house would swing 180 degrees and three airplanes which had been hidden in there would be brought into the yard, and after 40 seconds, would move into its former position. "And the airplane that didn't get off in time would just have to know what was coming to it." He offered some technical knowledge about the anti-aircraft truck he was playing with. He would not divulge his source, but facts, as well as a good fantasy life, were demonstrated.

When asked what the baby bird would do when its nest was blown away, he replied, "The bird would build his own nest." When asked about the elephant, said it would be "bigger and heavier."

There was good gross and fine motor coordination. He shuffled playing cards quite well. He asked to play Old Maid and this was done with lots of spirit and gusto. It was established that he could not read the names on the cards, e.g., one out of four tries was correct.

This was the only boy seen for the Project who ventured to give a month for his birthday. He was unwilling to state what month we were in, though he did talk of the summer season. He guessed the year when asked, saying 108. His three wishes were: (1) to fly himself like Superman, he illustrated with flowing gestures and said, "Fly";(2) "All the magic in the world," and he smiled in an impish manner; (3) a jet plane.

At the end of the hour he was asked to Draw-a-Person, and said, "I will draw you," at which he drew a big head and ears of a rabbit. Another head appearing below in the paper was egg-shaped with the egg laying on its side. The facial features were added, finally, in pencil. He drew a very immature, odd body which was not a stick figure and had a pair of shorts only for clothing. His remark was, "Here's you in your underwear out in the wetting." It should be said that a few moments before the drawing was begun, there was a cloudburst.

PSYCHIATRIC RE-EVALUATION

Tom's behavior was essentially the same as the initial contact, i.e., the same boundless energy, difficulty in following directions, and much aggressive drive. In the absence of the popgun, he spent the majority of the hour hitting Bobo's replacement around the room. He showed good strength and his coordination was above average. As he punched he talked rapidly and with an adequate vocabulary. He did not mention his mother or his father. Much of what he had to say was superficial, and he continued to speak with a kind of babyishness, but his words were understandable at all time.

The child was asked to make a drawing of anything he wanted, plus a drawing of a person. He drew an action picture in which a Nazi plane fired at an enemy fort. When asked who this fort belonged to, he said, "The Germans." He gave the same reply as last year to Draw-a-Person, saying, "I'll draw you"; but this time he was asked to try something else. He drew a man with ears and a face resembling a rodent. The bizarre distorted hands and fingers which were larger than the hand, were placed upon a trunk which dwindled away into tapering feet.

Conversation with mother: The child's mother stated that she had not seen too much change in her son. She said it was still hard to get him to do things. Also, she found it hard to do the things that she was supposed to do in her relationship with the child. She does feel, however, that he has been able to get along with a larger group than his usual number of two or three youngsters. But he may have trouble with certain friends because he is apt to be a little critical and not too forgiving.

Pediatric Clinical Psychology Examination

The psychological evaluation is exceedingly important in the study of brain injury, perceptual processing, or learning disabilities. From this source will come much information which the teacher needs, not only to know at what levels to pitch instruction, but so that he knows what psychological strengths and weaknesses there are. He will learn from this phase of the study what aspects of perceptual difficulties he needs to keep in mind as teaching materials are constructed for the child, as instructional procedures are employed, and as the general educational setting is created for the child. So important is this data that the educational program is severely limited if the psychologist is unable to provide for the teacher the detailed blueprint which is needed. The psychological evaluation of a learning disabled child needs to be repeated much more frequently than with other children who may have other types of disabilities, for the teacher needs to know from period to period what the changes are which the child is experiencing and demonstrating, and thus what modifications are required on the part of the school and home in order to continue meeting the child's needs appropriately. We have in mind here again the necessity of modifying the psychoeducational match in relation to the progress which the child makes under good clinical teaching.

STANFORD-BINET, FORM L (PRE-TEST) CA: 8–4; MA: 8–10; IQ: 106

Present intellectual functioning falls within the Average range with an IQ of 106 and mental age of 8–10; This is consistent with testing done when an IQ of 100 was obtained, mental age 7–4. Thus the rate of intellectual development seems to be quite consistent. The seven-year range of performance was from Year VI through Year XII. The Basal Age was at Year VI, while the ceiling was at Year XII.

All items were passed at Year VII with the exception of comprehension. In this item a situation is verbally described in which the child is expected to grasp the essential factors involved. For example, when asked what he should do if he accidentally broke something which belonged to someone else, he said, "Nothing." When asked what he should do if he were on his way to school and saw that he was in danger of being late, he said, "I wouldn't go at all then." Abstract ability, as in seeing the similarity between two things, was good, and he was able to make three good diamonds.

At Year VIII two items were missed, verbal absurdities and again, comprehension. Auditory organization, as in repeating sentences, was good, as was ability to see similarities and differences.

At Year IX two items were failed, verbal absurdities and repeating four digits reversed. In the absurdities, for example, when asked what was absurd about the statement that only recently a small skull had been discovered in Spain which was believed to be that of Christopher Columbus when he was about 10 years old, Tom said, "He wouldn't die when he was ten, because he wasn't old enough to die." Attention span, as measured by repetition of digits, was inadequate at this age level.

At Year X two items were passed. Eleven words must be defined to pass the vocabulary test at this level, which Tom did. He was also able to analyze a situation presented pictorially. He was unable to read even the simplest words at this level. For example, He read "I" for "a." He could not find reasons for various problem situations. He did not pass the word naming test. In this test the child is instructed to say as many words as he can in one minute. At least 28 words are expected at this level, and he was able to product only 18. He started out very well and named the objects in the testing room, but then he "blocked" and could not continue. He also could not repeat six digits.

At Year XI two items were passed, the memory for sentences and similarities of three things. This indicates that auditory organization, at least as far as meaning is concerned, is relatively good, as is abstract ability.

STANFORD-BINET, FORM M (POST-TEST) CA: 9–2; MA: 8–10; IQ: 96 (NORMAL VARIANCE WITH LEARNING DISABLED CHILDREN. CF PRETEST.)

Intelligence is Average, with a performance range of seven years from a Basal Age of Year VI to a ceiling at Year XII.

At Year VII one item was failed, memory for sentences. Tom transposed phrases and left out words.

Comprehension was failed at Year VIII. This item involves a problem situation presented verbally. In answer to an inquiry as to what a man should do if he came home and found that his house had been robbed, he said, "Go out and try to find the burglar."

At Year IX he was unable to draw designs from memory, rearrange a series of disarranged words so that they made a sentence, or make rhymes. He knew what rhymes are, as may be seen in the first series of responses, but was unable to produce enough rhyming words. He saw the absurdity in verbal absurdities, gave good similarities and differences, and repeated four digits reversed.

At Year X he was able to name more than 12 animals in one minute, and count the number of blocks presented on a card. He could not repeat six digits, define abstract words, or remember the details of a story that was read to him.

At Year XI two items were passed, verbal absurdities and abstract words. He was unable to find reasons for problem situations, copy a bead chain from memory, see similarities between three things, or repeat a sentence from memory.

All items were failed at Year XII.

AMMONS FULL-RANGE PICTURE VOCABULARY TEST
CA: 8–4; MA: 9–0

The mental age obtained on this test was only two months greater than that obtained on either of the Stanford-Binets. Tom passed a number of words that the average child of this chronological age is not expected to pass, including purchase, panels, sudden, sympathy, and gravitation. (It can be pointed out that the Peabody Picture Vocabulary Test is probably more commonly used than the Ammons, but this is a matter of examiner choice.)

GOODENOUGH INTELLIGENCE TEST (DRAW-A-PERSON)
PRE-TEST: CA: 8–4; MA: 6–3   POST-TEST: CA: 9–1; MA: 6–3

Both the pre-and post-test drawings are very crude for this chronological age level. The first drawing is a tightly compressed figure near the extreme upper edge of the paper, with huge, wing-shaped ears, and one single hair coming from the top of the head. The second figure lacks the facial detail of the first, but has the correct number of fingers represented. In general, the post-test figure was more poorly executed than the pre-test.

BLOCK DESIGN AND CODING FROM WISC

	Raw Score	Scaled Score	Equivalent Test Age
Block Design	14	11	9–6
Coding	20	7	6–10

All of the block designs up to Design 2 were done quickly and accurately on the first attempt. He could not form the diagonals in Design 3, attempting to rotate the complete design instead. On the Coding test, form B, 21 symbol substitutions were attempted, with one error.

BENDER-GESTALT TEST

On the pre-test 14 errors were made with 1 immature, 1 perseveration, 2 dissociations, 1 incorrect element, 2 distorted angles, 1 rotation, 3 enlargements, and 3 disproportions. Only 10 errors were made on the post-test with

1 immature, 2 perseverations, 2 distorted angles, 2 rotations, and 3 enlargements. The main improvement may be seen in fewer errors categorized as dissociation and disproportion.

SYRACUSE VISUAL FIGURE-BACKGROUND TEST

In the pre-test there were 8 correct responses to figure, 2 perseverations, and 1 background response. On the post-test, there were 10 correct responses to figure, 1 background reaction, and no perseverations. Thus improvement may be seen in accuracy and lessened perseveration, but no change was shown in distractibility by background stimuli.

TACTUAL-MOTOR TEST

He correctly drew the diamond, both with plain and with structured backgrounds. The other drawings have no resemblance to the stimulus figures.

MARBLEBOARD TEST

Marbleboard 1 was reproduced quickly and accurately. The drawing shows a good grasp of the basic configuration, i.e., overlapping squares. Marbleboard 2, however, proved to be too difficult. He counted the correct number of marbles for the horizontals, but could not construct the diagonals, despite many shifts and changes. His drawing shows two dissociated pentagons.

VINELAND SOCIAL MATURITY SCALE

Pre-test (11–19-75)		Post-test (5–15-76)	
Total Score:	65	Total Scores:	17
Age-Equivalent:	7–0	Age Equivalent:	10–0
Social Quotient:	81	Social Quotient:	109

The mother served as informant at both interviews. The post-test, social quotient is 28 points higher than the pre-test, reflecting the observed progress made in classroom behavior over the course of the year.

Tom can do several things at the present time that he could not do formerly, such as using a pencil for writing, going to bed unassisted, doing routine household tasks, bathing himself unaided, caring for himself at the table, going about home town freely, making telephone calls, doing small remunerative work, and being left to care for himself and other smaller children.

At the beginning of the year his mother commented that in doing things he was like a nine-year old, but in a group his behavior was more like that of a seven-year old. Although he does not contribute much information about his school activities, his mother feels that he is widening his circle of friends and is much more competent in dealing with other children now.

SUMMARY

Intelligence is within the Average range. Difficulty was noted on the *Stanford-Binet* with tasks requiring auditory organization, such as repetition of sentences from memory, problem situations, and memory for a story that was read to him. Vocabulary and abstract thinking, as involved in seeing similarities, were passed at a level higher than his chronological age would indicate. Visuo-motor tasks were also difficult for him, such as the stringing of beads according to an example presented by the Examiner.

Tom showed improvement on three of the five tests on which both a pre- and post-test is available for comparative purposes. He made fewer errors on the *Bender-Gestalt,* showing fewer dissociations, and disproportions. On the *Syracuse Visual Figure-Background Test* accuracy was greater and perseveration less, but there was no change in reactions to background stimuli. There was a great change in the rate of development of social skills and abilities, Tom now being able to do many things that were either absent or just emerging at the beginning of the year.

There is a great range of tests and parts of tests available to competent clinical or school psychologists. Some of the tests which may be particularly valuable to some psychologists are not mentioned in the example. This omission is not to be interpreted as either incompetence on the part of the examining psychologist or disapproval of the items by this author. The tests used and reported are simply those which this psychologist felt would most accurately provide the information desired. Quite a wide range of tests was employed. The reader may be interested to note that only one or two items of certain tests were utilized (e.g., from the WISC—*Wechsler Intelligence Scale for Children*). These were employed because it was believed they would produce specific information on specific psychological characteristics of the child. The total test was not needed.

From the psychologist's report, the reader will see included with some frequency many of the terms which were used in Chapter 2 in characterizing learning disabled children, i.e., perseveration, dissociation, visuo-motor difficulties, and difficulty with abstraction. Note, too, in this test, that the boy has many skills which are passed at levels above expectancy. There are many strengths here on which to build. One of these, of course, is his normal level of general intelligence.

STANDARDIZED TESTS

It is rare that in a public or professional meeting dealing with any topic of learning disability one fails to be asked, "What tests do you use with learning disabled children?" The reference point is always to commercial tests commonly employed by psychologists and educators in the schools or in clinics. In this chapter and the preceding one, frequent references, particularly in the case study, have been made to tests. In practice we make a much greater use of qualitative assessment than quantitative evaluation of children and youth with learning disabilities. The same perceptual issues which cause lowered achievement in reading, number concepts, and writing, for examples, will function to impair the child's performance on intelligence or achievement tests. This is another reason why the artifact of a definition containing an arbitrary IQ cutoff point is so important and should be reconsidered at all levels of program planning.

In this chapter there have been frequent references to data relating to quantitative tests, and in Chapter 2 to data relating to qualitative techniques of evaluation. Quantitative tests tell us little about the capacity of an individual child to function in specific perceptual areas. Qualitative assessment provides the basis of a total school and home management plan. The statistical inadequacies of most quantitative tests coupled with the perceptual and emotional problems of the child result in inadequate data at best. From this considered opinion, the use of quantitative tests has a primary relation to subsidy and fiscal matters in public schools. The results are not needed or appropriate in placement or curriculum development.

This writer often uses subtests from standardized psychological tests or scales, but normally does not observe time limitations or other administrative restrictions. For example, the Coding subtest found in the Weschler scales are very helpful in understanding the length of a child's attention span in a situation involving "new learning." The Block Design subtest, also found in the Wechsler scales as well as in other commonly used psychological performance tests, is helpful in understanding such processes as dissociation, closure, and perseveration. Some of the cards from the Bender-Gestalt or Benton's tests are most helpful, but the whole process loses its clinical value if quantitative scoring systems are applied to these types of measures. Quantitative scores are not good substitutes for clinical expertise. It is the latter which is needed with children who demonstrate perceptual processing deficits. Obviously we are stressing caution in the utilization of quantitative scores, systems, or other pseudo-objective techniques of evaluation. The emphasis should rather be on a careful assessment of the perceptual input and output processes such as are possible in a well-conceptualized task-analysis approach. Tests per se will not accomplish this.

Ophthalmological and Optometric Examinations

In Tom's case no special visual examinations were completed. They un-doubtedly should have been included, although none of the other examiners suggested that there was either a visual problem of seeing or a visuo-motor problem of usage severe enough to warrant this phase of the examination. A complete evaluation would have included tests for both visual problems.

It seems important to this writer that both ophthalmological data and optometric data be obtained on many learning disabled children. The ophthalmologist will be able to provide important data concerned with the neurophysiological function of the eye, disease processes which may be related to visual function, and information pertaining to possible operative intervention which may be indicated.

Occasionally one finds an optometrist and an ophthalmologist working together. This becomes a unique source of information and diagnostic assistance for those who will carry out the long-term programs for the child.

The Educational Evaluation

It is always interesting, but a bit shocking, to this writer that in assessing the problems of a learning disabled child the educational diagnosis is al-most always omitted. Even when school personnel themselves refer the child, there is often no educational diagnostic data submitted or scheduled to be done later. Only rarely does an interdisciplinary team in-clude an educator in the diagnostic phase. While the educator's contribution is not necessarily the most important factor, the information he is qualified to provide on learning disabled children is very important. It cannot be omitted. In this section we are emphasizing diagnosis, not the educator's more traditional roles of teaching or remediation.

Not only is the educational diagnosis of significance to the educators themselves, but also much of the information collected within the education evaluation can be of value to the other diagnosticians—medical and non-medical—who will be examining the child. An example of the type of evaluation which should be done is noted in the following case.

Gregory is a boy, slightly more than seven years of age, who was studied by an interdisciplinary team over a two-year period. During this time evaluations and re-evaluations were made in an attempt to understand his needs and to plan adequately for his present adjustment and his future school and social life. One portion of this continuous evaluation, of course, was the educational assessment. From the many samplings of his behavior two are selected for report here as examples of what we have mentioned. These evaluations were made by an educational specialist, not, in this case, the boy's teacher. Often the teacher herself may be the best person to evaluate the child from an educational point of view.

DECEMBER 1 AND 2, 1976

1. *Motor coordination:* He was able to perform all the tasks. His movements were characterized by a degree of rigidity. Rigidity was also noted in his cursive writing. His writing manuscript was jerky. His drawing of himself was adequate in terms of identification of parts, but it did indicate a rigid self-concept.

Summary statement: All of his body movements were characterized by degrees of rigidity and non-fluency. Motor training should be structured toward achievement of fluency.

2. *Visual perception:* He indicated some confusion in discriminating between blue and purple. His form discrimination was fairly adequate, but limits were quickly reached in terms of complex and fine discrimination, i.e., (1) he could not perceive form relationships in the figure background puzzle, (2) he could not perceive the relationships of interlocking geometric forms, (3) he dissociated in the block design, 4) he did not have closure on the drawing of the diamond.

Summary statement: He has difficulty in perceiving patterns and compositions. Laterality seems to be a problem. (1) His horizontal line was slanted, (2) he tended to rotate as he drew horizontal lines. He needs help with left-right discrimination. Reversals in "*h*" and "*b*."

3. *Auditory perception:* He was able to reproduce environmental sounds adequately and was able to locate the source of the sound.

4. *Oral expressive language:* He appeared restricted in oral expression. He did not use complete sentences. He tended to answer questions asked by the teacher. He was not free to be spontaneous. He needed the external structure presented by the teacher. The content was relevant and coherent. He needs consistent support and guidance in more adequate oral expression.

5. *Reading:* He was fair in comprehension of beginning consonants. Rhyming was no problem. He was able to structure a logical sequence of events with the pictures. He was weak in recall.

Summary statement: He appears to be functioning at the level of reading readiness although his capacity level appears to be a higher level.

6. *Arithmetic:* He was able to relate pictures (dominoes) to arithmetic numbers. He was unable to relate these to words, e.g., *one, two,* etc. He was able to count from 1 to 50, but this appeared to be rote.

Summary statement: He appeared weak in real number concepts. He cannot work word problems. He cannot add or subtract. He needs concrete experiences with quantities as a basis for adequate abstractions.

SUMMATION

1. Gross and fine motor movements lack fluency.
2. Appears to be functioning at concrete levels in all areas.
3. Visual perception of pattern and composition is weak.
4. Visual discrimination of figure from background is weak.
5. Body image is weak.

GENERAL RECOMMENDATIONS

1. Set up tasks on the child's shelf in such a way that he is performing with different media for each. That is, follow a coloring task with a puzzle followed by tracing, etc.
2. Go slowly in each area, but not to the extent that the child becomes bored or anxious.
3. Drill, as such, will only reinforce perseveration and poor working habits. Vary the task each day.
4. Encourage good posture while child is sitting at his desk. Insist that he keep his right elbow on his desk and use the left hand as a helping hand.
5. Teach the child cursive writing only. Do not allow any manuscript writing on the child's part.

SPECIFIC RECOMMENDATIONS

1. Copying geometric forms
2. Puzzles

3. Cutting and pasting
4. Pegboards
5. Writing—cursive
6. Numbers—concrete—abacus
7. Phonics—beginning consonant sounds
8. Sequence—pictures and stories
9. Reading readiness

CLASSROOM OBSERVATIONS, OCTOBER 4, 1975–JANUARY 17, 1976

In following the school day routine, Gregory goes into the planned schedule of activities and moves comfortably in this routine. Only rarely does he deviate from the routine by requesting a drink of water, candy, etc. At these times, we have observed that Gregory asks permission to do so in an acceptable manner.

Gregory's relation to his peers at the first of the year was observed to be more "along-side." He watched the other members and laughed at them, but only occasionally did he interact with them. The interaction with members of the group was on a one-to-one basis in situations which usually promoted distractible behavior.

At present, observations of peer interaction reveal that Gregory is more aware of the other boys in the class and participates in conversations between two or more class members. He antagonized individual members of the class directly and also indirectly by soliciting help from another member.

At the beginning of the year, Gregory played with the work materials at length before getting into the work activity with them. He frequently interrupted his work to manipulate materials, scan the floor, make trips to the waste basket, and rock in his chair. There were frequent outbursts of defiance and refusal to do the work. His anxiety about the amount of work to be completed was further reflected in his shuffling through the papers on his work shelf.

At present, Gregory gets himself into the tasks assigned. He generally works through each assignment without interruption by distractions in the room or by the work materials themselves. He works toward completion of the day's work, and frequently calls for help in this way: "I need help so I can get finished." He responds positively to help in most instances. But when he is unable to secure help and reinforcement within a very short time after he has requested it, Gregory becomes frustrated and negative.

However, at the present time Gregory's control is maintained over a longer period of time. Formerly, loss of control was revealed in his protruding bottom lip, scowl, and slouched position in his desk. These bodily expressions gave way to shouts, loud banging of fists on his desk, and tears. This overt behavior, however, is occurring much less frequently now than in November.

TUTORING SESSIONS

Perception. In November, we observed that Gregory in some instances was able to focus on a target and move with it. Generally, however, his eyes jerked to overshoot the moving target or neglected to move with it away from the starting point. We have been working daily with ocular pursuit training to promote better visual tracking and longer fixation span. In reproducing peg board designs, Gregory tended to overshoot the starting and stopping points.

At present, Gregory still has difficulty following a moving target smoothly. Since November he has shown improvement in his ability to control eye movement during activities on the mat. His performance on the peg board tasks indicates his awareness of a beginning and an end to a line and most of the time he is able to keep within these bounds. His span of eye fixation is still very short.

Gregory indicated uneasiness in his initial entries into rooms or new areas of space. He wandered aimlessly about, in several directions with no apparent goal. He tended to rotate his papers. In using chalkboard exercises and the Getman "Physiology of Readiness," our purpose is to assist Gregory in organizing space and fixing on one point during physical involvement.

Motor. We observed a lack of fluency and a presence of rigidity in Gregory's gross motor movements. At present he shows anxiety and lack of confidence in performing physical tasks. There was generally increased hyperactivity during this kind of program. We are working with Gregory to develop his coordination of gross movements, thus reducing anxiety and building self-confidence.

Gregory consistently shows that he understands how to completely relax his body. With obvious effort, he is able to control movement of his head and arms. At the chalkboard a great deal of improvement can be attributed to his ability to relax. He has achieved fluency and rhythm in these activities and is able to evaluate his own work accurately.

Reading Readiness. The reading readiness tests administered revealed weaknesses in the areas of:
1. Word recognition
2. Opposites
3. Picture association
4. Comprehension

To aid and develop these areas our planned activities at present consist of a phonics program introducing initial consonants and noting familiar consonants in the final position. Gregory responds very well to the phonics program. When this particular activity is mentioned in the schedule for the day, he usually claps his hands and smiles.

For the development of comprehension and a story sequence we have directed conversation time with Gregory. This is usually about a topic that he has previously mentioned. For example: his dog Buttons; neighborhood

Figure 19. Results of a Primary Mental Abilities Test indicating the wide variation in test scores achieved by a learning disabled (PPD) boy, aged 7.

baseball game, etc. These topics are purposefully reintroduced by the teachers for further development of Gregory's language patterns and story sequence.

To promote picture association and comprehension, there is a planned story time for each day. Just before Christmas, upon completion of a story, Gregory began taking the book, looking over the pictures and often laughing about a particular picture. He would then spontaneously retell the incident of the story that went with this picture.

With the progress that Gregory has demonstrated in the past ten weeks it would be anticipated that a developmental program would continue to produce significant improvement.

This continuous evaluation of Gregory was requested by his teacher because of her feeling that the boy had reached a plateau in his school learning achievement. A reorientation of the teacher to Gregory and to his learning problem was desirable. Some objective measures of this plateau behavior are to be observed in Figures 19, 20, and 21.

In the *Primary Mental Abilities Tests* which were administered in February 1975, and nine months later in November 1975, it will be noticed that there is some gain in verbal meaning and in spatial relations. However, in perceptual speech, in number facility, and in the total test score there is little change in areas of reading, arithmetic, and language as measured by the *California Achievement Test* noted in Figure 21. There is indeed some regression in the last evaluation as compared with the two earlier ones.

The total picture of Gregory is, of course, missing from this presentation. However, it is not the direction of growth with which we are concerned here. These data indicate the nature of the material which parents should ascertain are being collected about their children and the kinds of data which should be a part of the interdisciplinary diagnostic conference program for all learning disabled children.

Motor skills evaluation. The final aspect of child growth and development which will be mentioned here and which should form a portion of the total diagnostic interview is that of motor development. The reader will have noted in the educational diagnostic material the fact that several times attention was called to Gregory's motor incoordination and lack of "fluency." Three sources of information regarding assessment of motor skills are available for parents. The first is Getman's volume, *Physiology of Readiness.* The second is the excellent volume by Dr. Newell C. Kephart, a psychologist, called *The Slow Learner in the Classroom.* The third, by B. J. Cratty and Sister M. Mary, is *Perceptual-Motor Efficiency in Children.* These authors outline in great detail procedures to be used in

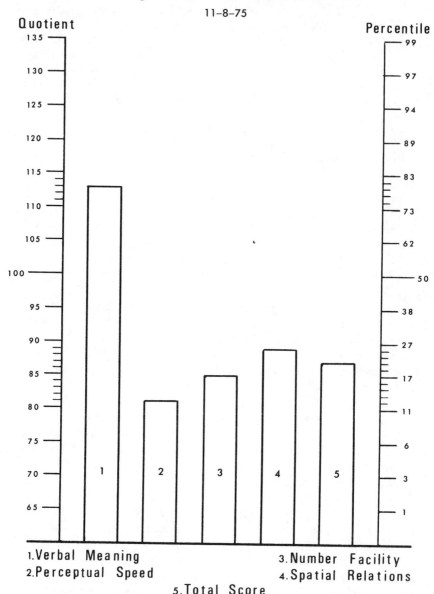

Primary Mental Abilities

11-8-75

Quotient

Percentile

1.Verbal Meaning
2.Perceptual Speed
3.Number Facility
4.Spatial Relations
5.Total Score

Figure 20. Primary Mental Abilities Test administered nine months later than that illustrated in Figure 19. Note that there is still a great deal of variance between subtests in the later administration, and that there is little difference in overall results between the two administrations. This is a good example of the plateau characteristic so often observed in learning disabled children.

California Achievement Test

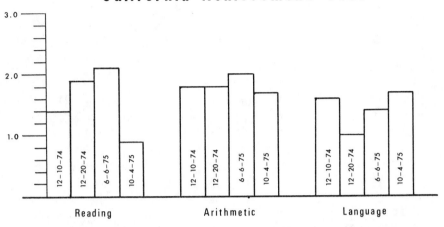

Figure 21. Plateau characteristic in four consecutive administrations of the California Tests of Achievement to a learning disabled child. This is often manifested in learning disabled and emotionally disturbed children and is typical of their performance prior to their fuller understanding of the emotional problems and to marked achievement in visual-motor skills.

assessing the motoric skills of learning disabled children. If the individual assessing the motor development of a child follows the suggestions of these authors, an excellent amount of information will be assembled upon which many logical decisions regarding the child, his education, and his home activities can be based. Further discussion of this problem will be included in a later chapter in this book.

EARLY CHILDHOOD AND YOUTH

To this point discussion of diagnosis in the areas of learning disabilities has concerned itself with the traditional elementary school-aged child. Two other age groups need attention, although neither has been given the attention of professional educators or psychologists in the extent warranted.

Infancy and Early Childhood

Questions are often raised by concerned parents and teachers relating to the earliest age at which diagnosis of learning disabilities can be made.

Obviously, the greatest amount of effort diagnostically has been with children between 6 and 12 years of age. Diagnostic instruments are relatively well perfected for children of these ages. More important, an obvious problem exists of which parents and educators are aware. Something is present to diagnose. The problem is there, and the diagnostic problem must be to ascertain its scope, intrinsic nature, and impact on total learning.

With infants and very young children, unless there is an obvious birth injury known or factors related to a high-risk pregnancy, the child must be viewed in terms of normative gross development. The emphasis must essentially be on gross-motor development, although on occasion fine-motor development (particularly related to sucking movements as discussed in Chapter 1) can also be evaluated in comparison to what is known about normal development. Although there are infant scales of intelligence, these are essentially of a motoric nature. Tests of perceptual processing are either unsatisfactory at the very young ages or do not exist at all.

It is important, however, that efforts be made qualitatively to evaluate infants particularly in those instances where there have been high-risk pregnancies or where obstetricians or midwives observe or suspect something related to the delivery which may result in maldevelopment. There are several scales available to the professions which can assist in such an evaluation. In general these are gross versus specific, but they do provide a reasonable yardstick by which parents and professionals can monitor the growth and development of the very young child. The *Denver Developmental Scale* is an example of this type of instrument, and it is one which has received rather wide usage.

The *Early Intervention Developmental Profile,* a technique developed by the staff of the early intervention project for handicapped infants and young children at the Institute for the Study of Mental Retardation and Related Disabilities, University of Michigan, has been demonstrated to have much value in assessing major developmental milestones with children whose cognitive, motor, social, self-care, or language skills fall within the 0–36 month developmental range. The authors of the *Profile* state that it provides a systematic means of screening a child's skills, selecting appropriate objectives for treatment of developmental delays, and designing an appropriate, individualized curriculum based on a developmental model. This scale is concerned with the assessment of a child's functioning in six developmental areas—language, gross- and fine-motor development, social growth, self-care, and cognitive skills. Language, cognition, and motor development are particularly related to what may become in later years recognized as a perceptual processing or learning disability problem. Although a simple scoring system is provided, the *Profile* essentially provides a standardized way in which a child's growth and development can be viewed against what is known of normal growth trends and patterns. Such an item as that noted for the 0–2 months age level, "Moves limbs, head, eyes in response to voice, noise," may in the opinion of the trained observed of young children portend significance if maldevelopment is recognized. The aim of this effort is to monitor physical behavior of the infant and young child, later cognitive and language development, and to be alert to either developmental lags or outright maldevelopment. Sequential and continuous assessment of these problems in children can lead to the initiation of therapeutic programs early on, and go far in minimizing the impact of such developmental issues on learning. Early discovery and intervention may not be the entire solution to the problems of learning disability, but these efforts can go far in assisting the child to a fuller realization of his potential. A full reference to the *Profile* will be found at the end of this chapter. It may be helpful here, however, to illustrate briefly the nature of the information which the *Profile* will provide when used as a guide by professional personnel in the evaluation of very young children with suspected problems.

Martha P was the product of a supposedly full-term and normal pregnancy and delivery. She weighed 8 lbs. at birth and was discharged at 2 days. She was brought into the emergency room at 12 days for a reported apnea spell. Records indicate that the physicians questioned this story. Martha has been seen for repeated ear infections. Martha was first seen at five weeks for a developmental assessment, but she was extremely sleepy and did not perform well. She showed no head-righting responses and lacked head control such as might normally be observed in a child of that age.

GROSS MOTOR AND REFLEXIVE DEVELOPMENT

Martha was assessed at 13 weeks. At this time her head control in an upright position had improved. She was able to lift her head up to 45 degrees, but not sustain it for any longer than 5 seconds. Her head-righting response in prone position was inconsistent. She had a neck-righting response and used this to turn from her stomach to her back. She would bear some weight on her feet when held upright, which indicated integration of primitive stepping responses. As would be expected for her age and degree of head control, she shows a Moro response and an asymmetrical tonic neck reflex. Her arms and legs move in a normal fashion in random activity. Mother reports that Martha does move about in her crib when placed on her stomach. Her gross-motor and reflexive development appear slightly depressed for a normal newborn. They are at a 2–3 month level.

RESPONSE TO ENVIRONMENT

During the first session, Martha was non-responsive both to auditory and visual stimuli. When she was seen at 13 weeks there was a marked change. The baby was extremely alert to visual stimuli. She maintained excellent eye contact with an adult. She was still not responsive to any available auditory stimuli: voices, bell, clapping, drum. No startle to loud noise could be elicited.

SUMMARY

Martha was formally evaluated at age 13 weeks. At this time due to her lack of good head control in a prone position, she is functioning motorically slightly below her chronological age level. Her motor and reflexive development is at a 2–3 month level. This slight delay may be due to the fact that she has not been positioned on her stomach or offered sufficiently interesting stimuli to promote better head control. This bears monitoring, but should not raise undue concern regarding any lag in motor development. Her continued lack of response to auditory stimuli bears immediate investigation through audiology.

The above excerpt from the infant's chart was completed by a physical therapist. While other members of an interdisciplinary diagnostic team evaluated the child, the material quoted here is of interest. First, recommendations for parent education and home training are suggested. Certainly the auditory evaluation should be undertaken. However, some normal children at 13 weeks do not respond fully to auditory stimuli, so parent concern in this area should be kept minimal until complete data are available. However, both auditory and auditory-motor evaluations should be made, recognizing that the latter will be difficult to determine accurately at this young age. Continued monitoring of auditory perceptual processing should be undertaken if auditory acuity is found to be normal or nearly so. This child may develop in a perfectly normal manner. There is nothing in this data to indicate that she definitely will not. However, head and neck characteristics indicating possible developmental problems do exist in contrast to what appears to be normal lower-extremity development. When one recognizes the nature of the neurological development of the fetus and newborn child, the relationship between the physical development which Martha shows, and what *might be* seen as motor and processing deficits when she reaches five or six years of age, a bona fide reason exists for the careful and continuous monitoring of her development. Her development may proceed normally.

Then again, if it does not, a rigorous training regimen can be instituted at a very early age which may have significant preventive impact.

ADOLESCENTS AND YOUNG ADULTS

Children with perceptual processing deficits do grow and mature into adolescents and young adults. It is known that there is sometimes a remission of the psychological characteristics associated with learning disabilities, but this is by no means the rule. It is also known that appropriate educational programming and teaching techniques can and often do go far in assisting the child to lead a more normal life. But some children arrive at adolescence still with serious learning problems active as deterrents to a full life. There are many psychological and educational techniques available by which thorough analyses can be made of the continuing needs of such young people. There is no appropriate reason here to delineate a total testing program, for this would duplicate what is common knowledge to most clinical and school psychologists as well as to educational diagnosticians. It should be enough to remind ourselves of certain rules and principles that should be recognized.

1. If the youth is seen as a learning disabled person, a complete assessment of all perceptual processing abilities needs to be undertaken. Tests must be utilized which not only have a high interest level, but which at the same time provide a full developmental range. For example, while the Goldstein-Scheerer *Color Form Sorting Test* may be excellent in the area of abstract-concrete behavior for children and early adolescents, the psychologist may need to employ a more advanced scale for later adolescents and young adults, e.g., the Vigotsky (Hanfmann-Kasanin).

2. Perceptual-motor tests are generally developed for young children. Care should be exerted to secure a test in this area which encompasses older children or youth. For example, the Berry *Developmental Test of Visual-Motor Integration* is suggested by the author to be appropriate for youths through the chronological age of fifteen years. Oftentimes, however, professional personnel attempt to apply scales conceptualized for younger children to the older age group. This is not an appropriate decision.

3. It is essential that the pre-vocational and vocational futures of adolescent learning disabled youth be kept in mind. Such tests as the *Purdue Peg Boards* not only give information regarding vocational aptitudes, but can also provide much information regarding the eye-hand coordination skills of the youth, the latter being an essential characteristic of learning disability if deficiencies are apparent.

4. Assessment of the adolescent learning disabled child must go beyond the pencil-and-paper stage of testing. We have stated that emotional overlays often accompany the perceptually handicapped child of elementary school age. This in large measure is due to the relatively continuous failure history experienced by the child. Adolescence is also a time of emotional tension under the best of circumstances. It is important that the normal growth problems of adolescence not be seen as the result of or the cause of the learning problems of the youth, but they be viewed in an objective light as normative. Obviously, emotions cannot be separated into water-tight compartments relative to growth stage or etiology. It is helpful, however, if the emotional status of the adolescent is viewed by adults in terms of development as well as in terms of failure problems. In this manner it is often easier for adults to work with the young person in assisting him to confront his total adjustment situation realistically.

5. Finally, it is important that the youth with learning disabilities be evaluated in terms of his or her social skills. Social acceptance, particularly by peers, is often a function of the individual's emotional adjustment and academic or physical skills. The young man or woman who carries into adolescence the residuals of childhood learning disorders may have difficulty in establishing social relationships and friendships which will bring satisfactions. The basis of competition on which so many social relationships are established may be beyond the youth; whether they be boy-boy or boy-girl relationship is of no consequence. Skills in sports, driving, dancing, as well as the carry-over of an elementary school reputation of failure may well continue to isolate the learning disabled adolescent from the rich social relationships which are normally a vital part of adolescence.

SUMMARY

A discussion of the role of diagnosis in the life planning for learning disabled children and youth has been included in this book for parents in order to give them some idea of the nature of this aspect of the professional problem and to what they must expose their child if, indeed, others are going to be able to help him. Diagnosis is not the end of the program; it is only the beginning. Too few parents are given an understanding of what areas of their child's life, as well as of their own lives, must be sampled in order to find a possible recipe which will further the child's development. The many professional fields represented by men and women who have competency with children must bring their knowledges together. Out of this interprofessional union of skills may come a better understanding of the child and later of the youth.

As important as diagnosis is in planning for the home and school adjustment of the child, *continuous evaluation* is at least of equal importance. The child is going to make growth of some sort and in some degree. He will not stand still indefinitely. It is absurd to think that an initial diagnosis is going to provide guidance for a teacher or parent for long periods of time. The teacher will plan his teaching program and provide specialized teaching materials for the child or youth in terms of what he has been told about him. As the child progresses these materials continue to meet his needs only at the place he originally was unless the teacher knows the type of growth which has taken place. From the concept of continuous evaluation comes the best of diagnostic teaching, the essence of a good educational program for children and youth with learning disabilities.

If dissociation were a significant factor in the learning abilities of a child initially, and if after some specialized teaching this is less a factor than originally, the teacher needs to know it. He needs to know it because now different types of teaching materials are required by the child. Obviously teachers can make many of these evaluations themselves, and they do. However, they need the support of objective assessment made by someone divorced from the day-to-day situation.

There are several aspects of the child's educational development which should be re-evaluated approximately once a month in the early years of his special education. These re-evaluations the teacher should be prepared to make himself. A full psychological appraisal based on the type of data collected in the initial diagnosis should be completed once every six months for the first three or four years.

The interdisciplinary diagnostic team should not lose sight of the child when diagnosis is completed. Not all the specialists will be required, but a minimum team should have an obligation to follow the child for several years. Included in this ongoing staff would be the educator, the psychologist, the speech pathologist, and the pediatrician or the pediatric psychiatrist.

SELECTED REFERENCES OF SPECIAL INTEREST TO PARENTS

Cratty, B. J., and Mary Sister M. *Perceptual-Motor Efficiency in Children.* Philadelphia: Lee and Feberger, 1964.

Cruickshank, W. M., and Hallahan, D. P. *Perceptual and Learning Disabilities in Children.* Syracuse, N.Y.: Syracuse University Press, 1975.

de Hirsch, K.; Jansley, J. J.; and Langford, W. S. *Predicting Reading Failure.* New York: Harper and Row, 1966.

Francis-Williams, J. *Children with Specific Learning Difficulties.* Oxford: Pergamon Press, 1970.

Kephart, Newell C. *The Slow Learner in the Classroom.* 2nd ed. Columbus, Ohio: Merrill, 1971.

Kirk, S.A., and McCarthy, J. *Learning Disabilities: Selected ACLD Papers* Boston: Houghton-Mifflin, 1975.

Haeussermann, Else. *Developmental Potential of the Preschool Child.* New York: Grune & Stratton, 1958.

SELECTED REFERENCES OF SPECIAL INTEREST TO TEACHERS

Ayres, A.J. *The Development of Sensory Integrative Theory and Practice.* Dubuque: Kendall/Hunt, 1974.

Capobianco, R.J. "Diagnostic Methods Used with Learning Disability Cases." *Exceptional Children* 31 (December 1964): 187–93.

Hasford, P., and L'Abate, L. "Screening Children with Learning Disabilities." Paper read at International Conference on Measurement in Education, Atlanta, Georgia, 1967.

Haeussermann, E. "Estimating Developmental Potential of Pre-School Children with Brain Lesions." *American Journal of Mental Deficiency* 61 (July 1956): 170–80.

Hunt, B., and Patterson, R. "Performance of Brain-Injured and Familial Mentally Deficient Children on Visual and Auditory Sequences." *American Journal of Mental Deficiency* 63 (July 1958): 72–80.

Koppitz, E.M. "Diagnosing Brain Damage in Young Children with the Bender Gestalt Test." *Journal of Consulting Psychology* 26 (1962): 541–47.

Peter, L.J. *Prescriptive Teaching.* New York: McGraw-Hall, 1965.

Rapaport, D.; Gill, M.M.; and Schafer, R. *Diagnostic Psychological Testing.* New York: International Press, 1968.

Scherer, I.W. "Prediction of Academic Achievement in Brain-Injured Children." *Exceptional Children* 28 (October 1961):103–106.

Taylor, Edith M. *Psychological Appraisal of Children with Cerebral Defects.* Cambridge, Mass.: Harvard University Press, 1959.

Wedell, K., and Raybould, E. C. *The Early Identification of "At Risk" Children.* Birmingham, England: University of Birmingham School of Education, 1976.

Wherry, J. "The Diagnosis, Etiology, and Treatment of Hyperactivity in Children." In *Learning Disorders,* edited by J. Hellmuth. Vol. 3. Seattle: Special Child Publications, 1967.

4

Stimuli Control and the Educational Program

I T IS IMPORTANT that parents have a thorough understanding of the type of educational program needed for their learning disabled and perceptually handicapped child. Most parents are, of course, concerned about their child's progress in school; oftentimes they are confused by the school program. If the program is properly conceived to meet the learning disabled child's needs, it will be different from that experienced by the parents themselves as children or by the other children in the family. It is important that parents understand the educational program because much of what is appropriate for the learning disabled child in the school setting is applicable to the home, as will be outlined in later sections of this book. If parents are thoroughly informed concerning the nature of the school program and know what it should be like, they are in a position to cooperate more fully with the teacher and thus help develop a total life program for the child.

It has been implied throughout this volume that parents are a most important segment of the team which will work with the learning disabled child. The parents will have an obligation to assist with much of the child's learning experience in the home to assist with the child's motor training program, and to do this effectively they must understand what the school is attempting to do. We do not mean to suggest that parents should carry on reading practice at home, nor are we suggesting that an arithmetic drill be a part of every evening's activities. This would most certainly be inappropriate. If the teacher requests parental assistance on certain things, indicating what is to be done and how it is to be accomplished, the parents can enter actively into these aspects of school learning. We are thinking now, however, of the many adaptations of educational theory which can be made to home-life education in terms of eating habits, dressing habits, motor training, and related matters. There are some pamphlets and books written on these problems. While they have been written for professional educators, there is much included in them which may be helpful also to parents. A list of these suggested additional readings is included at the end of this chapter.

In beginning this discussion of life planning for learning disabled children with a chapter concerning education, we do not mean to imply that the school program alone will solve the child's total problem. His adjustment to school, home, and the community will be the result of several simultaneous programs, some involving the child alone and some involving only the parents. Education in the classroom, though very important, is but one aspect of the total solution.

TEACH TO THE DISABILITY

Earlier we stated that teachers must teach to the disability of learning disabled children. This is a slightly different approach than that used with other types of handicapped children. When dealing with other physical handicaps an attempt is made by use of prosthetic devices to remove the disability, thus making possible the use of customary teaching methods and materials.

For example, the hard-of-hearing child is given a hearing aid so that he may hear normal sounds. A child with defective sight is given glasses so he can see the blackboard and read normal print. The crippled child is fitted with a full-leg brace in order that he may walk normally. The teaching materials prepared by specialists for use with mentally retarded, visually handicapped, hard-of-hearing, and crippled children are similar to those used with normal children.

But it is not possible to outfit a learning disabled child with a corrective device. Professional educators in their conceptualization of learning disabled children sometimes fail to appreciate this important distinction. The disability is there, and it is going to remain there in just as active a form after the child is placed in a specialized type of educational setting as it was before his diagnosis of perceptual processing deficits was made. While the growth and maturation processes will work in favor of the learning disabled child, growth and maturation will not increase the child's ability to learn rapidly enough, and growth and maturation will not prevent development of the secondary problems of emotional disturbance.

The problems of educators and parents in dealing with learning disabled children, then, are quite different from those involved with children with only physical disabilities, and the distinction can be confusing. Instead of providing prosthetics which make it possible for the child to adjust to the normal world, it is necessary for adults to modify the environment to meet the needs of the learning disabled child. This modification will be necessary for as long a period of time as it takes the learning disabled child to learn to meet the demands of society. We must, therefore, teach to the disability; we must plan programs that take the disability into consideration. We must never lose sight of the nature of the child's handicap or its implications for environmental adjustment.

THE EDUCATIONAL SETTING FOR THE NORMAL CHILD

To understand the educational needs of the learning disabled child, one must know what a good educational setting is for normal children. In the modern elementary school, classrooms for children are wonderful and exciting places. Creative teachers attempt to provide stimulating situations in which young children can learn and grow. Good teachers try to make their classrooms interesting so that their students will be motivated to learn.

In one typical third grade room the teacher has succeeded in her task; she has provided an environmental setting that is rich and stimulating. In this room are reading, library, science, and transportation areas. The windows are decorated with seasonal pictures, and children may be seen playing and cars and trucks passing outside. On the bulletin board are displayed drawings and examples of the better accomplishments of the children. Colored curtains are at the windows, and folding screens, effectively placed, make the room more useful. The teacher has provided plants and an aquarium filled with interesting plants, fish, and water animals.

In this rich educational setting are from twenty to thirty children, each dressed differently. There are desks or tables and chairs for the children to occupy as well as other furniture. The teacher is wearing attractive, brightly colored clothing, and her jewelry fascinates the children.

There are functional things in this classroom too: a clock, a pencil sharpener, and perhaps a sink with drinking facilities. The walls of the room, the floor, the furniture, and the woodwork are of different materials and colors. There is activity. This is a classroom rich in stimulus value.

Not only has the teacher made the classroom a pleasant place in which to live, but she has created a stimulating setting in which children will be motivated to learn. Normal children thrive in this type of school setting. This classroom environment is what most parents wish for their children. An environment of this type makes education come alive, and teaching in this fine setting is effective; the facts taught about science and other subjects seem alive and real to the children.

Other aspects of the school environment also concern normal children. Eating at the school cafeteria is exciting; other children are present, and it is quite busy. Generally the normal child can tolerate this experience; but even some normal children find the confusion of the cafeteria too much, and they have trouble eating. The auditorium experiences, musical activities, free play on the schoolyard, the competition of gymnasium games, the tension of a fire drill, the halls of seemingly endless length to a second or third grade child—all these things and others are generally well assimilated by the normal child.

THE EDUCATIONAL SETTING FOR THE LEARNING DISABLED CHILD: SCHOOL

The normal child can accept the type of educational environment which we have just described because of his ability to ignore, block out, or adapt negatively to those things in his operational area which are not essential to the specific task at hand (see Chapter 1). Every teacher knows that by the end of the day even normal children are less able to learn than they were early in the day when they were rested. Generally speaking, however, the goals which the teacher hoped to accomplish for most of the children through a rich school environment have been accomplished.

Think now of the nature of the learning disabled child (the PPD child). Think back over the characteristics earlier attributed to him and decide for yourself whether or not he will be a successful participant in the classroom just described. *Often the best classroom in your community for normal children is the worst classroom for learning disabled children.* One must seriously question whether or not mainstreaming for perceptually handicapped children or youth is the logical or educationally appropriate milieu. It would appear that *mainstreaming and perceptual processing deficits in learning disabled children are not universally compatible concepts.*

Figure 22. A nonstimulating classroom planned for hyperactive learning disabled children who have perceptual processing problems.

This paradox is easily understood: the needs of the two groups of children are quite opposite. Into the rich classroom for normal children is placed a boy who is unable to refrain from reacting to stimuli, whose attention span is short, and who is further characterized by motor disinhibition, figure-background problems, and a general attitude of defeat because of past failures. How can he be expected to adjust in the highly stimulating environment? Some children may be able to succeed in the regular grade, but the betting odds are against this if the child's problem is anything but very mild and in the face of the fact that teachers rarely are given any preparation for understanding the essentials in educating accurately diagnosed learning disability problems.

The first, and perhaps the most important, requirement of a setting for learning disabled children is that stimuli be reduced to a minimum. Figures 22 and 23 illustrate a properly prepared classroom. This room, adapted from another function to the purpose of educating learning disabled children, is not perfect, yet it is a good room and can serve learning disabled children well.

Many details are difficult to discern from the photographs, but it is clear that there is present little of a stimulating nature. The walls, floor, and furniture are all of the same color. The transparent windowpanes

Figure 23. Another view of the nonstimulating classroom prepared for hyperactive learning disabled children. Note the enclosed shelves. Door leads to adjacent toilet facilities.

have been replaced with opaque glass so that the children will not be distracted by stimuli from the outdoors. Wooden doors enclose all the shelves so that the boxes, books, and other teaching materials needed by the teacher will not distract the child with their different colors, shapes, and sizes.

Noise created by the children within the room is minimized by the wall-to-wall carpeting and soundproof ceilings. A pencil sharpener was removed when the teacher observed that the sound of pencils being sharpened distracted some of the children from their tasks.

There is nothing in the room except items essential to the tasks immediately at hand. The teacher has no desk; her materials are kept elsewhere in the building. There is no wall calendar, nor are there bulletin boards or chalk boards. There are no science corners, reading corners, aquariums, or other things parents look for and expect when visiting their child's neighborhood school.

This is what we meant a few pages earlier when we said that since it is often impossible, because of perceptual processing problems, for the child to adjust in or to the normal world, it is necessary for adults to modify the environment to meet his particular needs. This child has some very specific needs. He needs to be free from having to react to the unessential. If educators truly believe in the concept of meeting the needs of individuals, and if this concept is to be the basis of an action program instead of a cliche, then for a child who needs to be free of interfering stimuli there will have to be constructed a learning and living environment with as many stimuli as possible eliminated. This is teaching to the disability. It is not implied that the learning disabled or hyperactive child will always require this stimuli vacuum. He will need it only long enough for some success experiences to be had and until his ego is strong enough for him to feel self-assured and secure. Then other arrangements can be made for him. At this point in his short life, however, he is a handicapped child, educationally and psychologically. If he is to be helped, then he must be provided with the type of clinical teaching and other clinical services which his condition warrants.

In a stimulus-free learning environment the child has a greater chance to see, understand, and have learning experiences from the material the teacher places on his desk. His perception of what he should look at is not interfered with by external stimuli, for these are at a minimum. Stimuli reduction alone goes far in meeting the child's needs and in making it possible for him to assimilate ideas successfully. When the child's attention is not distracted by the unessential in the environment, his attention span increases. An increased attention span provides the teacher with more time for teaching and the child with more time for appropriate learning.

Furthermore, when a child is not distracted by unessential stimuli in his environment, he is less fatigued. Over the years this writer has learned with interest and some anticipation to expect a certain inquiry from parents after the child has been participating for some time in the type of clinical teaching setting here described.

"What are you doing to my child?" asks the parent.

"Why do you ask? What is the problem?"

"There is no problem, but he has changed a lot. We used to dread his arrival home from school. It was a pitched battle from the time he neared the house until we finally got him into bed—and sometimes long after that. We prepared ourselves for his coming home, but it was always an unpleasant tussle. Now, although most of his problems are still present, we can at least live with him on a reasonably pleasant basis. As a matter of fact, the other evening we actually played together, and it was fun for all of us. Going to bed is still a problem, but he is much more willing to comply than before. What has happened? What have you all done?"

The answer to this parent's inquiry is an easy one. Actually, the teacher has done practically nothing by this time because he has had the

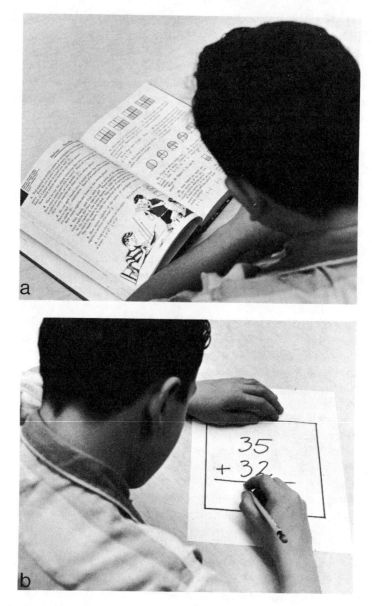

Figure 24. The child above (a) is forced to respond to visual stimuli. His arithmetic book possesses so many unessential details that he cannot attend to the specific problem (figure vs. background) he is asked to solve. b illustrates the manner in which the teacher prepares the arithmetic lesson for this child. Each problem is presented separately in the absence of extraneous background stimuli.

child for only a few weeks. The one thing that has been done is to reduce external stimuli. The child's need to function in a less stimulating situation has been recognized. Adults have responded to his need to be free from environmental confusion. This is in part what is meant when educators are told to meet the individual needs of children.

Human beings are endowed with a given amount of physical energy. In normal persons this energy reservoir is sufficient to carry them through their complicated day and still have enough of a reserve by the time 5:00 P.M. rolls around to go out to the theater, visit friends, go bowling, or to take part in one of the many other social activities in which adults engage. There are times, however, when even adults come close to the end of their reserve, and they remind themselves that they "are at the end of their rope" or are "operating on frayed nerves!" Normal adults, and frequently normal children, are then able to retreat from the pressures of their activities, nap or sleep through the night, and prepare themselves physically to meet another day's activities.

The energy of learning disabled children is utilized considerably by their constant physical reaction (visual, auditory, tactual) to the unessential aspects of their environment. Normal individuals conserve their energy by ignoring most of what goes on in their environment. A secretary may be so intent on what she is doing that she is oblivious to twenty other workers in the general office, their machines, and activities for many minutes at a time. The subway rider can become so engrossed in his thoughts or his newspaper that he fails to realize he has traveled from 14th Street to 125th, and it is now time to get off. This is not the pattern for the PPD child. He is unable to ignore, and his energies are utilized in reacting to every detail of every "thing" he focuses upon with any of his senses. The reduction of stimuli in the classroom has allowed him to return to his parents at the end of the school day as a more relaxed child—a child with sufficient energy left to cope with the complexities of home living. To the parent's question of "What are you doing to my child?" the answer is, "We are giving him fewer things to react to now which gives him a greater opportunity to react more appropriately to you when he comes home from school."

WHAT ABOUT THE HOME?

Parents, after they have seen their child's schoolroom, often ask, "Should we do the same to the rooms in our home?" The answer, of course, is "No." The home is a place for all members of the family including the learning disabled child. It cannot be stripped of things as a classroom can.

Retreat is Honorable

It is important, however, that some place in the home be modified to meet the child's needs. The logical place, and least expensive room to modify, is the child's own bedroom. It is not usually too difficult to reduce the stimuli in this room. Plain wooden doors can be put on toy shelves. Curtains and bedspreads can be of solid-colors rather than designs. The room may even be carpeted. The walls, curtains, furniture, and floor covering should be of the same color. Apparently it is not important what color is chosen, just so it is a pastel rather than an intense tone. This writer has observed children in schoolrooms utilizing light pink, green, blue, gray, and tan.

The child should know that when he feels "tired," "frightened," "fearful," "tense," or whatever word he understands, he may retreat to his room and remain there as he desires. He should not be sent to the room as a disciplinary measure, for unpleasant connotations should not be associated with this place of quiet and retreat. Many times the presence of strangers in the home or stimulating activities will make it desirable for the child to leave and be alone in a setting nearly free from distraction.

The goal is *not* to protect the child from all stimuli. The goal is to provide a setting wherein *the child can deal correctly* with a limited number of stimuli. Thus, care should be taken to see that the child participates in appropriate social activities. He cannot be carried around in a wrapping blanket, of course, and there will be times when the best-laid plans will go awry. Thought on the part of parents, however, may go far to minimize the exposure this child will have during these years of adjustment. This author recommends the reasonable use of both television and motion pictures for learning disabled children. In a darkened movie house or in a semidarkened room for television, the external stimuli are reduced almost to a minimum. The only thing to attract the child is the lighted movie or television screen. He can attend, and he can have a wonderfully good time, behaving as he should throughout, so that at the end of the show the parents can warmly compliment him for having been a good boy. Not only has he enjoyed himself, he has received a compliment. He has had a success experience.

Parents and teachers unfamiliar with the type of educational setting we have described often ask if it is not depressing to the child. This has not proved to be the case. As a matter of fact it is the feeling of those who have worked with children under stimuli-free conditions that the reverse is true. These children tend to be so confused perceptually, although they do not consciously realize their problem, that they find the nonstimulating environment a place where they can relax, live, and reorganize themselves without being threatened. The schoolroom with its therapeutic atmosphere as well as the child's own modified room at home serve to make possible a reorientation by the child to his environment. It must be stressed that changes in the child are slow and often not at all obvious to those who have daily contact with him. It may be weeks, months, or even years before major changes are observed in him. The majority of children are able to modify their behavior, although it is a trying experience for some of them.

If Eating is a Problem

A second matter of concern to parents is that of the eating habits of their learning disabled children. We discuss this matter again in another section; here we discuss the gains to be made in establishing better eating habits by control of the eating environment itself. Other things will need to be done too, but the reduction of stimuli is of first importance.

As you sit at your dinner table with your family around you, analyze the situation, assuming there is a family of five at your table. Many things on the table are really unessential to the specific action you are about to take, i.e., cutting a piece of food on your dinner plate. If there are five individuals, there will be at least five plates, five forks, five knives, and five spoons. There will be cups and saucers and glasses of water and milk. Dishes filled with vegetables and other foods are on the table, and there may be a center decoration of flowers or candles. Napkins, salt and pepper shakers, and a variety of other items may appear. People are present, and they are moving and talking. Dishes are passed, and eating utensils cause noise. Once again, most individuals find this enjoyable and can adjust to it. But keep in mind the hyperactive learning disabled child who is also at the dinner table and who may be so highly distracted by what he sees that he is unable to eat properly. Because he is hungry, eating may become a mere physical operation of hand-to-mouth activity. He grasps the food and forces it into his mouth irrespective of decorum, the feelings of others, or the admonitions of his parents. Since others can take only so much of this behavior, problems result. Correction is followed by a scene, and the child is sent away from the table. Everyone is upset, for everyone knows that something is wrong, but no one seems able to assist the child.

This scene should not be permitted to take place. The situation should be carefully evaluated, and without overtones of punishment, the parents should arrange for the child to eat alone in a situation where there is little to distract him and where one parent or an older brother or sister can sit at the table with him to converse and to assist in certain important ways. A small table placed in the corner of the room against walls which are free of pictures or other decorations may be an ideal place for the child. The child should have in front of him only what he needs at the moment, i.e., a plate with his food and a single fork or spoon. The number of unessential items should be kept at a minimum until he has learned to deal adequately with those he already has. Then other utensils or dishes can be added as the child becomes able to tolerate stimuli. If the table top is extensive in size, it is wise to place a solid but brightly colored place mat under his plate. The brilliant color serves to reduce the visual field and to assist the child in focusing on his plate. The learning disabled child needs everyone and everything he can get to help him perceive his world accurately.

TESTING AND THERAPY SETTINGS

The assumptions regarding the value of a stimuli-free environment also apply to settings other than the schoolroom or the child's home situation. It has been this author's observation that learning disabled children, when tested by a clinical psychologist, will perform much more satisfactorily in a small room which is devoid of distractions. Too often all of the armamentaria of the psychological profession are on display in the psychologist's office, and these serve as distractors to the learning disabled child. Pictures and diplomas on the wall, boxes of test materials on shelves, a desk top full of reports in progress, and other similar items reduce the possibility of optimal test results by a learning disabled child. In any good psychological clinic the room for the actual examination should be separate from the professional office used by personnel. Children should have an opportunity to put their best foot forward. The evaluation of their mental capacity should not be distorted by distractions, such as the office clutter, over which they have no control.

The speech therapist, too, should be aware of the need for a non-stimulating setting in which speech therapy or language development may be carried out. Anatomical charts and models, professional books and journals, and the teaching materials which the therapist uses will serve as distractions. What amount of attention the perceptually handicapped child might be able to invest in the therapist is drained off into unrelated and unprofitable activities.

The application can be carried into still another professional field. In the cerebral palsy clinic, occupational therapists and physical therapists often complain that certain of their clients are unable to respond with profit to their instructions. One such child, observed by the author, was known not only to have cerebral palsy, but also to be characterized by much perceptual disturbance. The physical therapist was attempting to direct this child's attention while the child was lying on his back on a treatment table in a room with three other therapists, three other treatment tables, and three other patients. There were so many unessential stimuli in the room that the child in question was simply unable to respond properly to his own therapist. Most of the time which the two people spent together was wasted. When this was pointed out to the therapist, curtains were pulled around the treatment table so that the child's attention was not distracted from the therapist. Significant gains in the physical therapy aspect of the child's treatment program were soon noticed.

Motor training within the school setting likewise should be carried on in as stimulus-free environment as it is possible to achieve.

The environment recommended here may seem sterile and cold, but, on the contrary, the clinical teaching classroom, despite its lack of stimuli, can be a warm and friendly place. Color is used; the teacher and the assistant are warm and friendly; and the small group activities engaged in by the children allow social contacts. The most important fact is that the environment prompts learning.

OTHER CONSIDERATIONS FOR THE SCHOOL PROGRAM

The class for perceptually handicapped or learning disabled children should be a *self-contained unit*. It is more advantageous to the children, for example, if toilet facilities are attached to the classroom. All the activities of the school day will be carried on in the classroom. At least in the beginning of the child's educational therapy he will be a nonparticipating member of the wider school community. As we have suggested earlier, we see nothing in the literature or in general practice which would convince us that the present emphasis on mainstreaming is anything but a disservice to most perceptually handicapped and learning disabled children. If educators would only analyze the total situation, it would appear easy to understand that the philosophy of mainstreaming and the nature and needs of perceptual processing deficits in children simply do not harmonize in favor of the child. Normally he will *not* participate in *auditorium experiences,* though exceptions may be made on occasion when he is in good control of himself and if the teacher knows in advance that the auditorium activity will be relatively nonstimulating. For the most part, however, auditorium programs will be too stimulating for this child. It will be difficult to return him to his special class and to get him settled down sufficiently to be able later to have success experiences in the lessons his teacher has prepared for him. Many months may pass before he is ready for this type of school activity.

Another school activity which needs consideration with learning disabled children is the *fire drill.* In spite of the care with which school officials plan these drills, they nevertheless are exceedingly exciting to all children. Some learning disabled children may lose an entire day of positive learning because of the tension and stimulation resulting from participation in a fire drill. Many school principals work out separate arrangements with teachers of hyperactive learning disabled children. In temperate climates there is no problem. During a drill the children are lined up at the door of the room leading, as is customary, directly to a patio or play area. They do not leave the building, however. On other days when none of the tensions of the drill are present, when the other children are still in their rooms, the teacher and assistant give the learning disabled children separate practice and instructions about what to do, where to go, and how to get out of the building in an emergency. In still other schools in colder climates, the procedure may be the same. The children in the class for learning disabled line up prepared to leave their building, but they do not leave their classroom. They would leave their classroom only on a special signal which is prearranged by the principal and the teacher. One person in the central office is charged with giving this signal in case of a real emergency. Again, at other times special drills are given to this group of children when the stimulation of hundreds of other children moving through the halls is absent. The child's energy is thus reserved for his learning activities.

The *cafeteria* of the school poses another adjustment problem for learning disabled children, and it is wise to avoid using it until the child has full control of himself. Lunch is better served in his own classroom where the environment better suits his needs.

It is obvious by now that the concept of stimulus reduction, to be effective, must be consistently carried out throughout the total school and home program. *Physical education* and free play periods in the schoolyard are not included in this program except under special circumstances which are discussed in later chapters. Competitive games requiring quick judgments and many choices are beyond the ability of most learning disabled children at the development stage of which we write. At a later time, they will be able to tolerate these important aspects of their education. The most important aspect of the education of learning disabled children, whether in the home or school, is to experience success. Environmental control to achieve this end is paramount.

Music and musical activities need to be evaluated with great care in the early phases of the therapeutic educational program of learning disabled children. It is generally assumed that rhythmic tunes are good for group activities and games. This is undoubtedly true with normal children who are able to tolerate all that goes into music and the musical activities of rhythmic games. The learning disabled child cannot. Music, as an auditory stimulus, surrounds the child. He has trouble localizing it, and often he is disturbed by it. (Chapter 8 will outline the circumstances under which music may be used.) Rhythmic games performed with music accompaniment involve just too many motor and auditory stimuli, too much movement, too much awareness of visual stimuli, and too much opportunity to come into close motor contact with other children to warrant their use in the early months of training. For the hyperactive child this excess stimuli can prove disastrous. These activities will be utilized ultimately in the program, but they will come later after greater emotional integration has been achieved by the child. This, like many other things included in the program for learning disabled children, is the reverse of the program for normal children for whom music forms a large part of the school and social life in kindergarten and in the elementary grades.

What has been said of music applies also to *unstructured art experiences*. Finger painting, often considered to have therapeutic value for emotionally disturbed children, may be too threatening to some learning disabled children to be utilized as a part of the general activity program. Certain children will be able to perform satisfactorily and will be exceptions to every point we have made in these last few pages. As a rule, however, unstructured art activities should be delayed until the child has achieved success experiences and until he feels secure.

We have been deleting things from the school program rather rapidly in the last few paragraphs. A thoughtful teacher and parent may well wonder what *is* going to take place during the school day. Is there anything which is to be taught? Chapters 7 and 8 will approach the matter more positively and indicate what is to be included. Thus far the emphasis has been to call to the reader's attention those elements of the school or home situation which may involve choice, motor activity, reaction to unessential stimuli, or other elements which might better be left out of the daily experience of the PPD child.

Teachers of perceptually handicapped and learning disabled children should plan very carefully for the period immediately after the child's arrival at the school in the morning. This is a crucial time of the day. Whether the child has ridden the bus to school or walked, he has been exposed to many different situations. Some children, following a long bus ride to school, arrive at the special class distraught and extremely tense. The potential for failure is great when tension is present, and teachers must use care to insure that assignments given the child at this time are accomplished successfully.

THE PARENTS' ROLE

Parents have a very special role to play in the life of the learning disabled child. Their role may sometimes be an almost impossible one, particularly if there are other children in the family. The parent must constantly be an arbiter between the child and the neighborhood. The parent will need to be a thoughtful, patient interpreter of the learning disabled child to other parents, to group leaders such as den mothers, and indeed oftentimes to school personnel themselves. It is essential that the learning disabled child have success experiences with his neighborhood friends. He cannot be kept in isolation from them. Yet his hyperactivity and instantaneous motor response to other children may often bring him into physical conflict when in reality his intent was quite innocent. His lack of motor coordination may cause him to be the last man chosen for the baseball team. His short attention span may disturb his playmates just as it disturbs family members and classmates. His need for friends is obvious, however, to anyone who has observed perceptually handicapped children trying to become involved with others of their own age.

The parent will have to be a wise judge to determine the point at which the child's perceptual problems and limited tolerance begin to become sources of interference to good adjustment with others. At this point the child should be withdrawn from neighborhood play and his energies diverted for a while to activities in his own back yard or home. The other children will appreciate this adult wisdom. They will be more likely to welcome the child back into their group again if they know that things will never be allowed to go so far that his uncontrolled behavior will require them to defend themselves against him.

Parents will need to observe the child to ascertain the amount of stimuli and the kinds of situations he can tolerate. Anticipation of new experiences will often disturb a learning disabled child for many days in advance of the event as well as for a period of time afterward. A birthday party, for example, is better announced just a day or so before or in some cases on the exact day rather than to permit a long buildup weeks ahead. Such a party may involve only one or two friends rather than a large group, and the party should be brief. The author is reminded of a group of learning disabled boys with whom he once worked. The tile floor of their classroom was to be covered with a wall-to-wall carpet to cut down the auditory stimuli within the room. The children were informed sometime ahead that the carpet was to arrive, and the teacher went to some length to prepare them for the change which would take place in their classroom. The carpet finally was installed. In spite of the preplanning, or perhaps because of it, the new rug was a veritable trampoline for some of the children for several days. On one occasion the author, having witnessed all the uncontrolled motor behavior he thought necessary, said to one of the boys, "Keith, surely you can control yourself by now. Certainly you can adjust to this carpet." At this Keith replied, "Well, it is a new situation, you know, and you know what new situations do to us!" In spite of the clinical sophistication of this boy, new situations do create much tension, and they must be understood by parents so that negative experiences can be kept to a minimum. Parties, holidays, and similar events are "new situations."

Parents too will serve their children well if they can anticipate events and ascertain their impact on the learning disabled child. They will serve their child well if they can continually interpret his behavior to their neighbors and friends, not from the point of eliciting pity but to provide understanding and to assure other adults that the parents are themselves conscious of the child's problems and are trying to solve them. The role of the parent is not an easy one at best. It can be challenging and rewarding, however, especially when the child begins to learn, improves his behavior, and earns greater social acceptability. Stimuli reduction, then, is the first element in a broad plan of home and school education for the learning disabled child.

RELATIONSHIP STRUCTURE

In this chapter we have been discussing the importance of environmental structure. Teachers and parents also are a part of the environment of learning disabled children. Although we shall be discussing the parent role from time to time in subsequent chapters, it is important to view parents and other adults also as a part of the environmental structure of these children. Just as children come to learn appropriate adjustive mechanisms to a structured and stable classroom or home environment, so children can learn to adjust to parents who demonstrate the same qualities. The initiative, however, must come from the adults. The child cannot structure parent behavior except as a reaction to the child's controlled or uncontrolled behavior. Behavior models for perceptually handicapped children are essential to their growth and development, even more than for the normal child who can rather quickly determine what is appropriate or inappropriate in teacher or parent behavior. Under the best of circumstances, it is not easy to grow up in this world. For children who have difficulty in processing the stimuli which come to them, the problem is doubly difficult. Stable, consistent, predictive relationships between the child and his parents are essential. This applies to teacher, father, and mother as well as to any other adults who may be living in close proximity to the child.

In recent months the father and mother of a seriously perceptually handicapped child have visited with the author for counseling regarding their son. The son's problems could quickly be assessed and constructive planning undertaken. The parent's reactions to the boy as well as to each other were considerably more complex, however, and became the subject of relatively long-term counseling. One example serves to emphasize the points being made in these paragraphs.

A second child, two years younger than the 9-year-old Billy who was under immediate consideration, lived in the home. The mother was a typical busy housewife, concerned for herself, her home, and her family. She was deeply concerned for Billy, and spent an unusually large amount of time explaining him and his behavior to the neighbors, arbitrating child quarrels, and defending his presence in the neighborhood community. She was exhausted by the end of the day. The father, a junior executive in a local manufacturing firm, managed, on the pretense of his work and his developing career, to leave the house in the morning before Billy was through with his breakfast. He arrived home in the evening after six o'clock in time for a quick dinner and shower before he left for bowling on Mondays, Rotary Club on Tuesdays, the Toastmasters Club on Wednesdays, poker with his boss regularly on Thursdays, and a hoped-for engagement with or without his wife on Fridays. Saturday, depending on the weather, was reserved for golf with business associates. There was no time for the family, and it appeared to the counselor that much of this frantic father behavior was contrived to avoid Billy and his problems. The father's own image was damaged because of the behavior and school problems of his son. How can a relationship be established between the two? The father had inadvertently opened the door.

"You say that you regularly get home from the office at six P.M. and immediately take a shower before dinner," commented the counselor.

"Yes," said the father, "that's always the routine."

"How long does it take you to complete your shower?"

"Fifteen to twenty minutes at the most. I like to relax under the hot water."

"Is there any reason why you and Billy couldn't take a shower together?"

"Yes, . . . then again, I suppose no," responded the father, attempting to avoid what appeared to be the inevitable.

"Then," said the counselor, "do it. In this way you will at least have a few minutes each day with your boy."

The father did follow this request. The shower activity was fun for Billy. The spatial area was small. Parent-child relationship was just about as structured as it could be. Failure experiences were practically nil. Fun was a part of the relationship. Success was essentially built in to the activity. The father reported that both he and Billy looked forward to this experience, and that it was indeed a success. While "shower therapy" is not necessarily a recommended approach to all learning disabled children, it nevertheless was the basis of the beginning of a strong, consistent relationship between this father and son. Some weeks later during a counseling session, the father again opened another door. In a rather wistful comment to the counselor he stated: "It would be nice if there were other things Billy and I could do which provided us such satisfaction." It didn't take long for other suggestions to be made and for some of them to be accepted and tried.

The essential point here is that activities which produce success for the child (and for the adult), which can be consistently planned, and which can be predicted as thing to happen insofar as the child is concerned, must be built into the daily life management plan. Out of such activities can be structured a strong parent-child relationship, the basis of healthy growth and development.

On still another dimension parents and teachers can provide structure. Their physical presence can be significant to the perceptually handicapped child, and as such can be of great assistance in the child's attempts to organize himself in relation to his environment. The world of the learning disabled child is a chaotic one from his point of view. Things do not appear to go together well. If the adult can intercede for the child and assist in the recognition of a more ordered world, the relationship between the child and the adult can be strengthened greatly, so that the child comes to see the adult as a source of support.

In thus describing the adult's role, we are not suggesting that it be a domineering one. It will be a role in which the adult will be dominant, although the dominance will give way to the child's own dominance as the child learns to control and direct his life in terms of the environment. The distraction of the environment can be minimized for the child in many inconspicuous ways by the adult. For example, as the child stands in a line waiting to leave the classroom, the teacher may move to stand by him, perhaps placing an arm around the child's shoulder. In walking along the sidewalk, the mother or father may from time to time place a hand gently on the child's shoulder or an arm around his neck. Touching a child's arm or wrist by the teacher while she is sitting next to a child to whom she is giving some individual instruction; the parent to the child during the dinner; the parent or teacher to the child as they are sitting next to one another during an auditorium experience, a movie, in church, or in other large spatial area—in all of these examples, the adult is providing for the child a conscious reminder that there is a structure, not only to their relationship, but to the child's relationship to the larger environment in which he lives at that time.

One of this author's concerns regarding mainstreaming and the learning disabled child stems from the inability of the regular classroom teacher to have his or her presence felt by the child in a sufficiently consistent way. If the adult-child ratio could be significantly increased in those integrated classrooms wherein children with learning disabilities were to be placed, then our concern for the efficacy of the concept of integrating these children would be considerably lessened. The increased number of adults could in part have the same effect on the immediate teaching situation for the child as is obtained in environments where the stimuli have been reduced. This is not fully satisfactory, but the adult structure can go a long way to achieve this objective.

What an optimum teacher-adult-class ratio should be, we do not know. In a recent visit to a small but excellent school for these children, some thirty-five children were functioning in one group. All children had learning disabilities and most also had serious emotional problems. Nine or ten adults were assisting with structure in the group activities, although most of the adults were merely a presence in the situation, not actively participating in the direction of the children. No stimuli reduction had been attempted in a very large room. The greater the number of adults (to a point), the less need there is for stimuli reduction. The adults provide what might be considered an even better structured environment—one that does not modify the normal stimuli, but one in which, because of adult controls, the child learns to adjust to the appropriate stimuli. Again it should be pointed out that adult dominance and control is not the same as a domineering adult. The manner in which adults—teachers, parents, volunteers, high school students—are utilized in groups of children with learning disabilities is a matter needing careful examination. We have not yet learned how they can most effectively be integrated into a concept of structure where structure is seen as a tool of instruction and pupil growth.

SELECTED REFERENCES OF SPECIAL INTEREST TO PARENTS

Caldwell, B. "What is the Optimal Learning Environment for the Young Child?" *American Journal of Orthopsychiatry* 37 (1967): 8–21.

Clements, S. D. *Some Aspects of the Characteristics, Management, and Education of the Child with Minimal Brain Dysfunction.* Glen Ellyn, Ill.: West Suburban Association for the Other Child, pp. 3–4, 9.

Ilg, Frances L., and Ames, Louise B. *Child Behavior.* Glen Ellyn, Ill.: West Suburban Association for the Other Child, 1955, pp. 8, 10.

Lewis, R. S. *The Brain Injured Child.* Chicago: National Society for Crippled Children and Adults, 1963, p. 16.

Strother, C. R. *Discovering, Evaluating, Programming for the Neurologically Handicapped Child.* Chicago: National Society for Crippled Children and Adults, p. 13.

SELECTED REFERENCES OF SPECIAL INTEREST TO TEACHERS

Cruickshank, W. M. "The Learning Environment." In *Perceptual and Learning Disabilities in Children,* edited by W. M. Cruickshank and D. P. Hallahan. Syracuse: Syracuse University Press, 1975. Vol 1, Chapter 8.

_____. "The Education of the Child with Specific Learning Disabilities." In *The Education of Exceptional Children and Youth.* 3rd ed., edited by W. M. Cruickshank and G. O. Johnson. Englewood Cliffs, N.J.: Prentice-Hall, 1975, pp. 242–91.

_____; Bentzen, Frances A.; Ratzeburg, F. H.; and Tannhauser, Mirian T. *A Teaching Method for Brain-Injured and Hyperactive Children.* Syracuse: Syracuse University Press, 1961, pp. 15–16.

Strauss, A. A., and Lehtinen, Laura E. *Psychopathology and Education of the Brain-Injured Child.* New York: Grune & Stratton, 1947, pp. 131, 136.

Quay, H.; Wherry, J.; McQueen, M.; and Sprague, R. "Remediation of the Conduct Problem Child in the Special Class Setting." *Exceptional Children* 32 (1966): 509–15.

Kelman, H. R. "The Effect of a Brain-damaged Child on the Family." In *Brain Damage in Children: The Biological and Social Aspects,* edited by H. G. Birch. Baltimore, Md.: Williams & Wilkins, 1964, pp. 77–99.

Rappaport, S. R. "Personality Factors Teachers Need for Relationship Structure." In *The Teacher of Brain-Injured Children: A Discussion of the Bases for Competency,* edited by W. M. Cruickshank. Syracuse: Syracuse University Press, 1966, pp. 45–56.

————. "The Brain Damage Syndrome." In *Childhood Aphasia and Brain Damage: Diagnosis,* edited by S. R. Rappaport. Norristown, Pa.: The Pathway School, 1964, pp. 54–98.

————. "Diagnosis, Treatment, and Prognosis." In *Childhood Aphasia and Brain Damage: Differential Diagnosis,* edited by S. R. Rappaport. Norristown, Pa.: The Pathway School, 1965, pp. 53–106.

5

Adjustment to Space and Time

H AVE YOU EVER by chance arrived at a restaurant where you were planning on having dinner only to find that you were the first guest? The restaurant had just opened for the evening, and any table in the large and spacious dining room was yours for the asking. The *maitre d'hotel* graciously swept you into the room, saying that you could sit wherever you wished. What table did you choose? The one in the center of the room? Possibly. But the chances are that you took one to the side, in a corner, in a booth, or in some portion of the room other than the undifferentiated center area. "We'd like to sit along the side," you told the waiter. Why along the side? There may have been many reasons, but one of them which you probably did not recognize is that "along the side" there was a wall or other structure which provided a convenient spatial orientation for you, a structure which brought all of the other aspects of the room's space into a logical relationship with you.

The proper use of space is important in creating the most appropriate learning situation for learning disabled children. It should be recalled from the earlier definition of learning disability (Chapter 1) that one of the primary characteristics pertained to the child's inadequate ability to recognize spatial the temporal orientations. If the reader will refer again to Figure 21, he will note that the room pictured is somewhat smaller than a standard-sized classroom. This particular room, 14 feet by 22 feet, is quite adequate in size for the group of eight children who occupy it daily. This exact size is not necessary for all classes of learning disabled children, but as a general rule the room should be smaller than a standard elementary school classroom. The extent of space is related to stimuli factors; as space increases so stimuli increase. The converse likewise is true: as space decreases so stimuli decrease. The factor of spatial stimuli is one of two issues to be considered in thinking of learning disabled children. First, in keeping with the preceding discussion, it is important to reduce space if in so doing it is possible further to reduce the stimulus value of the child's classroom. The second factor is equally important. The smaller space permits the child to perceive the limitations of his environment more easily and to organize himself perceptually in relation to these limitations.

Many kindergarten children experience tension when they are taken as a group into the school's large auditorium. Not only is the auditorium new to them, but it seems so large that they cannot easily adjust to it. The tremendously large areas needed for the assembly of spaceships and rockets which will be used in probes to the moon have been commented upon as being a factor to which workmen and technicians must condition themselves. The author can recall the comments of his friends when they first attended the Paris Opera. For the first few minutes they were more concerned with adjusting to the vast auditorium than interested in the opera itself. Perceptually handicapped, learning disabled children likewise are concerned with space. Their instability in space, and the anxiety which this produces, undoubtedly is due to their faulty perceptual processes. Being constantly distracted by the unessential in itself produces feelings of spatial disorientation. They need constant reminders of where they are and of their relationship to other things. As positive learning occurs, these limitations to their physical environment may be relaxed as the children are able to tolerate more distractions. In the initial phases of their educational program, however, it is appropriate to use a small room as a means of meeting their needs.

The reader will also note the partitions in Figure 21 which form cubicles so that each child has his own work area. The cubicle performs two services. First, since the partition extends about ten inches beyond the student's back when he is seated, the child is not distracted by anything which takes place in the next cubicle. Visual distractions from neighbors are thus kept at a minimum. Secondly, the cubicle implements even further the concept of reducing space. The space in which the child works is now one over which he has almost complete perceptual control. He can touch the three sides of the cubicle, which at the moment is almost his complete environment, and he can frequently orient himself to place and continue the task he is doing. Jeffrey, a 10-year-old boy, was observed frequently to run his hands around the interior walls of his cubicle. When asked why he did this, his reply was, "Well, I've got to remind myself where I am, you know." He was not merely repeating concepts he had heard mentioned by adults but was serious in informing the adult that

Figure 25. The relationship of teacher to children in the nonstimulating classroom environment when cubicles are used. These carrels do not permit teacher-child eye contact. The carrels would be more appropriate to the teaching needs if they were each about 24 inches wider.

from time to time he found it helpful to be able to touch the limitations of his environment and to reorient himself in relation to it. One disadvantage to the carrels depicted is that they are too small. It is more satisfactory if the carrel is wide enough to permit two chairs. The child may use the space alone, but as needed there will be space for a second chair to be used by the teacher. This will provide an opportunity for eye contact between child and teacher and support the notion of adult structure mentioned in Chapter 4. A larger space will also permit two children to occupy a single carrel at the time the teacher believes this feasible and as a first step toward planning for learning in a more complicated and stimulating environment.

The author's point of view is that all school work requiring close attention by the child should be carried on in the carrel or cubicle. The child need not be forced to remain in his seat. Movement is permitted under circumstances to be described later. The child will have ample opportunities to change his position and move about. He may walk from his cubicle to the supply cupboard, leave the area to go to the water fountain, and be involved in other activities important to his adjustment. But lunch (which is considered a vital part of the educational program), instruction, and all other things significant to the learner's program are handled within the carrel.

Adults inexperienced with cubicles often feel that the children will not like them, that they are too confining, or that the child will feel restricted. The contrary is the truth; children do like them. There is, of course, as with everything else, a short period of adjustment to the new situation, but after this initial adjustment period learning disabled children express much satisfaction with the cubicle. The space is small enough for them to be its master, and they are in control of it psychologically. This is perhaps the first time in their lives that they have felt secure in space, and they are pleased both with themselves and with the teacher who has provided this comfortable working area. The young child may call the cubicle his "house," and the older child refers to it as his "office." More frequently, however, it is called just what it is, a cubicle or a carrel.

The size, lighting, and construction of the cubicle are three important considerations. The lighting must be standard candlepower, and the lights must be positioned so that when the child is working in the cubicle shadows are not formed as his head gets between the desk top and the light. Moving shadows will serve as visual distractors to the child. However, the light must not be placed low enough in the cubicle for the child to reach it, for then it becomes a stimulus to distract the motoricly disinhibited child. Incandescent light is preferable to fluorescent light since the latter may flicker or buzz for some time before burning out, creating stimuli distracting to the children.

Very careful carpentry is required in constructing the cubicle. A permanent installation is recommended over folding screens or other types of movable partitions, and in any construction the joints should be perfect. Cracks left at the corners or at the points where the desk top fits against the cubicle walls will serve as distracting visual stimuli which will produce motor responses, namely, the response of sticking the pencil point into the space and cracking it off. From experience, this author knows that faulty carpentry may indeed almost wreck the educational program. The desk tops should be bolted tightly so that they cannot be wiggled by hyperactive children, but they must also be designed so that they can be raised or lowered to fit children of different heights.

It is recommended that the walls of the cubicle be constructed of hard wood. A prime quality plywood may be satisfactory, and the surface should be free of all blemishes which may distract the child. The cubicle walls shown in Figure 25 are constructed of ¾″ plywood, and they are covered with several coats of paint. However, a small defect just the size for a pencil point was discovered at eye level by one of the boys. This defect soon became a small hole, and ultimately, as the child was distracted to this spot time after time, he drilled his pencil completely through the wall. Two boys now had a stimulus to work on! Before the wall could be replaced, a hole the size of a nickel had been neatly carved out of the partition. A formica-type covering on cubicle walls has been found quite satisfactory in some classrooms, since the wall can then be cleaned easily without repainting.

The author questions the use of a cubicle in the child's bedroom as a place for his work or play activities. The cubicle does not seem appropriate or necessary in this setting. The child's bedroom is usually a small room anyway, and a table placed in a corner will serve the same function as a cubicle when the child wishes to draw, color, play with models, or involve himself in other activities. If the child is distracted during eating, the mother might screen off the offending area with a folding screen or some other type of divider so that the child's attention can better be directed to the task before him. It is not recommended, however, that parents go to extremes within their homes to provide the type of learning situation appropriate for school.

Substitutes for cubicles have been tried by numerous teachers. In the opinion of the writer, they remain only substitutes. Three- or four-panel folding screens have frequently been utilized to separate children from each other. Being portable, they are just as easily moved and knocked over by the children as be adults. Furthermore, when the screens are set up around a desk, cracks appear at the folds permitting fingers, papers, and pencils to be inserted. These may appear to be inconsequential concerns, but any teacher of perceptually handicapped children will attest otherwise. Easels are used for isolating learning disabled children by some teachers, but these, too, have limitations.

Oftentimes a teacher of a regular class in which there is a learning disabled child has been able more adequately to serve the child on a temporary basis by utilizing the folding screen. This permits the child to be separated from the rest of the class during periods when the child's close attention is required for a particular task. The approach can work reasonably well in a regular grade, provided the teacher has made it clear that this is a method of meeting the individual needs of a child and that isolation is not a method of discipline or punishment.

Space considerations, then, are vital in an over-all plan for the education of learning disabled children. Reduction of space is the second element in a total program, the first being the stimuli reduction discussed in Chapter 4. Insofar as the child feels comfortable in space, is oriented to

Figure 26. One of several types of carrels available commercially. Note this one has built-in facilities for television, an educational technique which with proper environmental controls can be of importance to the child or youth with learning disabilities.

the space in which he works, and can feel a definite relationship between himself and his spatial environment, he will be in an optimal situation to attend and to learn.

There are many commercial materials which, particularly for the older child and adolescent, are helpful. One such study carrel is illustrated in Figure 26. This one is designed for the older youth, and it contains several built-in advantages.

First, it is large enough to permit the pupil and the teacher to work side by side at the same time. Its walls are high enough to reduce environmental distractions. It is likewise attractive, and the spatial area is sufficient to contain larger books and equipment which may be typical of the need of the adolescent pupil. Furthermore, the carrel is wired and equipped so that video taped material can be channeled into the carrel and be viewed and heard (through headphones) by the pupil himself. The positioning of the television monitor prevents distraction to other pupils seated nearby. As school systems move more and more to meet the needs of the secondary school-aged pupil with learning disabilities, the need for such equipment will become obvious. One has only to consider the facilities which most college and university libraries have afforded to undergraduate and graduate students to recognize the generally accepted need for reduction in distractions to *normal* learners. We hope the same thought will be extended to the pupil who, by reason of perceptual processing deficits, needs such facilities even more.

TEMPORAL ORIENTATION

To call children with learning disabilities confused is not completely erroneous. It is not wholly accurate either, but it does describe an attitude exemplified by such children on many occasions and toward many things. Confusion may on the one hand be the result of disorientation in space. It may be the result of an inability by the child to screen out unnecessary or intruding stimuli in an adjustment situation. As we have seen, it may also be due on other occasions to a misinterpreted or misunderstood structure in the parent- or teacher-child relationship. On still other occasions, problems of temporal disorientation may be a matter of significance.

Over centuries, people working together in societies have structured their lives in terms of years, weeks, days, hours, minutes, and sometimes seconds. Little goes on in social living but that it is related to a time base or frame. We get up at a given time, eat at other times, go to school, begin work, make social engagements in terms of a specific structure involving time. Some are more concerned for this aspect of structure than others and go so far as to organize their lives weeks, months, and sometimes years into the future. Adherence to an appropriate time-related structure provides a significant degree of security to normally perceiving individuals. Battles have been won or lost in terms of time orientations. The world populations sat in awe a few years ago as their attention was directed to television screens, and they became aware of the split-second timing necessary to complete successful earth-orbiting and moon-landing expeditions. Time became real and significant.

Children with perceptual processing deficits often demonstrate temporal disorientation. Their distracted lives, their attention to the unessential, their lack of internal controls leave them vulnerable to time in its passing. Teachers and parents are often frustrated by the many times each day (or often each hour) that a child with learning disabilities asks "What time it is?" "Is it time to get a drink?" "When will we eat lunch?" When can I talk to John? Did you say I could talk to John now?" So goes the day of questioning, seeking information, and striving through inquiry to orient themselves to time as others understand it. In one instance university students were asked to observe eight perceptually handicapped children for a full day in a special teaching unit, and to be primarily concerned for the children's orientation to time. The eight children were boys between the ages of 8 and 11 years, all intellectually of normal range, all perceptually handicapped in some manner. All questions or comments relating to time were recorded by the students who were observing the children from an adjoining room. Within the 5½-hour school day, the average number of time-related questions or comments was twenty-three. The range was eleven for one child, fifty-one for another. Because of their perceptual processing problems, there appears to be a need to orient themselves to the passage of time, yet the processing deficits themselves are the very reasons why the child finds it difficult to relate to things in a temporal sequence.

Time, of course, is an abstract concept. Children with learning disabilities tend to be able to deal with the concrete better than the abstract. Developing a concept of time, such as telling time from a clock, is usually well developed by the age of seven, often before. With the child characterized by perceptual processing deficits, the ability to use a watch or a clock may be a skill not acquired until eight, nine, or ten years of age. In a later chapter of this book additional material is furnished specifically related to clocks, calendars, and determining time.

The issues to which we address ourselves at this point serve primarily to illustrate the earlier definition of these children and their problems and to demonstrate the close interrelationships among the characteristics of learning disabled children which have thus far been discussed. There is no single characteristic as in some other type of exceptional children. The problems of the blind child, for example, while very complex insofar as learning is concerned, are specific to a more or less single entity—visual acuity or the lack of it. Children with perceptual processing deficits are characterized by interlocking problems which oftentimes defy separation. Temporal and spatial disorientation are in and of themselves significant characteristics. But these are the result of those other characteristics of failure to refrain from responding to interfering sensory or motoric stimuli, problems of figure and ground relationships, dissociation, and many others. Sometimes, in learning disabled children, one characteristic may be the cause of another; other times, the cause is a characteristic. These children represent the essence of complexity, and it is this fact which makes difficult a realistic understanding of them and more difficult the development of a realistic educational and life management plan.

REFERENCES OF SPECIAL INTEREST TO PARENTS

Kephart, N. C. *The Brain Injured Child.* Chicago: National Society for Crippled Children and Adults, 1963.
Lewis, R. S. *The Brain Injured Child.* Chicago: National Society for Crippled Children and Adults, 1963.
Radler, D. H., and Kephart, N. C. *Success Through Play.* New York: Harper & Row, 1963.
Strother, C. R. *Discovering, Evaluating, Programming for the Neurologically Handicapped Child.* Chicago: National Society for Crippled Children and Adults, 1963.

REFERENCES OF SPECIAL INTEREST TO TEACHERS

Bower, R. "The Psychology of Space Perception." *Special School Journal* 45 (1956): 22–26.
Cruickshank, W. M. "The Learning Environment." In *Perceptual and Learning Disabilities in Children,* edited by W. M. Cruickshank and D. P. Hallahan. Syracuse: Syracuse University Press, 1975. Vol. 1, Chapter 8.
_____. "The Education of the Child with Learning Disabilities." In *The Education of Exceptional Children and Youth.* 3rd ed., edited by W. M. Cruickshank and G. O. Johnson. Englewood Cliffs, N.J.: Prentice-Hall, 1975.
_____; Bentzen, Frances A.; Ratzeburg, F. H.; and Tannhauser, Mirian T. *A Teaching Method for Brain-Injured and Hyperactive Children.* Syracuse: Syracuse University Press, 1961, pp. 16, 17.
Dunsing, J. D., and Kephart, N. C. "Motor Generalizations in Space and Time. " In *Learning Disorders,* edited by J. Hellmuth. Seattle, Wash.: Special Child Publications, 1965.
Haring, N. G., and Lovitt, T. "Operant Methodology and Educational Technology in Special Education." In *Methods in Special Education,* edited by N. Haring and R. Schiefulbusch. New York: McGraw-Hill, 1967.
Kaliski, I. "Educational Therapy for Brain-Injured Retarded Children." *American Journal of Mental Deficiency* 60 (July 1955): 71–77.
Kephart, N. C. *The Slow Learner in the Classroom.* 2nd ed. Columbus, Ohio: Merrill, 1960. pp. 91–117.
Rappaport, S. *Public Education for Children with Brain Dysfunction.* Syracuse: Syracuse University Press, 1969.

6

The Role of Structure

FROM THE DESCRIPTION of the learning disabled child given thus far it is apparent that the child is often confused. His confused behavior results from his exposure to an overstimulating environment and his self-generated need to react. This child tries, but in his confusion his attempts are often futile. He wants to be loved, but his attempts to attract adult attention may result in rejection instead. This child's total life experience has been one of perceptual distortion and perplexity. The result is a child who is a mysterious riddle to those who wish to help him. Efforts to help are often rejected by the child who wants and needs help but cannot accept it because of his distrust of adults. A vicious circle operates constantly.

We have earlier stated that adults must modify their world to meet the needs of the learning disabled child. They must teach with his disability in mind. Distraction has produced failure which has produced more distraction. Somehow this endless chain of failure upon failure has to be broken. Radical steps may have to be taken to do so. We have seen that it is necessary to reduce environmental stimuli to a bare minimum, and we have further stressed the importance of reducing the learning space to dimensions acceptable to the brain-injured child. These two factors alone will help, but they must be supplemented by giving the learning disabled child a well-developed concept of *structure*. Through appropriate structure the child will be able to understand himself better.

Structure must be understood in terms of a theory of learning. The learning theory employed is fundamental—that of conditioning. We will not include a discussion of conditioning in this volume, for other books are devoted solely to explaining this concept. It is sufficient here to note that structure is necessary in order to assure appropriate responses to stimuli.

One of the unique problems of the learning disabled child is that, through his random responses to the multiplicity of environmental stimuli which surround him, inappropriate or partial responses are made. These are either absolutely wrong responses or responses which are wrong in the setting in which they are made. Immature judgment and faulty earlier learning fail to give the child the basis from which to make appropriate responses. These partial responses do not give personal satisfaction to the child; they are looked upon as failures by adults. For appropriate learning to take place, there must be an appropriate stimulus followed by a response appropriate to the social situation which in turn is followed by reward. The reward need not be tangible. It may be only the opportunity for insight to be developed so that the child understands and is satisfied that what he has done is accepted by society. This satisfaction motivates the child to make other similar types of responses. There is nothing particularly mysterious about conditioning; nor does its use represent a new point of view. Out of success experiences based upon conditioning comes self-satisfaction. Out of a series of satisfactions with self come new ego strength and strong self-concepts. The goal for the teacher or parent is the establishment of the kind of setting in which good conditioning can take place.

In the classroom for learning disabled children nothing should be left to chance. Structure must be employed at all times. Proper structuring of the child's environment should always be uppermost in the mind of the teacher. Some elementary educators protest against this emphasis on structure; structuring reduces opportunities for choice, we are reminded. Children must have opportunities to be creative, to plan, to decide, and to learn by self-directed experience, they say. Children must be given an opportunity to structure their lives and their own daily activities under the guidance of a permissive teacher. This may be the correct approach for normal children, as this writer prefers to believe. It is not correct for learning disabled children, however. Self-direction for them results in confusion and in additional fracturing of the ego.

Progressive education has many fine concepts and goals. When it is considered as an educational philosophy rather than as a religion, its methods can contribute to the growth and development of normal children in proportion to the wisdom and skill of the children's teachers or parents. The theories of progressive education, particularly the aspects associated with permissiveness, are predicated, however, upon a normal organism. These teaching theories and practices are to be employed with children who are assumed to have had positive experiences alone, with other children, and with adults. These children have had earlier successes from which they have built valid self-concepts and body images. Progressive education methods require children to make choices. Choices, however, are made by individuals who are relatively more mature and who have had previous successes with choice and are able to move from one situation to another without feeling threatened or becoming tense. No one of these characterizations fits the perceptually handicapped child.

The PPD child feels threatened by having to make choices. He is not yet able to deal with freedom, for freedom involves too many choices and too much exposure to the unessential stimuli which are his downfall. This child must yet demonstrate to himself that he is able to achieve and that he has a personality respected not only by others but by himself. This is a child to whom life is a constant struggle and for whom each day constitutes another major battle in the total war. His techniques of adjustment are so fragmentary that to place him in a permissive environment only serves to heighten his tensions and to increase and reinforce his feelings of insecurity and inadequacy.

If educators and parents wish to help this child, a different approach must be taken. The structured environment we advocate is not one of harsh rigidity. By structure we are not implying inflexibility on the adult's part nor advocating a return to the colonial school with its cold and rigid schoolmaster and the willow rod. Warmth and concern for human welfare, love and kindness, and fun and excitement kept at appropriate levels can all be incorporated into a concept of structure, and they must be. A sound concept of structure applied to an educational program provides the warp and woof on which, with adult guidance and help, the child can begin to construct proper frames of reference for his life.

The role of structure in our lives is an interesting phenomenon. We are so accustomed to it that its presence is relatively unnoticed. Usually we are aware of it only in its absence, and then we tend to seek it in order to aid in our adjustment.

Arriving in a strange city, we tend to look for landmarks around which to orient ourselves. Maps provide us with another form of structure in assisting us to become oriented to space. Music is recognized to have time, and that time is divided equally into bars which consist of subdivisions of notes, each with different time values. Some hear music as discordant or view paintings as unsatisfying when traditional structures are missing. For the average human life is segmented into years, months, weeks, hours, and minutes. The university student's classes are *scheduled* by semesters, credits, hours, and years. Time is a remarkable tool for structure. Many other examples could be provided. Structure or the need for structure is not innate or instinctive. It is learned. It is learned in the normal course of human development, and most such learning comes in the early years of a child's life.

The child with a perceptual processing deficit may, for the many reasons we have already mentioned, be unable to appreciate the everyday aspects of structure which his environment and the people in it try to provide. His disabilities result in confusion within the normal structural limitations of his environment. Perception of himself in space and in time is difficult, and when he cannot perceive himself in these dimensions appropriately he is viewed differently by his parents, his friends, or his teachers. He is confused and he is seen as being confused. To assist him in this vital aspect of adjustment, the structural cues must be accentuated. They must become more obvious and, for a period of time, more long lasting. It is within this framework that we consider structure and see its value for these confused and often perceptually disoriented children and youth.

The educational program must be constructive; it is a developmental program, not a remedial one. Too often public school programs for the learning disabled child are assigned to remedial reading teachers or are founded upon a concept of remedial education. Programs based upon a remedial concept are not likely to succeed since the issue is not one of rehabilitation; it is habilitation. New learning is the proper concept, not remedial teaching. The learning disabled child's learning background is filled with false starts and many stops. An evaluation of the child's education reminds the educator that the child has traveled down too many empty roads. He has rarely been able to see the relationships between one fact and another, between one learning experience and another.

If self-direction and choice are beyond the ability of the learning disabled child, the alternative is an adult-dominated situation. The implications of this are many, and one of the most important has to do with the selection of the adults themselves. Parents, obviously, cannot be selected, but teachers can be chosen and prepared to work with learning disabled children. Parents, too, as we will later indicate, can do much to adjust themselves to the needs of the learning disabled child during the period of his major educational development.

Although we will speak frequently in these chapters regarding the physical structure of the learning environment for children with learning disabilities, structure may be much more than bricks and mortar, more than study carrels, smaller spaces, and furnishings of a classroom. We stress these not only because they have proven helpful to many learning disabled children, but also because they lend themselves to illustration and discussion easily. Structure of almost the same magnitude can be provided by both adults and the nature of the educational program itself. At one point some years ago the author was attempting to develop the idea of a structured educational program in the Montgomery County Public Schools, Maryland. Nearby Dr. Fritz Redl was also developing a psychoeducational program for some serious emotionally disturbed children, six or seven in number. Redl and I discussed structural programmatic differences on several occasions. In the public school program, the author was working with several groups of children, ten children in each group with one teacher and a part-time aide. The environmental structure described here was established. In the Redl program at the National Institute of Mental Health, no effort at environmental structure per se was made, but for the six children there were as many as five or six times that number of adults. Structure in the latter program was provided by the adults. Adults were available to these children whenever decisions had to be made or whenever the child needed them.

We do not advocate such an adult-child ratio in the public schools. The NIMH program was experimental. The author has frequently observed and sometimes participated in programs for children with learning disabilities where there was one teacher with six or seven children. These have been exceedingly successful when the teacher has been sufficiently dynamic to be able to exert her influence on all of the children at all times and to assist them quickly to achieve a level of self-direction which relieved the adult of constant obvious efforts at structuring the situation. One of the most remarkable examples of this is to be seen in the Gateway School, where Elizabeth Freidus and her colleagues, with a minimum of environmental structure and modification, nevertheless provide a remarkably structured program by sheer dint of excellent programming and total devotion to the logical aspects of a good developmental experience for children. The impact of the adult personality on the appropriate behavior of the children is obvious to all.

TEACHER SELECTION

Teachers of learning disabled children must be selected with great care. Some information concerning the competencies needed by teachers of learning disabled children is already in book form. It is sufficient at this point to say that the teacher of the learning disabled child must be a patient person and one who is satisfied with relatively small gains. He must view a small gain as the possible forerunner of greater ones by the child. The teacher must be a flexible individual who can accept the unusual in both behavior and language. He must be shock-proof. The teacher must be comfortable with structure, be able to establish limitations, and be able to maintain limitations until the child understands that they are essential for his well-being, not hurdles to be challenged. The teacher must be able to function as an equal on the interdisciplinary teams composed of members who are concerned with the different phases of the total educational program. The teacher of learning disabled children must be creative and capable of maintaining an experimental approach. Since no two children are identical in their needs or capacities, the teacher's approach to each child must be in terms of what he knows of the child's past performance; but the approach must also be experimental and tentative in terms of whether or not the child is ready for the new material being presented to him. The teacher must be secure enough to retreat quickly if his teaching materials are too advanced for the child, and he must be able to make this retreat without threatening the child or making him feel that he has failed. Teachers who meet these criteria and who have received specialized preparation for this work are worth their weight in gold, and they become one of the most significant influences in the lives of many perceptually handicapped children. The characteristics needed by the teacher assistant are much the same as those needed by the teacher; matters related to the selection of teacher assistants are discussed later in this volume.

ENVIRONMENTAL STRUCTURE

Environmental structure has been discussed in Chapter 3. Its reintroduction here is for the purpose of bringing into focus the earlier comments regarding reduction of stimuli as a part of the structured approach. Control of stimuli produces the external structure to the educational program which is so important to the learning disabled child. The reduction of space and the use of the carrel help shape the environmental structure. The carrel makes it possible for the child to conceptualize his immediate physical environment and to relate appropriately to it. The carrel provides a physical structure for the child which serves as a substitute for the lack of structure in his personal life. It is something tangible, something firm and fixed.

Teacher Structuring

The teacher can serve in the same external capacity role. As mentioned earlier, teachers occasionally are concerned at the amount of physical handling they receive from some learning disabled children. It was suggested that such physical advances can be countered by the teacher's taking the initiative to maintain physical contact with the child. An arm around the child's shoulder or a hand on his head or arm assists the child in structuring himself in relation not only to the adult but to the total spatial situation of both individuals. When the children move through the halls to the school exit or come into the building in the morning and walk toward their room, it is particularly helpful if the adults present (the teacher, assistant, or volunteers) can unobtrusively take them by their hands or put an arm about their shoulders.

On arriving at school, the children, particularly if they have come by bus or taxi, may be overstimulated from the ride. Some children will regularly appear confused and uncontrolled. Recently a learning disabled boy, enrolled in the demonstration class in the building where the author has his office, reached school quite late. The teacher, assuming the youth was not coming to school that day, had already taken the other boys to the classroom. When the taxi arrived, the writer saw John. Realizing that class had already begun and that there was no one at the door, the writer went to meet the child. "Good morning, John. How are you?" was the greeting, but there was no reply. Instead the boy walked past and proceeded toward his room. Since responses are always expected from the boys, the writer called after him, "Good morning, John. Say hello to me, please." There was still no answer, and the writer stopped the child and turned him around so they were facing each other. The boy was obviously distracted. "Hello, John." Silence. "Good morning, John." Silence. The writer by now had John's chin in his hand and was directing the boy's eyes and face toward his own while another hand rested on the child's shoulder. "John, hello. Say hello to me. You know who I am." A long silence of perhaps ten seconds passed. Then John said, "Oh, hello. How are you. I'm late this morning."

John was distracted by the relatively long ride to school and in addition was tense because he knew he was late. He was unable to organize his tension, his need to be in class, his fear of what the teacher might say, and his language abilities sufficiently to recognize and speak to an adult who had always been friendly to him. The writer, structuring their dual relationship by holding the child and by patiently waiting for a response, was able to reduce tensions and to make the child understand that a relationship existed between them. There was no thought of punishment or discipline by either the child or grownup. It was simply a matter of establishing a structure which would permit the child to function appropriately. In a nonthreatening situation time was provided for the child to organize himself. The significance of the time required cannot be overstressed with perceptually handicapped children.

Oftentimes we have seen learning disabled children in a frenzy of emotion call to the teacher to "hold me" just before they reach a completely uncontrolled emotional pitch. They know from other times when stresses were not so great that they found security in the physical relationship with their teacher. Now, in a moment of fear, for emotional breakdowns are often very fearful experiences for the child, he calls for the person who brought him assistance before, namely, the teacher who held him. We feel that when a child asks for this type of physical reassurance from an adult, a considerable amount of insight has developed in him and that the child's request for help should be granted immediately.

The close physical relationship which children need with adults is another reason for careful selection of the teachers, who must themselves be secure and well-adjusted individuals. Following an emotional outburst, or when a child may have to be removed from a group because of his temporary inability to cooperate at any level, we have found it important to spend time with the child in trying to analyze the total situation with him. During this period, depending upon the age of the child, the child may be held on the adult's lap. This is done in order to establish a structured relationship between the two people. If the child is seated in a chair across the desk from the adult, there is little likelihood that contact will be made if the child is at all tense or disturbed. On the other hand, if he is standing by the adult or sitting on his lap, close interrelationships can be formed, security can be sensed by the child, and the emotional situation can be transformed into a positive learning experience.

In handling a child physically one must be careful not to place him in an embarrassing position in front of friends. If he is approaching preadolescence, this relationship could be intolerable for him if observed by his friends in other classes regardless of how much he might both want and need the contact. The teacher needs to be alert to these social implications and should either avoid contact completely when it might prove embarrassing or work out substitutes which will provide the structure which the child needs at these times.

PROGRAM STRUCTURE

Admissions to the Program

Structure is of concern to educators of learning disabled children at all points. The initial organization of the class at the re-opening of school each fall is a case in point. The diagnostic committee will have screened children for admission, and the superintendent of schools or his designated official will have indicated which children are to attend a given class with a particular teacher. During the weeks preceding the opening of the school, the teacher will have had an opportunity to study the diagnostic records carefully, and he will have had an opportunity also to discuss them with members of the diagnostic team. This teacher may actually have been the one who administered the education evaluations of the children initially, so that he already is familiar with much of the case data. In the event he has not previously had contact with the child, arrangements should be made for the teacher to visit the child in his home, talk with his parents, and perhaps at that time, in the informality of the child's familiar home surroundings, actually make an abbreviated educational assessment. Such a visit will give the teacher some firsthand understanding of the child's potential and skills.

After the teacher has acquainted himself with the group of children for whom he is to be responsible, he should be permitted to indicate the *one child* who is to come to school on the first day. The parents of the other children will be informed that their children will be admitted just as soon as possible. They have already been informed of the admission procedures and are aware of the waiting period before their child is assimilated into the special class. The balance of the children ultimately to be accepted remain in their former school placement or at home. The role of administration is significant here, for thorough understanding of the process must be provided the parents of "waiting children" by school administrators.

The teacher is expected to work with the child he has selected until that child is adequately adjusted to the special class situation. This adjustment may take only a day or so, or it may be as much as two weeks. The longer period is not necessary in most instances. Time must be permitted, however, for teacher and child to acquaint themselves with one another and for the child to become thoroughly conditioned to the nature of the program for him. It is also important that he is given an opportunity to assimilate the idea that other children will soon be joining him. When this has been accomplished the teacher will indicate to the administrator that a second child is desired for a given morning, and he will specify the child he feels will adjust best to the one who is already there and vice versa. This procedure continues until the entire group is assembled.

It has been observed that it is better to move too slowly in assimilating new children than to move too rapidly. If all children arrive on the same day in September or if assimilation of the group is too rapid, chaos will result. If a teacher finds that he has moved too rapidly in assimilating the learning disabled children into his class, he should have the administrative support and freedom to request that the last one or two be temporarily excluded to return later when the situation is really ready for them.

If this procedure is followed, learning disabled children will be able to acclimate themselves both to the special class environment and to the other children. It is not all easy; crises are bound to develop. Fewer eruptions will occur, however, if a step-by-step assimilation of children is used than if all the children are thrown together with little or no advance preparation. In the plan recommended here, the teacher can help each child anticipate the "new situation" of an additional friend in the classroom. This procedure may be repeated by the teacher after long vacation periods. Usually the assimilation is much more rapid at these times, however. At the beginning of each school year the plan of gradual adjustment of the group is followed even though some of the members of the group are returning for a second or third year. School administrators should place the responsibility of determining the order of the children's arrival on the teacher. The teacher, in turn, will develop the order on the basis of what he knows about the children and their ability to adjust to each other. The relative emotional maturity of the children and their social abilities, motor skills, and educational needs will all enter into the teacher's decision concerning which child enters the program first, second, or last. Administrators must have faith in their teachers and know that the teacher will move as rapidly as is advantageous for the child, to the end that all the children assigned to him are finally in school. It is poor policy to push the teacher to accept children more rapidly than is educationally wise from the teacher's point of view. Children will be harmed if assimilation is too rapid. The program can indeed fail under these circumstances.

The First Days

Structuring begins the first time the child comes to the school room. He should have visited the room informally before the beginning of school, but at that time no major indications of his role or the teacher's role will have been stressed. The initial visit is only for orientation purposes. When he has been admitted to the program for a long-term experience, however, and when he first arrives in the classroom, the teacher quickly informs him of the behavior limitations of the group and helps him understand these limitations as thoroughly as possible. It is essential that he know and understand the few things expected of him.

Initial structuring may begin with as simple a task as hanging up his coat and hat. "Good morning, John. Hang your coat on this hook when you get it off. It will go there every day. This is your hook. The others are for other boys who will join us later. You are to use only this hook, and your coat is to be hung in this way." If he can take his coat off by himself, the teacher helps him to see that the coat is in a position to be hung properly, not by a sleeve or through a buttonhole. "Let's try it now and see if you can hang it properly." The teacher will watch the child, and if she observes that the coat is going to be hung in ways other than the way which has been specified, she stops the action before a failure is experienced. The teacher may then put the coat in the child's hand the way it is to hang. He then takes the child's hand in his own, and together they hang the coat properly. "There, *we* did that right." The emphasis, notice, is now on *we*. The child is perfectly aware that *he* did not do it alone and that the teacher assisted him. There is no sense in talking down to these children. It is much better to be honest and forthright with them. "We" did it, and "we" will continue to do it together until the child is sufficiently conditioned to this activity to be able to handle it alone and to succeed. The emphasis is on success experience, and failure experiences or criticism should be avoided.

Now that the coat is on its proper hook, the hat is hung up in a given relationship to the coat. Again help is given if the child cannot accomplish the task alone. The lunch box goes on a particular shelf in a particular way. It may be that the child's perceptual disturbance is sufficiently severe that he is confused and unable to pick out his coat hook from a dozen others in front of him. The teacher may find it necessary to increase the stimulus value of the hook by painting it a bright color or by putting a special symbol or picture on the wall above John's coathook. It also may be well to identify the proper place on the shelf for the lunchbox. These tasks may seem elementary, but remember that the child fails tasks expected of others at his chronological age because he has few basic skills. It is essential that he learn these skills which he somehow missed as a younger child not only in order to build the motor skills that lead to more complicated learning, but also to build up the child's self-confidence—to make him feel that he is one who can achieve something.

Note also that these initial skills bring him into direct contact with an adult—with an adult who obviously wishes to help him succeed. Since this child is often fearful of adult and has no real basis for a strong relationship with them, these simple activities, which usually involve much success experience, also afford an opportunity for trust and confidence to be engendered.

From this point on, everything in the school day has an order and a correct procedure. The schedule is not overly rigid, but there is a recognizable structure to everything expected of the child. He is given a definite frame of reference for all of his activities, and nothing is left to chance. He will be shown how to attract the teacher's attention without unnecessary disturbance of the other children. He will see what kinds of things the teacher will do for him and what the teacher's assistant will do. He will be taught the routine of performing a task, having it checked for accuracy by the teacher or assistant, and returning the necessary materials to the cupboard across the room. He will be shown how to get the materials for another project from the cupboard, return to his cubicle, and again obtain instructions from the adult so that he can proceed. There will be time for fun, play, and relaxation during the day, but these activities, too, will be structured in such a manner that the child will know what is expected of him.

There are bound to be unexpected interruptions in the classroom, and the teacher and assistant should be prepared for them. A child may arrive in school having had an unpleasant encounter with a parent at home or with a bus or taxi driver en route. He may still be emotionally upset, and before the end of the day he may have a tantrum or emotional outburst. At this time the professional person, the teacher, must move in to work with the disturbed child while the assistant turns his attention to the other children. The assistant will ascertain that each child is emotionally secure and pause to speak with each of them, assuring them that soon everything will be all right. This effort will prevent the entire class from becoming upset. It can also elicit from the other children efforts to control themselves, and when they do they can be praised for their self-control. The assistant should also see that each child has the learning materials necessary for his assigned activity. If a child is not occupied and is at the same time witnessing an emotional scene, the tension may be too much for him, and he, too, may buckle emotionally. Children quickly become proud of their ability to control themselves under stress. Sometimes they even boast of their self-control and try to use their good behavior as a tool to accomplish other ends! It should be noted that, even in the circumstances just described, there is a definite preplanned procedure for the teacher and the aide to follow.

Luncheon as an Educational Experience

The school day for learning disabled children may be somewhat shorter than that for normal children, particularly during the early months when tensions are great and adjustment to the program is not yet complete. Since the lunch and nap periods are considered integral parts of the school experience, the shorter school day is being fully utilized. Some children may be unable to tolerate even this shortened day for some time. Administrative flexibility on the matter of school day length is essential.

In our experience it is better for the child to bring his lunch from home. Milk can be added from the school cafeteria, but the basic lunch is better provided by the parent. This procedure is more satisfactory for several reasons. First the lunch should include only those things which the child enjoys eating. This is no time in the life of the learning disabled child to have to fight an issue of food dislikes. This may happen if food from the school cafeteria is utilized and the child is suddenly faced with something he dislikes. The menu will often include certain things which the child does not like or cannot eat, and then a type of failure experience is at hand. Secondly, since much of the school program will involve both gross- and fine-motor movement training and since learning disabled children are usually characterized by poor coordination, foods utilized in the initial lunch experiences should not be those which require knife, fork, or spoon, or which can be spilled.

The teacher should tell the parent to send the quantity she thinks her child should eat and to include in the luncheon only items that the child has previously eaten and liked. The parent should prepare the lunch in such a manner as to simplify lunch time as much as possible for the teacher and assistant. Sandwiches, for example, should be cut into four squares, and each quarter should be wrapped in a separate piece of paper.

When lunch time arrives, a piece of colored construction paper, perhaps with a black border around it, will be placed on the desk top in the child's carrel or cubicle to assist him in reducing his visual field. Only one quarter of the sandwich will be unwrapped and placed before him. The child, we remember, has a tendency to be distracted by extraneous stimuli; there should be no extraneous objects on the table top while he is eating. The sandwich wrapping and all other food should be removed (see Figure 27), if the child is distracted by these things. Initially only the single stimulus should be present—the quarter of a sandwich which has been unwrapped. This is the target upon which his attention should be fixed; we want him to pick the food up and bring it appropriately to his mouth. If he can do this, splendid; if he cannot, the teacher will have to help him achieve the socially acceptable response. If the quarter of a

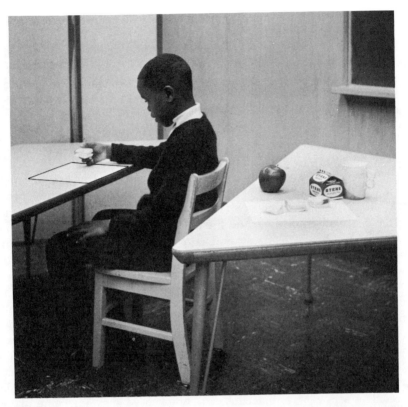

Figure 27. In this relatively nonstimulating room, the child's lunch is arranged in keeping with his known psychological needs and problems. Note that the cup is one which when partially filled with milk can be easily grasped by the child. A place for two fingers gives manual stability to him while he is learning accurate motor skills.

sandwich is grasped with the child's whole hand instead of by two or three fingers, or if it is smeared over his cheek, nose, or ear, it is obvious that he is not ready for this motor activity. The teacher may then cut the quarter into bite sizes, show the child how to grasp the piece with his fingers, and then guide the child's hand to his mouth. As the child shows success in this skill and can be complimented genuinely, two quarters of the sandwich may be placed on his table top. If he is distracted motoricly by the second quarter, the teacher must retreat to the level where success was achieved. Gradually, more and more stimuli (more and different articles of food) will be placed in front of the child always *within the limits* of his tolerance. It may take several months before the child will have learned to tolerate having his entire lunch before him on his desk and to eat it within socially acceptable standards.

Instead of the plain construction paper, other cues may be provided the child to assist in structuring the lunch experience. For example, a large piece of oak tag paper, construction paper, or plain brown paper can be used as a place mat. On the place mat an area may be drawn to indicate where the sandwich goes as well as for other types of food such as milk, a thermos of hot soup, dessert, spoon. The child may write his name on the mat as an added "drill experience" in learning to spell his or others' names.

Analyze for a moment the motor skills involved in drinking milk from a bottle through a straw. Usually two hands are brought together to hold the bottle. This involves coordination. The bottle is raised to the face (more coordinate activity), and the mouth seeks the straw (more motor activity). Finally, with the straw in the mouth, sucking movements are made (fine-motor activity), and milk should go into the mouth and be swallowed (fine-motor activity). Since some of the problems of these children go back to this initial inability to suck, it is doubtful whether this complicated task will be performed adequately at this level. Drooling and spilling often take place. What appears to be a simple task for a "big boy" is indeed a complicated task for one who does not possess the necessary motor skills. It is better that the child be permitted to drink from a cup, often with the adult assisting, in order that all of his disabilities do not militate against him to cause another failure experience. Drinking milk through a straw may, indeed, be a complicated task for some of the children; it may take several months for some of them to use their straws adequately.

Let us assume that the child is eating a meal at home. Earlier we described the extraneous stimuli of an ordinary dinner table. Let us assume now that the child has a figure-background reversal problem or is dissociating. The table, set as previously described, is covered with a brightly colored tablecloth. Place mats are used also, and on one of these is the child's plate. The plate is light blue and has an interesting design. On the plate are meat, mashed potatoes, and peas. The child is expected to eat these things with a fork, and to cut his meat with a knife and a fork, primarily because he is of the age when children should be handling utensils properly. However, this child has a figure-background problem. He may be confusing the peas with the plate design or the tablecloth. His distraction results in peas going in every direction when he tries to eat them with his fork. Motor incoordination may, of course, also be a factor in the lack of skills.

Although it may appear that we are painting an absurd picture, experience has not demonstrated it to be untrue. Perceptually handicapped children do have these problems, and they do behave in these ways. The problem can be minimized by structuring the situation and by careful parental planning. Instead of the print tablecloth, a solid-colored place mat should be used. Instead of a plate with designs, it is better to use a solid-colored plate. Instead of having three different articles of food on the plate at once, it will help the child if only one thing is put on the plate at a time, perhaps in small quantities. While the child is trying to learn, he should be permitted to do so in as uncomplicated a way as is possible. The examples that have been given are typical of the care with which all activities in the schoolroom, home, or elsewhere should be structured for the learning disabled child.

When the child in school shows improvement in dealing with his lunch, the teacher can plan to increase the stimulus value of the situation. If he can tolerate all of the items from his lunch box when they are placed on the table top in front of him and if he can at the same time eat it properly, he is ready for something else. This may be the first time that choice is presented to him. "Jeffrey, you are eating so well these days that I thought perhaps you'd like to try something different tomorrow. You may decide for yourself whether you would like to continue eating in your cubicle or to eat lunch with me at the table in the center of the room. If you decide to eat lunch with me, you may return to your cubicle at any moment you wish."

An escape valve should always be provided for learning disabled and hyperactive children. They must always know that it is all right to retreat, without losing face, to a level of behavior which they know is comfortable to them and to one which is within their tolerance level.

If, however, the child decides to eat his lunch in the center of the room where he is aware of all that is going on in the rest of the room and if he does so satisfactorily, the child is ready for still another step. These steps may be separated by intervals of several weeks or months in time. "You are doing so well with your eating and lunch, you may wish to have your mother stop sending lunch to school with you. You may go to the cafeteria and get your luncheon tray, then bring it back here to eat." If the child can withstand the stimulation of the halls and the cafeteria and still return to his classroom to eat satisfactorily, the next step is to permit him to eat his lunch in the cafeteria. Every step of the way is carefully planned, structured, and executed. The child knows that under tension he can always move back a step without losing the respect of the teacher or others. His capacity to tolerate stimuli and to function adequately in this phase of his development will also provide cues to the teacher regarding the child's readiness to return permanently to the regular grade of his neighborhood school. This decision can be made only when his achievements in other areas as well have reached a certain uniform level. Structuring makes it possible for conditioning to take place. From satisfying conditioning or learning, ego support develops to provide the child with more positive self-concepts.

Rest Can be Structured

The extent to which structure is pursued can be seen as it is applied to the rest or nap period, for here, too, learning must take place. Figure 28 illustrates the utilization of the cubicle during the nap period. Sometimes one child will need frequent periods of rest during the school day. It is thus excellent if the room is sufficiently large to accommodate a cot where this child can relax without disturbing the other children.

During their nap the children may lie on small mats. These mats, as can be noted in Figure 28, are a different color from the floor or carpet.

Figure 28. Use of the cubicles during a nap period to assist in providing structure for the children.

The use of different colors has a purpose; the contrast assists the child in observing the limits of his mat. It will provide a visual focus or structure to help orient him to this space.

Occasionally a child will be too insecure to relax when lying down on his stomach in the cubicle area. He is fearful because he cannot be certain what is happening in the space behind him. Sometimes the assistant can sit on the floor next to him. A hand on the child's leg or back will be sufficient to permit him to relax completely. At other times when the adult tries to help the child relax, sand bags can be placed on either side of the child's legs and back. The weight of the bags reminds him that something is behind him and permits him to relax and often to go to sleep. This technique has been recommended to parents whose children are unable to relax sufficiently to go to sleep at night, and many have found it satisfactory. Two bags made of canvas are filled with approximately ten pounds of sand each. In between is sewn a wide strip of canvas cloth long enough to fit tightly over the child's back or legs. Only the cloth tightly held in place by the sand bags touches the child's body. The bags of sand themselves rest on the floor or the bed on either side of the child. This gives the child sufficient support, permitting him to relax his fear of the uncontrolled space behind him, and go to sleep. Gradually, often over an extended period, the amount of sand can be reduced until the technique is completely discarded.

The examples used thus far have been concerned essentially with concrete activities. The presentation of instructional material must also be done in a structured manner. The individual elements—reading, writing, spelling, and number concepts—will be discussed in Chapters 7 and 8.

STRUCTURE AND PERSEVERATION

In an earlier section we mentioned that perseveration is a serious handicap to a child's successful learning and that it is also a difficult factor to prevent occurring. On the other hand, if the teacher is careful in the way he structures the child's daily program, much can be done to minimize this problem. Once again, however, the nature of the educational program departs from that which is appropriate for other children in elementary school.

The teacher of normal children will attempt to stress similarities. He will build one concept on another whenever appropriate relationships can be found. Spelling lessons grow out of the reading experiences, and social skills are closely related to both reading and spelling. This building upon similarities and the relating of one subject to another is appropriate for the normal child.

For the learning disabled or perceptually handicapped child, however, the similarities stressed with the normal child may in themselves serve as deterrents to learning, particularly if perseveration is one of the child's problems. The teacher should structure the learning disabled child's day-long series of learning experiences with as much differentiation as possible between one activity and the next. A pegboard activity will be followed by a word-recognition task. This will be followed by a block design problem which in turn may be followed by motor training, then by number concepts, then by paper-cutting activities, then by a walk, then by reading, and so on through the day. Activities scheduled next to one another should have a minimum of overlapping insofar as concepts, physical skills, or language activities are concerned. Differences are stressed, and in this manner perseveration may be kept at a minimum.

The teacher will also approach this problem from an intellectual point of view with the child. It is helpful to remind the child that perseveration is a problem for him, and this reminder will help him to keep in mind that with the completion of a given activity new ideas are to be developed with the next task. To reduce perseveration in a child who may have the beginning of reading skills, the teacher may put brightly colored swatches of paper between the words as signals to the child that one concept has ended and another idea has begun. In this case, instead of emphasizing the words, the teacher is emphasizing the space between words to keep the child aware of the shifts in the visual appearance of words and in the ideas the words represent. This careful attention to programming structure may go far in helping the child eliminate perseverative experiences in school activities.

THE RETURN TO THE REGULAR GRADES

Although the full story of the education and adjustment of the learning disabled child has not yet been told, there is another matter which is very important with relation to a discussion of structure. This is the procedure to be utilized in returning the child to the regular grades. When the teacher feels that the child is achieving satisfactorily and when his behavior appears to have been modified to socially acceptable standards, she makes a request for a final evaluation and a staff conference. If, in the opinions of the teacher, the school social worker, and the psychologist or the psychiatrist, the child is functioning realistically at the levels expected of him, he will be transferred back to his regular school.

The decision to effect the transfer is not reached quickly, nor is it implemented quickly. The social worker notifies the receiving school principal of the intended transfer. He and the social worker assigned to the receiving school are invited to a conference. At this time the child's progress is reported upon again. Care is taken to describe to the principal the nature of the program which the child has experienced and the type of teacher who it is felt would be able to deal most satisfactorily with the child as he now is. Generally among the several teachers in a building who are teaching the same grade there will be one who tends to be a bit more formal in his approach to children. This person is the one recommended for the child. Again, warmth of personality, interest in children, and flexibility are also essential. Since the child will come from a relatively structured program, he may be more comfortable for a while longer with a more formal than informal classroom—hence the recommendation for this particular teacher. It may be suggested at this point that when a receiving teacher is selected he be permitted to spend a day with the special class teacher seeing the child and examining the records and files of the child's work. A substitute teacher is utilized to free the teacher for these activities. At this time a decision is made between the sending and receiving teachers concerning the timing of the transfer. Usually the child should be transferred when the receiving teacher is ready to begin a new unit, not in the middle of one already under way.

When the time comes the child should be fully oriented to the arrangements which have been made for him. At this time it is important to assure him that he is being transferred because of his achievement, that he no longer needs the clinical teaching situation, and that he is ready to deal successfully with a regular school program. The transfer, however, should be gradual. The first day the child should stay perhaps only a half hour or perhaps only long enough to participate in a particular activity in which he has good skills. The receiving teacher will indicate to the special teacher when the time spent in the new room should be increased to an hour, to an hour and a half, to a half day, to a full day. This transition may take from two to six or even eight weeks to accomplish.

In advance of even the trial experiences described here, it has often been found helpful to permit the child to visit the new school or indeed any schools. He can return to his classroom and share with the other children what he saw, how he was received, and his general impressions of what he can expect in the future. When a final decision is made regarding the actual school to which he will go in the future, many visitations should be planned for the child.

In attempting to develop visuomotor skills and to establish good reading and number concepts, content typical of the regular grades may have been neglected in the clinical setting. The child should not be returned to the regular grades until he can join the grade at the appropriate chronological and achievement levels. During the transition period the receiving teacher should send back to the special teacher on almost a daily basis his suggestions for reinforcing the content which is then being considered in the new grade for which the child may not have a complete background. For example, the child may need some additional support in a different method for number concepts than the special teacher had stressed. Plenty of time should be allowed for the transition period. If the transition is handled carefully, the brain-injured child will be able to move from one setting to the other with relatively little disturbance or regression. The transfer becomes another success experience.

Although a decision may have been made to transfer the child back to the regular school, it must be recognized that a fragile package is still being handled. The child has obviously made gains. If there were no gains, transfer would not be seriously considered in most school systems. Regardless of the child's achievement, there is still growth to be made. It is astounding how often the issue of transferring children from one school to another appears to be a mere administrative decision. The human quality is forgotten. Moving a child, even the best adjusted, from the known to the unknown is a scary experience. For one who has had a history of failure and poor relationships with schools and learning, the timing of the transfer can renew anxieties and fears which may have been almost forgotten in the security of a clinical teaching situation. Good educational programs and the administrators thereof recognize this crucial situation, and often provide "transition teachers."

Transition teachers seek out the best possible location for the assimilation of the child under consideration. This person is the one on whom the responsibility rests for all the planning, visitations, parent counseling, and other matters relating to the return of a previously "sick" child to the normal environment. After the transfer has taken place, the transition teacher makes frequent visits to the child and his new teacher to let the child know he has not been forgotten, to ascertain that there is understanding and knowledge about the child on the part of the new teacher, to assist with suggestions where there are problems, and in other ways insure that the efforts of clinical teaching pay off to the child and his family in the community-based school program. Without transition teacher concepts, the whole effort may fail for many children.

The need for a close relationship between the two teachers is a valid reason for having the special class for learning disabled children located in an otherwise normal school situation rather than having it located in a clinic center or otherwise removed from elementary school buildings. There are occasions when trial transfer of the learning disabled child is desirable, and if he is enrolled in a total elementary school this can be accomplished without an excess of administrative protocol. The emphasis again, however, is on careful planning and structure of the total transfer experience for the child.

IN THE HOME

What has been said about structure in the school situation applies equally to the home. Structure should not be confused with rigidity or mere repetition that will lead to boredom. Meals should follow a schedule. Bedtime, bath or shower, recreation, and time for close contact with parents should be scheduled so that the learning disabled child can predict and anticipate the events. Scheduling, probably not a serious inconvenience to any other member of the family, is a necessity for the learning disabled child. Allowance must be made for unusual circumstances, but these circumstances should be infrequent so that the child will be able to adjust simply because he knows that an emergency has occurred or that some unforeseen circumstance requires everyone to change.

Parents will lessen their own tensions with the learning disabled child if they anticipate along with the child things which are both routine and unusual. The famous "new situation" will be just as much an adjustment hurdle in the home as in the school. For example, learning disabled children who are helped to anticipate the arrival of guests, the role of the visitors and the length of their visit, what adjustments will have to be made, and what modifications may be required in the family schedule will be better able to assimilate the new situation. Birthday parties, family trips, shopping excursions, and other similar events which change the child's normal day should be given some advance notice, perhaps only during the breakfast conversation, but nevertheless sufficient notice so that the idea can be integrated into the conscious life of the child. Parents should expect, however, that when routines are upset by unusual events, children are going to be more hyperactive afterwards. Parents can go far in maintaining a stable atmosphere within the home by simply reminding themselves of what the child may be like when he returns from a trip to the zoo with his father and by not being startled or frustrated by a temporary new level of hyperactivity.

ELEMENTS OF STRUCTURING

Teachers and parents must recognize that skills are required to establish a well-structured learning and living environment. This is not a matter to be left to chance, nor is it a responsibility which can be delegated to one individual alone. In the home both parents will have to come to an understanding regarding family management. There are several significant elements to structure, each important to the establishment of an adequate growth situation for learning disabled children.

The first of these is the *establishment of limitations*. Probably no social situation involving human beings is completely free of limitations. Until the individual is aware of what those limitations are, however, he is under a certain amount of tension. As the individual becomes aware of the limitations to his behavior, he can relax and adjust to the situation. So, too, with children there is a need to establish limitations in order that they will know what is being said here and the concept of permissiveness. However, if one analyzes the concept of permissiveness, one will see that limitations are involved in this point of view too.

In play therapy, a technique utilized by psychologists and psychiatrists in dealing with the problems of emotionally disturbed children, an attempt is made to develop a permissive atmosphere. An environment is sought that is free enough of limitations that the child's problems can come to the surface through play activities, role playing, and conversation and be understood by the therapist. It is assumed that this is possible only in the most permissive environment. But even in this environment, limitations are imposed on the child. They may be few in number, but nevertheless they are present so the child will have some focal point around which to organize himself and his relationships. The therapist, when greeting a child at the initiation of play therapy (or it may be a small group of children in group play therapy), may state, "This is a different sort of place than you have ever been before. Here you may do almost anything you wish. There are only two things we may not do [limitations!]. First, we may not break the toys purposefully, for they do not belong to us. Secondly, we will not hit each other." These limitations may change from situation to situation and from therapist to therapist, but some form of limitation will be established.

Children who function in a limitless environment are frustrated by degrees of freedom too great for their level of maturity. They find themselves in a situation over which they have little control. Complete freedom requires maturity beyond that of most children. In a completely permissive environment children become frustrated and confused because of the necessity of their functioning in a trial-and-error fashion.

When guidelines are established for behavior, children and adults immediately have a direction for their actions. A life of reason prevails.

Learning disabled or PPD children particularly are in need of limitations and structure, for their entire life has been one of confusion and psychological disorder. Their perceptual skills are faulty. They are hyperresponsive to details. At best, they are unable to plan their own courses of action. In an unstructured situation the brain-injured child gradually ends up an hysterical child, since he is completely unsure of himself and of the direction in which to move. In trying to act, he may fail. With limited, established goals there is some chance that he will succeed.

No more limitations should be established in the classroom than are necessary for a small group of learning disabled children to live together comfortably. It is important, furthermore, that the children be made aware of the limitations during the first contact which they have with the adult in the school situation. If today one ground rule is established and tomorrow a second and the next day a third, the child can never know exactly what is to be expected of him. Tensions mount under these circumstances, and the child's faith in the adult is disturbed. The limitations must be reasonable for the situation. They must be fair, and they must come from an adult who can convince the children that they are established in all honesty as a measure for better group living. The limitations may change from one situation to another—from school to home; from playground to Sunday school. Within each situation, however, the limitations will change only as the maturity of the children increases to a point where certain guidelines are no longer needed for group or individual accomplishment.

Secondly, with limitations established *the adult must accept the child at all times.* Punishment may be applied when the established limitations are exceeded. However, the child must be accepted at all times by the adult. The adult may reject the *behavior,* but he cannot reject the *behaver* and expect to be useful as an agent of change. Children will test the limits, and wise adults will anticipate this testing. Learning disabled children, particularly those who are emotionally disturbed and who have little reason to trust anyone, will test the limits to ascertain that the adult is really an honest person. The adult now has to prove himself. Adults should move cautiously, establishing only those limitations which are valid and absolutely essential to group harmony. Unfair limitation, or those made solely for the convenience of the adult, will quickly be challenged by the children. The learning disabled child must know that, even though he tests the limitations in a way unforeseen by the adult or uncomfortable to the adult, the adult still likes and accepts him. Insofar as he does not exceed the limitation in his testing, he is still operating within the es-

tablished frame of reference. When the child senses and accepts the fact
that the adult is fair and that he means what he has said, there will be an
immediate diminishing of the testing behavior. The period of testing requires secure and well-adjusted teachers or parents. There will always be
a honeymoon period at the beginning of a new school year or at the start
of a new program. Teachers and other adults can approach the end of this
period and the beginning of the period of limitation-testing in better
mental health if they know that it is going to come. It is quite inevitable
until the nature of children and adults changes radically!

A third aspect of this problem is that within the limitations *the learning disabled child must be accepted at all times in terms of the meaning of
the situation to him.* It is the opinion of this writer that many, if not most,
of the problems between adults and children stem from different understandings of the same situation. The possibility for learning disabled
children to misunderstand a given situation is great because of their
unique perceptual characteristics. It is essential, before challenging the
behavior of a learning disabled child, that the adult make an effort to
understand the situation or the meaning of the situation from the child's
point of view. This requires astute guess work at times, but if successful
the attempt to understand the child's viewpoint will facilitate communication with him.

A learning disabled, emotionally disturbed boy passed his teacher in
the hall while the latter was replying to some questions put to her by her
principal. The boy said hello to his teacher but received no reply because
the teacher was engrossed in conversation. The child interpreted this lack
of response, however, as a sign that the teacher disliked him. All morning
long the teacher was perplexed by the child's hostility and by her inability
to reach him. Finally, one of the other boys said, "Gregory thinks you
don't like him because you didn't speak to him this morning in the hall."
The teacher, who was on the verge of demanding a better attitude from
the boy, now took him aside and tried to analyze the situation on the basis
of the second child's comment. When the total situation was re-
constructed for both the teacher and the child and both could admit to
one another that there had been an error in judgment, the child was able
to relax and again feel he was wanted. The teacher was then able to obtain
the proper types of responses from the boy. Many examples could be
cited of misunderstandings which have developed from such dual meanings being attached to a single situation. Since the adult is the mature individual, the responsibility of ascertaining the dynamics of such situations
rests on his or her shoulders.

The final aspect of this problem of limitations and structure is the
matter of *consistency.* A child cannot adjust to a rapidly changing envi-

ronment; his environment should be both consistent and predictable. The total life experience of a child with perceptual processing deficits has been one of inconsistency and unpredictability. His fragmented relationships leave him with little basis for constructive development. If in addition to his own perceptual distortions the learning disabled child is confronted with inconsistency in his environment and unpredictable adult responses, learning and proper adjustment simply cannot be developed in sufficient measure. Consistency does not mean rigidity but implies on the part of the adult a coherence of behavior and a firmness of approach based on an honest appraisal of all relevant facts. Its result is congruity, harmony, and stability for the child. Consistency is desperately needed by learning disabled children, and wise adults will seek to provide it for them.

SELECTED REFERENCES OF SPECIAL INTEREST TO PARENTS

The "Brain-Injured" Child. New York: New York Association for Brain-Injured Children, 1960.

Clements, S. D. Some Aspects of the Characteristics, Management, and Education of the Child with Minimal Brain Dysfunction. Glen Ellyn, Ill.: West Suburban Association for the Other Child.

Hewett, F. M. "Educational Engineering with Emotionally Disturbed Children." Exceptional Children 33 (1967): 459–67.

———. The Emotionally Disturbed Child in the Classroom. Boston: Allyn and Bacon, 1968.

Ilg, Frances L., and Ames, Louise B. Child Behavior. Glen Ellyn, Ill.: West Suburban Association for the Other Child, 1955.

Nall, Angie. "Structured Living in the Home." In Ideas for Action, edited by Dorothy Knowlton. Texas Association for Children with Learning Disabilities.

Strother, C. R. Discovering, Evaluating, Programming for the Neurologically Handicapped Child. Chicago: National Society for Crippled Children and Adults, 1963.

SELECTED REFERENCES OF SPECIAL INTEREST TO TEACHERS

Cruickshank, W. M. "The Education of the Child with Brain-Injury." In The Education of Exceptional Children and Youth. 3rd ed., edited by W. M. Cruickshank and G. O. Johnson. Englewood Cliffs, N.J.: Prentice-Hall, 1976.

————; Bentzen, Frances A.; Ratzeburg, F. H.; and Tannhauser, Mirian T. *A Teaching Method for Brain-Injured and Hyperactive Children.* Syracuse: Syracuse University Press, 1961.

Freidus, E. "Methodology for the Classroom Teacher." In *The Special Child in Century 21,* edited by J. Hellmuth. Seattle: Special Child Publications, 1965.

Haring, N. G., and Phillips, E. L. *Analysis and Modification of Classroom Behavior.* Englewood Cliffs, N.J.: Prentice-Hall, 1972.

Kaliski, Lotte. "The Brain-Injured Child: Learning by Living in a Structured Setting." *American Journal of Mental Deficiency* 63 (January 1959): 688–95.

7

Teaching Materials

O f the five essential elements basic to the educational program for learning disabled children, three have thus far been discussed—namely, reducing stimuli, structuring space, and structuring both the learning environment and the teaching program. The fourth element, involving teaching materials, has implications for both home and school.

Parents need as much information as teachers about teaching materials, for parents are the purchasers of toys, games, and books for their children. Many items which are purchased lie unused on the toy shelves of the child's room because they are inappropriate for the child or because they are too complicated for the coordination and motor abilities of the learning disabled child. Children may easily become frustrated with the wrong toy, or they can be well pleased with a wisely purchased one. Toys and teaching materials for perceptually handicapped children should be selected with the child's learning disabilities in mind.

Several times in the course of these chapters the statement has been made that the teacher or parent "must teach to the disability." Obviously a teacher also addresses and emphasizes all of the abilities and strengths which a child with learning disabilities has. However, the teacher must also teach to the disability. This statement vividly comes to life in considering the teaching materials. For example, consider the matter of hyperactivity alone. It is known that the child is responsive to stimuli. The environmental stimuli, as earlier described, have been reduced as much as possible. The child is no longer distracted by things in his schoolroom or in the nearby area to any great extent. He is still a hyperactive child, however, and he is still responsive to stimuli. This being the case, he should be given stimuli to react to in the area where the teacher wants his attention directed and toward those things which are pertinent to his learning experience. Hence, the teacher should increase the stimulus

171

value of the thing to which he desires the child to attend. Throughout the pages of this chapter and the next, the reader will often note references to color. Through the use of color, it is possible to increase the stimulus value of the letter, line, word, or number concept which the teacher wants the child to recognize and learn.

Another child is characterized by a figure-background reversal problem as well as by hyperactivity. In this instance the teacher should not give him an arithmetic drill experience which perhaps contains a dozen problems on a single page. The twelve problems with all of the digits, addition symbols, and lines will constitute such a visually stimulating situation that the child may be unable to attend to a specific problem. He may be able to get the first problem correctly solved, because that problem is protected by the corner angle of the paper, and on two sides of it there are no extraneous materials. However, as he moves to the other problems, figure-background reversal soon begins to interfere. The child fails to respond correctly to the addition problems whose solutions in reality he knows. The teacher can modify his materials easily to assist the child. Instead of giving him one sheet of paper with twelve problems on it as we have described, the teacher will give him twelve pieces of paper appropriately arranged, each with one problem on it. There are now no surrounding stimuli to the problem which appears alone in the center of the page. There is little or no background to reverse. Furthermore, in providing him with a small packet of twelve pieces of paper, the teacher is providing him with pages which can be turned. If the child is characterized by motor disinhibition, the turning of the pages utilizes his motor hyperactivity *in support* of the learning experience rather than as a detractor from it.

Because of the close relationship between the teaching materials and the child's disabilities, it is necessary for the teacher to have a detailed understanding of what the child is like. This places a distinct responsibility upon the diagnostic personnel, particularly upon the psychologists. They must so carefully describe the child in terms of his perceptual and motor disabilities that the teacher immediately has a set of guidelines for the preparation of appropriate teaching materials. The teacher's own educational evaluation will give him further information, but essentially the educator will have to depend upon the psychologists for the much-needed information. Too often the psychological data is lacking in the very elements the educator needs in order to begin immediately to meet the requirements of the learning disabled child.

Let us further assume that the child has an attention span of approximately two minutes under ordinary circumstances. He may glance away from his work momentarily even during this short period; under normal conditions the child can attend to a task conscientiously for only about two minutes and then can effectively tolerate it no longer. In the clinical teaching program, the teacher must be aware of the length of the child's attention span. Everything that the teacher prepares for the child must have a successful beginning and end within the known limits of the attention span. This means that, prior to the child's arrival in the classroom in the morning, the teacher and assistant will have organized for him (and for each other child according to their individual attentional needs) a series of learning experiences or items, each involving only approximately two minutes' time, which will carry the child as far through the school day as the teacher desires. For some children the materials may be developed on a three-, four-, eight, or ten-minute base. Everything presented to the child should have a successful beginning and end within the child's attention span.

It is thus important that the teacher, or psychologist if he has time, measure the child's attention span frequently. Teaching materials must be geared to the increasing span. The attention span will increase as success experiences are achieved and as conditioning to attend takes place. If the child is capable now of attending for four minutes whereas three months ago it was only two minutes, his needs will not be met if the teacher continues to utilize two-minute teaching items. The materials must now be constructed and planned to utilize all of the time the child is capable of utilizing. This is a plan of education which in reality meets the developing needs and characteristics of the child. It is obvious why continuous evaluation and assessment are necessary.

Parents also need to be aware of the length of the child's attention span. Fewer parent-child altercations will take place if this matter is kept in the parents' minds. How long should the child be expected to play with a toy? How long can we expect him to attend to a card game? Obviously things with a particularly high interest level will extend the attention span much longer than those things which are not quite so interesting to the child. Thus some parents report that their learning disabled children will spend long periods of time in front of the television set. This is true not only because of the high interest value which the program has for the child, but also because the more or less darkened room in which the television program is being viewed reduces environmental stimuli sufficiently to keep the child from constantly being distracted away from the screen. This helps to extend the attention span. The short attention span is also another reason why learning disabled children generally should not be asked to eat their meals with the rest of the family, other members of

TABLE 2
RELATION BETWEEN SOME TEACHING MATERIALS AND PSYCHOLOGICAL AND MOTOR
FUNCTIONS

	Parquetry	Block Design	Peg Boards	Sorting	Matching
Eye-Hand Coordination	X	X	X	X	X
Seeing Design or Pattern as a Whole	X	X	X		
Fine Muscle Development		X	X	X	
Establishing Handedness	X	X	X		X
Concept of Spatial Relationships		X	X		
Depth Perception		X			
Left-to-right Progression		X	X		X
Organization of Approach to Task		X	X	X	X
Color Discrimination	X	X	X		X
Form Discrimination	X		X		X
Relation of Figure to Background	X	X	X		X
Increased Attention Span	X	X	X	X	X
Control and Limitation of Persevervation		X	X	X	X
Temporal-Spatial Relationships	X	X	X		
Size Discrimination				X	X
Classification and Grouping				X	X
Laterality			X		
Directionality			X	X	X

which are content to prolong pleasant experiences as long as possible, or they should be excused from the table when they are finished eating.

These comments regarding attention span are made in the recognition that the attention span of the child is a direct reflection of the situation itself and of the interest level. Many have observed the work of Elizabeth Freidus as she demonstrates before large audiences with six or seven children who are often characterized by extreme perceptual processing deficits, emotional problems, and behavioral disturbances. It is not unusual in these circumstances for the children to be occupied as a group

Sequence Patterns	Stencils	Cutting	Pasting	Coloring	Geometric Form Copying	Coding	Tracing	Puzzles
X	X	X	X	X	X	X	X	X
		X			X			X
X	X	X	X	X	X	X		
X	X	X		X	X			X
X	X	X			X	X		X
X					X	X		
X			X	X		X		X
X	X			X	X			X
	X	X	X	X	X			X
	X			X				X
X	X	X	X	X	X	X		X
X	X				X			
				X				X
	X	X						X
X								
	X	X						
X		X			X	X		X

for two-hour spans of time, sometimes for more. The keys to this situation lie in the splendid capacity of the adult to keep the situation structured within limitations which are appropriately imposed, to vary the activities in which the children are participating, and to provide educational experiences which have high motivational value. While Ms. Freidus is an outstanding educator, the techniques she employs are well within the capacity of good teachers to emulate. If this is done appropriately and regularly the cautions regarding attention span which we have emphasized in the previous paragraphs do not assume such importance.

BASIC CONSIDERATIONS*

The selection of all teaching materials must be on the basis of what they contribute to the learning situation for a given child. It is essential that all materials relate to the disabilities which the children show. For this reason, teachers and parents must evaluate games, activities, and materials carefully in terms of their educational value, in terms of their ability to complement some psychological disability which characterizes their child. Table 2 illustrates this problem with selected teaching materials and isolates for each the basic functions which utilization of the materials should accomplish.

Even a casual glance at the table will be enough to show that many activities listed appear to have the same goals. This is quite true. While there may be one particular goal which is served best by a given activity other goals may also be obtained through its use. Every activity provided to a learning disabled child should be analyzed to be sure that it is appropriate to meet the needs of the child.

The list of possible activities is not complete on the chart. In a good classroom, this kind of list is always open-ended, leaving room for additions, deletions, or modification. Activities given the child should be planned so that they will aid in attaining some particular goal.

It would be to the advantage of both student and teacher for the teacher to verbalize (at least to himself) the purposes behind each activity. This may prove quite a time saver over a period of months. A monitoring effect will also be gained through this constant evaluation and perhaps will prevent the teacher becoming overly enthusiastic with a new type of material. The fact that something looks good and appeals to the teacher or parent does not necessarily qualify it as a good teaching tool.

Time should not be wasted trying to separate the various types of activities. A single task may have implications and background learnings for reading, writing, and arithmetic. As the child's developmental level rises, his capacity to employ more complex materials increases. He may use his beginning reading skills to discover what his task is. Then his arithmetic learnings may help solve his problem, and his writing ability allows him to record his answers.

*Much appreciation is extended by the author to Miss Ruth Cheves, an outstanding educator of learning disabled children. Appreciation is also extended to Miss Gwendolyn Adams, formerly a teacher of hyperactive and learning disabled children in the Jefferson County Public Schools, Birmingham, Alabama, for her assistance in organizing this material in the way it is being presented.

BASIC TYPES OF EQUIPMENT

Presented in this section are groups of materials which have been found to be suitable for use with learning disabled children. Some will be useful just as they are purchased. Other items will need modification to suit the needs of a particular child. Equipment listed for construction of materials has proved useful to other teachers. On the basis of their experience and judgment, these things will occasionally refer to a brand name or type. Certainly no one would suggest that this list exhausts the possibilities. A good teacher will always be alert to new things which can be used. An evaluation of an item based on the principles described in this book may produce several new uses for it. Shortcuts and time savers in the area of construction are most desirable provided the quality of the material is not downgraded. Numbers or amounts are not given. They will vary depending on the needs of the children.

A.   Commerical items to be used essentially as purchased

1. Wooden 2" parquetry blocks
2. Wooden 1" colored cubes
3. Wooden 1" plain cubes
4. Wooden 6 × 6" pegboards
5. Wooden beaded pegs in colors
6. Wooden 10 × 10" pegboards
7. Wooden dowels in color
8. Stencils—animals, birds, fish, etc.
9. Parquetry *Design Blocks*
10. Mosaic Color Cubes
11. Magnet board and magnets
12. Alpha Brilliants
13. 1" paint brushes
14. Plasticene
15. Plain stamp pads
16. Stamp pad ink—red, blue, green, violet, black
17. 30" paper cutter
18. Primary typewriter—black and red ribbon
19. Record player and records
20. Geometric shape templates
21. Full-length mirror
22. Large crayons and small crayons
23. Pointed scissors, left and right handed
24. Rulers with ½" markings
25. Rulers with ¼" markings
26. Abaci and beads

B. Equipment for constructing materials

1. Magic markers with wide felt tips
2. Magic markers with thin pointed felt tips

3. Paper punches, ½″ and ¼″ diameters
4. Scissors
5. Rubber cement and thinner
6. Ruler and/or T-square
7. Papers
   a. Construction—red, blue, purple, yellow, green, orange, brown, black (no shaded tones)
   b. Poster—several colors
   c. Onionskin—(Plover Bond)
   d. Pressed board
   e. Manila drawing
   f. White drawing
   g. White tagboard
   h. White cross-section—1″,½″, and ¼″ ruled
   i. Colored tagboard
   j. Flint paper
   k. Adventure Brand (several types)
   l. Sand paper
   m. Emery paper
   n. Newsprint—white, yellow, blue, and green
8. Readiness workbooks
9. Ditto masters—red, blue, black, and green
10. Stamp print set—capitals and lower case
11. Stamp print set—pictures and words
12. Paper clips—small, regular, and jumbo
13. Contact paper (transparent)
14. Yardstick
15. X-acto knife or utility knife
16. Ballpoint pens—red, bue, black, and green
17. Masking tape
18. Transparent tape and heavy-duty dispenser
19. Large drawing board
20. Stapler and staples
21. Shears
22. Assorted rubber bands
23. Empty boxes in assorted sizes

C. *Workbooks (for cutting up)*

1. Ginn and Co.—*Tom and Betty, Games to Play*
2. Houghton Mifflin—*Getting Ready*
3. Scott, Foresman—*We Read Pictures, We Read More Pictures, Before We Read*
4. Row, Peterson—*The Reading Road to Spelling,* Grade 1
5. Lyons, Carnahan—*Phonics We Use,* A, B, and C Books

D. *Reading series texts (order guide for each)*

1. American Book Co.; Betts Series—grades pre-primary and elementary series
2. Lyons, Carnahan; Regular and Classmate editions
3. Sheldon Series; Allyn & Bacon

4. Pacemaker Series
5. The Rolling Reader; Scott, Foresman
6. Benefic Press: Cowboy Sam Series, Dan Frontier Series, Sailor Jack Series

E. Reading supplements and aids

1. Reader's Digest Skill Builders—grades 1–up
2. Science Research Associates Reading Program

F. Games

1. Five Pins Bowling
2. 10″ playground ball
3. Checkers
4. Go Fish
5. Animal, Bird, Fish
6. Mixies
7. Old Maid
8. Hearts
9. Crazy Eights
10. Busy Bee
11. Squares
12. Dominoes
13. Color Bingo
14. Gittermosaik
15. Bridge-It
16. Magnetic Tic-Tac-Tow
17. Double Hi-Q
18. Cars
19. Lincoln Logs
20. Tinker Toys
21. Plastic Bricks
22. Duffle Bag of Blocks
23. Jumbo Beads
24. Instructo-Work
25. Cootie
26. Constructo-Straws
27. Happy Little Train
28. Candy Land
29. Wonderful World of Color
30. Pyramid
31. Count to Ten
32. See & Say Consonant Game
33. Memory
34. Fit-A-Space
35. Lego blocks
36. Pegity
37. Etch-a-Sketch
38. Zoo Lotto
39. Farm Lotto
40. Bolt It
41. Plastik Stechbrett
42. Spin & Color
43. Easy 3's

G. Motor training equipment

1. Walking Board
2. Balance Beam
3. Gym mat
4. Whiffle balls and bat

5. Bean bags
6. Chalkboard—4 × 6′

7. Double size chalk
8. Playground ball

H. Sensorimotor commercial materials

There are numerous commercial firms which manufacture and distribute educational materials in the areas of sensorimotor function. Space limitations prevent listing or describing all of these materials. Often great care must be exerted to ascertain that claims for materials are supported either by theoretical appropriateness or by field testing with data which support educational claims of the publisher. As we have stated there are many firms offering materials to educators. Two firms are selected here as meeting many of the criteria we feel should be of particular concern to educators—Teaching Resources Corporation of Boston, and Developmental Learning Materials of Niles, Illinois. Both of these companies are specifically oriented toward children with learning disabilities; as a matter of fact they were organized with these children as a primary target group and in response to recognized needs of these children, their teachers, and parents for well-conceptualized and constructed educational materials. Both of these companies utilize on a continuing basis nationally recognized persons as consultants. These consultants provide in-depth critiques of materials which may be accepted ultimately by the firms for manufacture and distribution. Most of the time their products are also supported by field studies demonstrating their effectiveness or by field use during their formative stages, and the results of these efforts are integrated into revisions and modifications of the products. A selected series of examples of the materials provided by these firms is noted here. These are among the most helpful of their products, but others are also available.

Auditory-Perception and Language Materials

Lindamood Auditory Conceptualization Test, Teaching Resources Corp. (TR)
Auditory Discrimination in Depth, TR
Erie Program 1, 2, 3, 4, TR
Auditory Tapes, Developmental Learning Materials (DLM)

Visual-Perception Materials

(These materials often involve also perceptual-motor activities)
    Fairbanks-Robinson Program 1, 2, TR
    Denhoff Programs 1, 2, 3, TR
    Visual-Motor Skills, TR
    Perceptual Skills, TR
    Visual Discrimination Flip Books, DLM
    Visual Matching, Memory & Sequence Books, DLM
    Visual Sequence Memory Exercises, DLM

Teaching Resources Corporation also has excellent developmental materials in the content areas or materials based on carefully developed theoretical constructs which lead up to the readiness level and beyond. For examples of these materials (all TR) one should examine:
    Foundations for Mathematics, Units 1, 2, 3, and 4 (pre-kindergarten through 2nd grade)
    Fundamentals Underlying Numbers (pre-kindergarten through 1st grade)
    Fokes Sentence Builder
    Cursive Handwriting Development
    Language Skill Training

School supply stores and toy shops offer an overwhelming variety of items which purport to aid a child's learning. Sometimes claims made for such toys are accurate, and the toy or piece of equipment is enhanced by its appeal to children. Other materials may appear quite attractive to the adult viewer but prove totally unsatisfactory for a child.

In selecting commercially made games, it is important to pay attention to the appearance, sturdiness, tactual appeal. simplicity of operation, and the learning tasks toward which the items are pointed. Generally, wooden materials are more satisfactory than plastics. Care should be taken that colors and designs are clear and not too "busy." If there are any moving parts, they should function properly and resist damage from normal use. Directions must be clear enough that a brief reading by the teacher is all that is necessary before using games. Regardless of what games are available, the capabilities and interests of the child who uses them constitute the most important criteria for selection. The games listed here do not form a complete list of possibilities. The interest and ability levels indicated by them span a rather wide range. Familiarity and success with a game may cause a child to continue enjoying it even though he has progressed enough to use more involved or complicated ones. Happily, many of these games require the youngster to employ his beginning skills in arithmetic and reading and may even provide an impetus for further learning.

Materials for more conventional work tasks are not plentiful. The most frequent criticism is that there are far too many unnecessary details on most materials and that these tend to dissipate the child's energies before he accomplishes his task. It then becomes necessary for the teacher to prepare or construct the child's materials for learning, basing her efforts on the complete evaluation she has of him. This takes time and care, but it is a major determinant of the child's success.

There are several suggestions and directions which apply to the construction of teaching materials for disturbed children. These same techniques of construction will apply in many cases to material selected for use by other children with learning difficulties.

Perhaps the first thing to mention is the need to remove from the material *all* unnecessary details. The child's attention will go to the central problem or task if it is directed there and not enticed away by something added only for decoration. Normal children seem to react positively and to work well when their material is made "attractive" through the use of decorative devices. Disturbed children are victims of the same material when it confronts them and their energy is sapped by traveling from one interesting spot to another. While stressing the need for simple material, it should be pointed out that the commonly used readiness workbooks contain a wealth of suitable pictures and materials. Often, they can be used very much like the workbook by simply cutting out the pictures and mounting them on other paper or cards.

To be more specific, consider a workbook page which has rows of several bright yellow ducks on each. Since the aim of the page is to help teach right-left discrimination, all the ducks are facing right except one. Workbook directions say to make a cross on the one which is different. This same learning for a disturbed child would be prepared by cutting out the ducks and mounting each one on 3 × 3″ white poster paper. (By using this size cards as often as possible, material may be interchanged and recombined in many ways and storage is facilitated.) Around the edge of each card a *straight* yellow line is added which provides a limit and helps direct the child's attention to the duck. The child considers the pictures, puts together the ducks pointing right, and selects the different one, placing it in the spot designated by the teacher.

Another approach might be to cut two or three strips of these duck pictures, mounting them on green construction paper backed by tagboard or other fairly stiff paper. An envelope containing several small squares of green paper may be attached to the sheet by paper clip; and the child can be instructed to place them on those ducks which are different from all the other ducks on the row. When finished, if the project is completed correctly, all the ducks pictured in a row will face the same way.

Closely related to the need for reduction of stimuli (details) is the need for *accurate pictures* which present a true concept to the child. The child already has difficulty in perceiving the true nature of things without having to deal with pictures which portray familiar objects in a grotesque manner. Trees should be quickly recognizable as trees and not as animate, talking objects with eyes and arms. Pictured animals will serve the child much better dressed in their native pelts without the further adornment of aprons or vests.

It is difficult to overestimate the importance of neatness and care in the preparation of teaching aids. Errors of placement, erasures, spots of dirt or color can distract the child. Neatness is essential and may be achieved only with planning, practice, and proper equipment. The teacher, for example, will learn to use rubber cement rather than white glue on paper items, to increase the appeal of the material. Rubber cement forms a flat bond and does not cause wrinkles, another cause of distraction.

Since the child may have some difficulty coordinating himself sufficiently to pick up material and move it where he wants it to go, an effort should be made to produce a "feeling of firmness" in all his equipment. This does not mean that every item should be on heavy cardboard, but simply that the item should not be so flimsy that the child will be afraid of damaging it. He should know that he can move it about without its tearing or coming apart.

The sizes of the cards on which visual aids are mounted should be governed partly by the individual child's ability to deal with objects. When used alone, cards cut 3 × 3″ work very well, as do some items, such as domino cards, made 4 × 4″. When used with other things they might be slightly smaller. The advantages of storing, manipulation during construction, and interchangeability of items present a good case for customarily using similar-sized cards. An effort should be made to use sizes of pictures that are appropriate for the material under construction. The child will adjust more readily to similar-sized materials.

The use of a border serves a triple purpose. Borders seem to set limits to a task, to create a neater and more attractive format, and, in many cases, to provide the child with color cues. (Color-cued items are those that provide an extra hint to the child by using color. In the construction of the duck cards described earlier, a color cue would have been present if all the cards were yellow except the different one which was trimmed in blue.) This trim should be *straight and even throughout* and can be made so through the use of a ruler.

Red, yellow, blue, green, orange, and purple are the primary and secondary colors recommended for use in making these materials. The stimulus value of these colors is high, and when used as a background, they constitute a strong attraction for the child's attention. When used as part of the task itself, they provide a valuable means of attracting the child's attention while at the same time controlling and limiting any tendency he might have to perseveration. Thus, color may be used as a crutch or clue to the proper solution of the task; it may be used for its high stimulus value, or it may be used mainly for its esthetic appeal.

Problems presented in the early stages of a child's program should have only one possible solution; the materials used might be described as error-free. The child needs no opportunity to choose wrongly. By always getting the correct answer he experiences success instead of failure. When after many successes he is given an opportunity to do a task which may have two or three possible solutions, the task should be constructed so that if an error is made, correction is simple and no permanent reminder of the error remains. At this point tasks involving erasures should be avoided.

Time is valuable; it should be used constructively by teachers and pupils. The child should be properly evaluated and his strengths and weaknesses correctly assessed. On the basis of these evaluations materials may be prepared.

Teacher-Made Materials

In the preceding paragraphs we have focused on some commercial materials as well as some teacher-made materials. It is well to consider the latter for a moment. Most, but not all of the commercial materials can be matched by teacher-made materials if the teacher is thoughtful, well oriented to the educational problems of the children, and is enterprising. Ms. Freidus demonstrates a remarkable tactual-perceptual "game" for perceptually handicapped children. She fills a large shopping bag with one good-sized piece of fruit or vegetable for each of the children in the group, five to seven, for example. The bag may contain an apple, orange, grape-fruit, Spanish onion, large carrot, lemon, cucumber, or other common vegetable. The child may first be asked to identify—to guess—what is in the bag after lifting it, touching it, or probing. Tactuo-conceptual-motor activities are involved here. The child then puts his hand into the bag, held closed at the neck by the teacher. He feels an object, is asked to describe it fully, name it, and withdraw it to check for accuracy. The game has much motivation to children. It has excellent educational and diagnostic values. Fruit can be substituted by toys, pieces of cloth, wooden or plastic forms, or other sets or objects. All types of tactuo-perceptual activities can be developed from this simple activity. Significant insights can be obtained regarding both perception and conceptualization from this teacher-provided game.

A set of six or seven large empty cardboard boxes can provide other excellent diagnostic and learning activities. A group of six or seven children are lined up against a wall on one side of a large open area. "How can we get these boxes across to the other side?" asks the teacher. One boy volunteers and carries one box in each hand with several trips to the other side of the room. "How else?" asks the teacher. A second child carries two boxes in his hand and kicks a third. A third child lines up the boxes and pushes them as a long train across the floor. A fourth child places a smaller box inside a larger one, until all are stacked in such a way as to be able to carry them at one time. From a diagnostic point of view this simple activity can provide information regarding motor coordination, conceptualization of size and shape, and comparisons of size and shape, among other things.

The capacity of teachers to develop appropriate teaching materials is limitless. These two examples merely describe something of the nature of things which can be developed by a creative teacher. Obviously these are less expensive than commercial materials. They are destructible. They can be highly motivating, because no one has to caution the child to "be careful; don't break."

The following facts and suggestions will be helpful in teaching and preparing teaching aids:

1. Materials should be used which require only a few simple directions.

2. All equipment needed for a specific task should be close at hand.

3. The length of time required for a given task should be short enough to fit the child's attention span.

4. Little opportunity should be allowed for failure or error.

5. Follow developmental levels and keep tasks in sequential order. Refine to its most primitive level any task as much as the child requires so that a success experience can be achieved.

6. These children learn more quickly and understand better when dealing with concrete rather than abstract concepts.

7. Tasks should not be assigned until the child has the necessary background learning.

8. The child's day should be planned so that his tasks are varied; similar tasks should not be juxtapositioned.

9. Learning problems should be approached from as many different directions as seem appropriate. Do not be afraid to try something new if it is indicated, or to discard something which proves valueless or unworkable.

10. There should be no hesitation in returning a child to an earlier step of any subject when it seems necessary. He may need to relearn or may feel the need for reassurance.

11. Be alert to the possibility of the child's interpreting his task in a different manner than what was intended. If the unexpected learning is correct, capitalize on it. If not, attempt to correct his approach. If this seems upsetting, do it for him (with his help), then put the work away and go on to other things.

SELECTED REFERENCES OF SPECIAL INTEREST TO PARENTS

Avery, M., and Higgins, A. *Help Your Child Learn How to Learn.* Englewood Cliffs, N.J.: Prentice-Hall, 1962

Radler, D. H., and Kephart, N. C. *Success Through Play.* New York: Harper & Row, 1963

Strother, C. R. *Discovering, Evaluating, Programming for the Neurologically Handicapped Child.* Chicago: National Society for Crippled Children and Adults, 1963

SELECTED REFERENCES OF SPECIAL INTEREST TO TEACHERS

Blessing, K. "Use of Teacher Aides in Special Education: A Review and Possible Application." *Exceptional Children* 34(1967):107–16.

Cruickshank, W. M. "The Education of the Child with Specific Learning Disorders." *The Education of Exceptional Children and Youth.* 3rd ed., edited by W. M. Cruickshank and G. O. Johnson. Englewood Cliffs, N.J.: Prentice-Hall, 1975

Fernald, Grace M. *Remedial Techniques in Basic School Subjects.* New York: McGraw-Hill, 1943.

Jolles, I. "A Teaching Sequence for the Training of Visual and Motor Perception." *American Journal of Mental Deficiency* 63 (September 1958):252–55.

Kaliski, Lotte. "Educational Therapy for Brain-Injured Retarded Children." *American Journal of Mental Deficiency* 60 (July 1955):71–77.

Millison, R. *Education as Therapy: Suggestions for Work with Neurologically Impaired Children.* Seattle: Special Child Publications, 1968.

Miller, N. "Teaching an Emotionally Disturbed, Brain-Injured Child." *The Reading Teacher* 17 (March 1964):460–65.

Patterson, R. M., *Teaching Devices for Children with Impaired Learning; A Study of the Brain-Injured Child from Research Project 50 at the Columbus State School.* Columbus, Ohio: Columbus State School, 1958.

Strauss, A. A., and Lehtinen, L. E. *Psychopathology and Education of the Brain-Injured Child.* New York: Grune & Stratton, 1947.

Wade, B., and Wedell, K. *Spelling: Task and Learner.* Birmingham, England: University of Birmingham, 1974.

8

Visual Motor Materials and Activities

Some tasks are more difficult than others for learning disabled children. There are certain guides which may be used to predict the difficulty of a given task. For example, it is easier for a child to work with few pieces in a puzzle than with many pieces. The stimulation is not as great, and the task can be completed in a shorter time. As the child develops greater skills, the number of pieces can be increased appropriately.

The proper use of a number of colors serves the perceptually handicapped child better than the use of only one color or only a few colors. Each color change in a task catches the child's attention and forces him to see what is happening in his work. The greater the contrast between adjacent colors, the easier it is for him to use them. For instance, it would be much easier for him to distinguish blue from orange than blue from purple. Red and orange when placed side by side provide more difficult discrimination tasks than do yellow and purple.

It usually proves better for the child to use large items in his early tasks. More gross-muscle operation is required for manipulation of rather large objects than for small objects. Large-muscle development is required before small muscles can be effectively utilized. As a child becomes more skillful and more successful with large-muscle activities, reduction in the size of his materials may be indicated.

A learning task involving a motor activity will likely be more desirable than one which is mainly visual. The need to call into play additional muscles and parts of his body aids the child's learning in many things which require eye-hand coordination—for example, reading, writing, or steering a bicycle. This is also true of activities using ear-hand coordination or other sensorimotor combinations. Several of his sensory organs are later brought into focus on a single task, giving him more chances for a complete understanding of what he is doing. As he progresses, the need for motor activity as a major part of his work is lessened. Closely related to this is his need for concrete materials. With success on the child's part becoming somewhat of a habit, the teacher then may help him extend his learnings into more abstract areas.

While all of these things form a fairly reliable frame of reference with regard to sequence and difficulty, the most valuable guide will be the child himself. A good teacher will constantly evaluate each task presented to the child in terms of the past learnings on which it is built, its present usefulness, and the indications it shows for the future.

The child's stage of readiness and tool skills should be considered in planning the individual program for him. An individual program gives the child an opportunity to develop areas in which he is lagging behind or in which he has distorted understandings. He may work at a very low level in some tasks and at a much higher level in others.

In the teaching material described here an attempt is made to break down the needed learnings into small segments which will force the child to see what is involved in each task. His habits are gradually conditioned in a way that contributes toward his being able to participate in more conventional learning experiences.

It is quite unnecessary and inappropriate to try to separate perception skills from tool skills. Without the perception skills, there is little possibility of developing or utilizing the tool skills of reading, writing, and arithmetic. By examining the learning tasks described here and by paying close attention to the sequences, one will notice that the perception skill tasks move quite far into the tool skill areas. So, if properly utilized, these function smoothly together. In fact, it will be exceedingly difficult to tell where one leaves off and the other begins. The perception skills area provides a strong base on which to build future knowledge. The major goal of this area is to teach a child intentionally things which most children learn incidentally during earlier stages of normal development.

In the following pages learning activities are listed and are grouped together in the same order they should be placed in the educational program for the learning disabled child. Initially, it is desirable that the learning disabled child gain proficiency in recognizing forms, shapes, and configurations. After the child gains skill in recognizing these things, activities such as puzzles, coloring, and paper cutting are used.

FORM, SHAPE, AND CONFIGURATION PATTERNS

Activities discussed in this section constitute part of the direct antecedents to arithmetic skills. Basically, the task involves helping the
child to perceive color, form, and position. He is given "form cards" or
configuration cards which he matches (see Figure 29).

The cards should be cut from white poster paper or other heavy
board 3 × 3″ and a geometric figure should be drawn on each one.
Several cards should be prepared for a particular figure, and these should
agree in color so that all circles are red, all triangles green, and so on. The
child may be given all the cards and instructed to pick out the identical
ones; the color cues aid him in this task. Several other sets should be prepared with the entire set made in one color. For example, there might be a
set containing three triangles, three circles, three squares, three
diamonds, three rectangles, and three hexagons all cut from orange paper
and pasted on white.

Sets with configurations (more than one figure on each card) would
be presented next. Again, color cues should be used to facilitate the task
for the child. After the child has developed some facility in recognizing
and selecting the geometric figures, he may be given a set of the cards
containing several figures all in the same color.

The concepts discussed here have been carried over into "content"
with respect to the readiness stage for mathematics. In Unit I, in which
concepts for sets and curves are developed in *Foundations for Mathe-*

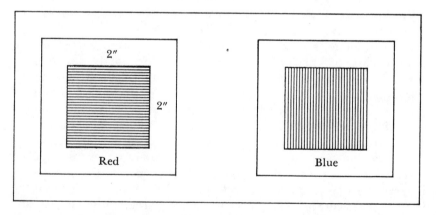

Figure 29. Examples of "form cards" provided for the child as a basis of practice
in the recognization of form, shape, and configuration. Reprinted by permission
from Cruickshank *et al.* 1961.

matics (see Chapter 7), much emphasis is placed on forms, shapes, and configurations lead to an understanding of sets. Other units do likewise, but also emphasize other factors as will be pointed out in subsequent paragraphs.

PUZZLES

Teacher-made puzzles, as well as those available commercially, in addition to their usefulness as a device for the development of perception,

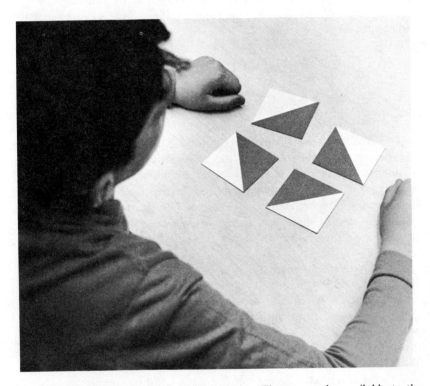

Figure 30. Much use is made of large puzzles. These must be available to the teacher in large supply with different puzzles illustrating different geometrical forms and different common objects. Puzzles employing intense colors are more appropriate for learning disabled children in the early stages of their educational experience. Permission to photograph and reproduce this illustration from Teaching Resources Corp., Boston.

provide opportunities for more extended learnings. The pictures selected for construction of the puzzles should offer many topics for exploration by the child and the teacher.

When a child first begins working with puzzles, he will probably be able to speak of the completed puzzle only in concrete terms. He may recognize and name specific items in the picture, but he is not inclined to go further. Through gradual expansion of positive conditioning and appropriate increase in awareness of reality, he should become able to deal with the same sort of picture in a more abstract manner. In addition to identifying the objects, he will begin offering explanations concerning their usage, location, size, availability, color, age, and so on. At perhaps the most mature level of interpretation, the child may be able to project his thinking about the picture into the future, telling what he thinks probably will happen next.

Construction

Rather large pictures, about $8\frac{1}{2} \times 11''$ and larger, may be selected from reading readiness workbooks, magazines, calendars, teacher drawings, and other inexpensive sources. Clear, accurate drawings, as free from distortions as possible, should be chosen. Colors should be clear and appropriate to the item depicted by them. It is best to avoid using pictures with large areas of identical color and those with large areas of subtle change. Although learning disabled children usually have some color perception, these two color usages offer an unnecessary and often frustrating challenge.

The puzzle may be mounted on pressed wood or thin plywood, thick cardboard, heavy bristol board, poster board, or backs of unusable commercial puzzles. When complete, the back of the puzzle should be a solid color, free of writing and other distracting elements. A dry-mount process is excellent for this mounting and may be done quite satisfactorily through the use of photographic mounting sheets and a household iron. While rubber cement also provides an excellent mounting adhesive, the white glues are less acceptable because of their tendency to cause wrinkles in the paper. Wrinkles become both visual and motor extraneous stimuli to the perceptually handicapped child. If rubber cement is used, care should be taken to see that the *entire* picture is covered and adheres to the mount board. When placing the picture on the board, make certain that a border about $\frac{1}{4}''$ wide appears around the picture. It may be one

Cut on wavy line

Figure 31. Illustrations of teacher-made puzzles which are appropriate for use with learning disabled children. Dozens of similar puzzles can be made in order that the teacher will always have some new material to present to the child in addition to having practice materials with which the child is somewhat familiar. Reprinted by permission from Cruickshank *et al.* 1961.

included with the printed picture, or it may be added with a magic marker or permanent ink pen.

The puzzle can be cut after a delay of several hours when the glue is dry. A very sharp instrument should be used to insure straight and accurate cuts. The simplest puzzle is made by using vertical cuts which produce only two or three pieces for the entire puzzle. For example, if the picture were of a bottle, the cut might sever the bottle into two pieces, top to bottom (see Figures 31 and 32). Puzzles for children at the next level should be cut horizontally into three pieces. After a child has had success with these two simple puzzles, a combination of vertical and horizontal cuts with a larger number of pieces would be appropriate. The puzzle should always be cut in such a way that an entire object appears in each fragment of the puzzle. Depending on the picture, this might be an eye, an arm, a chair, a book, etc. The number of pieces should be governed by the child's ability to deal with them.

Additional Comments

Some children may have difficulty in getting the parts to stay where they are placed. A flannel board placed on the child's desk serves well as a base on which to work. The puzzle parts need no special backing to be used on the flannel board. A flannel board is a simple teaching aid consisting of a board of any convenient size which has been covered with a piece of dark flannel material. On this board puzzles, letters, numerals, or

194

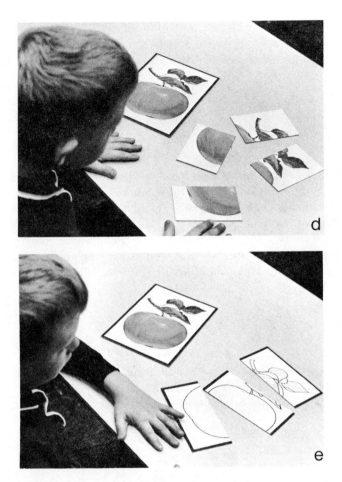

Figure 32. An example of an excellent commercially prepared puzzle for perceptually handicapped children. From *a* to *e* the reader will notice that the puzzle becomes more complicated and that fewer and fewer visual cues are provided. Heavy borders give way to undifferentiated space; color characterizing *a, b, c,* and *d* is reduced to line drawings in *e*. The puzzles are photographed and reproduced here through the courtesy of Teaching Resources Corp., Boston.

other items—themselves cut out of either flannel or another cloth or rough paper—are placed by the teacher or child. The materials do not slip, and the board can be used indefinitely without the need for glue, paste, or thumbtacks which complicate the learning situation for learning disabled children.

A shallow box may also be used as an aid in keeping the puzzle intact. A black border should be drawn around the inside edges of the bottom of the box, thus providing a bounded area in which the child will place the puzzle.

Goals

Through these activities it is expected that the learning disabled child will be able to progress from the point of recognizing individual parts to that of conceptualizing the whole. He will obtain experiences and satisfactions in completing a task successfully. He will be given practice in form perception as well as in color and spatial perception. The activity gives him practice in eye-hand coordination as well as providing him with activities through which handedness can be further established.

STENCILS

A square, or stencil 3 × 3″ is cut out of the center of an 8 × 8″ square piece of pressed board. Over the pressed board is placed a piece of paper, also 8 × 8″, with a large green dot in the center.

Typical Task

The child takes the crayon and by coloring inside the stencil makes a square.

General Techniques

He should color every part of the bounded area very carefully, "feeling" the shape as he colors.

Extended Learnings

The teacher should talk with the child, analyze with him what he has done, and seek understanding by the child of such questions as the following: What is the name of the shape you have made? How many sides does it have? Can you draw one with your finger on your desk? Do you know something which is shaped like that?

Goals

The goals of stencil activity are similar to those noted regarding the use of puzzles, namely, development of eye-hand coordination and practice in further establishing handedness and laterality. Stencils also provide the learning disabled child with practice in form perception, color perception, figure-background discrimination, size discrimination, and space perception.

Steps

A. Inside stencils (see Figure 33).
   1. Use one large sheet of pressed board containing one large stencil.
   2. Reduce the size of the stencil (not necessarily the board) and gradually add other stencils. An appropriate order is as follows:
      a. One square
      b. One circle
      c. One triangle
      d. One diamond
      e. One square and one circle (and the other combination of two shapes)
      f. One square, one circle, and one triangle (and the other combination of three shapes)
      g. One of each shape
      h. Two of each shape
      i. More than two using different colors
      j. Mixed shapes
      k. Other shapes

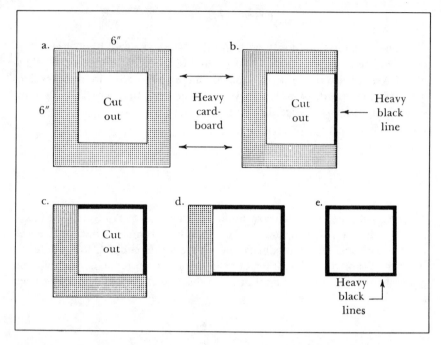

Figure 33. Example of an inside stencil. Note that for this particular experience, learning the concept of a square, the teacher has prepared four stencils in a series. Note also that in the beginning the child is further assisted by a heavy black line being drawn on the paper on the side of the stencil where the cardboard has been removed. Ultimately this line can become less and less obvious until it is not needed at all. Reprinted by permission from Cruickshank *et al.* 1961.

3. Where it is appropriate, as with a square, extend this task to help the child learn to color the shape without the "wall" which the board provides for him. This is done by cutting off one side of the shape at a time, substituting a heavy black line in its place. The child must then learn to confine his efforts to the marked area, seeing the shape in a slightly less concrete way.

B. Outside stencils. When control of the materials has been developed, the child may progress to "outside" stencils where he traces around the outer edge of a pattern placed on the paper. This is usually done as a part of some other task such as parquetry. It may be wise to use the same order of presentation at this time as was recommended for the inside stencils.

Additional Comments

While teaching shapes and learning to confine work to a given area are usually of primary importance here, a successful experience of making something is also a desirable result. By using various stencils, the child may "make" a picture containing recognizable objects. For example, stencils of a tree, a house, and a cat may be combined on one sheet of paper. These and all other activities discussed in this chapter are intended to extend in time over several weeks and months.

COLORING

Coloring actually is an integral part of other tasks and is separated here only for purposes of discussion.

The lowest level of coloring would be to use stencils as they are described above. One aid of stencils is to help the child limit his work to a given area. He should be encouraged to color the indicated space with enough care to make it pleasing to the eye.

After he has begun to learn that he colors inside the lines given him, a new task can be set. Several 1″ squares should be heavily outlined in black. The child's task becomes one of coloring the squares as indicated by the teacher. Variations of this can be made by increasing the number of squares and by having the child make pictures of them.

As the child becomes proficient with coloring, the teacher may present pictures of animals which have been outlined in black. The child is then asked to color within the black outline. Pictures, if they are large, may be taken from coloring books. It will be necessary to outline these in black also. Care must be taken that the pictures selected from the coloring books are large and offer no distortions to the child. The size of the pictures may be decreased as the child becomes more able to color within the given lines.

The width of the lines serving as the outline may also be decreased as the child becomes more able to stay within the lines. Rarely should the child be asked to draw a picture of his own. When a child is unable to control his hands, trying to draw his own picture can be quite a traumatic experience. This is true because, as we have discussed earlier in this book, learning disabled children generally have a poor concept of the human body or of animals or forms in general. To ask them to draw an original figure and then to color it in the early stages of their development is threatening and may lead to a failure experience.

CUTTING

Typical Material Equipment

The equipment needed includes construction paper on which geometric forms have been heavily outlined in black, scissors, and other items as required if this activity precedes a pasting task.

Typical Task

Cut the shapes from the paper, thus preparing them for use in subsequent task, such as on a flannel board activity.

General Techniques

Grasp scissors with thumb in top hole, middle finger in lower hole, and index finger used as a guide. Cut with long complete strokes following the outline.

Extended Learnings

Ask the child appropriate questions such as these: What shape is this? Can you point to the corners? How many sides does it have? What can you think of that is shaped like this?

Goals

The goals sought in cutting activities are similar to those mentioned in connection with puzzle and stencil activities. It is necessary to achieve these goals through as wide a use of different types of activities as it is possible for the teacher to employ.

Steps

Always construct these cutting tasks in such a way that the child uses what he cuts.

1. Child cuts short heavy line bounded on either side by thin cardboard. This cardboard, clipped to the lined paper, forces the child's scissors to cut paper in a straight line. The child in reality cuts through the middle of a channel formed by the cardboard pieces.

2. Use procedure above but place cardboard on one side of line only.

3. Child cuts 1″ squares with heavy black outline as the only guide.

4. Increase size of square to about three inches.

5. Child cuts two strips of 1″ blocks.

6. Child cuts three strips of 1″ blocks.

7. He cuts half-round which has been heavily outlined in black using edge of paper for straight side.

8. Right-angle shape at one corner of paper is drawn showing the child how to cut a corner.

Additional Comments

For all cutting tasks with these children, use 6″ pointed scissors designed for either right or left hand as the child requires. Pointed scissors are used so the child may have a clear and accurate view of where his cut will be, and they should be examined before being given to the child to be sure that they operate properly and do not offer too much resistance to a simple cutting operation. During the early steps, simple pictures may be made from the shapes by pasting them on paper and adding a few simple lines with crayons. Later, the cutting may be used in conjunction with a desired learning in arithmetic, parquetry, etc. These cutting activities will occupy a lengthy period of time, often an entire school year or more as varieties of experiences are provided for the child.

SORTING

Sorting is so similar to matching (to be discussed later) that it needs only a few additional comments. The same items are suitable for sorting as for matching, and the principles followed are the same. Perhaps the only difference is that sorting uses several similar objects rather than pairs. For example, a set of animal pictures may be sorted by the child into farm animals and zoo animals. If given a set of pictures showing clothes, he could sort them into sets of girls' clothes and sets of boys' clothes. Sorting is helpful in teaching children to classify groups of objects.

LACING CARDS

A lacing card is a device used in teaching children to match items in pairs. Down one side of a sheet of brightly colored paper are pasted one-half the items, with sufficient space left between each item to avoid the child's becoming confused. Down the right side will be the "partners" of the items arranged in different orders. All of this should be mounted on cardboard and bound on the edges with tape. Beside each item a hole is punched all the way through the board. The children are instructed on how to use shoestrings through the holes linking the items which match. It may be more satisfactory to glue the strings in such a way that they come through the holes on the left side. This simplifies the child's task because he only has to place the string through one hole to link a matching pair.

The wide range of picture sizes suitable for making a lacing card allows it to be easily tailored for the individual. Perhaps 6 x 10″ would be the smallest practicable size, but the only upper limit on size is handling ease.

MISSING PARTS

By emphasizing the appearance of a familiar object, the child is taught how each part of the object contributes to the whole. This teaching may be done in several ways. Perhaps it is easiest for the child to use a set of four cards, each containing a picture. Three of the pictures are identical, and the remaining one is the same except that one part is missing. For example, each picture might show a dog, but one dog is missing his tail. A child who is able to place together the three identical pictures may be unable to tell what is missing from the other picture. It may assist him to examine the pictures carefully, section by section, to see where the difference occurs. The parts not under consideration are covered.

There are two kinds of parts which may be omitted: (1) One which touches the contour (outside) of the object or person; (2) an internal part missing with the contour identical in each picture.

SIMILARITIES AND DIFFERENCES

Matching and sorting are perhaps the two most useful techniques for this learning. Small cards lend themselves very well to this area. An effort should be made to begin with tasks requiring little discrimination. For example, color matching would require no consideration other than color. More complex tasks involving several considerations would be a very late developmental task. The teacher should always explore with the child the questions: "Why are these things alike?" or "What makes these different?"

Another possibility is that of using animal picture cards which could be sorted two ways; an arrangement would have all mother animals in one group and the babies in another. Pairing the mother with her baby shows that they are similar animals. These activities are basic to the next steps related to content, for example in mathematics. These are essentially sequential steps which are carried further in Unit 4, Comparing Sets and Numbers, in *Foundations for Mathematics,* mentioned earlier.

PEGBOARD DESIGNS

Typical Material Equipment

1. 6 × 6″ pegboard with 100 holes (10 rows with 10 holes each) (see Figure 34)
2. Design 3 sides of a 10-dot square colored on ½″ squared paper
3. Colored pegs needed to construct design
4. Plain paper 5 × 5″
5. Crayons

Typical Task

The child constructs a given design on the board, and when he has completed his design, he reproduces the geometric shape with crayons on the plain paper. Care should be taken to make the drawing as nearly the same size as the design as possible.

General Techniques

1. Work from top to bottom first
2. Move next from left to right
3. Follow an orderly procedure
4. Use the dominant hand
5. Do not rotate design
6. In drawing, show the concept of lines, rather than dots or circles

Extended Learnings

In conversation with the learning disabled child the teacher or parent should seek to ascertain the child's understanding through such requests or questions as the following: Show me the top of your board. Show me the bottom of the board. Can you show me the left side? The right side? Do you know what the name of this shape is? Which line did you make first? Which did you make next? Which peg did you put in last? Which is the longest line? The shortest? Can you tell what color the line on the left is? What color is the top line?

Goals

The goals inherent in these activities are in many instances similar to those described earlier in relation to other types of activities. For example, the use of pegboards, like cutting or activities with puzzles, gives the child practice in establishing handedness, eye-hand coordination, form perception, color and space discrimination, and in judging laterality. In addition, however, skills basic to arithmetic as well as to reading and writing are inherent in the pegboard activities. Concepts of left-to-right progression are established. Attention span may be increased. Practice in figure-background discrimination is possible as are temporal-spatial relationships. Top to bottom progression is learned. Finally, the task is unique in its ability to assist the child in breaking up perseverative tendencies.

Additional Comments

By using beaded wooden pegs and pegboard to help plan the designs, the teacher should become aware of the many designs which may be

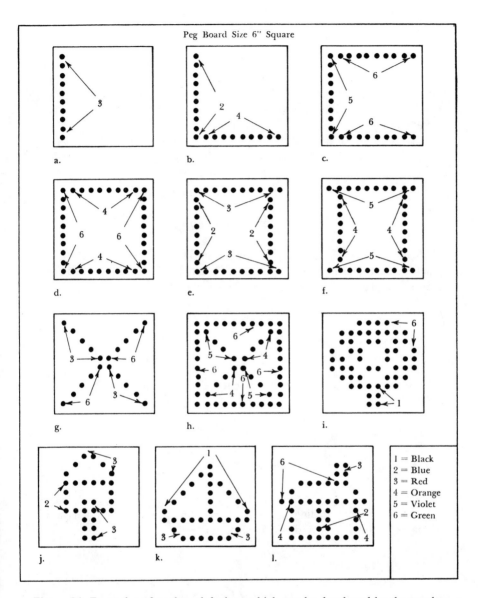

Figure 34. Examples of pegboard designs which can be developed by the teacher as models for the learning disabled child. These models proceed from what appears to be exceedingly simple designs as the straight line in example *a* to the complicated forms noted in examples *j, k,* or *l.* The teacher is cautioned not to proceed too rapidly from simple to complex. She must move with the child and constantly ascertain accurately his level of tolerance. The example above, with additional modifications which the teacher may make, is often a full year of activity with pegboards. Reprinted by permission from Cruickshank *et al.* 1961.

constructed with these materials. The possibilities for variations of shape, size, and position are almost limitless. It is essential that the child be aided in seeing shapes as wholes which he is able to construct. Ideally, he will learn the relationship of parts of a shape to the whole. He should develop some appreciation of the relative sizes.

GEOMETRIC FORM COPYING

Typical Material and Equipment

A sheet of 12 × 18″ newsprint divided in 4½ × 6″ sections outlined in black is used. On this sheet are four different colored geometric drawings with an empty section beside each one (see Figure 35).

Typical Task

With crayons the child reproduces each shape in the blank space to the right of it.

General Techniques

The child should operate in a left to right manner, finishing each drawing in order before proceeding to the next one. The preferred hand should do the work as the other hand holds the paper in place.

Extended Learnings

First, this activity assists the child in naming each drawing. This gives him added vocabulary and a frame of reference when he uses these same shapes and strokes in other tasks. Also, colors and numbers of lines may be identified by the child as he responds to appropriate questioning by the teacher.

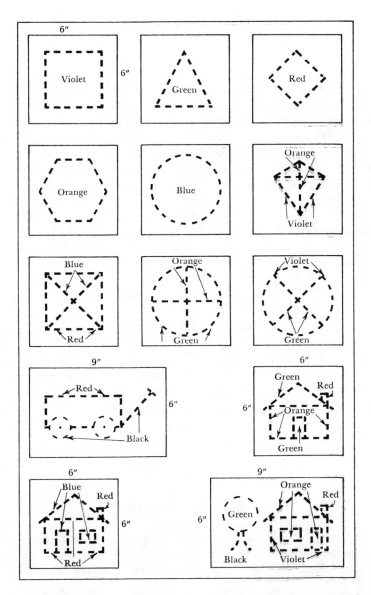

Figure 35. Examples of models provided to the learning disabled child by the teacher in geometric form copying. Note the recommended and extensive use of contrasting colors in forms which can employ two or more colors. Examples illustrated here proceed from simple to complex and are intended to serve as progressively more difficult activities which may extend in time over several months of activity for the child. Reprinted by permission from Cruickshank *et al.* 1961.

Goals

In considering these activities the teacher should keep in mind the goals inherent in the activities which have been previously discussed in this chapter. Most of them also apply to the copying of geometric shapes. In addition particular stress is placed on those skills essential to an appropriate grasp of prereading and prewriting abilities. Copying geometric figures gives the child practice in the integration of patterns of visual stimuli, in directionality, in increasing his attention span, and in controlling and limiting perseveration. Likewise the task is not so complicated that the child has a good opportunity to complete an idea and thus have a success experience basic to further appropriate conditioning.

Additional Comments

This material is closely related to the tool skill of writing as well as to the readiness aspects of reading and arithmetic. It is designed so that there is a tendency to first copy the parts of some shape or form and then use these same parts to make a whole. Thus it is emphasized that a whole is made up of unified parts in a given relation to each other. This task should be refined in any way necessary to meet the requirements of the child.

MATCHING

Typical Material Equipment

Pairs of 3 × 3″ cards (pictures) are prepared so that each pair of cards bears the same animal. For example, two cards should each depict a cow, and so on through the pairs, some of which are suggested below.

Typical Task

The child takes the shuffled cards and matches the pairs. The teacher should be certain not to give the child more pieces to manipulate than he can tolerate at one time.

General Techniques

The child should consider his cards as a group to see which things might go together. When he has matched a pair, he stacks them one on the other and places them toward the top left area of his desk. Other pairs, as matched, will be placed to the right of the previous stack. His preferred hand should be used.

Extended Learnings

The teacher should ask the child appropriate questions such as these: Why should these two cards go together? What animal is this? Where does he live? How large is he? How does he protect himself? What are baby (animal names) called?

Goals

As an activity basic to later successes with reading, writing, and number concepts, matching involves all the goals of developing eye-hand coordination, establishing handedness, directionality, left-right progression, size and color discrimination, and the ability to discriminate between figure and background. The activity also forces an expansion of the child's experience. The classification of objects is experienced in these activities. Increased attention span is required. Multiple stimuli are employed. Concept development and vocabulary development on an oral basis are experienced by the learning disabled child. There is the beginning element of abstraction involved in these activities, and these are basic to the abstractions required of the child in reading and in number concepts which will come to him somewhat later.

Steps

Begin with a few (perhaps two) pairs, increasing the number of pairs gradually as the child is able to work successfully with more stimuli. At first, identical pictures or forms on color-cued cards will allow the child to understand exactly what he is to do. Later color cues may be omitted, and eventually the pictures or forms may be similar rather than identical. He should develop the ability to see what the pictures have in common even though it may require careful attention to detail. For example, the pictures may be all of the same breed of dog, but pairs of them have on identical colors. Or perhaps pairs of them are engaged in the same action, such as running or sitting.

Additional Comments

The types of things which lend themselves to matching are countless. A partial list is included here. From these the teacher should select those which are within the child's ability to grasp. Too rapid exposure can result in failure experiences.

1. Color to color
2. Shape to shape
3. Configuration to configuration
4. Picture to picture
5. Picture to word
6. Picture to sentence
7. Pattern to pattern
8. Symbol to symbol
9. Configuration to symbol
10. Symbol to word
11. Object to word
12. Word to word
13. Rhyming pictures
14. Antonym (pictures)
15. Synonyms (pictures)
16. Sums (6 + 3; 4 + 5)
17. Shapes in different sizes
18. Identical items (missing parts)
19. Gross likeness
20. Gross difference
21. Size
22. Internal detail
23. Actions
24. Parts of a whole
25. Lower case letters
26. Capital letters
27. Lower case to capitals

The teacher of learning disabled children should be guided in the choice of items by the child's other learnings. For example, it would be useless to ask the child to match pictures and sentences unless he is able to read the sentences. On the other hand, he may be able to match words before he reads, because this is a visual perception task as well as a reading task. This task is a good way to parallel other tasks and approach the same desired learning from another way.

HEARING AND DISTINGUISHING SOUNDS

During the preadmission evaluation of the child, an audiometric examination may show that there is no defect in his auditory mechanism.

However, he may still experience difficulty in identifying a particular sound. Because of audiomotor perceptual problems, he may also seem unable to listen to and follow directions or understand what is said to him.

The problem is to help him develop his ability to listen. He must learn what to listen for and how to listen for it. In the structured classroom verbal expressions are limited but when used are short and to the point. The auditory perception materials developed by the Lindamoods, mentioned in Chapter 7, can be very helpful in this regard as can the Erie Programs.

During the period when he is doing tasks in his cubicle, the child should be able to receive most of his needed instructions from the material itself. Any comments or words from the teacher create another stimulus for him, and, of course, he reacts to it. As he matures in his ability to listen, a more verbal situation should evolve.

Many approaches to this learning are available. Some require easily obtained equipment, and others capitalize on the sounds in the environment. For example, ask the child to turn his back to the teacher. Bounce a ball two or three times and ask the child how many times it bounced. He must answer in terms of what he hears rather than what he sees. A similar activity is to have him count the number of pencil taps he hears. Stirring in a cup or tapping a cup gives him an opportunity to identify both the sound and the instrument making the sound. These are "games" which parents can play with their children at home, although when parents utilize these as games in the home they should be stressed as games and not as an extension of the learning experience of the school. They do have a recreational value, and this characteristic should be emphasized in the home.

Classroom sounds such as those made by closing a door, knocking on it, ringing a bell, sharpening a pencil, or turning on the water are familiar to most children, but some learning disabled children need specific help in selecting them from among all the other noises near them. There may be an auditory figure-background reversal.

The eardrums of hearing people are constantly being beaten upon by sounds so numerous and so varied that we usually pay no attention to them. It is only when our equipment is alerted to note some pertinent sound that we really notice it enough to say we are aware of it. Outdoors we often hear a medley of such sounds as those made by birds, dogs, and autos, yet notice none of them particularly. Learning disabled children in the special class need help in selecting certain sounds which they should hear. As urgent a reason for this as any is the need to hear danger signals.

Contrast is in itself a relative matter. These children need help in establishing reference points so that they may distinguish between loud and soft sounds and judge whether sounds are low or high in pitch.

In attempting to teach them to follow directions, present only one thing at a time until many successful experiences have been accomplished. Then increase the complexity a little bit, taking care to have them execute each in the proper sequence.

Reading to the children provides opportunity for the development of listening skills. Both poetry and stories may be used for enjoyment as well as for teaching. One obvious way to use poetry is to let the child select the rhyming words. When he does this rather well, he may enjoy supplying words which fit the poem and rhyme with the proper mate word. Specific things may be selected for a child to listen for in a story. Tell him before he listens to the story what will be expected of him. He may be asked questions about what he has heard. First, of course, the questions should be concerned with concrete answers, and later a gradual expansion into abstract thinking may be attempted.

When the child is ready, carefully selected music may be used. Such music offers another opportunity to help develop listening skills. Since a child may tend to become overstimulated by music, it may give him a chance to practice self-control. This is usually an area requiring a great deal of learning and teacher planning.

The use of music may be begun by playing recordings of quiet music during rest period. Familiar songs will perhaps point out the need to correct the child's pronunciation of some words. This is definitely part of the task of hearing and distinguishing sounds. Some words should have their meanings clarified.

Stories in music, loud compositions such as marches, soft melodies or lullabies, records which employ familiar sounds are all assets to developing listening ability. These may be used effectively, however, only when the child has achieved some ability to attend and to localize stimuli.

An alert teacher will find many occasions through the day to help a child use his auditory equipment more successfully.

BLOCK DESIGN

Typical Material Equipment

Use a full-sized pattern, colored strongly and pasted on poster board paper with a ¼" black edging or border. Also needed are enough one-inch cubes in required colors to build the complete design (see Figure 36).

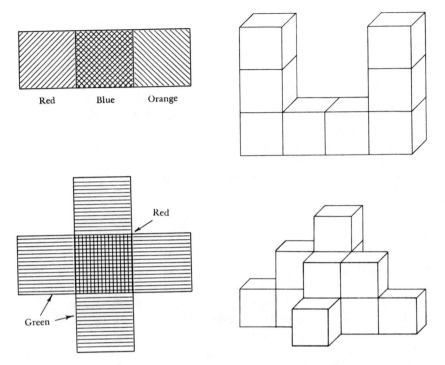

Red   Blue   Orange

Red

Green

Figure 36. Examples of block designs which may be used with learning disabled children. Teachers will conceive of many other designs which can be used. Reprinted by permission from Cruickshank *et al.* 1961.

Typical Task

Child builds design on his desk and is asked to interpret what he has done as the teacher asks questions.

General Techniques

1. Build from left to right as design permits.
2. Use organized approach to upper levels.
3. Place blocks exactly as shown in pattern, that is, touching or not touching as shown.

Extended Learnings

The child should be asked to:
    Point to the first block.
    Point to the last block.
    Show the third block.
    Show the highest row.
    Show the lowest row.
    Tell how many blocks he used.
    Count the yellow blocks, etc.
    Make the same design again without looking at the pattern.

Goals

The psychoeducational goals and skills which are inherent in these activities become more complex than some related to earlier tasks discussed in this chapter. All of those goals previously mentioned are also related to the block design activity. Such things as eye-hand coordination and color discrimination as well as practice in establishing handedness and control of perseveration are basic to most of the preacademic activities described. Similarly, further experience in understanding spatial relationships, practice in left-to-right progression, and in differentiating figure from background are all provided by the former activities as well as by the block design activity. More specific to the block designs, however, is the experience which the child receives in seeing and organizing a pattern or design as a unified whole. Much practice is obtained through these techniques in the organization of an approach to a task. Attention span may be increased in this way if the specific activity can also be made to have inherent interest for the child. Through the block designs the child is given insights into the problems of depth perception, for in a very concrete manner the activity involves three-dimensional elements. Finally, of course, this activity provides the child with practice in fine-motor movement and in fine-muscle development.

Additional Comments

By using the 1″ colored cubes (see Figure 37) to help plan the designs, the teacher should become aware of the many possibilities of this device. The

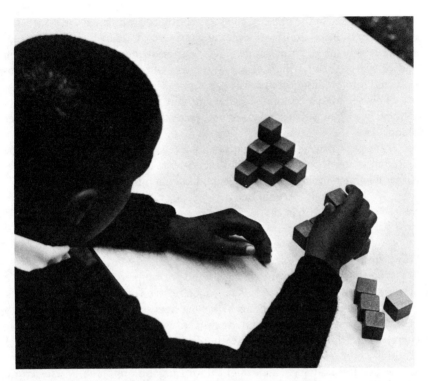

Figure 37. Much use is made of cubes in teaching learning disabled children concepts of quantity, depth, and spatial relationships. With young children larger cubes than those shown here may be used for easier grasp and control.

number of designs is limited only by the ability of the teacher to create new ones. The difficulty of the designs is controlled by the number of cubes used and also the combination of color. The child may do well with a given design and be quickly ready to move to another design. The teacher may also increase the difficulty by giving the child more cubes than are needed to complete the design. Some children may be unable to deal with this increase of cubes. This, then, should be delayed until he is ready.

RECALL

Long- and short-term memory problems were included in the definition of learning disabilities given in Chapter 1. Drill, in and of itself, is probably of minimal help to the child. Repetitious activities which can be integrated meaningfully into the life of the child through games which involve reasoning can be of great assistance. The materials described in this section and elsewhere in this chapter are suggestive of materials which can be integrated into meaningful drill-types games.

This technique combines visual and motor functions. The child's task is to view a geometric design and then transfer it in space to another plane.

A set of cards in various colors on white serve very well. They may be joined by rings at the top edge. This allows one card at a time to be visible. The following simple sequence is a good beginning set:

1. A single vertical line
2. One horizontal line
3. A circle
4. Cross
5. Square
6. Triangle
7. Diamond

Other designs may be used as the child progresses.

The teacher should provide the child with paper the same size as the viewing cards and with the crayons which he needs. Tell him what his task will be. Expose a card as long as he feels it necessary. When he is ready to draw, cover the card and let him draw what he remembers. If he draws incorrectly, let him look again. Gradually decrease the exposure time and gradually increase the difficulty.

A related activity which might afford a good opportunity uses cards containing pictures of familiar objects. When the card is presented to the child, it is covered completely with a plain card. This cover is gradually moved down the page, exposing a little bit of the picture at first and increasing the visible amount as it moves down. The child identifies the object as quickly as he can. He must draw on his experiences and recall the object, attaching a name to it.

Another version might be made from small objects which can be looked at as long as the child desires. Then, when a cover is placed over them, the child recalls as many as he can. He might also be asked at another time to view a set of several objects. Then, while he is turned away from them, one or two are removed. His task is to name those which are missing.

LEFT-RIGHT DISCRIMINATION

An excellent way of approaching left-right discrimination is through the use of color-cued materials. A large piece of cardboard divided in the center (top to bottom) is placed on the child's desk. The word *left* and the word *right* are written on large cards, the former with red color, the latter with green color. A red symbol is placed on the left side of the large dividend cardboard; a green symbol on the right side. The child matches the red word *left* to the red symbol, the green word *right* to the green symbol. Other forms of the words *left* and *right* are presented, e.g., Left-Right; LEFT-RIGHT. The colors used originally are continued during this matching phase to provide an additional clue. The next step would be to do the same tasks without the benefit of a concrete colored symbol. The child now simply matches the words with his remembrance of which was the left side of the card and which was the right side. Gradually the cue of color is withdrawn and the words are all presented in black ink again to be matched with the right and left sides of the large divided card.

Expand this activity by adding color-cued arrows and pointing hands made with a rubber stamp, pointing left and right. Matching is again practiced. Sentences using color cues may be written on a strip of tagboard and cut apart for the child to reassemble according to a pattern. Samples might be "This is left" and, "This is right." Matching these is attempted.

Although it is certainly to any child's advantage to know that a single word may have several meanings, it would probably help his learning process here to tell him his work is "correct" instead of "right." There is a great deal of activity related to left-right discrimination (as well as top to bottom) included in Unit 3 (Motor Development: Lines and Places) in *Foundations for Mathematics.* The activities mentioned there as well as those described in this section are basic to an understanding of and ability to work with numbers and numerals.

PARQUETRY

Parquetry blocks constitute a stage above the utilization of block designs which were discussed earlier. Although the block designs can be developed in a definite series of steps from simple to complex which utilize two- and three-dimensional arrangements, the forms nevertheless always involve only right angles. The child has been exposed to circles through the utilization of stencils, but in general the square has been emphasized. Straight lines have been accentuated to this point. With the utilization of parquetry blocks the concept of the oblique is presented to the child. Forms which depart from the standard square can be conceptualized in a concrete manner.

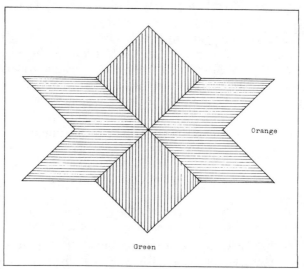

Figure 38. Examples of parquetry block designs. These designs can be modified by the teacher in an almost unlimited number of ways. Thus much variety can be provided for the child. Care must be taken, however, to provide the child with sufficient repetition of materials so that he has a definite feeling of success with the designs. The teacher must not move from simple to complex too rapidly. Slow growth will insure significant gains at a later time. Reprinted by permission from Cruickshank *et al.* 1961.

Typical Material Equipment

1. Full-sized design or pattern cut from high-gloss paper and posted on poster paper. The design should correspond in size and color to those of the parquetry blocks themselves (see Figure 38).
2. Parquetry blocks required to construct the design.
3. Plain paper the same size as that on which the design is mounted.
4. Colored shapes matching the given design.
5. Paste.

Typical Task

1. The child builds the given design with blocks, using the pattern as a guide.
2. When correctly done, he places colored shapes on plain paper making the same design.
3. He pastes them in place, making his paper look like the pattern.

General Techniques

1. Use the preferred hand.
2. Operate as nearly left to right as possible.
3. Use an organized approach.
4. Do not rotate pattern or paper on which design is being pasted.
5. Paste should be applied only to the corners of the shape through the use of the index finger of the preferred hand. This leaves nine clean fingers to assist with the placing of the shape.
6. Sides of shapes should touch each other as on the given pattern.

Extended Learnings

Ask the child questions such as the following:
    How many blocks did you use?
    What shape is this?
    Show me the square.

Which shape is red?
Which shape has three sides?
Show me a shape which has all sides the same length.
How many sides does a square have?
Can you think of anything which has a shape like this?

Goals

The goals which the teacher of learning disabled children has in mind in utilizing parquetry blocks involve tasks which make it possible for the child to deal with the increased stimulus value of the materials. Different colors and the different shapes of blocks and the designs expand his notion of the complexity of form. Fine-motor activities are involved in cutting on lines, in pasting within an outline, and in the assembling of the blocks themselves on top of the design. Color discrimination, recognition of form, eye-hand coordination, figure-background discrimination, and practice in increasing the attention span through the use of interesting semi-concrete materials likewise are elements which are inherent in the parquetry materials.

Additional Comments

This activity should be used parallel to those things which complement it and enhance the learning task for the child. Other approaches to geometric shapes are found throughout this section. Be sure that when this activity calls for cutting and pasting, the child has already been introduced to the correct method. Then this will afford secondary tasks which involve practicing these skills in a meaningful way.

Earlier in this chapter we mentioned that the activities discussed here are the direct antecedents to arithmetic skills as well as being closely related to the skills involved in reading and writing. We stated before that the educational program for learning disabled children is not a remedial program. It is a program of new learning. For a child who, in terms of chronological age, has passed the preacademic state of his development, he must still be given a formal educational opportunity to demonstrate his skills in the preacademic activities described in this chapter. It will not take long for the teacher and the child to become aware of those skills in which the child is deficient. When these become known, the teacher must then provide the same type of practice and learning experience in stencils, cutting, block design, or other activity with this child as would be done with a child who was both by reason of chronological age and experience much younger. Experience has demonstrated that it is useless to skip over aspects of the learning process simply because a child may be chronologically older.

PERCEPTUAL-MOTOR TRAINING AND ACADEMIC ACHIEVEMENT

There are those who minimize, if not decry, the employment of perceptual-motor training, stating that there is no evidence that it is related to achievement in reading or other academic skills. If a one-to-one relationship is demanded, then the critics of perceptual-motor training are correct. There is no such correlative evidence, and it is doubtful if there ever will be. What is the rationale of perceptual-motor training? Let us examine the normal child and the concept of readiness.

The child under six years of age (generally speaking), whose mental age is also less than six years, is characterized as being at a preacademic stage of development. It is often stated that the child is at a "prereading readiness stage" or simply at a "non-readiness stage" for the assimilation of abstract concepts. A complete *readiness* concept also involves a degree of neurophysiological maturation as well as psychological maturation. The structures of the eye and of the ear (as well as carpal and metacarpal bone growth) appear to reach a stage of near-adult maturation between 5½ and 7½ years of age in normal child development. These aspects of child development, while significant in the total concept of readiness, are not the immediate focus of our comments.

If one analyzes children at the prereadiness levels, one sees many characteristics wherein they appear comparable to children with learning disabilities who are several years older. For example, preacademic or prereadiness children are often, if not always, characterized by figure-ground disturbances, dissociation, perseveration, closure problems, short attention span, and a variety of other characteristics. As a matter of fact, one of the interesting and difficult challenges for the clinician is to make an accurate differential diagnosis of children under six, discriminating betweeen normal immature prereadiness development and perceptual processing maldevelopment which may accompany the child into later growth periods.

To bring the child to a readiness stage by the time he has reached the first grade, a number of techniques are employed by good nursery school and kindergarten teachers. Puzzles, motor development toys and equipment, eye-hand coordination activities, color-form sorting activities, form boards, and an almost endless list of other equipment and supplies characterize most such readiness programs. In another vocabulary all of these things are perceptual-motor training activities, of either a fine- or gross-motor variety. All are accepted as vital to good preschool and early childhood education programs. All are seen as intimately related to the development of skills of eye-hand coordination, eye-foot coordination, ear-hand, or other forms of audiomotor coordination, to say nothing of the more subtle influences which skill acquisition in these areas has for the development of ego strength, positive body image, good self-concept development, and a willingness to risk the self. The establishment of success is a paramount requisite to further growth. All of this is basic to a concept of readiness which in turn is basic to the child's acquisition of abstract concepts inherent in reading and mathematics.

Few if any educators deny the importance of the activities briefly described here as being anything other than basic to the development of readiness—readiness to read, readiness for number concepts, for handwriting, and for other abstract skills. Reading readiness activities do not in and of themselves result in reading. There is no one who claims a one-to-one relationship. The emphasis is on readiness to learn. Without success experiences in readiness activities, it has long been recognized that achievement in reading, for example, will be delayed until these prereading skills are achieved. In reference to educable mentally retarded children and youth, Bluma Weiner long ago spoke of the necessity of a "prolonged preacademic program" to bring such pupils to a readiness stage—a level which might, in the group of youth about whom she wrote, be at a chronological age of nine, ten, eleven, or later years.

The needs of the learning disabled child are twofold—namely, the need for readiness activities coincident with early physical and psychological growth and development (as for all children), and the need for an added emphasis on these activities as a result of a perceptual disability. The needs of the learning disabled child are the same as for the normal child except that the perceptual processing characteristics of the former are not only developmental, but are also deficits impeding learning. Learning disabled children need readiness activities too. By chance or otherwise, readiness activities, when applied to children with learning disabilities, have come to be referred to as perceptual-motor training activities (which they are). The purpose of perceptual-motor training is not to teach reading, but, through the total impact of success experiences in perceptual processing tasks in the areas included within a good concept of perceptual-motor training, to bring the child to a level of readiness to read. In the learning disabled child, this stage may be reached at any chronological age, depending on the severity of the perceptual processing problem. Until the readiness level has been reached, the employment of perceptual-motor training is logical and appropriate.

There is no one-to-one relationship between any perceptual-motor activity or series of activities and the acquistion of specific abstract skills. The total impact of success experiences acquired through these activities brings the child to a level of readiness to read and possessed of a motivation to wish to continue success experiences in different kinds of learning situations and learning activities. The child is willing to risk, because he has demonstrated to himself that he can succeed in something.

Perceptual-motor training contains another positive attribute. A. Jean Ayres makes a strong point, emphasizing what others before her have stated, that the development of intelligence is in large measure a function of appropriate movement in response to a stimulus. Neurophysiologists speak of this phenomenon as *neurobiotaxis*. This is not a new concept, but is one widely recognized, particularly by those who recognize intelligence in large part to be a reflection of the individual's environmental stimulation and reaction to it. Perceptual-motor training is accepted as fundamental within this concept, for in all ways its activities require the child or youth to make a specific motor response to a specific stimulus or set of stimuli. Trial and error behavior or responses are discouraged, for such random motor activities too often result in failure. Structured perceptual-motor activities, which insure successful responses to stimuli, are encouraged, for these lead to an enhancement of the self-image, and they provide for the child a basis for making choices in subsequent situations.

We cannot agree with those who criticize perceptual-motor training, with those who raise doubts but who have themselves not analyzed the situation fully. There are fundamental developmental reasons, neurophysiological and psychological, for the employment of these activities which will bring the child to the point of being able to accept subsequent instruction with profit to himself. In turn, this instruction leads to reading and to other abstract and concrete skills. To criticize without positive substitutionary suggestions or plans is to confuse and to déprive children and their parents in ways which are predictably harmful. Perceptual-motor training is neither the ultimate nor the total program. It is a logical and significant single element in a complete program for children with the serious problems of learning.

SELECTED REFERENCES OF SPECIAL INTEREST TO PARENTS

Golick, M. *Deal Me In!* New York: Jeffry Norton, 1973.

Lewis, R. S.; Strauss, A. A.; and Lehtinen, E. *The Other Child.* New York: Grune & Stratton, 1947.

Radler, D. H., and Kephart, N. C. *Success Through Play.* New York: Harper & Row, 1963.

Kauffman, J. M., and Hallahan, D. P. *Teaching Children with Learning Disabilities: Personal Perspectives.* Columbus: Merrill, 1976.

SELECTED REFERENCES OF SPECIAL INTEREST TO TEACHERS

Abercrombie, M. L. J. "Marianne Frostig Developmental Test of Visual Perception." *Perceptual and Motor Skills* 18 (April 1964): 583–94.

Cratty, B. J. *Developmental Sequences of Perceptual Motor Tasks.* Freeport, N. Y.: Educational Activities, 1967.

————. *Teaching Motor Skills.* Englewood Cliffs, N.J.: Prentice-Hall, 1973.

Cruickshank. W. M.; Bentzen, F. A.; Ratzeburg, F. H.; and Tannhauser, M. T. *A Teaching Method for Brain-Injured and Hyperactive Children.* Syracuse: Syracuse University Press, 1961.

Fernald, Grace M. *Remedial Techniques in Basic School Subjects.* New York: McGraw-Hill, 1943.

Ford, M. "Auditory and Tactual Visual Integration in Relation to Reading Ability." *Perceptual and Motor Skills* 24 (1967): 831–41.

Frostig, M., and Horne, D. *The Frostig Program for the Development of Visual Perception.* Chicago: Follet, 1964.

Frostig, M., and Maslow, P. *Movement Education: Theory and Practice.* Chicago: Follet, 1970.

Getman, G. N., and Hendrickson, H. H. "The Needs of Teachers for Specialized Information on the Development of Visuomotor Skills in Relation to Academic Performance." In *The Teacher of Brain-Injured Children,* edited by W. M. Cruickshank. Syracuse: Syracuse University Press, 1966.

Getman, G. N. "The Visuomotor Complex in the Acquisition of Learning Skills." In *Learning Disorders: Volume I,* edited by J. Hellmuth. Seattle, Wash.: Special Child, 1965.

Jolles, I. "A Teaching Sequence for the Training of Visual and Motor Perception." *American Journal of Mental Deficiency* 63 (September 1958):252–55.

Kaliski. L "Educational Therapy for Brain-Injured Retarded Children." *American Journal of Mental Deficiency* 60 (July 1955): 71–77.

Kephart, N. C. "The Needs of Teachers for Specialized Information of Perception." In *The Teacher of Brain-Injured Children,* edited by W. M. Cruickshank. Syracuse: Syracuse University Press, 1966.

_____. "Perceptual-Motor Aspects of Learning Disabilities." *Exceptional Children* 31 (December 1964): 201–206.

Klein, G. "Practical Applications for Perceptual Training." *Exceptional Children* 34 (1967): 50–55.

Marshall, E. D. "Teaching Materials for Children with Learning Disabilities." In *Perceptual and Learning Disabilities in Children,* edited by W. M. Cruickshank and D. P. Hallahan. Syracuse: Syracuse University Press, 1975.

Mink, L. "Adaptation of the Montessori Method in Developing Visual Perception in the Special Child." In *The Special Child in Century 21,* edited by J. Hellmuth. Seattle: Special Child, 1965.

Wallis, E., and Lozen, G. *Exercises for Children.* Englewood Cliffs, N.J.: Prentice-Hall, 1966.

9

Developing Abstract Concepts

O UR INTENT here is not to present a complete discussion on educational methodology. Many excellent volumes consider more completely than space permits here the matters of teaching children reading, writing, spelling, and number concepts. We will indicate certain emphases which are significant to the education of learning disabled children, and our hope is to provide to parents an inclusive view of their child's needs and something of how, with the assistance of teachers and others, these needs may be met. Many of the approaches we suggest are typical of the approaches taken with normal children. However, major differences do exist in the way material is presented to the child, the setting within which it is presented, and in the structured approach generally followed. These aspects of the program have been discussed in previous chapters.

The content to be used in teaching a learning disabled child to read must be different from that for the normal child. This is true primarily because the learning disabled child who is a nonreader usually will be from two to five years older than the typical beginning reader in the first grade. Keeping the child motivated is a very real problem, impossible to ignore if the teacher and parent hope to stimulate the child to want to learn. One cannot teach the nine-year-old nonreader with the same subject material that one uses with a six-year-old child. Although the older child functions in many ways as a preschool child, it is not valid to assume that the teaching materials utilized with first and second grade children are appropriate for him. Although he must be approached as a nonreader, the material presented him must have a high interest level. Since appropriate material is not always available, many teaching materials will have to be written and produced by the teacher.

In Chapter 8 a sequence was suggested for strengthening learning skills involved in form perception and recognition and in the other preacademic skills basic to abstract reasoning. Similarly, we suggest that, in abstract learning, the learning disabled child be advanced from number concepts to writing to reading in that order. While this sequence does not eliminate overlapping, it takes into consideration the degree of abstract reasoning involved in the three areas. The learning disabled child's tendency to understand the concrete more readily than the abstract may be exploited to his advantage if number concepts are given first emphasis by the teacher. Reading skills, which involve the greatest abstract ability, will generally be achieved more readily by learning disabled children after skills in number concepts and writing concepts have been established.

NUMBER CONCEPTS

The discussion related to the development of number concepts is based on the *Foundations for Mathematics* by W. M. Cruickshank, E. D. Marshall, and M. A. Hurley, referred to in Chapters 7 and 8 (Teaching Resources Corporation). This four-unit program is intended to bring the child to a level of achievement comparable to the second grade, at which time it is expected that the learning disabled child (or others) should be able to use whatever basic arithmetic program may be employed in a public school system. Closely related to *Foundations for Mathematics* is *Fundamentals Underlying Numbers* by John W. Wilson and Edward Uprichard (Teaching Resources Corporation), the latter containing a wealth of pre-arithmetic readiness activities and materials. We also find the Stearn's *Structured Arithmetic* materials to be of immense help with children with learning and perceptual disabilities.

> The goal of *Foundations for Mathematics* is to provide the child . . . with a base for satisfactory performance in elementary school mathematics. Four separate units have been developed to give the child competence in the skills and concepts of (1) sets, including the introduction of color discrimination, and curves, including lines and planes; (2) exploring sets and size comparisons; (3) motor development involving lines and planes; and finally, two levels of sophistication in the comparison of sets. . . . The teaching materials in this series are intentionally focused on the most primitive levels of these concepts out of which more abstract levels of mathematics are developed. In the authors' experience, a child with a learning disability is often characterized by the fact that he has not mastered certain broad, funda-

mental concepts. For example, the understanding of the primitive level of the concept for line segment (which may be behaviorally evidenced by the ability to identify straight line segments from other paths, or the ability to construct line segments and other curves) is needed before a child can be expected to form a cross, figure, or symbol by intersecting two line segments (such as a numeral *4* or a letter *t*). The failure to achieve this understanding may be demonstrated as a visual-motor problem, which may seriously influence the child's ability to read or spell adequately. Remediation in this instance calls for *new* learning. It may require teaching at least the primitive level for curves and their relationships to one another.

Early experiences in arithmetic are always concrete in nature. A child learns the concepts of *more* and *less* as he compares his collection of rocks to that of his friends. He discovers *little* and *big* when told that he is too little to go alone or that when he gets big like his older brother he can have a bike. *Large* cold drinks appeal to him more than *small* ones he receives. Time takes on meaning when he learns that he must take his nap *before* he plays and that *tomorrow* is his birthday. One-to-one correspondence is stumbled onto when he receives two bits of candy—one for each finger he holds up.

These and countless other daily happenings in the life of a preschool child furnish him with a wealth of concepts and information from which to proceed to the formal study of arithmetic. The preschool period might be thought of as a prereadiness period during which the child learns to perceive form and to understand objects in time and space. During his readiness period his early learnings are checked for accuracy and reinforced so that his concepts will be correct. Then, before he knows it, he is "working arithmetic."

Unfortunately, a learning disabled child often lacks enough of the right kind of experiences to set him on the track to more advanced learning. This lack, frequently, is accompanied by a serious problem in perception. Although a child's visual equipment may appear to be intact, the impressions he receives may not be in accord with reality. Since he fails to perceive properly, his concepts are incorrect. Before he can continue into the very orderly and precise study of arithmetic, he must be helped extensively with his perception problem.

The materials and methods described in the section on perception can assist in forming an excellent core of learnings for the disturbed child in preparation for his study of the tool skills. If these materials and methods are presented in the correct order and coordinated properly, the child may be able to move smoothly into arithmetic experiences which are new to him. It is a rare child who knows nothing in this area when he first enters the class—counting, some vocabulary, and a little addition or subtraction—and it is imperative that the teacher discover and use this to the child's advantage.

Solid objects which may be manipulated easily (e.g., the blocks shown in Figure 37) give the child an opportunity to overcome a tendency to perseveration or disinhibition by giving him something to handle. If he moves an object each time he counts, he must stop counting when there are no more objects. He is likely to adopt some of these concrete objects as "crutches" for his work, but this is acceptable. As he becomes secure with the concepts he will voluntarily abandon them when they are no longer needed. His materials should be designed so that he has a definite point to begin and end each task. New material will need to be repeated more than in a classroom for normal children. An effort should be made to demonstrate the same concept in as many different ways as possible. However, these different approaches should be spaced so that they add to learning rather than create confusion.

Prereadiness and Readiness (Level I)

In additon to other techniques for teaching form perception, exercises in form recognition are needed at this developmental level. Cards are used to present a "matching" task; also, an alert teacher can use the same cards to help the child with quantitative and qualitative vocabulary. The form cards which are used are color cued—one color on white. The configuration cards also are color cued, also using only one color on white, preferably black on white (see Figure 39).

Introducing Numbers and Symbols (Level II)

Mentioned several times in this section is the technique of matching. The learning intended to be derived from matching is that a configuration, word, printed symbol, or spoken word may all be ways of expressing the same concept. For example: ---, "3," "three," and ". . ." are ways of indicating what is understood as the "threeness" of a number. Sequential steps would include the following:

1. Matching 3 × 3'' cards of number symbols. (In all matching tasks follow order of steps already described with regard to the use of color.)

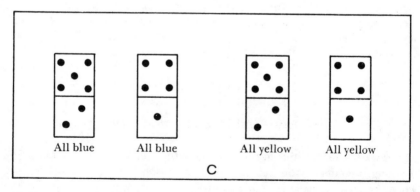

Figure 39. Numerical configurations: *a.* basic number concepts; *b.* combinations of number concepts utilizing multiple color cues and stimuli; *c.* domino-type numerical configurations utilizing same color throughout each configuration but different colors for different configurations. Reprinted by permission from Cruickshank *et al.* 1961.

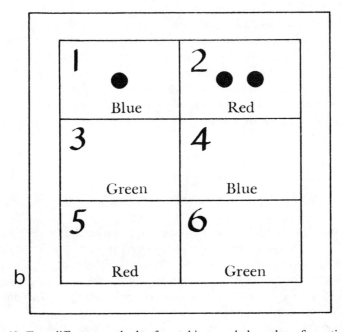

Figure 40. Two different methods of matching symbols and configuration cards. Note that in *b* space is left for the child to fill in, with the appropriate color, the numerical configuration called for. Reprinted by permission from Cruickshank *et al.* 1961.

2. Matching symbols and configuration cards (see Figure 40).

3. Matching name and symbol.

4. Matching name, number, and symbol.

5. Using reference chart. Make this for the child to have with his equipment in his storage space.

6. Providing worksheets. Several types may be used depending on the child's needs and ability to deal with stimuli used. Color cues would govern the earliest levels. A child might be given a sheet of paper divided into four sections. In each section would be a number symbol in color. The first two squares are completed for him so that he knows just what to do. His task is to paste the correct number of gummed shapes in the remaining sections. Later the same type of task could employ all one color or just black. He could also use a stamp pad and the eraser of a new pencil to create the configuration. When he is able to do this successfully, he could use crayons to draw the necessary objects.

It is impossible to overemphasize the value of teachers' using a reliable teachers' guide to arithmetic throughout the rest of the child's school experience. Such a guide would provide a complete outline for a developmental study, and the sequence would probably be reasonable. Countless suggestions for enrichment and reteaching are placed throughout most such books. While it may be impractical or unsuitable to adopt ideas directly from such a guide, suggestions contained there will form a secure basis for variations and adaptations which would be very suitable for disturbed children. The teacher needs only to keep in mind the individual child's abilities and disabilities and the recommended principles of construction.

Counting (Level III)

At this level there are a number of techniques which the teacher may use in developing further the child's sophistication with number concepts. Symbols have already been learned by the child. The effort at Level III is to associate symbols with abstract concepts involving sequence and quantity. Some of the ways in which the teacher may do this are included in the following suggestions:

Concrete objects may be used. In this situation the teacher may place several blocks before the chld. The child is then asked to give the teacher one block, two blocks, three blocks. etc.

A large *pegboard* may be employed. A peg board 10 × 10″ is recommended for this purpose. The teacher should tape a 1″ strip of tag-board down the left edge of the board. On it (and beside the rows of holes) she should write number symbols in colors. The child's task is to place the appropriate number of pegs in the row beside the number symbol, using the indicated color. Questioning is appropriate as, "Show me three." The child shows the teacher the three pegs and gives them to the teacher, counting each as he removes them from the board. The same sequence is employed with other numerals. In this task not only is the child receiving experience with number symbols and counting, but also with the association of colors and in eye-hand coordination as he puts pegs in the board and later removes them and gives them to the teacher. More important, however, is the association of abstract concepts of quantity with symbols.

Block-counting rods (see Figure 41) are used to develop numerical concepts. A 1″ board is cut into pieces about 5″ wide and 15″ long. Six rods are spaced down its length. In order, these rods will hold a single 1″ cube (with a hole drilled in its center the size necessary to fit over the rod), two cubes, three cubes, and so on up to the highest quantity the teacher desires to teach at this level. The child is asked to place the proper number of cubes on each rod, counting as he does. He should be assisted in seeing concepts of *more* and *less*. "Show me four." "Show me six." "Which is more?" "More" is taught first; later "less" (or "fewer") is introduced as a concept.

A *counting box* may be helpful as an additional technique in developing concepts of counting. Divisions are made in a relatively large flat box which is not too deep. In the bottom of each space resulting from the dividers the teacher places a numeral in color to indicate to the child how many objects should be placed in each area. Questions and activities as suggested with using the pegboard may be employed here also.

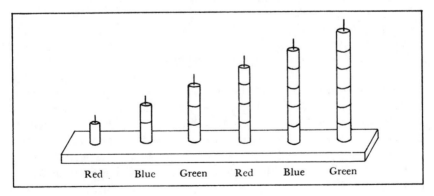

Figure 41. Design of a block-counting rod technique. Reprinted by permission from Cruickshank *et al.* 1961.

To further stress counting and number concepts the teacher may have the child *paste the correct number* of objects in the section indicated on a piece of paper; *stamping with a new eraser* of a pencil on a stamp pad and putting the appropriate number of dots where indicated on a piece of paper; or *drawing a specified number* of objects. These are all means of reinforcing this learning task.

Flannel boards and *magnetic boards* may prove valuable aids in developing number concepts and in counting. Eye-hand coordination is involved in this task as well, of course. The child arranges for the teacher a specified number of pieces on either one or the other board in relation to the number symbol which the teacher suggests to him: "Put five cubes on the magnetic board and count them out loud as you place them there."

Finally, the use of the abacus is most helpful in developing not only concepts of sequence and quantity, but also in developing a concept of spatial relationship. The teacher should use an abacus strung with beads from one through six. First the child is asked to push over one bead, then two beads, etc. He is then asked to "Make all the rows say 'three.' " He is then asked to "make all the rows say 'four,' " etc. More complex abacuses are employed as the child becomes able to handle adequately more complex numerical concepts.

Groupings (Level IV)

Some of the methods already discussed may readily be used in this area. Flannel boards and magnet boards are excellent additions to the pasting, stamping, and drawing which the child would use here.

Analysis of Configuration (Level V)

The beginning approach here should follow the configurations which appear on domino cards (see Figure 39) with which the child may be familiar. Place several 1″ cubes on the table in front of the child which are arranged, except for one missing cube, in a configuration similar to the domino. These are placed so that with the addition of one more cube they will correctly form the configuration with which the child is familiar. For example, three cubes might be placed in such a way that the one needed to show the numerical configuration of the domino 4 is obviously missing. The child is asked to add the cube necessary to "make the 4."

From this type of familiar configuration involving number concepts, the teacher can move to what is called a linear configuration. This simply means placing blocks in a straight line on the table in front of the child and telling him to add one, two, or three more blocks to make the desired number. For example, the teacher places three blocks in a straight line in front of the child. He is given a small supply of extra blocks, and from this he is told to add more blocks to the line to "make 4" or to "make 5." Later he should be able to draw the configurations or to cut out small pieces of paper the paste these on a larger piece of paper in the shape of the configuration which he is copying.

Addition Sign (Level VI)

Depend on color cues for much help here. Use blocks to show the child that one block *plus* two blocks equals three blocks. Pasting or stamping exercises may be used to arrive at the correct combination. Later the child will be taught to write the answer in numerical signs. His first addition problems should be presented in vertical form, i.e., on a single line. Horizontal addition may be used once proficiency is gained in the vertical method.

Numbers 7–10 (Level VII)

These numbers are introduced on an abacus strung 7 to 10, and the procedure is essentially the same as it was for teaching the numbers 1 to 6 (see the discussion of block-counting rods and Figure 41).

Addition (Level VIII)

Worksheets are employed in this level to a greater extent than before. The child uses an abacus, pushing over one bead, then two. When he does this, ask him how many beads he has moved. Show him how to write the numerical sign 2 on paper.

Subtraction (Level IX)

After the addition process is well established, the child begins subtraction on the abacus. The child is asked to push over four beads; then he is asked to push back three and tell how many are left. After he does this successfully several times, the problem is shown him on paper. Emphasize what the minus sign tells him to do.

A flannel board or magnet board may be useful in learning what "take away" means. Color cuing the plus and minus signs may be valuable help for the child as he encounters worksheets with mixed examples. Correct placement may be emphasized by placing individual examples on cards. Prepared paper on which the child copies the example in the correct form may prove necessary.

Column Addition, Sums to 10 (Level X)

The usual methods employed in the teaching of addition are appropriate here. In the beginning, however, the learning disabled child may need many more cues to assist him in correct computation than is ordinarily thought to be necessary with normal children. For example, each problem may need to be outlined in black ink if dissociation is a characteristic. Each problem may need to be presented separately on a different piece of paper if figure-background differentiation remains an active issue. The teacher may need to utilize heavy lines on one or another side of each problem if more structure is required by the child to help him orient himself to the space of the paper. Color cues may continue to be needed for many weeks to accentuate certain portions of the column addition problem, i.e., the addition symbol, the line under the numbers to be added, or the numerals themselves.

Simple Word Problem (Level XI)

Three steps are ordinarily characteristic of this level. First, the teacher merely presents the problem to the child verbally: "One ball and two balls are ——— balls." Second, a step which may take several weeks to achieve, the problem is *written* on a card and placed in front of the child as "1 ball and 2 balls are ——— balls." Finally, the problem is *written* as in step two but utilizing words instead of numerical symbols: "One ball and two balls are ——— balls."

Writing Numerals (Level XII)

Use paper with large squares. Down the left column should be numerals 0 to 10 and across the top, 0, 10, 20, 30, 40, and 50. Sprinkled on the page would be clues helping the child to monitor his work and check its accuracy.

Adding to 20 (Level XIII)

Use a two-string abacus and a tens pocket chart (see Figure 42) in addition to all the other materials already used.

Telling Time (Level XIV)

At this level the child, if he is ready, will be introduced to two time divisions, the whole hour and the half hour. In dealing with both time parts a large concept clock should be utilized (see *Concept Clocks in Color,* and accompanying manual of instructions, Teaching Resources Corporation).

Figure 42. Tens Pocket Chart. Use wrapping paper 13 by 15". Fold back 4", making the pocket chart 9 by 15". Staple the edges, and staple between the "Tens" and "Ones" pockets. The words on the face of the pocket should be written in color—a different color for each word. Colored counting sticks may be used singly and in bunches of ten. Reproduced by permission from Cruickshank *et al.* 1961.

Figure 43. Good examples of an hour and a half-hour clock used in learning the beginning concepts of time. In the hour clock the two hands are of different colors of plastic. These illustrations photographed and reproduced by permission of Teaching Resources Corp., Boston.

In dealing with the whole hour a clock which has different colored hour and minute hands is used. In teaching the half hour a clock whose face is divided in half with different colors utilized to depict each half is employed (see Figure 43).

Calendar

On the first school day of each month, the child should make a calendar. Making a calendar will help him become aware of the sequence of numbers, the number of days in weeks and months, the names of days and months, and the order they follow. It offers some opportunity for recording daily occurrences such as weather, attendance, accomplishments, etc. The calendar is an excellent "take-home" paper. The child can be justly proud of it, and he can quite easily find a place for it in his home.

A simple way to prepare the material for this project is to ditto forms leaving spaces for the numerals and names of the month and days to be filled in by the child. Above the calendar he can draw a picture or do a more structured task as indicated by the teacher. He should be given a pattern to follow for placing his numerals. The reader will observe that the child is now being asked to draw, to "fill in areas," and to perform other eye-hand coordination tasks which earlier in the preceding chapter were discouraged. The assumption here is that the child has made progress and is capable of performing these simple tasks. If he is not, then, of course, these procedures should not be used, and careful assessment should be made of exactly at what level the child should be and is performing. Teaching should not get beyond the child's ability to succeed.

PREPARED PAPERS

Dittoed sheets may be prepared which are adaptable for a large number of activities. For example, one sheets useful in several activities may be prepared by dividing a stencil into parts by the use of lines. Two-inch squares down each side, leaving the middle plain, are very usable for all kinds of matching activities. Large sections of four or six to a page may be used in arithmetic. The child puts the designated number of items in each section.

Devise several of these multipurpose type sheets. A great deal of time will be saved through their use, and they have the added advantage of appearing familiar to the child.

TRACING

This activity is closely akin to those involving stencils. The child is limited in what he can do by the way in which the material is prepared. A tracing technique may be used extensively in teaching cursive writing and may also be valuable in the teaching of forms or shapes. Establishing habits in areas such as arithmetic, where placement of numbers is done by convention, is another use of tracing. In some cases a child may trace something which results in a sort of "picture" that he may take home with him.

Tracing may also be used by the child in making his monthly calendar. This may help him learn to write his numbers in counting order and write them so that the size is appropriate for the working area.

Commonly used tracing tasks involve nothing more than preparing the model to be traced on a sheet of tag-board. Over this is clipped the tracing paper. Sufficient clips should be used so that the paper does not slip. Again, color can be used to give the task a higher stimulus value.

Tracing books are available in the coloring book sections of stores. Some may be adapted just by removing the item to be traced from the book and mounting it on stiff board. Another version has tracing paper between two pictures with numbered parts. The directions tell the child which parts of either picture to color and provide a code to determine the color he uses. The result is a picture different from either of the originals. With care, this activity might prove to be satisfactory for some children.

WRITING

One of the problems often experienced by learning disabled children is the inability to see things as a whole. The picture of the totality, or gestalt, is lost in a series of short exposures to each individual part. When lines and circles are presented to the child as he is introduced to manuscript writing, they tend to remain just lines and circles. Perhaps he can say an "*a*" is made from a "nice, round circle and a short straight line." When he tries to produce an "*a*" he makes the circle and the line, but they do not touch each other. This dissociation of parts is found throughout his attempts at manuscript. The cursive method of teaching writing is recommended for learning disabled children. Manuscript writing is introduced much later, if ever.

If he shows a tendency to perseverate, he may continue making one of the parts of a letter long after finishing the letter. Because his writing does not look like what he has learned to read or tried to copy, it is as meaningless to him as to a casual observer.

The method of teaching a child cursive writing, which is recommended here, has been found to work well with children who have experienced great difficulty in learning manuscript writing. Obviously, a child is more likely to see "wholes" in cursive writing because the stopping and starting places come before and after complete words. The technique requires the child to use himself as a whole also. He must hear about the work to do, he must see the task and its tools. His large muscles and small muscles must perform the job, and finally his speaking mechanism must say what he has done. Through the combined efforts of these many parts of the child, his brain receives a correct impression of what is involved.

Starting points are clearly defined, and left to right progression is demanded by the structure of the task. By repeating this emphasis countless times in his work assignments, correct habits of placement and direction are set. There is little chance for reversals of letters in this approach. Purposeful use of color helps the child to see the strokes and directions. Locations of lines and direction of stroke may also be emphasized through the use of color. Gradually as the child learns to make letters, he also learns their names and the sounds they make. When he has begun to join letters into words, he learns to know what the words say. The movement into reading and phonics is smooth and natural, pointing out once more how truly impossible it is to completely isolate one learning from another.

The visual perception training already described utilizes many varieties of manipulative tasks and provides basic understandings which should precede early attempts at writing. This is not to suggest that a child should be made to wait until a given amount of perception items has been mastered. The perception items themselves should provide some clues pointing to certain parallels in the area of writing. As in all other areas, the technique of writing becomes a useful extension of earlier learnings. At this point the child begins to communicate with his world in another dimension, a dimension which encourages him to feel quite grown up and knowledgeable. It is easy to see how closely related the tasks of learning to write and learning to read are. It often proves very exciting to a child to be able to spot in another place a word he has learned to read in school, but perhaps the biggest thrill is to write it all by himself.

It is important to remember the desirability of involving as much of the child as possible in his learning experience. In order to do this, the teaching of writing must be systematically planned. By adhering rather closely to a sequence of developmental learning, the child should acquire some facility for writing almost before he is aware of it.

The *first stage* utilizes the *clay pan.* This stage is sometimes omitted because the teacher feels it is unimportant. Far from that, it is perhaps the most important, because it is the most concrete. The exercise requires a shallow rectangular pan with a thin layer of clay covering the bottom inside. The child uses a sturdy wooden stylus to make his strokes in the clay. He copies the pattern which the teacher makes for him in the clay. This technique has several things to recommend it. First, the rim of the pan affords an automatic "fence" around the task, eliminating the possibility of operating in the wrong place and helping to reduce stimuli. Second, the natural resistance of the clay forces the child's muscles to work noticeably harder, thus forcing him to become very involved in the task. Direction and shape are emphasized through this kinesthetic experience.

The *second stage* is *tracing.* This requires that the child use crayons to reproduce what he sees through the tracing paper. The material is simple to prepare. White tag-board serves as the base. Large magic markers are used for making the appropriate strokes as presented in many cursive writing manuals. These strokes are made as large as possible but with an attractive space between them. Colors are used so that the child is forced to put down one crayon and pick up another each time. He should not be allowed to skip to another part of the page where he finds one in the same color. Left to right progression and top to bottom order, as well as good work habits, require that the child proceed in orderly fashion. To this sheet of prepared strokes, a sheet of onionskin paper is attached. Care must be taken that enough clips are used to hold the paper securely. The child's task is to trace the stroke with crayon.

The *third stage* of writing employs the use of *controlled lined paper,* which may be prepared through the use of ditto masters. Remember that the lines function in units and require considerable space between the units, so that the child does not become confused. In the early stages, the colored lines should be quite heavy. Teacher judgment concerning the individual child's ability is most important here. The child's first copying will be done by looking at the simple stroke and reproducing each individual stroke on the lines directly below the pattern.

The *last stage* in teaching writing of the developmental learning in cursive writing comes only after the child has demonstrated a free grasp of each of the three preceding stages and after he has learned some letters. It may prove necessary to supply the learning disabled child with controlled lined paper during his first attempts at *independent writing.*

A method of teaching cursive writing has been outlined in the paragraphs above in this section. Actually, were it available, the *Palmer Method* of teaching handwriting which was so popular during the decade of the 1920's has much to commend it to children in need of visual-motor training. This method whose popularity continued for more than thirty years, was based essentially on extensive training in both gross and fine motor skills. Libraries and school stock rooms could well be searched for old, and long unused, manuals. If found, a fine program for the development of writing skills for children with learning disabilities would be available.

As in all other learning experiences with this child it must always be remembered by all who may be working with him that progress comes very slowly. In fact, it may come so slowly that it is unrecognized until the whole year's work is evaluated.

READING

Who can say just exactly when a child first begins to read? Although it may not be difficult to notice when he selects a book to read, the chances are that he has already had a wealth of reading experience prior to that. Perhaps he has learned that certain combinations of letter shapes indicate which public restroom he uses. Brand names on his favorite foods are very familiar to him. Advertising on television usually presents words visually and auditorily. If he brings in the mail, perhaps he notices the names and addresses all look alike. Generalizations to other similar types of written material may result from such experiences as these. Then informal learnings raise the child's readiness for formal instruction.

The program of learning tasks outlined here does not depend on the child's having had these usual childhood experiences. These things are built into the learning activities in an orderly fashion. An effort is made to incorporate, in a gradual way, concepts necessary to the child's understanding of the printed materials which he will learn.

Almost before he knows it, he is beginning to read. His perception skill tasks present words to him from time to time and eventually employ short sentences. The careful use of these kinds of experiences will give him a small start toward a sight vocabulary.

The most obvious type of activity leading to reading is sequence stories. The child begins by "reading" pictures and follows the developmental sequence into reading words and short sentences. Later, after he has had more formal instruction in reading, he deals with paragraphs.

Activities which promote reasoning, logic, and other thinking skills are directly related to reading.

When a child is having noticeable success with form perception, left

to right progression, sequence stories, rhyming, and sorting and matching, he is probably ready to work more intensively in the area of reading.

Phonetic skills may be developed by using material which is designed
in a way similar to items for perceptual skill. Visual perception combined
with auditory skill will form the basis for the child's phonetic analysis of
words.

A task requiring the child to match letters is a logical starting place
for learning beginning consonant sounds. This should be followed by a
task requiring the child to match pictures that begin with the same sound.
When he is ready, the next step will involve matching pictures to letters.

When his skills with a sound seem strong enough, have him find
magazine pictures which begin with the sound. Outline the picture with a
felt marker. The child will then cut it out and paste it in a specified place.
He should also trace the letter which makes the sound and repeat the
sound.

Vowel sounds may be approached in a similar fashion. The child first
matches pictures which have the same vowel sound, then pictures to letters (vowel sounds). Matching sounds with words and pictures follow
next. He will perhaps need color cues for some time here. He again finds
the magazine pictures, and cuts and pastes them.

When he begins to use a book, be sure to examine the teacher's guide
very carefully. It will serve as a good compass pointing the direction
toward next learnings the child will need. There will also be included
many enrichment activities which may be adapted for use by the child.

With older children another approach may be more feasible. The
Fernald method is one which uses several techniques common to the
other material described here. Certainly, no one should attempt to use
this method on the basis of the brief information here, but some general
statements are worthy of inclusion.

The first step involves tracing a large copy of a word selected by the
child. He traces it with his finger saying each part as he traces. When he
is able to write the word without looking, he writes it on "scrap" and then
in his story. His new word is filed under the proper letter in his word box.
He continues to use this combination of visual, tactual, auditory, and
kinesthetic approaches until he no longer needs them. The first to go is
the tactual. He depends on his ability to see, hear, and reproduce the
word without tracing. Ultimately he learns new words just by looking at
them.

Several advantages to this approach seem apparent. The child is
likely to show more interest since he selects the material he uses. The se-
lections he writes need not be below his level of intelligence, or below his
age group. He is not forced into sounding out words when he is attempting

to read. This usually encourages him to want to read more. Obviously, if he has selected the words he wants to learn, they probably are from an area he wants to know more about. This automatically gives him a resource on which to draw when he finds these same words in a book. In a real sense, he may learn the skill of reading through what is usually thought of as "reading for pleasure."

GROSS-MOTOR TRAINING

It is to be observed in the daily schedule discussed later in this chapter that certain activities continue throughout the entire clinical educational period for the learning disabled or PPD children irrespective of the child's chronological age or level of development. Among these are, for example, the continued use of peg boards for eye-hand coordination, color discrimination, recognition of forms, and for other similar types of skill formation. Similarly, gross-motor training, which will be discussed in Chapter 11, continues just as long as the child is in the school program and frequently can be supplemented by similar types of activities in the home. Block designs, parquetry designs, and copying geometric figures likewise are often continued for many months beyond the level when they are usually dropped from the teaching program. These children need much reinforcement to their learning of these concepts which are fundamental to all other learnings.

SEQUENCE STORIES AND CONCEPTS

Attention will now be turned to an examination of the procedures which should be employed by teachers of learning disabled children in helping children to higher concept formation in activities involving sequence, similarities and differences, sorting, spelling, and other basic skills fundamental to abstract thinking.

Typical Material/Equipment

A storytelling series of three or four pictures, each attractively mounted on separate sheets of construction paper.

Typical Task

Child places the pictures on his desk in the order in which events depicted took place.

General Techniques

1. Select the picture showing what happened first and place it toward the top left section of the desk.
2. Remaining pictures should be placed in proper sequence going from left to right as in reading.
3. Preferred hand should do the work.

Extended Learnings of the Task

Ask the child questions such as these:

What is this story about?

Can you tell it to me as it happened in the pictures?

What do you think might have happened then (after event in the last picture)?

What kind of day was this (weather, temperature)?

Would you wear different clothes on a day like that than you have on now?

Has anything like that ever happened to you?

Goals

The goals which may be accomplished through the media of sequence stories include many of the basic problems which the child demonstrates. Through this technique, he may be helped to develop appropriate figure-background relationships, temporal-spatial relationships, directionality, left-to-right progression, and even in some instances he will be assisted in establishing handedness. Inner language development is stressed and achieved in this manner.

Steps

1. Use two pictures which obviously show first event and last event.

2. After correctly placing the series, the child tells about the pictures.

3. Increase the number of pictures in series very gradually.

4. Very gradually increase the difficulty of the discrimination task. Use sequences that are less obvious in their order. These should require the child to look for fine points of difference as well as for gross differences.

5. To the series of pictures add one sentence describing each picture, but mounted on separate paper. The child must then order the pictures, following that with matching the sentences to the pictures. Color cues might be used with the lowest level here.

6. One picture and several sentences, mounted separately, would require the child to use the picture as a frame of reference on which to base the sequence of sentences.

7. Give the child several sentences which will necessitate his forming a mental image of the story as he places the sentences.

8. The child is given a series of short paragraphs, mounted separately, to place in order of occurrence.

9. Increase the length, difficulty, and number of paragraphs presented to the child.

10. Paragraphs dittoed, but out of correct order, are given to the child. He cuts them apart, places them in correct order, and pastes them on construction paper.

11. He arranges a series of pictures in order and writes an original *sentence* about each one.

12. The child arranges a series of pictures in order and writes an original *story* about them.

13. Child is given several paragraphs in order, but not making complete sense, and several separate sentences. He places the sentences and the ends of the paragraphs in such a way that they form an entire sensible story.

Additional Comments

The first steps of this activity require no skill of reading but form an essential prereading activity. The child will most likely require extensive practice of this kind to help him grasp the orderly sequence of material he will later read. Learning to anticipate what will probably come next is an invaluable aid to beginning readers. The emphasis is on *thinking*.

After the child is able to read, this activity can be carried quite far into his experiences, even when he is quite a competent reader. With adaptations and extensions this technique will move smoothly into the broader field of the language arts.

It has often been observed that sequencing of parts of a series leading to a product may be a very difficult activity for perceptually handicapped children (as well as for intellectually retarded children without perceptual processing deficits). For example, the activity is to bake a cake. In this example, there are many steps, i.e., reading the recipe, measuring several elements, preparing the baking pan, putting the mixture into the pan, preparing the oven, putting the pan into the oven, and so forth. If one goes back to the definition of learning disability, it will be recalled that long- and short-term memory were significant and frequently observed deficiencies in these children. Teachers and parents often observe the child to "lose interest" in the baking activity before the end result is accomplished. The usual routine employed is wrong. The process should be reversed from that normally employed. Instead of having the child start by reading the recipe, and then ultimately get all the ingredients into the pan, the first experience with cake baking would be to place already-mixed materials into the pan and place it in the oven. These tasks, one following the other, are all within the memory span of the child. Immediate success experience can be achieved without constant urging to renew interest or "pay attention" on the part of the adult. On the next occassion the activity might start with mixing the ingredients preparatory to placing them in the pan. A third experience would start with measuring some or all of the ingredients before mixing, etc.; a fourth, start with reading the recipe, and so on. In this example there may be quite a supply of cakes before total learning has been achieved, but the same reverse chain can be applied to cookie-making, lacing and tying a shoe (i.e., tying and lacing a shoe), table setting, and most other activities. The goal in such reverse sequencing of motor activities is to bring the end product as close to the reward point (i.e., praise, eating the cake, etc.) as is possible. Teach as close to the product as is possible in the initial stages of sequencing.

CHOOSE AND DO BOX

As a further elaboration of the sequence story technique or as an aid to the teacher in presenting this material in another manner, cover the top of a hosiery box with construction paper. On the outside of the lid paste a picture. Above the picture put the words "Write a Story." Below the picture write six or eight words that might relate to the picture. If, for example, you placed a picture of three cowboys on horses, the word list might contain horses, trail, ride, saddle, western, spurs, and boots. The child's task is to write the story using some of these words if he needs them.

The inside of the lid may be divided into two parts. The child matches the cards in the box with the label on the section. The items to be matched could be based on any type of grouping, i.e., size, color, name, categories, similarities, etc.

In the bottom of the box could be drawn pictures of clocks. The child writes on paper what the clock face says with its hands.

These are only a few of the possible arrangements which may be made in this way. Enough help should be provided in the task itself so that the child does not require additional help. Essentially, this should be an activity encouraging independence in the child. If possible, he should be allowed to select what he would like to do.

SPELLING

This is not usually taught during the regular school day, unless learning to spell certain words is a natural part of a task. Each child is given a loose-leaf binder which he carries home along with a box of letters and a small desk chart. Words are added each week, and the book is outlined precisely so that the child is able to work independently.

Each Friday he brings his book to school and receives the material for the following week. This consists of a page with a story on it and some lined paper appropriate for his level of writing. His week's assignments will follow an outline something like this (these instructions are written on the inside cover of the book):

Monday:	Read the story.
	Say the new words.
	Find the new words.
	Draw a line under the new words.
Tuesday:	Write your new words three times each.
Wednesday:	Spell your new words in the chart.
	Spell aloud as you take them out.
	Write a sentence with your new words.

Thursday: Write your new words two times.
Friday: Bring your work for the week to school.

On Friday his first task is to take the chart and put the words in alphabetical order. It is also test day, and he spells without looking. He also gives to the teacher another sentence using each word. After he learns to use a dictionary, he looks up two or three words one day and some more another day.

SORTING BOX

Several variations on this may be used depending on the items to be sorted and the materials from which the box is made. The device is simply one of providing sections into which groups of objects may be placed. In each section a symbol or sample of the group should be put so that the child knows what he is expected to do.

An excellent box of this type may be made from wood. On a base attach a sturdy upright piece 12 × 18″. Two rows of three boxes each should be attached through the use of *metal slots* so that any number may be used as desired. Thus the small individual boxes may be used with or without the supporting frame. Into them could be put almost any kinds of things from concrete objects to word cards. A holder on the front of each will provide a place for the child's sorting directions.

TYPICAL DAILY PLANS

In order for the parent to understand somewhat more fully the way the preceding experiences are integrated into a school day for the learning disabled child, two typical plans are outlined in the paragraphs which follow. The first plan, for younger children, contains suggestions for the organization of the preacademic activities all of which are involved in visuo-motor training, eye-hand coordination, and which are related to the psychological problems which he had. These materials are those essentially discussed in Chapter VIII. The nature of the daily organization of learning experiences will vary from child to child due to differences in the children's attention spans, learning characteristics, and psychological need. The reader will note that one of the major characteristics in the organization of the learning experiences is that one activity is followed by another of great dissimilarity. This is essentially done to assist the child in minimizing the effect of perseveration. The daily schedule for academic levels illustrates this particularly.

Typical Daily Plans for Younger Learning Disabled Children:
Basic Readiness Level

Gross-motor training
Peg design
Matching shapes (color cued)
Puzzle (teacher made)
Copying geometric shapes
   a. matching
   b. drawing with crayons
Block design
Stencil (coloring within form)
Phonics—matching pictures with
   the same beginning consonant
   sound

Colors—matching and sorting
Chalkboard training
Writing—tracing with crayons
Arithmetic—matching config-
   uration cards
Sequence patterns
   a. similarities
   b. differences
Things that go together—matching
   picture cards
Geometric shapes
Writing—tracing numerals

Typical Daily Plans for Older Learning Disabled Children:
Academic Level

Gross-motor training
Peg design
Workbook—(reading) Part of the
   page correlated with story read
   the preceding day.
Copying geometric shapes
   a. Sequence patterns
      (completing the design)
   b. Copying designs
   c. Similarities
   d. Differences
Dictionary work (alternate days)
   a. Definitions
   b. Dividing words into syllables
   c. Telling how many syllables

Block design
Arithmetic (alternate days)
   a. Reading problems to work
      and solve
   b. Examples
Chalkboard training
Writing
Phonics (suggested activity from
   Guidebook)
Alphabetical order
Arithmetic (alternate days)
   a. Clock
   b. Fractions
   c. Writing numbers from words
   d. Dollar mark and decimal

Parquetry design (alternate days)
  a. Make design
  b. Cut and paste and make the
     design
Language (suggested activity from
  Guidebook)

Arithmetic
  a. Tens and ones
  b. Rote counting by 2's, 5's,
     10's, or 3's.
Spelling

The reader should note carefully the sequence which has been suggested both for the basic daily readiness program and the academic program. In each there is a planned order of presentation of the materials. Both programs begin with activities involving gross-motor training. From this the readiness program progresses to fine-motor activities involving peg boards, matching shapes, puzzles, copying, and so on through the program. The academic program also begins with gross-motor activities, and this is followed by some form of fine-motor activities prior to the initiation of the daily learning experiences of number concepts, writing, and activities broadly related to reading and language skills.

It will also be noted that both activity sequences take into consideration what has earlier been said about the perseverative nature of many brain-injured children. Thus, dictionary work is followed by block design activities, not by some activity involving language concepts. Arithmetic is followed by chalkboard activities, which is followed by writing, which is followed by another activity unrelated to the preceding one.

It is obvious that these are merely suggested models. Where fractions have been included in the example, short division, multiplication or other aspects of number concepts may be included for another child in accordance with his developmental needs.

SELECTED REFERENCE OF SPECIAL INTEREST TO PARENTS

Lewis, R. S.; Strauss, A. A.; and Lehtinen, L. E. *The Other Child.* 2nd ed. New York: Grune & Stratton, 1951.

SELECTED REFERENCES OF SPECIAL INTEREST TO TEACHERS

Bryant, N. O. "Characteristics of Dyslexia and Their Remedial Implication." *Exceptional Children* 31 (December 1964): 195–200.

Cruickshank, W. M.; Bentzen, Frances A.; Ratzeburg, F. H.; and Tannhauser, Mirian T. *A Teaching Method for Brain-Injured and Hyperactive Children.* Syracuse: Syracuse University Press, 1961.

Cruickshank, W. M., and Hallahan, D. P., eds. *Perceptual and Learning Disabilities in Children.* Syracuse: Syracuse University Press, 1975. In Vol. 1 see: Kephart, N. C., "The Perceptual-Motor Match"; Cruickshank, W. M., "The Psychoeducational Match"; Gaddes, W. H., "Neurological Implications for Learning"; Turton, L. J., "The Development of Linguistic Aspects of Learning."

deHirsch, K. "Concepts Related to Normal Reading Processes and Their Application to Reading Pathology." *Journal of Genetic Psychology* 102 (1963): 277–87.

Fernald, Grace M. *Remedial Techniques in Basic School Subjects.* New York: McGraw-Hill, 1946.

Freidus, Elizabeth S. "The Needs of Teachers for Specialized Information on Number Concepts." *The Teacher of Brain-Injured Children,* edited by W. M. Cruickshank. Syracuse: Syracuse University Press, 1966.

Frostig, Marianne. "The Needs of Teachers for Specialized Information on Reading." *The Teacher of Brain-Injured Children,* edited by W. M. Cruickshank. Syracuse: Syracuse University Press, 1966.

Gardner, R. W. "The Needs of Teachers for Specialized Information on the Development of Cognitive Structures." *The Teacher of Brain-Injured Children,* edited by W. M. Cruickshank. Syracuse: Syracuse University Press, 1966.

Kaliski, L. "Arithmetic and the Brain-Injured Child." *The Arithmetic Teacher* (May 1962): 245–51.

Kephart, N. C. *The Slow Learner in the Classroom.* 2nd ed. Columbus: Merrill, 1960.

Nudd, E."Perception of Pictured Social Interactions by Brain-Injured and Non–Brain-Injured Children of Normal Intelligence." *Exceptional Children* 24 (February 1958): 242–48, 281

Reed, J., and Reed, H. "Concept Formation Ability and Non-Verbal Abstract Thinking Among Older Children with Chronic Cerebral Dysfunction." *Journal of Special Education* 1 (1967): 157–61.

Strauss, A. A., and Lehtinen, L. E. *Psychopathology and Education of the Brain-Injured Child.* New York: Grune & Stratton, 1947.

Wade, B., and Wedell, K. *Spelling: Task and Learner.* Birmingham, England: University of Birmingham, School of Education, 1974.

10

Adolescents with Learning Disabilities

The ADOLESCENT with learning disabilities is one for whom little or no planning has been done in any coordinated manner—nationally, at the state level, or locally. Some few programs are in operation, but these are sporadic, often short lived, and many times opportunistic. A very few are good or long-standing in nature. The learning disabled elementary school children of the late thirties and forties are in some cases grandparents now; those of the sixties should be in the fullness of their lives. Whatever their status, particularly if it is positive, it is very likely *not* because of their school experiences, but in spite of them. If their lives are not being spent optimally, it is largely the responsibility of ineffective school programs, for even at the elementary level educators have hardly scratched the surface of the problem with meaningful and appropriate programming. At the secondary and college levels, almost nothing has been accomplished.

WHAT YOUTH TELL US

Few have concerned themselves with groups of learning disabled adolescents. There are some exceptions to that statement, but generally this is true. In my own professional practice, this is certainly the case, yet recently we have gone back over many folders of children and have been able to select quite a large number of those who now are junior-senior high school students and a much fewer number of students in community colleges or other types of higher education. Others are now employed in their communities. There are also many more examples of those who did not succeed in any of these avenues of education or work.

254

It is dangerous to use examples, for one can appear to prove most any point from a single example. However, we shall write briefly about some examples, and see what these young people tell us. From these statements we can attempt to make some generalizations and to suggest what is needed educationally.

A seventeen-year-old male is known to his friends by the name of *Luke*. His intelligence level is normal. He presents many perceptual processing deficits, although by no way are they as severe as six years earlier when he was first seen. He has failed his driving examination once, but anticipates that with tutorial help he will pass it on the second trial. "We can't get into driver education, you know," he reminds me. "They [the public school personnel] don't trust us. The driver school will take us, though—anything to make a buck. I am sure that I can do it the second time. The guy at the academy says that the driving examination is written at a third grade level, and I can do that." "How do you get around," I ask. "My pal has a car, and he drives. We do OK, or I guess I should say I do OK." Is driving an important issue for adolescents insofar as their psycho-social adjustment is concerned? Is this a matter which should be of concern to educational planners?

On another occasion Luke's case notes are of interest in a different sphere. We were visiting with him about the residuals of the perceptual-motor problems with which he and the clinic staff were working, and somehow the discussion veered to Luke's girlfriend. "Hell, I got problems I know," said Luke. "I've had those problems all my life and I guess I always will. Susie doesn't seem to mind. I mind, but Susie doesn't. She's a swell gal. I'll have to bring her in to meet you. You know, Dr. C., I don't have any perceptual-motor problems when Susie and I get into the back seat of John's car—what a gas!" Do these two vignettes, when generalized to the larger group, indicate concepts regarding the content of curriculum for adolescents who also have learning disabilities?

Alec is sixteen. He has been seen periodically in a good diagnostic facility since he was six years of age. He is a classic example of a child with perceptual processing deficits severe enough to have required that he receive individual tutoring for two years, that he be placed in a special clinical teaching program for three years, and later that he be assigned to a resource room through his so-called junior high school years. In high school, however, Alec was "mainstreamed," as his principal states in a letter to the clinic director. As a fourteen-year-old student, moving along in terms of social promotions, Alec demonstrated three years ago that he was functioning with a fourth-grade mathematics achievement, strong third-grade total reading scores, and an estimated intelligence score in the low one hundreds. While he had made a good social adjustment in the more sheltered situations, he started to deteriorate markedly concomitant with the mainstreaming experiences of the upper secondary school. At sixteen, where is he? He has had three severe brushes with the police. He is on marijuana and other drugs. His academic achievements are at a standstill. He had no genuine success experiences within his recall. He says to me, "It's like I don't exist in those god-damned teachers' classrooms. Mr. Carver didn't even say 'pardon me' when he stepped on my foot the other day. He just glared. I go to school only to please my dad and mother. To hell with the rest of them."

When one compares Alec and his present achievement levels, his progress, his attitudes, one sees a completely different individual than when he was in elementary, or even in junior high school, programs. He is lost. He has no basis for genuine achievement in the programs of the non-adjusting high school. He is receiving no attention from teachers, for they consider him as a failure and as a block to their content-oriented teaching. They do not understand him, and they do not want to be bothered to do so. Our questions are: Is mainstreaming a valid concept with the severely learning disabled? Is Alec, as representative of hundreds of others in similar situations, to have his life spoiled, his parents distraught, because of a fad of mainstreaming which is based on not one iota of valid research? Who indeed is the culprit—Alec or the educational establishment?

A third example consists of fifty sets of parents with whom the author has worked. These are all parents of male learning disabled children older than fourteen years of age. They are asked, "What are the hopes you have for your children?" What are their answers? In order of priority, the parents say:

1. I want my child to be able to get and hold a job.
2. I want my child to be socially and emotionally happy.
3. I want my child to be able to make appropriate decisions.
4. I want my child to have a girl friend. This later was expanded to a girl friend or a boy friend, since three parents stated their sons were undoubtedly homosexual.
5. I want my child to have the opportunity to enter the armed forces.
6. I want my child to have good sexual experiences.
7. I want my child to be able to function properly in the community insofar as purchasing, banking, and related matters are concerned.

These seven wants were the responses of the ten or more parents to each of the above-listed items. There were thirty-three other wants covering the total spectrum of adolescent–young adult adjustment and learning. A valid question is: Is there a curriculum obvious here in these "wants"; i.e., vocational or prevocational, human sexuality, social achievement, and academic?

Karen is a sixteen-year-old young lady with whom we have had contact since she was four. At four Karen was the bane of her family's existence. Characterized by hyperactivity and all of the psychological attributes by which children with perceptual processing deficits are described, Karen was a classical so-called learning disabled child. The community in which she lived was small and had no facilities for nursery school, preschool, or significant individual adaptations for troubled children at the elementary school level. Already a child with emotional problems as an overlay to her basic perceptual difficulties, adjustment problems were intensified when Karen was placed at six years of age with an aunt in a neighboring large city where university clinic facilities were available for her. She was enrolled in a clinical teaching situation at the university for four years until she was ten. Significant strides were made in terms of perceptual-motor reorganization, in the acquisition of basic learning skills, and in social adjustment. At ten she was placed in a neighborhood elementary school on a part-time basis, still living with the aunt and seeing her parents only on infrequent weekends or holidays. The trial placement in school appeared to be satisfactory; at least the school could tolerate Karen's problems and worked with the university program to maintain her positive growth. By twelve, Karen's primary problem was social and emotional. Her parents did not really know her and were pleased to write her off to her aunt. This did not help Karen, although the aunt was more than genuine in her interests in Karen. The aunt remarried at this juncture. Karen entered puberty and also faced the problems of adjusting in a junior high school. While academic success was sufficient to support her in elementary school, it was not sufficient to carry her into the junior high school with success. The change in the life pattern of her aunt, the physical changes of her own life, the inability of her academic experiences to provide success acceptable to her and her peers, and the inelasticity of the junior high school to support her with that which she needed accentuated her emotional problems. These were further complicated by the time she reached fourteen in a rampage of sexual activity which gave her a reputation throughout the school. She was socially labeled to the point of no return. For her, success experiences had been achieved. However, adults had other plans. It appeared wise to return her to her parent's home and into a new social climate not ladened with at least the former sexual cues, and where a different reputation might be created. Frequent trips to a therapeutic setting were initiated. The small high school into which she was entered in her parents' home community was traditional and had no member on the staff who understood or truly accepted the problems of children in need. College placement was the school goal, and the percentage of graduates who went on to college was high. Others dropped by the wayside.

Now at sixteen, Karen is hopelessly lost. Her sexual success patterns were begun again, and are well established. Therapy has a minimal influence. A discrepancy of six years exists between chronological age and academic achievement age. Perceptual processing deficits are not now a major factor, although even without the social and emotional situation she experiences, Karen would need assistance in order to improve her academic success rate. The question is: Who is at fault in the general ruin of Karen's young life? The state, which provided no support for services she needed as a child? The parents, for not having moved to a larger community and thus maintaining a wholesome relationship with their daughter? The university program, for isolating her from the realities of an elementary school program? The inflexibility of the secondary school programs? The aunt who unfortunately got married? The secondary schools for not having provided total guidance and counseling to Karen when she arrived in its classrooms? None or all of the above?

The day before *Jeff* arrived at a clinical teaching classroom as an eight-year-old, he had been permanently excluded from the Boys' Club facilities in his city, because he had ripped up three pool-table covers. With that evidence added to the boy's already growing file, the public schools likewise excluded him. The relationship between the two actions is possible to see, but cloudy at best. For three years Jeff prospered in varying degrees in the clinical teaching program of a nearby university. The first year was more than difficult for both Jeff and the staff, but progress through careful nurturing, a highly structured teaching program, parent involvement, and well-prepared teachers paid off, and Jeff gradually turned failure into success experiences. At the end of three years, a part-time trial placement was undertaken in the community schools with supportive resource facilities available. The educational program for Jeff continued within the frame of reference of his previous special class experiences. His achievement continued. His social adjustment did not regress, except for the usual problems of a preadolescent child's adjustment. Jeff was continually promoted on a chronological age basis through the junior high school years. Always he was given one-to-one support either at the university clinic on an out-patient basis, or with carefully supervised university students on either an outreach or practicum basis. As he reached sixteen years he was transferred to a vocational high school where the status quo *maintenance* of his academic achievement was the only goal in that area of his development, but where prevocational testing and training was the primary concept. He was given a variety of community-based, supervised, prevocational experiences. Often there was failure, because this once-classical perceptually handicapped boy still was characterized by a residual of processing deficits, although his understanding of his problem was complete and his compensatory mechanisms were plentiful. There were frequent contacts for purposes of guidance from the high school to university personnel, and the parents were fully supportive. Jeff had his problems; there is no denial of that. He sowed his wild oats in a variety of adolescent ways. The security of his home and the closeness of his relationship with one of the university faculty members was a great support as he experimented with fast driving, beer, girls, marijuana, more fast driving, the police, and with aggressions against adults generally. The goal was to keep what may be considered normal adolescent behavior separated from the perceptual processing deficits and his learning problems in the minds of all who worked with him.

A prevocational placement in supermarket employment, the second in this type of activity, appeared to be a success. The manager asked if he wanted to work full time during the summer. Jeff was eighteen by then. He was told that if he did accept the job, he would be counted on to be on time, courteous, clean, off beer during working hours, and more important, he expected to build his skills with numbers, for he would be doing stock clerk and inventory work that summer. Fortunately, this was a success. He started going with a girl. His job continued into the fall. He dropped out of school. He and his girl started to live together. A baby arrived. They decided they could and should marry. Parent support was evidenced throughout. At twenty-two Jeff is still with the supermarket chain. He is now assistant night manager. His wife helps him with those things he needs to know and read where his skills remain deficient. The food chain knows something of his background from the original school placement. The manager sees no reason why in the future he should not move at least one step further up the employment ladder. Interestingly, his relationship with the university faculty member has always been maintained—originially as a professional in his special teaching situation, later as an anchor in times of trouble, and at the moment, although several hundred miles separate them, still as an anchor, but also as a good friend.

Greg is nineteen, a young man whom the author first knew as a boy of seven years of age. He has completed his junior year in a high school in a large middle-class community. When Greg was smaller he had dozens of problems which brought him into conflict with the teaching staffs of two schools. He made great strides during the three years he was in a clinical teaching situation in the nearby university clinic, and he was later transferred back to the public schools. Although currently he has a diagnosis of dyslexia, he was earlier seen as a child with most of the classic symptoms of perceptual and learning disabilities which we have described here. Greg was always an appealing boy, one who could attract attention by his good looks. His behavior soon belied his otherwise cherubic outward expression, and he was in constant conflict with teachers or other authorities. His early case record reads like a horror story.

However, Greg had achieved the rudiments of learning skills by the time he was eleven. He prospered in the public schools, although with a tremendous amount of effort on his part and that of his parents and some teachers. Junior high school was a real crisis for Greg, for the inability of the schools to adjust to his needs plus the onset of normal adolescent growth and behavior mitigated against him. It was sometimes touch and go. However, he made it, and completed the eleventh grade. Mathematics ability was at least at grade level if not above. Reading was at a minimal eighth grade level.

His twelfth grade program was to be planned. At this point two things happened. First, the guidance counselor of the high school insisted that his records from his seventh and eighth chronological years be submitted for study. It is difficult to understand the reason there was a need for these records. In the hands of an uninsightful person, these records could only do harm. The fact that exceptional children do often cease to be exceptional was completely ignored by this guidance counselor. The relationship between Greg's needs at seven years of age to his needs eleven years later is hard to understand. The clinic director wisely refused to release the records. The guidance counselor responded by saying that they were not needed anyway, for Greg's fifth grade records had been found "tucked away" someplace, and these would serve the desired purpose. The desired purpose was never specified.

Secondly, Greg and his parents were told that Greg could probably be granted a diploma at the end of the twelfth grade, but that it would be stamped "Dyslexic." What in the name of conscience this would accomplish is hard to understand. Furthermore, in many states such labeling of such a document is illegal, and suit could be instituted against the Board of Education, the superintendent of schools, and the building principal. More such suits ought to be initiated in defense of children and youth who have struggled and succeeded. When challenged regarding this potential action, the reply by the high school principal was "Well, Greg's a fine boy and has done a god job, but I couldn't possibly give him one of my diplomas without somehow noting all the problems he has had." Advocacy has a place in every community. In Greg's case, still not fully resolved, advocacy against such bureaucratic attitudes and possessiveness is certainly warranted. Such, however, are the problems that well-intentioned adolescents with learning disabilities must often face as they attempt to succeed within the secondary school arena.

RESPONSES TO YOUTH'S NEEDS

We have described a set of children with learning disabilities. Grown into youth and young adulthood they present a variety of problems, some sad and as failures, others modestly successful, and at least one with the potential of reasonable adult adjustment. What generalizations can be made?

In spite of the commonly held statement, not all children with perceptual processing deficits grow out of them as adolescence appears. Some may, abut we have no broad-based data to illustrate that this is a firm and general rule by any means. We hope that all will outgrow their deficits, but in the face of reality, thousands carry their problems into adolescence and adulthood. Maturity seemingly does have a leavening effect, however. Adult insights which can be developed in the youth assist in the individual's adjustment.

In going back over the comments made by the young people referred to here, what are their specific concerns? Several are immediately apparent: a need for driver education; a need for human fulfillment; a need for success experiences; a need for techniques to provide positive social acceptance; a need for freedom (under appropriate adult monitoring) for social and personal experimentation; a need for pre- and ongoing vocational evaluation and training; a need for personal security in social situations; a need for training and education at interest and capacity levels; a need for information regarding marital responsibilities and child growth and development; and a need to be able to be an adolescent without misinterpretation.

If these needs, not an exhaustive list by any means, are logically grouped, three major categories become apparent: (1) human fulfillment, (2) educational, and (3) vocational. Let us examine them in this order.

Human Fulfillment

It must be understood from the beginning that the handicapped are not asexual beings. There is an absolute myth held by many parents and a large segment of society in general to the effect that human sexuality is something which does not affect the handicapped. "Thank God. I don't have to worry about my son and his virginity," said a father to the writer on one occasion. "He'll always be one. He can't walk." It's only wine and song for my boy," commented a mother. "He'll never have to worry about the women in the verse. But then, he doesn't have that need, what with his handicap." "Do perceptually handicapped people have normal sex drives?" writes a parent. These comments and questions reflect ignorance.

Perceptually handicapped youth and adults do have sex drives, of course. They also have more than the need for the mere physical relationships in sex. Human fulfillment or human sexuality encompasses the totality of the concept of love in its broadest definition. Human fulfillment means a parental and social concern for the physical well-being of the youth, for his emotional and social well-being, and for freedom to grow normally into these spheres of human behavior. The security of two parents who are accepting, and the satisfactions learned by the youth through the structure of a good early childhood and elementary education, make it possible for the young man or woman to experiment, to test this dimension of human experience, and to broaden his or her own horizons of experience. Parents often must worry, must hold their peace, must exert self-control as well as extend a minimum of specific direction for the adolescent. The extent of parental worries about their children's behavior will be a reflection of the depth of the dialogue which has existed between and among family members from early on. All that one would wish between parents and normal children must also prevail between parents and youth with learning disabilities.

It must be recognized that in our society the child of eight is an independent, voting adult a decade later. From the point of physical maturity, the learning disabled is not different from any other youth of comparable age level. That youth, whether man or woman, has needs on occasion to experiment with his body, to push it to the point of physical exhaustion, and to learn pride in his body and what it can do. The youth has need, depending on circumstance, to engage in sexual behavior of his choice with the security of knowing that he is ready for it, is intellectually prepared, and is supported in his actions by an accepting society. Like Jeff, the young man with the severest of perceptual processing deficits, the learning disabled youth with the support of family and friends must move unhesitatingly into marriage, if that be *his* or *her* desire, and be able to engage in the totality of a married life including the rearing of his own children. Is this asking too much of society? The role of the schools appears obvious. Can society, by whatever dimension, arbitrate that youth with perceptual processing deficits be denied those things which go to make up a full life? Years ago Professor Franklin Bobbitt of the University of Chicago used to speak of human fulfillment as the attainment of "the good life." He was ahead of his time by four decades at least.

Where are the essentials of the good life learned? First they are learned through the modeling of two secure parents. In the greater number of instances they are learned through the total program of the schools—a place where today human fulfillment and all it implies is usually ignored or vigorously avoided.

Perceptually handicapped and learning disabled youth have all the needs of all youth. The home and, particularly, the schools, cannot disenfranchise handicapped young people in this area of development. The schools need to face this challenge and the parents must support these areas of learning. Human fulfillment cannot be left to chance, to the gutter, to word of mouth, to fear. Nor by avoiding the issue do parents or the larger society have the right to impose on these young people fears, guilt feelings, psychological impotence, or other negativisms which are controlling and self-defeating. Youth with a history of perceptual and learning disabilities have had enough of such life tones. They do not need now to warp their lives further. The learning disabled youth and young adult has a human right to the beauty of human sexuality in its richest forms.

Educational Needs

The fact that youth with these problems exist means that something must be done about them at the junior-senior high school levels and, for a smaller number, in the community college or other types of higher education programs. This will be difficult because the educational settings are content oriented rather than individual oriented.

The fact that the secondary schools are not presently receptive to the individual differences of children presents a totally new and somewhat different challenge for parents with youth with learning disabilities. It is essential, from my point of view, that parent organizations, having begun a reasonable program for young children, again muster their energies and begin a national, state, and local attack on public educational facilities to open up the secondary schools to youth with perceptual processing deficits.

What must be available in the long term for these children? First, there must be sensitive teachers and administrators who understand or who are brought to understand the unique individual differences of this population of youth.

As we have already stated, secondary school teachers are generally content oriented, often to the point where their view of the *learner* of the content is blurred or completely lost. Certification programs for secondary school teachers contain a maximum of subject matter courses and a minimum of information about human beings, their childhood and adolescent development. Concepts of individualization of instruction are read about but rarely integrated into a way of a teacher's life or practical application. College preparation is a goal, even often a nonverbalized goal, held by many of those teachers who work in center-city schools or with disadvantaged populations of youth. The focus of all too many teachers is on the number of their pupils who pass the New York State Regents examinations, earn Merit Scholarships, who enter the university directly out of high school, or obtain high scores on the SAT! To recall a high school graduation is proof. Scholars are rewarded. Even some athletes are recognized for their prowess. Where is the recognition of the learning disabled youth who, by sheer dint of a good education, of supportive parents, a unique teacher, and his own persistence, has achieved a high fifth-grade reading ability and success in four prevocational experiences? That youth's diploma, if there were one, should be embossed in gold and he should be given a standing ovation. Who in the schools ever genuinely rewarded Jeff for becoming an assistant manager of the night shift in the grocery store? Educators speak of meeting the individual needs of children, but rarely do they or the schools they work in demonstrate this point of view. If the learning disabled child is to be accepted into the secondary schools, the schools must be characterized by administrators, teachers, and programs which are truly responsive to the nature and needs of the youth they purport to serve. What is the point of this?

If secondary educators are to meet the needs of a large number of youth with learning disabilities, at least three things must be accomplished. First, teacher education programs must provide a thorough understanding of the nature and needs of young people who arrive in junior and senior high schools still characterized by educationally and socially debilitating perceptual processing deficits. Preservice teachers must have a broad orientation to all types of exceptionality, but since this book is focused on the perceptual processing deficits and the learning disabled child, it is this group to which we give consideration now. Secondly, teachers in service must receive or be given the opportunity to learn about these young people and to understand ways in which they can be assisted. Mainstreaming without teacher orientation will definitely be a failure.

Finally, if the youth arrives at the secondary level with perceptual processing deficits which are functional to his disadvantage, his total educational achievement level also will probably be limited—reading, number concepts, and related areas of school learning. If this be the case, it is logical that there must be included within the teaching corps of the secondary schools some elementary educators who, by reason of their specialized training and preparation to work with children characterized by perceptual processing deficits, can meet effectively the continuing needs of such youths. The needs of learning disabled youths, *if the processing deficits are still present and apparent,* is for exactly the same type of educational training activities as used with younger children. Obviously these have to be adjusted to a higher social interest level, spoken vocabulary, and to the youth's greater experience.

The author is reminded of a twenty-eight-year-old first sergeant in his hospital during World War II who could not sign his name, who found it difficult to judge distances, who was originally in a special training unit set by the Army for high-grade retarded soldiers, and who needed his company clerk to read orders, regulations, and other items which arrived on his desk. He had taught himself techniques of adjustment, and he succeeded. Others are not so fortunate.

Don is a twenty-three-year-old married man who was referred by his employer for assistance. He was in charge of a large department in industry. He could not write or read. His wife assisted him, and he did well on his supervisory job. In the clinic his perceptual-motor skills were at times below expectancy for an early childhood level. How he reached maturity as a well-adjusted young man almost defied logic. He willingly entered into private therapy which began at a reading readiness level and included color-form sorting; recognition of the meaning of line segments, forms, and shapes; recognition of letters and numerals; and perceptual-motor training of a very primitive level. Motivation, of course, was high and played a role. Within a two-year period this man was reading at a strong third-grade level, was signing his name to his own handwritten checks, and was emotionally elated at his progress. His personal irritation related to his anger at not having been given the opportunity to advance a decade earlier.

It is this type of radical educational adjustment which must become one of the characteristics of the educational program for learning disabled youths in high schools. The secondary schools must make available highly individualized learning and teaching programs which are geared to the residual needs of the youth and which will—when he is an adolescent—provide him with genuine success experiences seen as such by both him and his parents and accepted as such by his less handicapped peers. This means that Gallagher's tutorial concept will follow these youth into the secondary school, along with the special teaching program as may be required for small groups, the resource room, and a healthy and appropriate program of integration where possible. We reiterate that if these individual educational adaptations are required at the elementary level, we must face the fact that they may also be needed in some cases at the secondary level. The provision of each and all of the techniques which we have mentioned will mean that youth with needs characterized from extreme to mild may be served. The cost of this can only be offset by an understanding and real appreciation of what the failure to provide will mean in terms of life span, lowered tax payments, welfare costs, delinquency manifestations, police and jail costs, psychiatric fees, and unhappy lives which damage the whole community in the long run.

Vocational Education

A focus must of necessity be placed at a minimum on at least the type of prevocational education, community trial placement, and vocational placement which Jeff experienced. The technical or vocational school concepts so often found in community schools is little different from content-oriented English, history, and science teaching. There are many such facilities which have a rigorous admissions policy, sometimes more restrictive than college-oriented academic programs.

Simply stated a mechanism has to be found whereby exploratory prevocational and vocational experiences can be provided to youth who retain significant perceptual processing deficits. These young people are important. Their needs must be met. Prevocational and vocational educators must be found whose interests and values can be directed to this population of adolescents. There must be a close working relationship among all educators who have direct contact with the child who retains perceptual processing deficits. There are more things which many of these young people can accomplish—driving a car included for some—than there are those which are unobtainable. This is an area which is almost completely unexplored by educators. It cannot remain in this ignored status longer.

Not one of the items briefly discussed here is beyond the reach of a society which cares. Since it does not always care, private organizations will have to provide pressure. Professionals are not strong enough to do this alone.

It is absolutely necessary that youth with perceptual processing deficits be seen for what they are. What is normative in their growth and development and what is specific to their learning disability? Normal growth and its adolescent problems must be separated from the processing deficits by those who work with these children and youth. As Luke reminded us, he has few if any perceptual-motor problems when he is out on a date with his girl friend. He functions then as a normal man. Yet the very fact that Luke must remind us of this is his way of saying he would like to be able to talk about it with someone who can help him put this aspect of his life in perspective. There is most frequently an emotional overlay observable in the young people about whom we speak, a carryover from childhood as the result of a life history of failure. This is a learned response to a failure experience. It is not an inherent characteristic of perceptual deficits. If this adjustment is carried into adolescence and is mixed with the daily emotional tensions of adolescent-adult growth, then another type of support is involved. Somewhere in the community there must be available to these youths an adult friend or a counseling service which understands their needs. This does not always have to be a formal service. A buddy system is often successful. A big brother or sister concept works well in many instances. A school counselor may be helpful. We could go on. The point we make is not to describe such a program, but to insist that it be planned into the life of the youth in some manner.

In the preceding pages we have emphasized our long-standing opinion that structure as a tool of instruction is a vital and necessary factor in the learning and development of children with learning disabilities. The confusion which the child experiences as a result of the unpredictability of the perceptual processing problems can only be offset by the thoughtful and intelligent structuring of his learning environment and program. With the onset of puberty and the child's growth into adolescence, emotions, physical development, and social expectancies regarding him constitute further sources for confusion and tension. Although the specifics of structure must change and accommodate the older youth, the necessity for a structure which will provide him with the security he seeks (but often also rejects) must be provided. Here the art of parenting or teaching becomes obvious. The capacity to provide freedom to explore and to develop within the adolescent peer culture must be granted the youth while at the same time leaving him with the knowledge that an adult structural base is constantly available to him which he can use as a yardstick for his learning, growth, and behavior.

Adolescence has often been described as a period of contradictions—simultaneous love and rejection of adults; emotional stability and moodiness; fastidiousness and complete disregard for personal cleanliness and care of possessions; charm and gross vulgarity; desire to be wanted and complete rejection of those who would attempt to own or control. Within these dimensions, each with a pendulum which may swing with a different speed, the adolescent often finds himself in a vortex of misunderstanding—misunderstanding of himself and of the social situation around him. The need for structure, an external framework which he can use to learn and experience an orderly pattern to life, is greatly accentuated during these years.

The Lukes, the Alecs, and the Karens of this nation—representative of thousands of youths and young adults—are not going to grow like Topsy into acceptable adults except by chance. This nation cannot afford such careless planning. We are at the point where the plank in our national charter for these children guarantees life-span planning. Nothing less is acceptable.

SELECTED REFERENCES OF SPECIAL INTEREST TO PARENTS AND TEACHERS

Morse, W. C. "The Learning Disabled Child and Considerations of Life Space." In *Perceptual and Learning Disabilities in Children,* edited by W. M. Cruickshank and D. P. Hallahan. Syracuse: Syracuse University Press, 1975. Vol. 1, Chapter 11.

Newman, Ruth G. *Psychological Consultation in the Schools: A Catalyst for Learning.* New York: Basic Books, 1967.

————. "The School-Centered Life Space Interview as Illustrated by Extreme Threat of School Issues." *American Journal of Orthopsychiatry* 33 (1963): 4.

Siegel, E. *The Exceptional Child Grows Up.* New York: Dutton, 1974.

Valett, R. E. *The Remediation of Learning Disabilities: A Handbook of Psychoeducational Resource Programs.* Palo Alto: Fearon, 1967.

————. *Learning Disabilities: Diagnostic-Prescriptive Instruments.* Belmont, Calif.: Lear Siegler/Fearon, 1973.

————. *Prescriptions for Learning: A Parent's Guide to Remedial Home Training.* Belmont, Calif.: Fearon, 1970.

11

The Overall Program

W E HAVE BEEN describing the nature of the educational program essentially as it pertains to the classroom, but the concept of the educational program for learning disabled children must often extend considerably beyond the school. Three elements are particularly important in the total planning for learning disabled children, namely, motor training, psychotherapeutic supports, and language development.

MOTOR TRAINING

The place of motor training in the education of perceptually handicapped children is an important one. There is some difference of opinion, however, concerning the relationship of motor training to the total program. There is little question among professional educators of learning disabled children that the great majority of these children need both gross- and fine-motor movement training and that they need it regularly over long periods of time. Motor training, however, cannot be the total program, nor should it be allowed to substitute for other aspects of the total educational and therapeutic program. Not all learning disabled children need long programs of motor training in order to achieve satisfactory levels of physical and personality integration.

On the other hand, enough has already been said here about the learning disabled child and his characteristics of incoordination and lack of motor skills to emphasize for the reader this author's concern that an appropriate program of motor development be followed. The problem in question admittedly has not been the subject of sufficient research, a

statement largely true of the total field of programming for learning disabled children. One study, however, has provided some evidence that there
is no relationship whatsoever between a child's "creeping" ability and his
reading skills. Until more research is offered in support of this point of
view, parents and professional persons should be cautious of any school of
thought which puts its total emphasis on a single aspect such as motor
training. The only published statements in support of creeping as an important medium of neurological organization are those of the advocates of
the point of view, who base their opinions on theoretical rather than on
objective experimental results. In spite of this, some parents in their
desperate effort to assist their children go to great extremes insisting that
their children creep rather than walk for extended periods of time. Time
has already indicated in some of these cases that the decision was an erroneous one; in others, time yet must tell whether positive or negative out-
comes are to be achieved.

Most of the authorities we have cited in this book are of the opinion
that motor training *in an appropriate relationship to other facets of the
total program* should be an integral part of the child's daily schedule. It is
strongly recommended that the decision concerning how much time is to
be devoted to motor training be made only in connection with a carefully
developed interdisciplinary evaluation. A determination should be made
on the basis of the child's total developmental history and current status.
In general, we have found it wise to include in each child's school day
from fifteen to thirty minutes of intensive gross-motor training (see
Figure 44). Sometimes more time is assigned, perhaps a second period
later in the day. The teacher should always be aware of the motor aspect
of all learning, and this aspect should be emphasized appropriately in the
activities which make up the balance of the school experiences.

This author has witnessed some weird approaches to the education of
children based upon motor training when the educators had no systematic
understanding of its role. In one school system, whether he needed it or
not, every child in the elementary school spent some time each morning
creeping and crawling in the school gymnasium, and in addition the
children practiced swimming motions lying on their stomachs on the floor.
This was the full extent of the motor program. In another school situation
all children underwent the creeping regimen. Some of these children,
several of whom were severely mentally retarded, had been creeping for
as much as five hours a day for as long as eighteen months. It is hard to
justify either of these extremes, although this author will undoubtedly be
criticized by many for questioning the validity of the approach. Suffice to
say that at this writing there is not one published piece of research which
would support either example we have given or which would give support

Figure 44. Motor training, here utilizing a walking rail, is an integral part of the daily educational program of perceptually handicapped or learning disabled children.

to an approach to learning disabled children which is based solely on the repetition of these primitive motor skills. In the first example, the elementary school children who are perfectly well coordinated and who need no motor training are being required to undergo it when their time could be better used in other activities related to learning. The children who do need the experience will be helped more if the training is more structured and presented on a more individual basis. In the second example, one wonders what the self-concept of a child is after eighteen months of crawling. What is his attitude toward the adults who insist upon such unusual behavior? What kind of a body image is envisioned by the child? What is the basis for wholesome parent-child relationships in this type of educational milieu? These are questions which parents who are seriously concerned about their children should ask themselves and also answer honestly and accurately before placing a child in such a program.

We have already said that well-conceived and appropriately balanced motor training is important. It is an essential aspect of the total educational and therapeutic program for learning disabled children. It is but *one* aspect in several, however. The total consists of education, speech and language development, psychotherapy, parent counseling, *and* motor training. We have previously stated that interdisciplinary diagnosis is necessary; we now also state that interdisciplinary programming is a second absolute for learning disabled children. Each of the five ingredients just mentioned is essential. Their individual weights in a given child's program will depend upon the child's needs as they are known through both the initial diagnosis and the continuing evaluations. Motor training, it can be observed, is one element in the total picture of life planning for the child.

It is essential also to differentiate between motor training and the usual physical education program in an elementary school. There is a difference. The physical education program may place an emphasis on physical fitness, and to that end children may engage in a variety of exercises and compete with each other for high achievement in them. The motor-training program is concerned essentially with the development of motor coordination and the appropriate utilization of motor skills. The physical education program accomplishes its goals partly through the use of competitive games and sports. The motor-training program is not concerned with competition whatsoever, and most of its activities are carried on in an individual instructional setting. Some of the skills which the learning disabled child practices and uses may, of course, be related to the activities of baseball, soccer, or tennis, but improvements in ability to participate in these games are coincidental to the primary purpose of the motor training. Motor training is intended to bring the child into a full awareness of his body as an effective tool to learning. Motor training must have as its purpose the development of a good body image, and this may develop only from the child's recognition that he is the master of his body and his knowledge of how it is to function for him in all situations. Gross-motor functions will be emphasized which lead to fine-motor functions.

Both Gerald N. Getman and N. C. Kephart have outlined the nature of the motor-training program completely, and it is unnecessary to repeat again what has been said better elsewhere. Kephart emphasizes the signifi cance of the "perceptual-motor match," a process by which "perceptual information is matched to earlier motor information." "Through this matching procedure, perceptual data come to supply the same consistent body of information that the previous motor data supplied. By this means a consistent body of information, which can be translated back and forth between motor and perceptual abilities, is established." In different words, this is essentially the statement which Ayres makes and to which we have made earlier references, i.e., intellectual growth is an appropriate response to a motor act. The significance of what Kephart says can hardly be overemphasized. There is a close interrelationship between motor activities which are initially of a gross, exploratory nature in early childhood and perceptual skills of later developmental years. When the child has experienced motor activities normally, and appropriate to his stages of development, and when perceptual skills are equally practiced and experienced, they can in reality become cues for the child which permit him, vicariously, to experience whole sequences of motor acts without actually having to participate in them. In psychology this is referred to as "cue reduction." He understands without having to engage in the direct activity what the teacher means when he says, "He cut the paper along the straight line at the top of the page," or when the parent says, "Please sit down and eat now. Pick up your knife and fork and cut your meat." The child understands, without having to be shown, that he is expected to cut his meat; he does not have to experience the task before he can accomplish it again. The child can understand what the teacher means when he hears him say that someone cut along a straight line. Auditory and visual cues are substituted for motor activity. This is possible, however, only when successful motor activities have been experienced in the life of the child. When they are lacking, as they usually are in learning disabled children, some time each day must be spent in developing these missing abilities.

Ray H. Barsch has added the concept of *triordination*. He points out that the term "motor coordination" is really not accurate, although it is popularly and widely used. He stresses that with the problem of motor training, the adult must keep a different perspective in mind, namely the

fact that "the human organism moves on and around a set of three or-
dinates. He moves vertically, horizontally, and on the depth axis." Motor
training, then, is not just a matter of putting two things together—it is a
matter of harmoniously converging all three planes into a working relationship to guarantee movement efficiency. Movement efficiency broadly
defined is indeed the ultimate to be desired as a result of a good program
of motor training. Movement efficiency must be thought of not only in
terms of gross bodily movement, but movements of the eye along the
printed line, such as the visual conception of a problem on a blackboard
and the correct translation of it in writing on the paper in front of the individual, or the auditory recognition of the emergency call of the mother
("Look out!") and the proper withdrawal of the hand from an electric
wire. Barsch appropriately suggests that all motor training is developmental. Not only is two-dimensional experience required, i.e., walking on
a "walking-rail," but with the same equipment the child needs experience
in walking the rail while targeting on a point in the distance without
watching foot placement or other cues. Each of these situations involves
the appropriate interpretation of the perceptual stimulus into an equally
appropriate movement. The existence of the human organism is dependent on the development of these relationships.

The Parents' Role

In the area of motor training the parent can play a very significant role
which can be both independent of what the school is doing and supportive
of it. In the informality of the home there are many ways in which parents
can provide interesting activities for their children which are related to
the child's motor development. These activities should be planned, and
educational personnel are usually happy to help parents make appropriate plans. It is again suggested that the parent become familiarized
with the Getman motor-training program as it is so well outlined in the
Physiology of Readiness, cited in the list of references at the end of this
chapter. It is wise too for the parent to discuss this matter with the school
personnel to ascertain what things can be done to support the school
activities which may already be in progress as well as to be certain that
the home activities which are being planned are indeed the correct ones
for the child.

Beyond the specific motor-training program, however, the parents
can provide for the child almost unlimited opportunities for gross physical
activity. If the child's own home is not equipped with a backyard for play

activities, then frequent trips to a neighborhood park should be scheduled so the child can experiment with and play with a variety of equipment. In the home backyard, parents can frequently provide climbing apparatus, balancing boards, walking rails, "Jungle Gyms," swings, basketball nets, and many other types of things which give the perceptually handicapped child practice in motor skills and in eye-hand coordination. "Pogo Sticks," dart games, various types of target activities, strength-development equipment, bicycles and tricycles, scooters, and other forms of leg pumping equipment are useful in play activities. Parents, the father in particular, will need to give a considerable amount of time to the learning disabled child, patiently helping him to develop the triordinate skills which will give him a feeling of command over his body. Time spent in learning to catch a baseball, getting a basketball through the hoop, or hitting a practice golf ball can be fun for both father and child and at the same time provide the child with the gross-motor practice essential to the development of fine-motor skill necessary in activities of the classroom and dining room and in dressing and writing.

The types of motor activities just described should be carried out free from the distractions of other children. The learning disabled child will usually not be able to perform as well as other children of his own age, at least initially. If several children are attracted to the activity, competition is bound to develop, and the learning disabled child will probably lose interest and drop out of the play. On the other hand, if father and child can use this as a time together when comparisons are not being made constantly, sufficient success can be insured for the learning disabled boy so that the experience not only is a healthy one in terms of motor training, but can be a splendid basis for strong parent-child relationships. Good feeling will then carry over into areas where skills are not so well developed and where parental guidance is more frequently demanded—eating, for example.

These motor-training periods at home should follow a consistent schedule, as has previously been suggested in discussing the need for generally structuring the child's day in both home and school. If the father cannot participate in the activity, then perhaps an older brother or sister can do so. At other times, a neighborhood high school boy who is patient can be employed to spend an hour or so each afternoon after school in supervising and in participating in appropriate motor activities with the learning disabled child.

This author has mixed feelings about the utilization of the ordinary swimming pool for motor-training activities. The swimming pool provides opportunities for recreation as well as motor training; kicking and arm movements can be practiced in a variety of ways more easily than on land.

If the child enjoys the swimming pool, in general he should be encouraged to use it. Many learning disabled children, however, are not ready for the typical swimming pool. Some children become disturbed because of the spaciousness of the room in which the pool is situated. The perceptual problems of some children make it difficult for them to understand what they are expected to do. The ripples on the surface of the pool, the echoes in the room, and the splashes and resulting drops of water constitute distracting stimuli for the child. Consequently some children are just plain scared, and it is better not to urge the continued use of the pool. Sometimes, however, even when the child is insecure, he can find satisfactions if his activities are centered in a shallow part of the pool and are restricted to one corner of the pool area. Here the two sides of the pool come together and constitute sufficient structure to permit him to adjust. It is the feeling of the author that swimming pool activities, while excellent for the purposes of motor skill development, should be carried on individually whenever possible.

Parents rarely give enough attention to the nature of toys which are purchased for their children. In purchasing toys for a learning disabled child, the parent should keep in mind both the mental age of the child and the developmental skills which the toy or game may require. Much excellent fine-motor training can be provided a child in the activities of playing a game. However, it must be recognized that the attention span of a perceptually handicapped child is short and that the game behavior of the child is probably not the same as that of an adult. The adult must expect that often a game will not be completed because the child has been distracted by something else. Checkers, card games involving sorting or rapid movements and reactions, toys with large pieces that can be assembled into something else, and games requiring accuracy all provide opportunities for the development of eye-hand coordination within a pleasurable setting. Adult participation, however, is an essential. Rarely will the child's attention span permit him to carry on solo activities for any length of time. His perceptual problems will be sufficient interferences so that he will become discouraged quickly if the adult is not present to keep the activity going smoothly and to motivate the child to continue.

The writer is well aware that he is asking for a great quantity of adult time, time which often is not available or which requires the sacrifice of something important to the adult. This time is needed when the child is young perhaps more than at any other time in his life and almost more than any other thing in his life—it is that important. Parents will have to make choices. The parents' choice will often determine whether the child makes the grade toward good adjustment to the maximum of capacity or a submarginal adjustment throughout his life.

A completely sheltered program is not advocated for the learning disabled child. Insofar as he can find satisfactions in group play and in competitive games, he should be encouraged to participate. Since most learning disabled children need individual motor training, we would suggest that group activities not be permitted to substitute completely for the activities which have been suggested in the preceding paragraphs.

The Motor Program in School

Although the motor-training program in the home should be informal, that of the school should be carefully planned and integrated.

Getman advocates a program involving six major phases, including practice in general coordination, balance, eye-hand coordination, eye movement, form perception, and visual memory. According to Getman, motor activity may be measured on a developmental scale from gross to fine, from broad general physical activities to those involving visual memory.

Practice in general coordination includes exercises involving head movements, bilateral actions (involving arm movements, leg movements, head and arm movements, arm and leg movements, bilateral arm, and leg movements), alternating actions of head, arms, and legs, and exploration of the body function in relationship to gravity. In the latter exercises skills involving jumping, hopping, skipping, rolling sit-ups, and other similar activities are suggested and outlined.

Practice in balance is primarily developed by utilization of the walking beam in varying ways. A walkingbeam can be constructed easily and without too great expense. The exercises which are recommended are not solely for the development of skills insofar as arms and legs or balance are concerned but also for the development of skills in relation to visual usage. For example, in the walking beam exercises, the child should be encouraged to walk the beam without watching the beam itself but focusing upon targets ahead of him or in varying relations to the beam. Getman recommends exercises involving forward and backward walking as well as those employing peripheral targets.

The chalkboard is the principal tool used in eye-hand coordination routines. As Getman states, the overall purpose of this phase of motor training is "to assist the children to gain the greatest possible integration of the visual-tactual systems of a foundation on which all symbolic interpretations and manipulations can be based." It is not useful to discuss these exercises in detail here; suffice it to say that they involve the visual-tactual concepts employing bilateral circles, horizontal lines, vertical lines, and abilities to function appropriately on a visual and motor relationship using other concrete experiences. These exercises are performed in order to adduce appropriate concepts. It is felt that these exercises, employing concepts which the normal child has experienced in a coincidental relationship to his total life development, but which the perceptually handicapped child has partially or completely missed, will provide the unifying experiences the child needs to permit his smoother function in still finer motor activities. Furthermore, it is suggested that these activities are an integral part of the base out of which learning disabled children, albeit belatedly, are able to construct healthy self-concepts.

The remaining activities Getman outlines and which are related to eye movements, form perception, and visual memory are not different from those discussed elsewhere by others. However, they are organized in a very convenient manner, permitting their easy incorporation into the child's program by the teacher or parent.

Kephart's program is much the same as those of Getman and Barsch. Similarly, the program advocated by B. J. Cratty has much to commend itself to parents as has that of A. Jean Ayres mentioned earlier. One major emphasis of the Kephart approach also utilized by Getman is *chalkboard training.* From exceedingly primitive activities involving scribbling, the child is guided to the development of directionality, space orientation, form recognition, and to concepts of length, parallel relationships, and proportion. These concepts in most children are acquisitions coincident to their normal growth and experience. They are nevertheless concepts which are basic to the individual's adjustment. In the perceptually handicapped child, because of the neurological insult, they are aspects of development which must be consciously taught and learned.

Since the normal child rarely needs any major assistance in learning these aspects of perception, elementary school teacher education programs rarely emphasize teaching them; elementary school teachers are rarely able to initiate this program. It is thus necessary for someone in the elementary or special education program to be assigned the responsibility of learning the concept and method of motor training. Knowledge of motor training is an essential aspect of the orientation of the teacher of learning disabled children.

Kephart also emphasized memory-motor training, and he employed the walking rail or beam as does Getman. He expanded on this phase of activities, however, by suggesting special activities utilizing the balance board, the trampoline, "angels-in-the-snow" games, and rhythms. In training for ocular control, Kephart was concerned with both monocular and binocular training of the eye, and he suggested a variety of ways in which teachers and parents may assist PPD children to achieve more mature visual motor skills.

As with other aspects of the total program for learning disabled children, motor training is not something which can be left to chance. It must be conceived as an integral part of the daily routine for a learning disabled child, and it must be carried out consistently and progressively in terms of the increasing skill potential of the child. Motor training should not be looked upon as something separate and apart from the other things which are on-going for the child. It is an integral part of the program, equal in importance to the child's other learning experiences. Furthermore, motor training should *accompany* the educational program throughout the duration of the child's early educational experience. While gross-motor skills and perceptual-motor abilities will have to be acquired before the child can make appropriate responses to all forms of abstract learning, motor training cannot constitute the total program of the young perceptually handicapped child. The daily schedule suggested for a typical young learning disabled child illustrates the variety of activities in addition to motor training which can be used to fill the child's day, all of which are essential at the readiness stage of development. What is sought is an appropriate balance of activities, each significant in some way to the child's growth, not the overemphasis of a single activity.

PSYCHOTHERAPY

In an earlier chapter of this book it was stated that as a result of lack of good perceptual and motor skills and as a result of continued insults to the developing ego, the learning disabled child is usually also emotionally disturbed. A well-conceived program for learning disabled children will include some form of continued psychotherapy. It is essential that pediatric psychiatrists and pediatric psychologists be available to assume responsibility for continued therapy for the child. The psychiatric social worker who is familiar with children may also assume an important therapeutic role in this aspect of the program.

As the child is learning new skills, both abstract and concrete, he should be given an opportunity to develop insights into the reasons for his behavior. He must be able to develop true concepts of his role as a behaver in the seemingly unfriendly environment of the adult and peer worlds. Most of the learning disabled child's relationships have been unsatisfactory. While the child is being given opportunities to develop success experiences in school activities and in motor development, similar opportunities must be provided in the area of personal adjustment and interpersonal relationships.

Sheldon Rappaport and others have pointed out that the individual goes through a normal course of emotional development postnatally just as he goes through a definite prenatal fetal developmental cycle. Rappaport speaks of this as a postnatal "epigenesis," which is the continuation of the growth, learning, and adjustment that started as a cycle in prenatal life. We have already observed how the lack of fine-motor skills may initially impair the mother-child relationship and how out of these initial experiences the long-term relationship between the mother and child also may become distorted. It has also been suggested that the disturbance of the relationship between the mother and the child may indeed as well be expanded to have detrimental effects on the father-child relationship. The father's perception becomes confused regarding the child's impact on the mother's adjustment, and he tends to support the mother against the child's physical and emotional threats.

The culmination of this crescendo of tensions—tensions resulting from failure to develop along normal patterns, guilt feelings on the part of the parents in not being able completely to fulfill the expectancies of parenthood, and a succession of experiences in which the child is isolated from neighborhood children and school companions is an ever more damaged ego for the child and increasingly disturbed parents who struggle to protect their own egos. The parents are in a constant state of conflict as they try at one and the same time both to force the child into normal patterns of behavior and to protect him from the pressures of the community. The inability of the child to obtain positive ego satisfactions prompts him to fall back on those more primitive types of behavior which have brought him some feeling of status but which are nonetheless inappropriate to his chronological age. His acts prompted by uninhibited id impulses have little acceptance now, although he knows that at one time in his life experience these were excused, accepted, or expected as a part of his behavior. This was when he was a very small child, but time is of no concern to him now. The fact is that what he did then was accepted because he was a little child, and his behavior brought him satisfactions of a sort. Now that he is older and cannot satisfactorily develop modes of behavior acceptable to his parents and friends, he will utilize those earlier behaviors which did bring him a modicum of satisfaction. The earlier patterns are completely out of place; and the child knows they are no longer appropriate, but he must use something as an adjustive force. The immature, unsophisticated id behavior further alienates him from the very individuals whose help, love, and security he seeks. A vicious circle is evolving rapidly.

Psychotherapeutic assistance must be given this child; he cannot satisfactorily resolve his problems. He does not have the background of satisfactory learning from which to develop a new course of behavior. Dr. William Adamson speaks of this situation as one which requires a "total-life-relationship structure." The child is so far removed from the normal course of child growth and development and is so enmeshed in his abnormal perceptual-motor schema that without an agent who can help him to restructure his life relationships, he may never reach a level of personality integration and learning acceptable to society. The id-ego conflicts will continue as dynamic, unintegrated forces on into his adult life. While a well-constructed and well-executed educational program alone can go far to provide the stability needed by the child, it has been our experience that the psychotherapeutic program must parallel education to insure maximum benefit to the child.

A psychotherapeutic program, not always easy to implement with young children, is possible if well-prepared personnel are available. It is not the intent of this author to instruct clinical psychologists or psychiatrists in therapeutic procedures. However, our experience with learning disabled children over the years indicates that some modifications in traditional clinical practice are warranted. The nature of the learning disabled child's problems minimizes his ability to profit from the customary approaches of the non-directive therapies either in counseling or in play therapy as it is traditionally practiced.

In play therapy, as we have already noted in an earlier chapter, the goal is to provide a permissive unlimited environment so that the child's play, role playing, and verbalizations will assist the therapist in understanding the dynamics of the child's personality and thus to be able to assist the child in the construction of new insights and new patterns of satisfying behavior. The hyperactivity and distractability of the learning disabled child militate against all that is in the permissive setting. In it there is too much freedom for one who is unable to deal with choice. There are too many environmental stimuli in the play therapy situation for one who is unable negatively to adapt to the unessential.

Experience has demonstrated that play therapy, carried out with learning disabled children within the bounds of the traditional approach employed with emotionally disturbed children, generally ends in chaos. On the other hand a therapeutic milieu which is much more structured can give the learning disabled child the support he needs, and yet it can be sufficiently permissive to provide a setting within which the psychotherapist can effectively work. If the psychotherapeutic program can be carried on side by side with a well-structured educational program, both will benefit. The success which the child experiences in the educational setting will carry over to the psychotherapeutic experience and will be an important factor in the development of new insights by the child.

The learning disabled child needs the psychotherapeutic program just as much as he needs the educational program. He has a tremendous need to talk with someone who will help him provide his own structure to integrate his understandings of himself and the developing picture of what he is really like in terms of his disability and in terms of the adult's expectancies of him. The nature of this experience cannot be adequately handled in the classroom by the educator in spite of the fact that the educator must be prepared to deal with material produced by the child which has much psychological implication. The long-term therapy responsibility is that of other disciplines. The experience which the learning disabled or perceptually handicapped child has in therapy is the element which ultimately crystalizes for him a "total-life-relationship structure," which Adamson sees as the ultimate achievement of the total program for the child.

RELATED PSYCHOTHERAPEUTIC SERVICES

Service to Teachers

We have found that the teachers of learning disabled and hyperactive children must also be provided with counseling—psychological or psychiatric. Probably all teachers of emotionally disturbed children will need some counseling.

Teachers of learning disabled children will be among the finest in the teaching profession. They should be well prepared for their work, and they must possess all of the personal characteristics mentioned earlier in this book. However, even the best teacher working under optimal conditions will find himself under constant and unrelenting pressures by these children. The teacher, as Sheldon Rappaport stated, must serve as an *ego bank* to the child, who alone is without ego supports. The teacher must constantly give of himself to the child, for the child is unable to help himself. The child must constantly receive in order to survive. The teacher must always understand and accept the child, and his belief in the child must be genuine and expressed. The teacher must be a perpetual source of strength, for the child has little strength of his own. The teacher must represent for the child the essence of consistency, for without external consistency the child falters. The teacher indeed must be everything that the child is not, and this means that the teacher must have tremendous resources of personal strength and wisdom. Many such individuals already serve children well. With a teacher like this, the concept of "relationship structure" which Rappaport describes is a reality for the teacher and the child: "Relationship structure . . . means the ability of the adult [parent or teacher or therapist or other] to understand the child sufficiently well at any given moment, through his verbal and nonverbal communications, to relate in a way which aids the child's development of impulse control and other ego functions."

Many times in the course of a day the teacher will question his own behavior in certain situations. At times the child's behavior will be beyond the ability of the teacher immediately to analyze. Sometimes the child responds in a completely different and unexpected manner than the teacher anticipated. When the child challenges the teacher's authority, almost the last ounce of the teacher's emotional energy must be given. Understandably, then, these teachers become frustrated and confused from time to time. They need the assistance of objective points of view to maintain a healthy personal balance and a good continuing relationship with the children.

We have found it essential to include in the teacher's schedule several clock hours per month of psychological consultation. Customarily we have used two two-hour sessions per month during which the teacher has the services of a psychiatrist, psychologist or psychiatric social worker. During this time the teacher does not necessarily enter into a clinical relationship such as would be established between a therapist and a patient, but seeks to reorient himself to his responsibilities. An opportunity for the teacher is provided to analyze his relationships with the children with the assistance of good professional personnel. "What does Gregory's behavior mean to me?" "Did I do something to trigger Mark's aggression to David?" "What are the implications for the adjustment of all the children if I modify my behavior and standards in a certain way?" Conscientious teachers often become rather involved with the children they are teaching. They get children's behavior confused with their concepts of not only the children but their feelings about themselves. These and many similar and related matters can be quietly discussed in a counseling session to the end that the teacher returns to the children with an objective point of view rather than one which internalizes the problems of all the children. In this way objectivity is maintained. In this manner the teacher can in truth function as an ego bank. Resources are maintained by the teacher from which children with deficits can continually draw. We feel this to be a significant supportive service to the total educational process for learning disabled children.

Parental Needs

It is not the intent of this author to prescribe psychiatric services to parents of learning disabled children. Yet it is the author's experience that many such parents need personal counseling and sometimes therapy. The complex problems of relating constantly to the child, of having a continued responsibility for other children, of maintaining a home with all of its complexities, and of keeping the relationship between husband and wife strong and rewarding are things which overtax most adults. We urge parents to seek personal assistance; they need help for the same reasons that their children's teachers do. Parents, however, are often hesitant to seek help from psychologists or psychiatrists. They are embarrassed because of what they feel their friends or relatives may say about them. The problem of rearing a perceptually handicapped child satisfactorily, however—and most friends and relatives will be aware of this—is a bigger one than most individuals are able to handle alone. Mature and intelligent parents recognize their need for support and singly or together will seek continuing counsel from appropriate professional sources.

LANGUAGE AND COMMUNICATION DEVELOPMENT

Along with motor training and psychotherapy there is a third element in the total educational program for learning disabled children: consistent and intensive attention to language development and communication skills. Problems in these areas are usually sufficiently complicated that a specialist other than the teacher is required. A speech pathologist will work closely with the teacher, and the teacher and pathologist will find a close interrelationship between their two aspects of the child's total program.

Speech is one of the most complex of all human learnings. In the normal individual without central nervous system disturbances, speech appears to be a simple and habitual thing. We have always talked. We cannot even remember when or how we learned. Communication, however, which requires listening, speaking, hearing, and writing, calls for complicated neurophysical activity, auditory-motor activity. The perceptually handicapped child may find his poor ability to communicate a severe handicap in attempting to learn and adjust to society. It is difficult because speech constitutes a code, and an abstract code at that. Abstraction is one of the abilities in which learning disabled children many times show a deficit. To understand the symbol code and to be able to interpret incoming signals into appropriate output is often completely beyond the ability of a perceptually handicapped child. The seemingly simple act of speaking requires a highly refined and fully integrated central nervous system.

Thus it is easy to understand why so many learning disabled children are diagnosed as having "delayed speech," retarded language or speech development, or are sometimes referred to as children with "language disorders." Some school systems, as mentioned in Chapter 1, actually have called their classes for learning disabled children, classes for children with language disorders. While speech impediment is not characteristic of all learning disabled children, most learning disabled children have some speech difficulty. The different levels of proficiency in speech and communication illustrate the great differences in individual learning disabled children. Deficiencies in speech and communication may be detected and assessed at a much younger age than can other retarded areas in a child's development.

The characteristics of hyperactivity, dissociation, visual-motor disturbances, perseveration, and all of the others mentioned in this volume are basic factors in the lack of adequate communication skills in the learning disabled child. Each of these psychological characteristics—manifestations of perceptual processing deficits—is characteristic of auditory perceptual processing as well as visual processing (or processing involving other sensory modalities). The speech pathologist will design an educational program to provide the learning disabled child with training in listening, interpreting, and responding through speech and language, keeping in mind many of the characteristics of a good learning experience discussed earlier in the book. Communication skills in learning disabled children do not readily correct themselves, nor do these skills develop spontaneously. Parents must appreciate that speech training and language training are not frills but are as essential for the total development of the child as is anything else mentioned in this book.

THE TEACHER ASSISTANT AND PUPIL LOAD

As many parents of learning disabled children will quickly attest, one hyperactive child can be a full load for an adult. The story of the learning disabled child, as he has been described in these pages, illustrates the complexity of his problems, and it also indicates the care with which specialized teaching materials need to be prepared for him. There is no research which conclusively indicates what the optimum class size should be for learning disabled children. More than twenty years of experience and observation of educational programs, however, have convinced us that the optimum teacher-pupil ratio is no higher than ten children for each teacher *and* a full-time teacher assistant. In the more nearly ideal situation there would be only eight children, roughly similar in chronological age and mental ability, per each teacher and assistant.

We have had experience on several occasions, when, in order to meet the needs of the children, it was necessary to reduce the number still more for an extended period of time. On one occasion an excellent teacher supported by a full-time assistant was assigned eight learning disabled hyperactive children. The children's emotional problems were so great that it was quite impossible for the teacher to accomplish his mission in any respect. After considerable trial, and following careful reassessment of the situation by the interdisciplinary staff, it was decided to reduce the group in size to four children and to restructure the situation much more gradually when in the future it was determined a fifth, sixth, or seventh child might be added. When this was done, results began to be observed which had not been achieved before.

Certainly it is essential that administrators view this program differently than they view their regular elementary or even special education programs which serve other types of disability groups. PPD children deviate from normal child growth and behavior more than any group. Within a group of learning disabled children there will be many individual differences, and no basis exists initially upon which group activities can be organized by the teacher. The entire educational and psychotherapeutic venture is a matter of individual instruction, or as educators often state, one-to-one teaching and learning. The tendency of learning disabled children toward displays of emotion, and the tendency of all the children to become disturbed at one child's outburst, is another reason small homogeneous groups of children should be taught. The short attention spans and the great variety of other psychological characteristics which each child demonstrates in different degree mean that a competent teacher can spread himself only so thin before ineffective teaching becomes a fact. With all of these variables in mind, most public and private school programs for learning disabled children have been organized around a good teacher, a good assistant, and at most seven or eight children. These are important considerations for parents to keep in mind as they work cooperatively with school officials in behalf of their children.

One essential of a good educational program for learning disabled children is a teacher assistant. This individual is an important factor in achieving success. Few commercially prepared teaching materials exist for learning disabled children, and all but occasional material will have to be made by the teacher for each child. One person alone cannot be expected to prepare this material, for it all has to be done after the school day when the children have left. A great deal of teaching materials have to be prepared, for one task may occupy only a few moments because of the child's short attention span. Many separate teaching and learning items must be prepared for a given child for a single day. The total amount of material which a teacher must have arranged before the children arrive each morning becomes a staggering total. The teacher assistant will be the factor which makes this preparation for the children a reasonable possibility.

The teacher assistant, in the absence of other personnel, can also be utilized in motor-training activities, in assisting with luncheon teaching, in providing periods of relief for the teacher, in supervising rest periods, and in performing other duties which indeed are innumerable. The teacher assistant plays a vital role in working with the teacher when a child has an emotional outburst. The assistant works with the other children, making sure that each of them has what he needs in order to accomplish his assignments. The assistant reassures the other children who may be insecure because of the behavior of the disturbing child, and makes it possible for the professional teacher to devote full attention to the one child who needs it. Two sets of hands are almost constantly needed in a group of learning disabled children.

The assistant should be familiar with children but need not be professionally trained. As a matter of fact, we have discouraged the utilization of professionally prepared persons as assistants because too often this results in differences in approach in the classroom. The assistant must be a good follower, one who will carry out the directions of the teacher fully and faithfully. The children must never become confused about which adult is the authority. Patience and concern for children with problems are the major prerequisites needed by an assistant. We have had excellent experience with mature women who have reared their own children, but who may have no more than a high school education. The personality characteristics of an assistant are far more important than the level of educational attainments.

Volunteers

The program for learning disabled children should be set up in such a manner as to utilize the services of selected volunteers. It is generally more satisfactory to use volunteers who are not parents of any of the children in the program. Too frequently parents become involved in the operational and administrative phases of the program, which should be avoided if possible. Volunteers can be used to help in the construction of teaching materials and can assist in the motor-training activities. They can provide transportation services for certain children who otherwise might not be able to attend the class. A group of retired men in one community has provided an excellent program of motor training for several classes of learning disabled children. Volunteers who work in direct contact with children must be carefully screened. They must receive an orientation and should be given continued guidance in their work.

SECONDARY SCHOOL EDUCATIONAL PROGRAMS

The emphasis of most educational programs which now exist is on the learning disabled child in the elementary school. It is difficult to know how early one can initiate a program for learning disabled children and have it be effective. It is assumed that the earlier a program can be started for a child, the better. Good programs for five-year-old children are in existence, and they are proving their worth. The concept of prevention of learning and adjustment problems, however, is an important one. If children can be provided with the techniques of learning and personality adjustment while young, and if they can be directed along lines which bring them feelings of success and ego strength, some of the problems which are so typical of nine- or ten-year-old learning disabled children may not come into existence at all. It is our experience, however, that many learning disabled children will still need special assistance when they are old enough to enter junior high school; a smaller number will need help at high school age. In Chapter 10, the importance of planning for secondary school youth has been stressed. We include this issue here again to emphasize the importance of this chronological age group in the overall program of education for children and youth with learning disabilities.

The junior high school is a particularly crucial period for learning disabled children. If a child needs help at that age, he will not only have as dynamic factors in his life the psychological problems which have been here described, but he will also be characterized by the problems of pre-adolescence. These are in themselves often very disturbing. The hyperactivity, the sensitivity, and the new growth and awareness of self which so typifies the preadolescent child serve to accentuate the adjustment problems of the learning disabled child. Schools must plan to carry an increasingly smaller number of these children into special educational programs within the secondary school. Whether it is better to have the special class for children of junior high school age in the junior high school building or as an additional upper class with other similar types of classes in an elementary school is still an open question. In spite of the administrative problems which are created, we feel that the classes should be conducted in the school appropriate to the students' ages. For the junior high school classes, it is recommended that the teacher be one with elementary school professional preparation. If the child at this age still needs the special class, the chances are that he will also need the techniques of education which have been described in this book. Most junior high school teachers are completely unfamiliar with them, whereas teachers well-prepared in elementary education area special education methodology are able to meet the demands of the preadolescent child in the junior high school setting.

THE ADMINISTRATOR'S ROLE

The administrator of any school building has a significant role to play in the total program of education for children and youth with learning disabilities. The first responsibility of the administrator is to understand the nature and needs of the child with learning disabilities, to appreciate the unique psychological characteristics of this group of children, and to understand the difference between remedial education and developmental education. If these issues are grasped, the administrator is in a secure position with respect to his leadership role in relationship to the program.

It is important also to recognize that the needs of the child and the teacher are essentially *instructional and developmental,* not diagnostic or pupil personnel. Too often special education programs are under the supervision of the director of pupil personnel in a given school system. This is alogical. Diagnosis is not what the teacher needs; instructional direction, assistance, and materials are the primary needs. The relationship of pupil personnel services is no more logical for the child with learning disabilities than it is for the normal child, and certainly no one would concede that pupil personnel services should be responsible for the instruction and curriculum of the normal educational programs. Administration needs to understand the place of special education in the total administrative process of the school system. Special education's relationship to pupil personnel has historical precedents which are no longer seen as valid. Special education for these and other exceptional children is primarily a matter of the school system's division of instruction. These are essential points of view for the administrator to hold, if valid educational programs for the learning disabled children of the school system are to be pursued effectively.

The administrator must be as committed to the education of children with learning disabilities as to any other child. In another book —*Misfits in the Public Schools*—we have carefully described how thoughtless administrators have ruined educational programs for these children by inappropriate statements, behavior, or unnecessary adherence to rules and regulations in spite of the fact that well-prepared teachers were available who knew what they were doing. Teachers, regardless of their level of expertise, cannot operate effectively if there is anything but complete support on the part of the building administrator. The education of these children and youth is too complicated. The teacher must know that sound administrative support is available at all times as the unique and difficult needs and problems of these young people are being met.

SELECTED REFERENCES OF SPECIAL INTEREST TO PARENTS

Cruickshank, W. M.; Paul, J. L.; Junkala, J. B. *Misfits in the Public Schools.* Syracuse: Syracuse University Press, 1969.

Getman, G. N., and Kane, E. R. *The Physiology of Readiness.* Minneapolis: Programs to Accelerate School Success, 1964.

Kephart, N. C. *The Brain Injured Child.* Chicago: National Society for Crippled Children and Adults, 1963.

Long, N.; Morse, W.; and Newman, R. *Conflict in the Classroom.* Belmont, Calif.: Wadsworth, 1971.

Radler, D. H., and Kephart, N. C. *Success Through Play.* New York: Harper & Row, 1963.

SELECTED REFERENCES OF SPECIAL INTEREST TO TEACHERS

Barsch, R. H. "Teacher Needs—Motor Training." In *The Teacher of Brain-Injured Children,* edited by W. M. Cruickshank. Syracuse: Syracuse University Press, 1966.

Cruickshank, W. M., and Hallahan, D. P., eds. *Perceptual and Learning Disabilities in Children.* Syracuse: Syracuse University Press, 1975. Vol. 1, see Cruickshank, W. M. "The Learning Environment," Chapter 8; and Morse, W. C. "The Learning Disabled Child and Considerations of Life Space," Chapter 11.

Cruickshank, W. M.; Bentzen, F. A.; Ratzeburg, F. H.; and Tannhauser, M. T. *A Teaching Method for Brain-Injured and Hyperactive Children.* Syracuse: Syracuse University Press, 1961.

Gaddes, W. H. "The Needs of Teachers for Specialized Information on Handedness, Finger Localization, and Cerebral Dominance." In *The Teacher of Brain-Injured Children,* edited by W. M. Cruickshank. Syracuse: Syracuse University Press, 1966.

Getman, G. N., and Hendrickson, H. H. "The Needs of Teachers for Specialized Information on the Development of Visuomotor Skills in Relation to Academic Performance." In *The Teacher of Brain-Injured Children,* edited by W. M. Cruickshank. Syracuse: Syracuse University Press, 1966.

Grzynkowicz, W., and Kephart, M. *Learning Disabilities: Last Lectures of Newell C. Kephart.* Fort Collins, Col.: Kephart Achievement Center, 1975.

Kephart, N. C. "The Needs of Teachers for Specialized Information on Perception." In *The Teacher of Brain-Injured Children,* edited by W. M. Cruickshank. Syracuse: Syracuse University Press, 1966.

———. *The Slow Learner in the Classroom.* Columbus: Merrill, 1960.

Knoblock, P., and Goldstein, A. P. *The Lonely Teacher.* Boston: Allyn and Bacon, 1971.

Kroth, R. *Communicating with Parents of Exceptional Children.* Denver: Love, 1975.

Reitan, R. H. "The Needs of Teachers for Specialized Information in the Area of Neuropsychology." In *The Teacher of Brain-Injured Children,* edited by W. M. Cruickshank. Syracuse: Syracuse University Press, 1966.

12

Psychoactive Drugs in the Treatment of Learning Disabilities

Maria J. Paluszny

THE WIDESPREAD USE of stimulant drugs in children in recent years has caused much concern and public reaction. At a Congressional hearing in September 1970, Dr. Ronald Lipman of the Federal Drug Administration testified to the effect that about 150,000 to 200,000 children were being treated with psychostimulants (Grinspoon and Singer 1973). That estimate is probably very low, as national reporting systems are inadequate, and since 1970 the number of such children treated by drugs has probably increased.

As frequently happens in a heated debate, "pro" and "con" sides develop. Some physicians feel that in many cases psychoactive drugs are very useful in children with learning disabilities. Wender (1971) in his interesting book states: "I am obviously opting for a trial of stimulants (amphetamine or methylphenidate) therapy in all children in whom the diagnosis of MBD is suspected. On the other hand, many physicians, psychologists, educators, and parents feel drugs are being "over" used. Eric Denhoff, a pediatrician concerned with research in amphetamines, wrote in 1971: "Soon it became evident that these drugs were being used indiscriminately—prescription would depend mostly upon a description of behavior by a teacher or a parent." The purpose of this chapter is not to take sides in this debate, but to consider drug therapy according to the following points: (1) The history and research on drug therapy in learning disorders; (2) the "for" and "against" arguments to consider in deciding to use psychostimulant drugs; (3) preparation and management of school, parents, and child when psychostimulant drugs are used; and (4) types of drugs and their actions.

Maria J. Paluszny, M.D., is Associate Professor of Psychiatry, Medical School, and Assistant Director and Chief of the Clinical Services Division, Institute for the Study of Mental Retardation and Related Disabilities, University of Michigan.

HISTORY AND RESEARCH

Early Studies

The first reported study on the use of psychostimulants in children was done by Charles Bradley in 1937. He described thirty children who were hospitalized for a variety of behavioral disorders ranging from "specific educational disabilities with secondary disturbed school behavior to the retiring schizoid child on the one hand and the aggressive egocentric epileptic child on the other." When these children were placed on benzedrine, fourteen of the group showed a "remarkable" scholastic improvement. The improvement was noted in all school subjects. It appeared promptly the first day benzedrine was given, and disappeared on the first day it was discontinued. Five children showed an increase of symptoms or no response.

From the first report on the effectiveness of psychoactive drugs in children, a variety of studies followed. Typically, however, many of the studies were anecdotal. These generally consisted of descriptive observations, rather than well-controlled studies using a research design. Barbara Fish (1971) describes this very well when she stated: "Almost all of the 350 children per year admitted to the in-patient service (at Bellville Hospital) in the 1950's received a thorough trial with drugs. The routine in that bygone era was to start with a trial of dextroamphetamine sulfate (Dexdrine) (5 mg/day up to 20 mg/day) in any child who did not respond to the ward program and psychotherapy alone. If dextroamphetamine sulfate failed, he was then given a trial on phenhydramine, and if that failed, he was given diphenylhydantoin sodium."

Later, methodologically more adequate studies evolved. Subjects were chosen according to definite criteria. Typically, double-blind studies (where the family as well as the physician did not know whether the drug administered was a placebo or not) were used. In addition, various rating scales were developed to assess the child's improvement more objectively.

Many studies, however, still focused on the child's activity level. The child was assessed according to his activity level being diagnosed "hyperactive," and improvement was judged on the basis of decrease of activity. To assess the degree of activity, rating scales for parents and teachers were developed. While in the laboratory, electromechanical devices often were used to record the child's movements. The stabilimetric ("wiggle") cushion, that records the child's movements while he is seated, and the actometer, a modified self-winding calendar which records movements while the child moves about the room, are two such research devices.

From the rather gross measures of activity, researchers moved to more subtle assessments, namely, assessment of arousal, attention, and general abilities. Psychostimulant drugs were evaluated as to their effectiveness in changing a child's academic progress as well as decreasing motility. Simultaneously, physiological reasons for the child's "deviant" behavior were sometimes assessed, with studies being done to determine the possible site of action of these drugs. In addition, a variety of studies comparing the effectiveness of numerous drugs were carried out on children with perceptual problems.

Although research on psychostimulants has come a long way from the early days of putting all disturbed children on drug therapy, one may well ask the question, where does research on psychostimulants stand now? The answer, of course, is not simple. Just as an army has its soldiers in different positions on different fronts in a war, so research makes uneven progress in different areas of knowledge. Occasionally, parts of the army may even retreat. Likewise in research some investigations may contradict others and new avenues must be found. In general, however, recent studies in psychostimulants have assisted professionals to make progress in defining possible mechanisms of action, in delineating types of actions, and which in a few instances resulted in some follow-up investigations.

Mechanisms of Action

Frequently it is assumed that psychoactive drugs have a paradoxical reaction in children. In adults, after all, Dexedrine and Ritalin (methylphenidate) act as energizers, "pep pills," even as anti-depressants. In children, these drugs appear to have a calming effect. Is there any way that the same effect of a drug could produce such dramatically opposite results? Laufer (1957) described a mechanism by which such apparently contradictory findings are explained. According to Laufer (and H. Gastaut who originated this test) the "photometrazol threshold" is a method for diagnosing diencephalon dysfunction. The test consists of injecting metrazol slowly intravenously while the subject is stimulated by a powerful flashing stroboscope light. Meanwhile, an electroencephalogram (EEG) is being recorded. The end point is indicated by a characteristic discharge in the EEG. If a significantly lower than normal dose of metrazol is needed to evoke this response, it is assumed that a dysfunction in the diencephalon is present. It is useful here to review some aspects of the diencephalon.

The diencephalon is the most rostral part of the brain stem. On a sagittal section of the brain, it appears to lie deeply imbedded in the cortex of the brain. The two most important areas of the diencephalon are the thalamus and hypothalamus. The major function in both these areas appears to be concerned with appropriate balancing to prevent under or over functioning. In the hypothalamus the balancing is concerned with appetite and the physical expression of emotions. The cortex is primarily concerned with subjective experience of feelings, but the hypothalamus is involved in the physical component of feelings—increasing heart rate, blood pressure, flushing, pallor, etc. The thalamus, likewise, appears to have a regulatory function, but in relaying numerous sensory impulses to the cerebral cortex. Processes of correlation and integration occur here, as well as the selective focusing of attention. It must be remembered, however, that awareness does not occur until the impulses are transmitted to the cortex (Gatz 1968).

From the above description if can be seen that the diencephalon acts as a screen and sorter for sensory input before the stimulus is transmitted to the cortex. If a dysfunction is present in this area, and thus the diencephalon cannot function effectively, then the cortex is overwhelmed by stimuli being unable to handle the excessive input. Laufer used the photometrazol test to demonstrate that such a mechanism is involved in children who show a "hyperkinetic impulse disorder" on an organic basis (his description of these children is synonomous with the term "learning disabled child"). He found that these children showed a lower photometrazol threshold. Furthermore, when these children were placed on amphetamines, their photometrazol threshold increased to normal levels. Laufer concluded that these children had an organic impairment and suggested that it was specifically a dysfunction of the diencephalon.

Two theories have been advanced for the possible mechanisms of the diencephalic dysfunction. One possibility is that the diencephalon functions ineffectively, thus not screening the cortex from unnecessary stimuli. The second possibility is that the cortex shows a maturational lag and thus cannot handle all the stimuli transmitted from a diencephalon that does not show a similar maturational lag. In either case, an imbalance between the two parts of the brain appears to be the problem.

Unfortunately, although an interesting and valuable theory, Laufer's work in the area of photometrazol stimulation has not been replicated by other investigators. Other investigators, however, have addressed themselves to the problem of amphetamine action on the central nervous system. Basically, much of this work suggests that amphetamines may act as a stimulant on the brain stem, thereby increasing alertness; focusing attention on a specific stimuli, thereby decreasing response to other stimuli. Secondly, since the reticular formation of the diencephalon regulates incoming stimuli to the cortex, stimulating the diencephalon would increase the monitoring function and thus inhibit or reduce extraneous stimuli reaching the cortex.

Although these mechanisms of hyperactivity and psychostimulant action seem very plausible, the findings yet are inconclusive. For example, some animal studies done by other investigators have suggested that at least some types of hyperactivity could be due to cortical lesions, and such hyperactivity also appears to be responsive to amphetamines (Davis 1957).

Types of Actions of Psychostimulants

ACTIVITY LEVEL

As already mentioned, much of the earlier work on the use of psychostimulants focused on the apparent calming effect they produced on hyperactive children. Scales for parents and teachers were developed by which to rate hyperactivity. Various mechanical devices were used to measure activity levels in a laboratory setting. Whalen (1976) has written, "Given the diversity of instruments used to tap activity levels, it often became difficult to compare studies across laboratories. Problems of reliability and validity emerge even with single measurement device. Johnson (1971), for example, found '. . . different readings resulting from slight variations according to where the actometers were attached to the subjects.' " However, despite such methodological problems, some gains have been made in studies on the effect of psychostimulants on activity. In a controlled study comparing Ritalin (methylphenidate), a tranquilizer (thioridazine), and a placebo on the behavior of twelve boys with emotional difficulties in a special education classroom, Sprague, Barnes, and Werry (1970) found a significant reduction in activity as measured by the stabilimetric cushion when the children were on Ritalin. The placebo group did not show a similar reduction of activity. In addition, Ritalin increased attention and cooperative behavior in the classroom for these same children.

Other investigators have found confusing results. For example, in a study by Millichap and Boldrey (1967), motor activity as measured by the actometer was *increased* on Ritalin. Yet the subjects were rated as improved by parents and teachers who felt there was less impulsivity and improved motor coordination. Another group of investigators found that Ritalin reduced seat movement of hyperactive children when they were working on a structured task but not when they were playing (Sleator and von Neumann 1974).

Because of such findings, investigators began questioning the previously held opinion that motion is an adequate measure of assessing improvement. Researchers began exploring the premise that activity level is not the critical issue, but rather the direction and the focus of the activity is crucial. Thus, the improvement noted by parents and teachers when a child was placed on psychostimulants could be a result of the child's better organized, goal directed activity and decreased distractibility, rather than an overall decrease of motion.

Satterfield *et al.* (1974) found that children with learning disabilities and hyperactivity showed a low central nervous system arousal level (as measured by skin conductive levels and slowing of EEG). When stimulants were given, these children showed an increase in CNS arousal and a concomitant raise in inhibitory levels. From these findings, they postulated that psychostimulants raised inhibitory control over motor functions in inappropriate motor behavior, but increased motor activity that was goal directed. Satterfield suggested that this allowed the child to selectively attend to a learning situation.

LEARNING BEHAVIOR

Once investigators of psychostimulants began relating activity levels and distractibility with learning ability, other studies followed on general cognition and drug effectiveness. These studies, however, have yielded inconsistant results. In reviewing this area, Whalen (1976) points out that usually children with hyperactivity or learning disabilities do not show an impairment in general intelligence, reading achievement, language skills, or complex learning. Furthermore, she feels that "even when such decrements are found, there is no clear evidence that psychostimulants enhance performance in these areas. Some studies of hyperactivity and learning disabled groups yield clear drug induced improvements in verbal or performance I.Q., while others reveal few or no differences." This becomes even more complicated if one considers the implication of a study by Gittelman-Klein and Klein (1976) which indicated that even though Ritalin improved a number of cognitive perceptual processes in children with learning disabilities, these gains were not associated with concurrent increments in reading performance. They state: "Unless vocabulary, information, comprehension and expressive skills are improved in children with learning disabilities, little hope of classroom change can be anticipated. . . . Another possibility is that the learning capacity of the children was significantly enhanced by the stimulant but in the absence of concurrent special education, the children were unable to capitalize on and make more use of their improved skills." Whatever the specifics, it appears that learning involves an interplay of several skills. Improving one aspect may not show a significant effect in the total.

Furthermore, little research as yet has been done on the transfer of learning from a drug-facilitated learning situation to times when the child is drug free. Apparently there is frequently a failure in animals to transfer learned behavior from drug to non-drug states. In addressing this problem in children, Sprague *et al.* (1970) found that in one such study children showed improvement in discrimination during the acquisition phase while on Ritalin, but when retention was evaluated, they showed better long-term learning with a placebo!

It is obvious from this discussion that the area of improvement of learning ability with psychostimulants still needs much exploration.

Follow-Up Studies

SHORT-TERM

Short-term follow-up studies have been used as predictors of medication response. Various investigators have attempted to define what features of a child's psychopathology will determine the child's response to psychostimulants. Part of the problem appears to be a confusion of terminology. Some investigators use the terms "learning disability," "hyperkinetic impulse disorder," and "minimal brain dysfunction" interchangeably. Others do not. The degrees of anxiety and behavioral disorders on a psychogenic basis varies from group to group; thus as Fish (1971) points out, diagnostic categories are frequently confusing, and it is difficult to generalize results across studies. However, even with these problems of nomenclature, Satterfield *et al.* (1974) have recently found a correlation between indications of central nervous system (CNS) dysfunction and response to Ritalin. Satterfield demonstrated that children who have low CNS arousal levels and who have low CNS inhibition levels are the ones that show the best responses to Ritalin. In keeping with

Laufer's earlier model, these findings suggest that psychostimulants re-store CNS arousal and inhibitory functions to a normal level. However, Satterfield cautions that medication alone is not the solution: "for management purposes the hyperactive child is best considered a multi-handicapped child requiring a multiple modality treatment."

LONG-TERM

In 1970 when a Congressional hearing was held considering the use of psychostimulants in children, only one follow-up study was then reported involving sixty seven cases after thirty five years of experience of treating children with psychostimulants!

Following the Congressional hearings, former HEW Secretary Elliot Richardson appointed a national "blue ribbon" committee under the chairmanship of Dr. Daniel X. Friedman of the University of Chicago to study and report on the use of medication to control the behavior of elementary school children. The committee members, ultimately focusing only on the use of the amphetamines with children, had the resources of the United States government available. The final report of the committee to Secretary Richardson noted the extreme paucity of any carefully defined or controlled research on this significant and often-utilized treatment form. A strong recommendation was made by the committee members urging the federal government to stimulate research in this field and, through its own research agencies, to initiate its own studies. Since that time, a few more studies have been added, but most of these studies are short-term research projects. Follow-up studies are still sparse and this remains the *bête noire* of psychostimulant research.

It is generally believed that the motoric components of hyperactivity disappear around adolescence, but according to some recent follow-up studies, this assessment is not completely accurate. Apparently while the intensity of the hyperactivity, distractibility, aggressiveness, and excitablity tend to decrease with age, Weiss *et al.* (1971) reported that these youngsters still scored higher on each of the above factors than their peers. There were other problems with these adolescents, namely, many had social and academic problems as well as problems with peer acceptance. The majority of these children had been treated with psychoactive drugs (chlorpromazine or dextroamphetamine). Whether drugs were used or not, the basic personality problems were essentially the same.

In another study comparing twenty men to their brothers after a twenty five-year interval, Borland and Heckman (1976) found that about half the group showed a number of symptoms of hyperactivity. In addition, almost half had some psychiatric problems. Interestingly, the group as a total had achieved educationally on a comparable level to their brothers. However, they were below both their brothers and their fathers in socioeconomic status. Unfortunately, the authors do not differentiate as to how many of these men had been treated with psychostimulants.

Thus it does not yet appear that using psychoactive drugs improves the long-term outcome of these children.

One positive finding, however, in a study by Bock *et al.* (1975) on psychostimulants, indicates that possibly earlier studies *on growth interference* may not be as great a problem as once thought. In this study, children on psychostimulants showed the same growth as their peers. Furthermore, the same study indicated that placing a child on psychostimulants *does not* predispose him in any way to future drug addiction.

From the above discussion of research in psychostimulants, it is evident that, although there are many areas where our knowledge of these drugs is inadequate, at least some progress is being made. Unfortunately, the progress is still insufficient to give a definite "yes" or "no" answer to the question, should a given child take psychostimulants? In order to answer that question, the specific child and his or her environment must be considered in detail.

THE DECISION TO USE PSYCHOSTIMULANTS

The first part of this decision is so obvious that it should seem ludicrous even to discuss it—namely, that a careful evaluation of the child is made. Unfortunately, this obvious step is frequently omitted or performed in such a perfunctory way that little useful information is gained. Fish (1975) points out that a myth exists in the use of stimulants, that "stimulants are the drugs for the hyperactive child." She further elaborates that stimulants are frequently used on children who represent mixed diagnostic categories; for some of these children, psychostimulants are appropriate, but for others they are not.

For the purpose of this discussion we can omit the details of diagnosing children with learning disabilities as this has been considered in earlier chapters. However, from a psychiatric viewpoint, in evaluating children for possible medication it is imperative to assess how much of the apparent "hyperactivity" is a motor expression of anxiety. Children with neurotic problems, transient situational reactions, or other emotional problems frequently may appear hyperactive. Furthermore, psychotic children, and even some children with behavior disorders, may show hyperactivity coupled with learning disabilities. In these children, however, the pathology is quite different from the usual child with learning disabilities. In fact, both the overtly psychotic child and the child whose behavior disorder is so severe that he resembles the psychotic child usually show a lack of response to stimulants.

Once a diagnosis is made and primary emotional problems or severe emotional problems have been ruled out, what other factors should be considered in deciding if medication should or should not be used? Is it reasonable, for example, to use a trial of medication on all hyperactive learning disabled children in whom severe emotional problems have been ruled out? Although some physicians may feel this is warranted, we feel there still are too many negative aspects to the use of drugs in children to do so. Thus, such a decision can only be made after reviewing both the general issues involved and the specific characteristics of the individual child.

General Issues

Several philosophical issues must be carefully weighed in all cases before medication is given.

PLACEBO EFFECT

This does not appear to be a serious problem at first glance, but considering the incidence of the placebo effect is estimated at 30–35 percent (Beecker 1955), then it is obvious that a problem exists. If, in giving medication to 100 children, 30 improve, conceivably that same number would improve if only a placebo were used. Furthermore, with such a high placebo effect, how is it possible to determine if the drug is effective in an individual case? Obviously it is impossible to be certain, but if other forms of intervention have been tried first, chances of placebo effect are decreased.

SIDE EFFECTS

These will be discussed later in greater detail. Generally, with therapeutic doses of psychostimulants, side effects involving the CNS such as insomnia or anorexia are rather common. In addition, occasional paradoxical reactions are seen. Instead of decreasing motor activity, the child sometimes becomes more active, more impulsive, and more aggressive. In instances of a paradoxical reaction, the drug is discontinued. If side effects are found, often these may be only transient, disappearing after one or two weeks of therapy. Occasionally, however, the medication may have to be stopped because of excessive side effects.

LONG-TERM EFFECT

As mentioned earlier, long-term follow-up studies on psychostimulants only now are coming into the literature. Some of these studies are changing previously held opinions. For example, earlier studies (Safer *et al.* 1972) on psychostimulants indicated that children who had been on psychostimulants showed a depressed growth curve. One study (Bock *et al.* 1975), however, did not show similar results. The overall height of the adolescents who had been on psychostimulants was comparable to the control groups. However, another study (Cole 1975) raised the concern that psychostimulants may cause cardiovascular effects such as hypertension. It appears in still another study (Simpson 1976) that this hypertension is probably not a sustained type.

These and other long-term effects of psychostimulants can only be assessed after many more follow-up studies are done on a variety of physical and psychological variables.

Case-Related Issues

In considering a child for therapy with psychostimulants, the child's overall environment and personality must be assessed.

NEGATIVE ASPECTS

First, the negative factors will be considered and the danger signals pointed out to alert for possible misuse of medication.

Psychostimulants should only be given under a physician's supervision. In the past, some physicians have placed a child on psychostimulants, writing the prescription so that it could be renewed indefinitely. Now, federal drug regulations prohibit the renewal of psychostimulants. A new prescription must be written each month. Unfortunately, some physicians still will write prescriptions without following the child with periodic physical examinations and medication checkups. Before any child is placed on medication, a responsible physician must be designated who will follow the child. If such continuity is unavailable, psychostimulant therapy should not be initiated.

The parental attitude toward the child should be supportive, firm, yet understanding. Unfortunately, parents not infrequently seek medication to alleviate not the child's problems, but their own. "He is an aggressive child who disrupts our entire household," the parents will tell a physician. The physician, feeling sympathetic, prescribes medication to "help" the entire family, forgetting his responsibility to the primary patient. Although the physician's reaction is understandable, medically it makes about as much sense as prescribing a sedative for a child in acute pain so that the entire family can get some sleep.

Before medication is tried, modifications in the household should be attempted. As discussed in other parts of this book, a child with learning disabilities can be greatly helped by a predictable environment that eliminates excess stimuli. Making suitable adjustments in the child's environment may not only preclude the use of medication, but even more important, it can give the parents a feeling of being active partners who can significantly help their child. This role for the parents will minimize the feelings of helplessness and self-blame parental behavior so frequently seen in families which have a "different" child.

An even greater problem for a physician prescribing medication is the unreliable or unpredictable parent. Many parents do not follow directions as to how the medication should be given. Many such parents will discontinue medication or increase the prescribed dose on a whim or their own notion of how the medication should work.

For example, I once evaluated a nine-year old boy who appeared drowsy, yet irritable. He was quite thin, and said he did not enjoy food, "not even candy." While I watched him, I occasionally observed muscle twitches of his face and hands. The reason for these signs and symptoms became quite clear when I questioned the mother. Seeing no improvement on 30 milligrams of Ritalin per day, the mother elected to steadily increase the dose. She was giving her son 120 milligrams per day when I saw the child! (The *maximum* dose of Ritalin is less than 60 milligrams per day). The opposite reaction on the part of the parents is likewise frequent with psychostimulants. Namely, the parents take the child off all medication without consulting a physician. The parents say that the child looked "groggy" or they wanted to see if his teachers would notice a difference or they give a similar illogical reason. Examples of this type of parental decision could be reported *ad nauseam*.

Most parents would not dream of changing the dose of an antibiotic or another drug without consulting a physician. Yet when psychoactive drugs are involved, whether it is a tranquilizer or a stimulant, parents somehow feel that they can regulate the dose according to their own observations of the child's behavior. Thus, not infrequently, the child is not on a steady program. As will be discussed later, psychostimulants are often discontinued during the summer or other vacations, but these periods are planned for and anticipated by the child's physician.

To summarize, as far as the family is concerned, psychostimulants should not be used if the family cannot follow directions or by those who instead devise their own drug treatment program.

Currently in many states the school is responsible for providing a suitable program for every child regardless of the child's handicap. Understandably, many school systems are having problems in their attempts to meet all the necessary demands. However, this should not be an excuse for not providing a program. Just as a child should not be placed on medication solely to make life easier for his family, likewise a child should not be placed on medication to simplify the school's problems in providing an adequate program. In other parts of this book, a positive learning environment for the child with learning disabilities is described. Both the parents and the child's physician should insist that such modifications are attempted first before a medication regimen is established.

Some schools, like some parents, have difficulty in handling a child appropriately once the child is placed on medication. Usually, it is largely a question of giving the school personnel some guidance in appropriate behavior. Occasionally, however, the school setting is so inflexible that a child who is "different" because he is on medication cannot be accepted. The most blatant example of this is the school principal who insists that the child cannot take medication while in school.

For example, a principal once told me that the school could not accept the "responsibility" of a child taking medication while on the school premises. He insisted that the youngster involved go home every noon to take his Ritalin. As the family lived a considerable distance from the school, the child's mother had to drive him back and forth at noon just so he could take his pill! Such an arrangement places an unreasonable burden on the family.

The child's perception of why he is taking "that pill" is critical. Again, the attitude is usually amenable to explanations and modification. If, however, the child sees his medication as a type of punishment for being bad or proof that he is "sick" and "different," medications should not be given until these misconceptions are corrected. Furthermore, in the overly dependent child who willingly sees his medication as a means of external control over his behavior, or who willingly abdicates to medication all responsibility for his actions, using medication may create more problems than it solves.

Finally, the greatest problem in using psychostimulants with children who have learning disabilities is the potential negative effect on everyone involved. This particular negative effect is extremely important and cannot be overstressed. Frequently when a child is placed on psychostimulants, the physician, the parents, and the school are lulled into complacency. Feeling that the medication is solving all the problems, they do not provide other therapeutic measures. The child's educational and emotional needs are not addressed, and his problems can be expected to increase with each passing year.

POSITIVE ASPECTS

As pointed out earlier, under some circumstances psychostimulants should not be included as part of the therapeutic plan for the learning disabled child. However, with adequate preparation, psychostimulants can be a very important adjunct to the total treatment plan.

First, it must be pointed out that ideal situations do not exist in real life. There are no ideal families or ideal school systems. Environment can only be modified to a certain degree. Once that degree is reached, then one must look to the child's behavior to see if that can be modified so that the child will be accepted in his home, his neighborhood, and his school.

Each family has a different tolerance for accepting a "different" child. This varies from the quiet, constricted family which cannot cope with a normally rambunctious child, to the family which not only accepts but integrates a multi-handicapped or psychotically aggressive youngster into their everyday family life. Most families fall somewhere in the middle of this spectrum. Despite counseling or other supportive help, the child's family will not change completely. Thus, not infrequently some of the changes must be made by the child.

The following case will serve to illustrate this:

Peter, a six-year old first grader, was referred to a guidance clinic because of school problems. After an evaluation, he was found to have normal intelligence but severe learning disabilities. In addition he was hyperactive, impulsive, and difficult to control. Peter's classroom teacher and his principal easily accepted suggestions to modify his school setting. His family, however, presented an entirely different situation. Peter lived with his grandparents, as his mother (who was mildly retarded) disowned him as a child resulting from a "rape." Peter's grandfather was a chronic alcoholic who on retirement spent most of his time drinking and criticizing his wife and other family members. The other family members consisted of Peter's uncle, his wife, and their infant son. These young people were unemployed, constantly argued about money, and on occasion were in trouble with the authorities for smoking "pot." In addition to the permanent household members, there were constant comings and goings of other family relatives. Peter's natural mother with her children would spend a few days there after an argument with her husband. Another of Peter's uncles would suddenly arrive to sleep off a weekend binge, or a cousin would stay over for a few days while looking for a job. In addition, there were frequent crises and disasters—illnesses, auto accidents, arrests for drunken driving.

The grandmother often bailed family members out of jail, loaned them money, cooked, and generally cleaned up after everyone. She behaved like a "professional martyr" who was totally incapable of setting structure or limits.

Early in therapy it became evident that the family situation would not change and that if Peter were to survive, he would need some assistance. When psychostimulants were added to Peter's program, a definite decrease in his hyperactivity was noted. Apparently the medication decreased Peter's responsiveness to the excessive stimuli in his home.

In conforming, complacent families a child may be placed on psychostimulants for a different reason. In these families the "different" child often is labeled and treated as if he were unlike other family members. If psychostimulants can effect enough of a behavioral change, this child is no longer considered unacceptable and a dramatic change may be seen. Previously criticisms levied at the child created an angry response in the child. These responses were expressed by more anger and met with more criticism from the parents. Now, with the child showing behavioral improvement with psychostimulants, a positive "snowball effect" is seen. The youngster behaving in a quieter manner, more in keeping with his brothers and sisters, is praised, accepted, and a pattern of positive reinforcement is setup.

In summary, children with learning disabilities are not placed on psychostimulants to relieve their families. After the family has made as many changes as is possible for them, the child may be tried on medication in an attempt to help him cope with his family.

Ideally the child should have a modified school classroom as described in other sections of this book. If, after modifications have been made, the child's overactivity and distractibility are still serious problems, stimulants may be tried. It should, however, be remembered that there is some question if long-term learning under the influence of stimulants is as effective as drug-free learning.

Under the negative aspects of stimulant therapy it was mentioned that the child may abdicate control over his impulses, feeling that, the "magic pill" takes over for him. On the positive side, however, it is not infrequent that stimulants decrease the child's hyperactivity and impulsivity, so for the first time, the child feels that he is in control. The following example illustrates such a reaction.

John, a ten-year-old boy with learning disabilities, impulsivity, and aggressive behavior, was placed on psychostimulants. Following this his impulsivity and aggressive behavior markedly decreased. When asked how he thought this occurred, John replied: "The pills give me time to think. I still get mad, but then I think if I want to hit someone or not. If I decide I still want to hit them, then I hit them. But I don't have to do it if I don't want to."

From the foregoing discussion, it can be seen that several rules can be applied to stimulant therapy in learning disabilities. First, a thorough evaluation of the child must be made. Second, the child's environment of home, school, and community is assessed. A program is developed consisting of modifying his school and home environment, which may sometimes involve therapy or guidance for the child and the parents. Other times only suggestions about modifying the child's environment may be sufficient. Finally, psychostimulant drug therapy is considered in the context of the child's reaction to it, as well as the potential for total responsiveness from the child's environment. This should all be done keeping in mind that the medication is only an adjunct to these other modifications, yet an adjunct that at times can offer significant symptomatic relief.

PREPARATION AND MANAGEMENT WHEN PSYCHOSTIMULANTS ARE USED

Once the physician involved has made the decision to use psychostimulants as part of the learning disabled child's therapeutic program, the critical factor in making the program successful is communication. As part of this, the physician must inform the parents, the child, and the school officials of what specific drug will be used and what side effects could be expected. In addition, the physician must allow the significant people involved to ask questions and help them to correct any misperception on drugs. Later, when the child is on a drug program, it is important to continue to keep the channels of communication open.

The Parents

The parents frequently expect the psychostimulants to be a "magic cure." This may cause them to become lax in helping the child to cope with the environment in other ways. The television set may be left on while Johnny is doing his homework, or the parents may forget to tell Johnny that they are all going on a trip, surprising him minutes before the trip is to take place.

After Johnny has been on medication one week, the parents may complain that the medication is not only not working, but Johnny is worse! In order to prevent such a response, it is imperative that the child's environment be a stable one during the first week or two of drug therapy and no other radical life changes are made. Otherwise, it is virtually impossible to evaluate the drug's effectiveness. Another rather common misconception which parents have about psychostimulants is that the child will become an addict. Although psychostimulants can be addictive in adults, producing at times severe psychological dependency in addition to physical habituation, such reactions have not been reported in children. This should be carefully explained to prevent parents from precipitously discontinuing the medication.

As well as allowing time for the parents to air their concerns and to ask questions, it is critical to review with them all details concerning the medication—side effects, paradoxical reactions, and details regarding administration. Frequently what a physician considers self-evident is not so evident to a patient's family. The following incident will illustrate this point even though the medication involved was not a psychostimulant.

While working in the emergency room as an intern I treated a sixteen-year old girl for an acute asthmatic attack. While on her first date the girl began wheezing, and her boyfriend rushed her to emergency. As part of the treatment I had a nurse give the girl an aminophylline suppository, then gave her several more to take home in case an attack recurred. Minutes later I received an angry call from the girl's mother.

"Doctor," she said, "I was wondering if you are a veterinarian. Only a horse doctor could expect a child to swallow such huge pills!" Obviously in the excitement, the girl forgot to tell her mother how the medication was administered in the emergency room. This incident taught me to be sure instructions are *always written.*

One such detail of administering medication is the time interval between pills. Parents occasionally believe that with psychostimulants as with other drugs the total daily dose is critical. Thus, if they forget to give the Ritalin at noon and in the afternoon, they will give the child a double dose later in the day. Such "making up" for a missed dose can cause problems. After about four hours the effect of Ritalin begins to wear off. If no further dose is given, the child will act essentially as if he were off medication. If later he is given a regular dose, the treatment will be resumed. However, if the child is given a double dose he will be over-medicated. Furthermore, if this occurs late in the day the child may experience insomnia.

The School

The principal and the child's teacher must agree where and when medication is to be taken. Usually it is best if this occurs during some natural break in the day, such as lunch. The child should not be called out of his class to go to the principal's office as this increases his and everyone else's feelings that he is "different."

The physician is in the best position to guide the school in this respect. It is not sufficient for the physician to just write a note to the school indicating that the medication is to be given. A school conference with the physician and parents in attendance is probably the best way to discuss how drug therapy will be implemented. If this is impossible, at least a phone conference with the school should be arranged.

During such a conference it should be stressed how, by giving medication, a child's self-esteem can be enhanced, or how he can be made to feel he is "bad" and only the pill converts him into a "good" child. For this child, the teacher can have a critical role in improving his self-esteem or reinforcing the feeling that he is "bad" without his pill. When appropriate, complimenting the child on his school achievements can help much with the development of self-esteem; at inappropriate times, reference to the medication can leave long-lasting negative effects. For example, a teacher frequently asked a child on stimulants if he took his pill before he came to school. Without recognizing it, she asked this each time the child acted up. Soon the youngster began asking for "two pills" so that she would be "good" at school. It was only then that the teacher realized she was implying that the child was "bad" if he did not take his medication. School personnel should be altered to such seemingly innocent comments.

Furthermore, if communication between physician, school, parents, and the child is maintained, there is no need to inquire if the child has had his medication. Prior to modifying drug therapy, the physician must notify the school of the impending change. If the school was not notified about a change, the teacher could safely assume that the child had taken his morning dose.

Generally, one would expect that the physician and/or the parents would initiate communication to be certain that the child's total treatment plan is integrated. If this does not occur, however, perhaps the school can take the initiative in "educating" the physician and parents by calling a conference.

The Child

As has been stated in an earlier chapter, children with learning disabilities frequently have a poor self-concept which in time can add to the child's difficulties. Such children may show behavior problems or neurotic difficulties which necessitate therapy through personnel in a guidance clinic or other similar facility. If a child is in therapy, the therapist can explain why the psychostimulants are used and together with a physician answer any questions the child may have regarding his medication or behavior. If the family physician is prescribing the medication and no other therapist is involved, then it is important that this physician talk directly to the child. Having the parents act as a communication link between the physician and the child interferes with the child's attempt to develop a trusting relationship with the physician. Also without direct communication, the physician cannot check on the possibilities of inappropriate dosage or side effects.

It should be explained to the child that the medication will aid him in controlling his actions, that the pills are not magic and will not make him into a different person, nor will they make all his problems disappear. Telling a child the story about John (described earlier), stressing how John felt his medication gave him time to decide what he wanted to do, is a useful technique in explaining drug action to children.

Before durg therapy is started the child should be told about possible side effects with the instructions that such symptoms must be reported to his parents. When the child comes for check-ups he again should be reminded and asked about side effects.

The Physician

The physician must be responsible for monitoring the medication. He must accept and carry out this responsibility. Routine medication checks should be done at least every three months. At such times, the parents and the child should talk with the physician, and programs should be modified if necessary. In addition, the child should have a comprehensive physical evaluation every 6–12 months. Likewise, as already mentioned, the physician should have direct communication with the school, especially with the child's teacher. Preferably a school conference should be held each year, so that the new teacher can meet all the members of the child's therapeutic team.

TYPES OF DRUGS AND THEIR USES

Typically the psychostimulants have been described as the preferred drugs for children with learning disabilities. Other types of medication have been favorably compared to the stimulants, but for one reason or another, over time, these drugs have not gained acceptance. First, these less-accepted drugs will be considered to analyze why they are less successful in the treatment of learning disabled children. Then, after some general comments on initiating drug therapy, Benedryl, Dexedrine, Cylert, and Ritalin will be described.

Drugs Other Than Stimulants

Tranquilizers, antidepressants, and a variety of other drugs have been used in the search for a more effective drug in the treatment of perceptually and learning disabled children.

PHENOBARBITAL

This hypnotic has been used with adults for a calming effect. In children, however, its effect is frequently one of increasing anxiety and hyperactivity. It should *not* be used with hyperactive learning disabled children. In those children who in addition have convulsive disorders it may be a necessary part of the anticonvulsant regime, but other anticonvulsants should be considered first.

THORAZINE (CHLORPROMAZINE) AND MELLARIL (THIORIDAZINE)

These drugs are typical of the major tranquilizers. They are effective in reducing hyperactivity, particularly in severely disturbed children. Typically these drugs are used not with the usual learning disabled child, but with the child who, in addition, has a psychotic disturbance or a severe aggressive behavior problem. Some researchers believe that the decrease in activity is a result of the drowsiness produced by the drugs rather than a physiological improvement. Adverse effects tend to occur more often with these drugs than with the stimulants. Sometimes even acute toxic reactions are seen (e.g., allergic reactions, blood dyscrasies). Though these reactions are less frequent in children than adults, nonetheless, *such drugs must be used with caution.*

TOFRANIL (IMIPRAMINE)

This antidepressant has been used successfully in the treatment of enuresis. Usual doses in children average 50 mg per day (1–2 mg per kg weight per day). In the treatment of hyperactivity and learning disabilities, successful usage has also been reported. However, in this disorder the dose used was substantially higher, i.e., 100–200 mg per day. Such higher doses *have caused serious side effects.* Children taking 4–10 mg/kg a day have experienced convulsions. Furthermore, a study by Winsberg *et al.* (1975) showed that even on 5 mg/kg per day children may show electrocardiogram changes. Largely as a result of this study the U.S. Food and Drug Administration, in 1975, warned that only a dosage up to 2.25 mg/kg is to be used in the treatment of children.

CAFFEINE

In 1973, a pilot study indicated that children who drank two cups of coffee per day showed a decrease in hyperactivity. A second study (Huestis *et al.* 1975) comparing caffeine, Ritalin, and Dexedrine with a placebo showed that although a slight improvement was seen, this was not significantly greater than the placebo. The authors suggested that a similar study should be done on a larger sample. At this time, however, it does not appear that caffeine is a very effective drug for the treatment of learning disabilities.

LIBRIUM (CHLORDIAZEPOXIDE)

This is one of several minor tranquilizers used. Though findings have not been uniform, most investigators believe children who show hyperactivity on an emotional basis respond best to this drug. It is less effective in the hyperactive learning disabled child.

MISCELLANEOUS GROUP

The two most interesting therapies in this group consist of megavitamin therapy and the elimination of food additives, the results of both still requiring much more definitive research and confirmation.

Pauline (1968) defined orthomolecular therapy as "the treatment of mental disorders by the provision of the optimum molecular environment for the mind, especially the optimum concentrations of substances normally present in the human body." Hoffer and Osmond (1960) proposed that because of a series of biochemical reactions, children with schizophrenia may be benefited by the use of large doses of vitamins (mainly niacin, Vitamin C, and B_6). Later Cott (1971) applied this therapy to children with learning disabilities. Although Cott reports favorable results on a clinical basis, controlled studies have not been done.

Feingold has hypothesized that artificial dyes and other additives in foods may increase hyperactivity associated with learning disabilities in children. He has advocated elimination of these substances from such children's diets. Though on a clinical level Feingold has reported improvement, controlled studies are lacking.

General Comments on Initiating Therapy

Whatever drug is used, be it in adults or children, theoretically the smallest dose which will produce the desired effect is the therapeutic dose. Since this varies somewhat on an individual basis the general rule is to start the child on a small dose, gradually increasing the dose every few days. The initial dose is usually estimated on the child's weight. That dose is increased until a relief of symptoms is seen, or until side effects are seen, or until the maximum recommended dose is reached. If side effects develop or the maximum recommended dose is reached but the symptoms still persist, that medication is discontinued. After a few days' wait to be certain that there is no remaining blood level of the drug, a new medication may be instituted. If the desired effect is seen but side effects are also seen, the dose is titrated down so a balance is established between a minimum of side effects and maximum effectiveness.

In most medications, continuity is important. The exception to this rule is the use of psychostimulants. Generally it is recommended that psychostimulants be discontinued over long vacation periods. Many therapists feel that such rest periods prevent the development of tolerance to medication or possible toxic effects (or even effects such as interference with growth). These rest periods can also be used to assess how the child appears with no medication, and this can allow for dose adjustments.

As mentioned earlier monitoring of the drug therapy by a physician with medication checks being done about one in three months are necessary. Likewise, the child should have periodic general physical examinations with routine laboratory work (complete blood count and urine analysis). In addition, the responsible physician may feel that other tests such as liver function tests should be done from time to time.

Drugs Most Frequently Used in Learning Disabilities

Typically, the psychostimulants are the drugs of choice. Occasionally, however, Benadryl is also a useful adjunct in the therapy of these children.

BENADRYL (DIPHENYLHYDRAMINE)

This is one of the oldest and safest of the psychoactive drugs. Basically it is an antihistamine, but it also has calming properties. It has been used with very young hyperactive children and also as a nighttime sedative with older children. Though not specific to learning disabilities, its anti-anxiety effects are useful in clinical practice, particularly as side effects are rare.

The most common psychostimulant used in learning disabilities are the amphetamines, Cylert (pemoline) and Ritalin (methylphenidate). Each of these drugs will be considered according to the description and general action of the drug, dosage, side effects, and special considerations.

THE AMPHETAMINES

This group consists of similar substances with minor chemical variation. The two major forms are optic isomers (isomers are substances which have identical molecular composition, but their spatial arrangement is different, i.e., they are mirror images of each other). Dexedrine (dextroamphetamine) is the d-isomer. Cydril (Levamphfetamine succinate) is the l-isomer. A mixture of the two forms is Benzedrine (amphetamine). It is felt that the d-isomer is the most potent, the mixture of the two forms is less potent, and the l-isomer is the least potent. However, a recent study comparing the d-isomer and l-isomer to a placebo indicated that even though Dexedrine appeared generally superior, the difference between the two forms was not significant. Furthermore, in twenty five subjects who showed a favorable response, three responded only to levamphetamine while five responded only to the dextroamphetamine (Arnold *et al.* 1976). This study is mentioned since from these findings it appears possible that a child who shows no response to one form may clinically show improvement to the other form of the isomer. However, as the various forms have similar actions only Dexedrine (d-amphetamine) will be discussed in this chapter.

DEXEDRINE (DEXTROAMPHETAMINE)

This is a sympathomimetic amine with CNS stimulant activity. As the drug acts on the autonomic nervous system, peripheral actions of increasing blood pressure and stimulating respiration are seen. In adults it is primarily used as an appetite supressor in the treatment of exogenous obesity, and as a stimulant in the therapy of narcolepsy. Unlike other stimulants, Dexedrine does not cause or potentiate the likelihood of seizures, so it can be used in persons who have convulsive disorders. However, because it frequently has an effect on appetite, it must be used with caution in persons who have diabetes as the insulin requirement may be changed.

In persons who have even mild hypertension, it should not be used because of its tendency to increase blood pressure. In children it is used as an adjunct with other therapies in learning disabilities for those children with the concomitant behavioral problems of hyperactivity, impulsivity, distractibility, and emotional lability. However, it is not recommended for children under three years of age.

As with all other drugs the smallest dose that produces the desired effect should be used. In children 6–12 years of age 5 mg/day is the starting dose and the medication is increased by 5 mg/day in intervals of about one week. In this age group probably 20 mg/day is an average dose and 40 mg/day should not be exceeded. The medication can be taken as an elixer, tablet, or sustained release capsule.

In children, the more severe problems of chronic intoxication that have been reported in adults are *not* seen (namely, drug addiction and occasionally a severe paranoid psychosis). However, side effects of insomnia, anorexia, irritability, headaches, dryness of the mouth, and other gastrointestinal problems are seen in children. Occasionally in children a paradoxical reaction is seen, i.e., the child becomes more hyperactive and disorganized.

CYLERT (PEMOLINE)

In this drug, the CNS stimulant activity is generally felt to be similar to the other stimulants. However, it has somewhat less effect on the autonomic nervous system; thus it is less likely to produce effects on blood pressure or respiration. Cylert is a new drug, having been on the market only a short time, so long-term follow-up studies are unavailable as yet. Likewise, comparative studies of Cylert with the other stimulants are not available in the usual research literature.

This medication is long lasting, reaching a peak of action in 2–4 hours. Most of it is excreted by the kidneys within 24 hours, but traces can be found in the blood up to three days later. Since it is primarily excreted by the kidneys, the drug should not be used in persons who have kidney damage. Likewise, some changes have been found in the liver in susceptible individuals.

The usual starting dose is 37.5 mg/day in children who are six years and older. Because it is long lasting, the drug is given in a single dose. The average dose is 56–75 mg/day, and 112.5 mg/day should not be exceeded.

The most frequent adverse effect with this drug is insomnia. Weight loss may be seen in the first few weeks of therapy, but usually this is only a transient reaction. Other negative effects reported included gastrointestinal symptoms, irritability, headaches, and drowsiness, and even hallucinations have been documented.

RITALIN (METHYLPHENIDATE)

As a psychostimulant in treating children with learning disabilities and related problems, Ritalin is at least as effective as Dexedrine. Some children, however, may show a positive response to Ritalin and not Dexedrine, and *vice versa*. Generally, it is felt that Ritalin has fewer adrenergic effects (i.e., seems to effect the sympathetic nervous system less) than Dexedrine.

As with the other psychostimulants, the medication is not recommended for children under six years. Since in earlier studies it was felt that Ritalin (and other stimulants) had a negative effect on growth, this is still a caution. [As mentioned earlier, Bock *et al.* (1975) presented a conflicting report on this finding.]

Ritalin appears to lower the convulsive threshold, thus potentiating the likelihood of seizures in susceptible individuals. Likewise Ritalin inhibits the metabolism of several other drugs so that if a child is on other medication readjustments in the other drug may be necessary.

As with all medication, susceptible individuals may develop hypersensitivity. Other adverse reactions include, irritability, insomnia, anorexia, skin rashes, dizziness, and headaches. In some individuals, blood changes (anemia, leukopenia, and thrombocytopenia) have been reported.

Usually the drug is given in the morning with a total of two or three doses being given. The last dose should *not* be given in the evening, as this increases the likelihood of the child being unable to sleep. As with all medication, the child is started on a small dose, and the dosage is gradually increased. The average dose is 20–30 mg/day, and rarely should the dose exceed 40 mg/day. No long-lasting or sustained-release form of the drug is available.

SUMMARY

Psychostimulants are at times a very valuable adjunct in the therapy of the learning disabled child. As with all medications there are risks as well as benefits which must be carefully weighed in deciding whether or not a child should be placed on drugs. Careful monitoring is necessary throughout drug therapy, and a team approach of the patient, the physician, the school, and the parents should be involved. Two important cautions must be exercised in using drug therapy with children who have perceptual processing deficits resulting in learning disabilities. First, drugs should never be substitutes for other types of therapy or educational programming; they should constitute a single element in the total regimen. Alone, the results of drugs will generally be unsatisfactory.

Secondly, communication between all members of the team of persons concerned with the learning disabled child must be open at all times. As Morse has stated elsewhere, "we should begin to recognize that the child grows up in a total milieu, and it is this total milieu which is the remedial environment." Appropriate use of psychoactive drugs may be an important dimension in the total remedial environment.

REFERENCES

Arnold, L. E.; Huestis, R. D.; Smeltzer, D. J.; Wemmer, D.; and Colner, G. "Levoamphetamine as Dextroamphetamine in Minimal Brain Dysfunction." *Archives of General Psychiatry* 33 (March 1976): 292–301.

Beeker, H. K. "The Powerful Placebo." *Journal of the American Medical Association* 159 (1955): 1602–606.

Bock, L.; Langford, W. A.; Mackay, M.; and Sum, G. "Childhood Chemotherapy and Later Drug Abuse and Growth Curve: A Follow-Up Study of Thirty Adolescents." *American Journal of Psychiatry* 132 (4) (April 1975): 436–38.

Borland, B. L., and Heckman, H. K. "Hyperactive Boys and Their Brothers." *Archives of General Psychiatry* 33 (June 1975): 669–75.

Bradley, C. "The Behavior of Children Receiving Benzedrine." *American Journal of Psychiatry* 94 (1937): 577–87.

Cole, S. B. "Hyperkinetic Children: The use of Stimulant Drugs Evaluated." *American Journal of Orthopsychiatry* 45 (1) (1975): 28–37.

Cott, A. "Orthomolecular Approach to the Treatment of Learning Disabilities." *Schizophrenia* 3 (1971): 95.

Davis, G. D. "Effects of Central Excitant and Depressant Drugs of Locomotion Activity in the Monkey." *American Journal of Physiology* 188 (February, 1957): 619–23.

Denhoff, E. "To Medicate—To Debate—Or To Validate." *Journal of Learning Disabilities* 4 (November 1971): 467–69.

Feingold, B. F. *Why Your Child is Hyperactive.* New York: Random House, 1975.

Fish, B. "The One Child One Drug Myth." *Archives of General Psychiatry* 25 (3) (September 1971): 193.

Gatz, A. *Manter's Essentials of Clinical Neuranatomy and Neurophysiology.* Philadelphia: Davis, 1968.

Gittelman-Klein, R., and Klein, D. F. "Methylphenidate Effects in Learning Disabilities." *Archives of General Psychiatry* 33 (June 1976): 655–64.

Grinspoon, L., and Singer, S. "Amphetamine in the Treatment of Hyperkinetic Children." *Harvard Educational Review* 43 (4) (November 1973): 515–55.

Gross, M. B., and Wilson, W. C. *Minimal Brain Dysfunction.* New York: Brunner/Mazel, 1974.

Hoffer, A., and Osmond, H. *The Chemical Basis of Clinical Psychiatry* (Springfield, Ill.: Thomas, 1960).

Huestis, R.; Arnold, L. E.; and Smeltzer, D. "Caffeine Versus Methylphenidate and d-Amphetamine in Minimal Brain Dysfunction: A Double Blind Comparison." *American Journal of Psychiatry* 132 (8) (August 1975): 868–70.

Laufer, M. "Hyperkinetic Behavior Syndrome in Children." *Journal of Pediatrics* 50 (1957): 463–74.

Millichap, J., and Boldrey, E. "Studies in Hyperkinetic Behavior: II Laboratory and Clinical Evaluations of Drug Treatments." *Neurology* 17 (May 1967): 467–71.

Pauling, L. "Orthomolecular Psychiatry." *Science* 160 (1968): 265.

Safer, D.; Allen, R.; and Barr, E. "Depression of Growth in Hyperactive Children on Stimulant Drugs." *New England Journal of Medicine* 287 (1972): 217–20.

Satterfield, J. M.; Cantwell, D. P.; and Satterfield, B. T. "Pathophysiology of the Hyperactive Child Syndrome." *Archives of General Psychiatry* 31 (December 1974): 839–44.

Simpson, L. "The Effect of Behavioral Stimulant Doses of Amphetamine on Blood Pressure." *Archives of General Psychiatry* 33 (6) (June 1976): 691–95.

Sleator, E. K., and von Neumann, A. W. "Methylphenidate in the Treatment of Hyperkinetic Children." *Clinical Pediatrics* 13 (1974): 19–24.

Sprague, R.; Barnes, K.; and Werey, J. "Methylphenidate and Thioridazine: Learning, Reaction Time, Activity and Classroom Behavior in Disturbed Children." *American Journal of Orthopsychiatry* 40 (4) (July 1970): 615–28.

Weiss, G.; Minde, K.; Werry, J. S.; Douglas, V.; and Nemeth, E. "Studies on the Hyperactive Child." *Archives of General Psychiatry* 24 (5) (May 1971): 409–14.

Wender, P. *Minimal Brain Dysfunction in Children.* New York: Wiley, 1971.

Whalen, C. "Psychostimulants and Children: A Review and Analysis." *Psychological Bulletin* (in press).

Winsberg, D. G.; Goldsteim, S.; Yepes, L. E.; and Perel, J. M. "Imipramine and Electrocardiographic Abnormalities in Hyperactive Children." *American Journal of Psychiatry* 132 (5) (May 1975): 542–45.

13

Parents and Families

MUCH HAS BEEN LEARNED about children with learning disabilities in the decade since the publication of the first edition of this book. However, from what has been said thus far it is apparent that, like the problems facing the King of Siam, the learning disabled child is a "puzzlement." He is a puzzle to professional persons, and he is a most complex puzzle to his parents. Many parents will remind us quickly that the word *puzzle* is hardly appropriate, for puzzles, they say, can be solved. This puzzle is still so complex that few of the pieces can be fitted together, and certainly no universal solution is in obvious view. We hasten to agree that the learning disabled child is one of the most complex problems which could face parents, for it oftentimes would appear that the child is completely normal. From all outward appearances this is the case. "Some parents feel that because a child looks perfectly normal, and in some cases has a normal behavior pattern, there could not possibly be anything wrong with him."

In talking with many many parents of learning disabled children, the author is frequently reminded of how isolated these parents feel from other parents in their communities. It has been the author's impression that parents appear at first to withdraw into themselves as they strive to understand the complex problems which their child presents and as they try to adjust their hopes for their child with what appear to be insurmountable odds facing him. It is easy to understand how alone parents can feel. It is also apparent from what we have said in this book that indeed parents are not alone. They will undoubtedly find many others in their community who are faced with the same problem. Parents, we have said, can be supportive of one another in their mutual attempts not only to understand the problems facing their child, but to bring into focus for themselves a meaningful plan for their personal and family adjustment.

320

In this chapter we try to share with the reader who may be learning about the problem of learning disability for the first time comments, feelings, and suggestions from some of the parents with whom we have conferred over the years. We do this in the belief that parents may find feelings of satisfaction in realizing that many others have faced and are facing problems similar to their own.

Occasionally the parent of a learning disabled child will be ill-advised by a professional person who may fail to see evidence or who more likely may not have sufficient evidence to make a firm diagnosis. If one does not recognize that his child has a problem, certainly he will initiate no constructive solution. In cases where there is doubt remaining, parents need to request periodic re-evaluations until such a time as the problem is either confirmed definitely or is clinically ruled out of consideration.

Once a child's problem is discovered and recognized, planning becomes essential. Planning for this child can be discouraging, or it can be a challenge intelligently accepted and logically met. At best, however, it will be time consuming and tiring. It will require an infinite amount of patience and wisdom.

In this book the reader has been exposed essentially to the author's point of view. There are a number of outstanding educators and psychologists in the United States and elsewhere who are doing excellent work with learning disabled children. While in some details their work and methods differ from what has been outlined here, it is important to note that basically there is little difference in the approach which they take to the learning disabled child and his education or training from that discussed here. Different vocabulary is sometimes employed, but an analysis of the essentials of the methods which they use in comparison to those discussed here show relatively little difference—none of them basic differences. Marianne Frostig as well as Sheldon Rappaport, each working with these children in different parts of the United States, view the learning disabled and perceptually handicapped child with somewhat greater emphasis on psychoanalytic concepts and ego psychology than the author does. Nevertheless they are in essential agreement with the author insofar as methods, techniques, materials, and general approach to children are concerned. Similar statements can be made regarding the important work of Ray Barsch and Gerald Getman. Both of these men place a very heavy emphasis on the development of motor skills—Barsch in terms of triordinate concepts of motion, mentioned earlier; Getman in terms of visuomotor development. However, these are not at variance with this author's point of view, and it would appear that these two researchers also feel that much if not all of what has been said in this book coincides with their methods or at least is not antagonistic to them.

Elizabeth Freidus, formerly a student of Alfred Strauss, brings to the learning disabled child the same point of view as this author does, coupled also with a keen insight into the growth and learning problems of children. Her approach, also strongly based in ego psychology as well as in the learning theory of conditioning, varies only in details from the concepts discussed in these pages. Newell Kephart, as earlier stated brought to the learning disabled child a thorough understanding of the early work of Werner and Strauss and added a broadly based training program which resulted from detailed and exact diagnostic procedures. Again, while details of method may differ slightly, the essential assumptions concerning dynamics, methods, and approach are similar. Haring and Phillips likewise employed the approach indicated here with emotionally disturbed hyperactive children without significant change from what we have described.

With the exception of the extreme use of motor development and the unusual emphasis on crawling employed by one group of people, commented upon earlier in this book, parents should realize that there is more unanimity of point of view among the leaders in this phase of special education than there are differences or conflicting points of view. There are those who place a greater emphasis on one phase of the training programs than others, but these are indeed relatively minor considerations. There is indeed an unusual degree of agreement. The work of James Gallagher, employing a tutorial approach with mentally retarded brain-injured children, emphasizes elements which are identical with those of the author. Gallagher, however, has stressed the method in a tutorial arrangement with a single child, whereas the work of this author has been with small groups of perceptually handicapped children who were usually intellectually normal. Fundamental differences, however, do not exist between the two writers.

We feel that the general agreement we have noted is an important consideration for parents. Often parents become confused as they move from one professional person to another by what appear to be and often are fundamental differences in diagnostic and treatment methods. Certainly there are many differences of opinion in the educational methods employed in other fields of special education with other types of handicapped children. Parents of learning disabled children can generally assume that there is basic agreement within the professions regarding the manner in which their children should be treated. There is little question but that if this book were written by one of another of the individuals we have mentioned in the preceding paragraphs different emphases would be made by them. Essential agreement would be observed between authors, however, in most major points which have been made.

PLANNING FOR THE WHOLE FAMILY

Parents of learning disabled children are frequently concerned about meeting their responsibility for the perceptually handicapped child when there are normal children in the family.* The learning disabled child demands much more time than a normal child. Parents, realizing this, often feel guilty for not being able to give their normal children as much time as they give the learning disabled child.

It has been said that parents seem to love the handicapped child more than the brothers and sisters. Well, whether we love them more or not is hard to say, but I do know that we have more patience with the handicapped child. One parent told me that her answer to that question was the same answer her mother had. Someone asked this mother which one of her eight children she loved the best. She replied, "The one that needs me most." I think it is normal for a parent to try to compensate with this child because we are afraid that the world might cheat them out of so much. As we study and learn what is considered normal and not normal, we also become aware of other people's problems. Even the so-called normal child seems to get more understanding from us. We realize that everyone has problems and people cannot be judged and censored by us.

This desire to meet the responsibility for normal as well as learning disabled children has been similarly expressed by many parents with whom the author has counseled. "If I give Chuck all the attention that he demands and that I know he really needs, what memories will Billy and Sue have of their mother? I don't want them growing up to hate me for what I was unable to do for them." Another mother said. "It seems that I never have time for the two older ones. I always have to give so much attention to Roger. I am sure that the others must think I don't love them sometimes."

"Tom's birthday party was just about ruined last year," reported still another parent. "He had planned for it for so long, and I wanted to make it a real celebration for him, That day was the worst Timmy had had for months. I had to give him so much attention that before we were through both Tom and I almost wished we had never heard of birthdays."

*Many parents have shared their feelings about their children with the author as this book was being prepared. One parent in particular made her feelings about these children readily accessible, providing the author with typed notes and a tape of comments. Quotations appearing in this chapter, except as otherwise indicated are those of Mrs. Edna Thompson, Birmingham, Alabama, a parent of a learning disabled child. The author is much indebted to her.

These are typical misgivings experienced by mothers and fathers as they attempt to be wise arbiters. Their attempts at parental leadership fail so frequently that they begin to doubt their abilities as parents.

It is quite true that the learning disabled child will demand much attention, in all probability considerably more than that given other children in the same family. The best laid plans to provide equitable amounts of time to each child often go awry because of unexpected situations which will occur in the normal course of the daily activities of the learning disabled child. This predicament is unavoidable, and both parents and their other children must come to accept it as a part of reality. If the problem is permitted to be magnified in the minds of the parents, guilt feelings will develop, and this useless waste of emotional energy will deprive all members of the family of the basis for wholesome relationships with one another.

Parents can do much in providing each child with sufficient attention by careful scheduling and advance planning. Fathers as well as mothers must enter into this important role. Eleven-year-old Tom will not resent the time his father spends with a younger hyperactive brother if Tom knows that his father generally will spend some time after work with him alone in playing catch, working on a model boat, in going to a baseball game, or in a hundred other ways having some time together alone. Arrangements need to be made so that one or the other parent can give time to the normal children without the presence of the learning disabled child. During these periods the other parent will be providing attention to the learning disabled child. The same parent need not function in the same role every day. However, it is important that the nonhandicapped children know that they can expect undivided time from their parents, and it is important for them to know when they can expect it. Knowing that it is possible, they may not always demand or utilize the time. They are satisfied in knowing that the time with their father or mother is available if they need it.

Normal brothers and sisters should come to have a feeling of love and warmth toward the handicapped child. It will assist normal children in accepting him if parents schedule private discussion sessions without the handicapped child's presence. The learning disabled child, who will also have his share of the parents' attention, will accept this arrangement if the whole matter is treated in a natural, straightforward manner. When the normal children learn that time is available to them when they will be able to command their father's or mother's undivided attention, they quickly come to appreciate what is being done. They return to the activities which encompass the entire family with a renewed ability to appreciate, tolerate, and accept realistically the often difficult behavior of their learning disabled brother or sister. In a family which practiced this type of scheduling, normal brothers and a sister not only reported (when they became teenagers) that they could remember no feelings of threat to themselves or antagonisms toward their parents, but that they took pride in the achievements of their younger learning disabled brother.

> I could always count on Dad giving me a few minutes of his time for my problems, whatever they were,when he came home from work. Sometimes this was only when he was taking a shower and getting cleaned up for dinner, but it was always my time. I grew to appreciate and value this time with him even though he must have sometimes been tired and wished he could do something else.

A college student reported:

> When I was in elementary school and my younger brother was always in my hair, my father would arrange to spend Saturday morning with him while I played with my friends, and Saturday afternoon he would spend with me in anyway I wanted. Those Saturday afternoons stand out in my memory as the highlight of my childhood. As I think back now, this idea which my parents had probably was the lifesaver for me. I could have been forgotten and I could have easily learned to dislike my brother and possibly my parents, for Manny was a real joker when he was growing up. I learned to love my parents for giving me time to be alone with them. And I learned to love Manny and to accept his behavior because I knew that it would not always interfere. There would be times when I could have Dad alone or have Mother alone, because they often switched.

Still another teenager reported:

> My parents always made it a rule when my brother and I were growing up that I'd have my birthday parties or other types of entertainment alone. This meant that the parties had to be smaller than they might otherwise have been, for while I was having a party, Dad would usually plan for Larry to go with him on a "private trip," as they called them. This was fun for him, and it made my parties a success. It was tough on Mom, for she would have to run the party herself, but she has often said that it was a happy pleasant experience for her too because she knew that the whole deal wouldn't be interrupted with a scene of some sort. Larry was three years younger than I and wouldn't have fitted into my group anyway, Sometimes they'd arrange for a babysitter or friend to take Larry, and then they'd both be around. That was great. Both Larry and I now look back on these arrangements with

good feelings. And I respect my parents for having the courage to plan for each of us separately. I guess that's the key to the problem. They did plan. It wasn't left to chance.

The young people whose comments have just been noted have the perspective of experience to which to resort. They also have maturity and experience available from which their insights can be drawn. The problem is often more acute for the brother or sister who is still very young and does not possess a lengthy experiential background. Recently in the clinic the author was seeing Tod, a nine-year-old boy with marked perceptual and learning problems. His older brother, Jon, aged twelve years, had accompanied Tod and his mother to the clinic. After spending some time with Tod, he and the clinician returned to the waiting room. Upon arrival there Jon blurted out, much to the consternation of the mother, "Well, Tod, are you still your damn old nasty hyperactive self?" This outburst, while overlooked for the moment, was sufficient for the clinician to suggest that Jon remain behind and go to lunch with him. Over lunch the two were able to discuss Jon's feeling about Tod, his parents, and numerous other familial issues, most of which centered around Tod and which Jon really failed to understand or appreciate. No one had helped him to do so.

"They're always talking about him," said Jon. "Never me. If you look at the tables in *our* living room and in *their* bedroom, all you see are books about hyperactive children, learning disability children, and a dozen other types of nutty kids. We couldn't go to camp last summer because there wasn't enough money to do that and to have my Mom and Dad go to a national convention in Seattle to learn about Tod. I guess I'm selfish, but everytime I want something that's important to me, like a skateboard, or a bike, or taking golf lessons, I am told 'Sorry John, we have to save that money to help out with Tod, you know.' Boy, do I *know* it. They don't have to tell me. I just can't wait to get old enough to really earn my money. I don't even have an allowance like the other kids in my class do—or some of them at least."

The emotional dam was broken, and Jon continued. "You know, we don't just have one baby sitter; we gotta have two. That costs money. I guess I like that though, 'cause it's two guys who come to take care of us. They're great and they play ball and stuff with me too. They never talk all the time about Tod like my folks do. They even stayed with us when they were in Seattle. Tod got along all right with them. He's different then. I almost like him. It's not fair the way my parents do everything for Tod and nothing for me. I even asked Bill (one of the sitters) if I could live with them. I know they have an extra room, 'cause I saw it once when I went to their house. That would be great—no more Tod." With that statement dessert melted into tears and a blubbered "What am I supposed to do?" Jon needs help too. His parents need assistance in providing as balanced a home life for both boys as is possible. This is a family which will profit from both individual as well as family counseling. When Jon agreed to permit the clinician to discuss his remarks and feelings with his parents, the latter were overwhelmed. "Dammit, he feels just like I do most of the time," commented the father. The mother's tears were added to Jon's. Out of this twelve-year-old boy's deep concerns for his own welfare, a long-term family therapy experience was begun with all parties, including Tod, participating and committed to seek ways to obtain a better family life experience.

Planning, scheduling, and careful family structuring will go far to insure parents' devoting nearly equal time to all the children. It will enable normal brothers and sisters more fully to accept the time which must be given to the learning disabled child because they know that their turn will come, and the learning disabled child ceases being a threat to the normal children by commanding all the adult attention. Guilt feelings are reduced on the part of parents, because they know that they are indeed building into the lives of their other children time to become acquainted, to have fun, to build respect, and to love and to learn about one another.

We say all this in the full recognition that the learning disabled child will demand much more attention than the other childdren, much more thought, and much more effort. "Our children are like blotters when it comes to soaking up emotions. There is so much misunderstanding of their problems everywhere. They are keenly aware of being accepted or not accepted, loved or not loved." Recognition by parents of learning disabled children of this awareness on the part of their children will make it possible for them to "love these children beyond what is ordinarily expected" without limiting the lives of other children.

LET'S SHOP AROUND SOME MORE

"Once you have a handicapped child—from the moment of confirmation—your world is changed, and not always for the worse," reports one parent. Most parents, as we have said previously, have some notion, frequently unverbalized, that there is a problem present in their child long before diagnosis is sought. Many times, however, parents who have limited background in child growth and development think that "this is just the way children are." "It's tough, but I guess it's the way with all kids," said a father. On these and other occasions it may be the teacher who first suggests to the parents that there may be a serious problem.

A first grade teacher had been doing some reading on aphasia and suspected that this might also be the cause of another child's difficulties. The parents were called in and when they had their child evaluated they found that she might benefit from the . . . School. This same child had a classmate in her room who seemed to have the same problems and learning disabilities. The teacher also called these parents for consultation. These parents were indignant. But they did realize that the child had a coordination problem, so they took the child to an orthopedic man. He certainly would be limited in diagnosing brain-injury. With this one doctor's opinion that this child was normal, the parents have dismissed the thought that anything can be wrong with their child.

These two experiences illustrate a problem which can have important ramifications for the child involved. In the first instance the parents, on receiving a suggestion of a potential problem, sought and found adequate diagnostic information. Thereafter they made appropriate plans for the child. In the latter situation the problem was emotionally received. The parents were unwilling to consider that something they could not see might actually be a problem. Rather than following the teacher's suggestion these parents, in reaction to the outward sign which they could see, went to a physician whose specialty was inappropriate. From the orthopedic point of view the child's problem did not seem a significant deviation from normal development. The doctor gave the parents an opinion that was correct from his point of view. Parental refusal to accept the problem for what it was and their willingness to accept only what they wished to hear served neither the child nor themselves.

Parents are often the first discoverers of the problem.

In many cases our parents knew something was wrong at a very early age. Long before the child started school, these facts were evident, because these children did not come along physically as fast as their brothers or sisters. Many of us learned about the problem when we visited the doctor, because the child could not speak properly. In our own case, the mystery of why our child choked on things like cookies and crackers at an age when all his contemporaries were eating them with great gusto was solved with the diagnosis. We learned that his tongue could not function because of the damage to his fine motor control. This included the fine motor control in his fingers also. I also suspected something might be wrong when he would throw his hands over his ears at every unexpected noise.

These are important clues which the parents themselves observed and which can be the basis for a referral.

Parents are often disturbed that physicians or other diagnosticians provide them with very limited information following evaluation.

I realize that I am about to step into dangerous territory. When something is viewed from only one angle, the parents' angle in this case, sometimes the perspective is distorted. We realize that there are many problems presented to the psychiatrist and pediatrician which are so similar to the problems of our children that it is natural for a professional to be reluctant to alarm a parent. The parent, so alarmed needlessly, might feel some bitterness toward the doctor for the hours of anguish when later events proved that there was no cause for alarm. This goes under the heading of "Derned if you do and derned if you don't." We might group teachers in a similar category. Teachers are also faced with viewing the problems of the children. Some of these parents have not been asking for or seeking any information when their children seemed to have a problem. The teacher then is sometimes met with hostility when she suggests that evaluating be done on the child.

The attitudes which have been expressed by this parent are all valid ones: valid on the part of the parent and valid on the part of the examining professional people. So long as there are people with the freedom to think independently and to do for others what they think best there will be these problems. We do not wish to change this. On the other hand, parents seeking information should be given it in order that they can guide their lives and those of their children. Physicians and psychologists should give parents as much information as they can even though in the end this information may, as a result of growth or further study, sometimes need to be modified. If the professional person says "the future may prove me wrong, but for now it will not hurt the child if we plan for him in this way; indeed it may help him," then the parents are willing to enter into a period of trial, of experimentation, of wait-and-see. The presentation of facts cautiously but honestly and fully will permit the parent to enter into the planning for the child. The parent in full possession of relevant information does not feel excluded from his correct responsibility. Parents given only half the facts because the entire diagnosis is not subject to conclusive demonstration are unable to give their full cooperation to any plan. They are often only more frustrated and tense. We have found that parents who are given the full story, even though it must be time after time called tentative, become both emotionally and intellectually involved with the child and the professional team.

Parents, too, have a responsibility in diagnosis. It is wise upon becoming aware that a complex problem of learning disability or possible perceptual processing deficit exists to seek the best diagnostic service possible. In an earlier chapter we have outlined what the nature of this diagnostic service should be. Parents should make inquiry of school officials concerning how to find the most complete and professionally reliable services. Often such facilities are close at hand; on other occasions some travel may be required. "Many parents had gone from doctor to doctor and from school to school until they were in a state of despair." Some parents likewise refuse to accept the reality of a situation and go from one physician to another or from one agency to another, not in reality seeking information with which to better plan for the life of the child, but seeking only the information which they want to hear. One set of parents who referred themselves to the writer presented him with a dossier regarding their child. It contained the reports of twenty-three physicians in seventeen different clinics! An ostrich-type approach does not lead to constructive action on the part of anyone.

Most interdisciplinary diagnosis is exceedingly reliable. The results of the first studies may not be conclusive, but they are undoubtedly sufficient to permit the making of initial plans. We have written already of the necessity of continuous diagnosis and evaluation. The search for conclusive information and understanding of the perceptually handicappped child may have to continue over a long period of time. If sufficiently broad initial diagnosis can be undertaken, however, parents will feel more secure. There will be plenty of information on which to start. If later, new data suggest a change in the course of action, parents should not assume that incompetency was at the basis of the earlier findings. At the later evaluations, the diagnosticians will be more familiar with the child, and the child himself will have matured to a point where he is more responsive to the diagnostic techniques which are available.

Parents and professionals must trust and respect each other. If parents can accept the idea that their responsibility is first to find good diagnostic facilities and then the idea that they will accept the findings of that diagnosis as a springboard for planning, they will be serving their children well. Parents who enter into the fact-finding aspect of the problem with the preconceived notion that professionals do not know what this problem is, that ultimately there will be a physician found who agrees with them, or that the school people don't really know how to teach or they would be able to reach the child—these parents will in fact serve no one. Indeed their continued search to support their own disbelief may delay the start of the educational program to the point where it may be too late to assist the child significantly. This is not a time to "shop around."

It is the opinion of this writer that parents should be as much a part of the diagnostic team as they wish to be. After all, who knows the child better than the parents who have lived with the child with learning disabilities? Trust in professional opinion, reduction in the random seeking of "additional information," and personal involvement in the development of an appropriate management plan for the child will come from participation in the parent-professional interdisciplinary team. The author is a colleague in an interdisciplinary training facility located in a large university. An Interdisciplinary Appraisal Services is a part of the facility. Here families of children with problems are regularly seen for extensive diagnostic assessments and for the development of the management plan. Parents are incorporated as fully as possible and as fully as they desire in all evaluations of their children—psychological, pediatric, nutritional, dental, educational, speech, and many other disciplinary appraisals. When the parent is not actually in the room with the child during an examination, arrangements for observation of the assessement through closed-circuit television is made. In the latter instance, an advanced graduate student or the case coordinator assigned to the family is usually present to interpret to the parent what is being viewed and its possible relationship to the problem for which the child was referred in the first place. Out of this exposure to the diagnostic procedure comes an appreciation for being made a partner in the process, an appreciation of what the child's problem really is, an understanding that there is no need for further seeking of other professional opinion, and a willingness to cooperate in carrying out the management plan jointly agree upon. The values of the interdiciplinary approach are many, for numerous opinions focused from different disciplinary points of view on the same problem bring confidence in the professional judgment with single disciplinary examinations cannot provide.

TO LOVE, HONOR, AND AGREE

In our parents, the confirmation of the handicap is accepted as a problem needing special education by both. When the parents do not agree, then we have a problem within a problem. I would venture to say that when both parents agree it is easier on the child. By this I mean agreement that a problem exists. I recall a situation a few years ago. A child had been evaluated and it was decided that he needed special teaching at the School. He had been a most unhappy child at home. His teacher had ridiculed him for poor work in some areas. He was able to function in the areas where he had no learning disability. He could not function where he had the disability.

The teacher could not reconcile the fact that he could do well in one area and do nothing in another. She thought that he was just being stubborn. The child was so unhappy and frustrated. He took out all of his hostilities on his mother. She was well aware that the child had a special problem. The father could not or would not admit that the child had any problem that was not normal. Even though the tuition was cut in half the next year, the parents would not send him back to the School. I saw the mother with the boy on a school day about six months after the next term of school had been in progress. I asked how the child was doing. She had let him stay out of his school that day bcause he was in such an agitated frame of mind. She also mentioned very quietly to me that he was back, as she put it, to beating her to death again. While this child was in what seemed the proper program all the hostilities had ceased in the home. This child has known nothing but failure since returning to the public school.

The failure of these parents to agree to the fact that a problem exists or to agree to the general nature of the problem resulted in this instance in the child being educationally hurt and the mother emotionally injured.

Fathers have a particular responsibility in connection with learning disabled and emotionally disturbed children. They frequently fail to notice their child's problem simply because they are so infrequently around the child. They may leave for work before the child is out of bed in the morning. They often return home after he is again in bed or so late as to be able to see the child only for a short time. "He's always all right with me. I don't understand why you can't get along with him." said one father to the mother of a hyperactive perceptually handicapped child. It is true that the child did perform quite differently when the father was there. However, the father was with the child for only short periods during the day and on week ends. When the father was home, there were two persons to operate the home. There were four hands to do what two had tried to do throughout the long hours of the week days. The father, when he returned to the home, was a new voice, a new set of standards, a different situation for the child, and as such he commanded the attention and notice of the child. The child thus did behave differently when the father was home. The child would be expected to behave differently in these circumstances. Since the father often is not in a position to view the child from the same perspective as the mother, he must accept with much faith the statements of the mother and the teacher that in truth a problem of some sort does exist. Until it can be demonstrated differently, parents must have faith in one another sufficient to permit facts to be exchanged. The marriage contract should include an agreement to agree where children are concerned! One diagnostician known to this author will see children in his clinic only when he has assurance from the parents that they will agree jointly to accept the findings and jointly to plan for the future of the child. The problem in reality is too much for one parent; it is impossible if one parent fails to support the other or insists upon a position contrary to the needs of the child.

GO TELL IT ON THE MOUNTAIN

It has often been observed by the writer that parental failure to agree is caused by one parent's fear of letting others know that a problem exists. Whatever the motivation, and there can be many reasons for this, the adult prefers to keep the problem secret.

> I have never been able to understand secretiveness for secretiveness' sake. About three years ago, a parent acting upon the suggestion of a doctor who was acquainted with both of us called me. At first I was at a loss to understand why the doctor had made the suggestion. Never had I met a person whose ideas were so alien to mine. Her child had been evaluated and was enrolled at the School. She asked me how I kept it secret. I told her that just the opposite of that attitude, I took the attitude that I wanted my family and friends to know of the problem so that my child or my husband or I would not be needlessly blamed for any behavior my child was incapable of controlling. She made the statement that she would much rather have people think that her boy was an unruly child than have them know that anything was wrong with him. She had not even told her parents or in-laws the situation. Her main reason for this behavior was that she was afraid some stigma would be attached to him, and that friendship would be denied him that he otherwise would have if he had not had a record of what she considered a mental problem. I need not tell you that this was one of the most confused women I have ever met. There seemed to be no closeness between mother and son, and the son did not even want her to attend any of the functions where parents were invited.

There are several important observations in this report. First, secretiveness in this case is the result of confusion on the part of the mother that learning disability or perceptual processing deficit is equivalent to mental illness or insanity. Nothing could be further from the truth. The attitude is typical, however, of many misconceptions. In reality this mother is not so much concerned that her child has a "mental problem" as she is to protect herself from the criticism of her friends. She implies that through her son she will be criticized for having passed on to him some sort of a mental condition. The parental ego is involved to the disadvantage of her son. Secretiveness is prompted by many things, most of which are aimed at protecting the individual who has the secret rather than protecting the learning disabled child. The child is used as the excuse for parental behavior.

"If I let it be known that my son is learning disabled or hyperactive, he will be excluded from the Cub Scouts and from many other experiences. He'll never have the wonderful memories I had as a boy," said one father. "In my company," said another father, "great stress is placed on family and family concepts. Promotions and my advancement in the executive aspect of my firm depends on my family as well as on my ability. If anyone is the office should learn that I have a learning disabled girl, my future would be shot. We have to keep it a secret." When this statement was investigated privately by the author with the president of the corporation involved, it proved to be erroneous. This fantasy, however, served as an excuse on the part of the father so that he never would have to face publicly the reality of his child. The parent's personal convenience was selfishly put ahead of the child's welfare.

A mother states, "If I should tell others that my son is learning disabled , it would certainly get back to my mother-in-law. She'd then have another excuse for reminding my husband that he shouldn't have married me in the first place. She has never liked me and tries to come between us all the time." The child's adjustment is sacrificed for the personal protection of the mother.

Another mother who was accompanied to the interview by her husband took just the opposite point of view. Looking to her husband from time to time for support, which she always found, she said:

> It was difficult for us to admit that we had any sort of a problem in our boy. He was the first of three. It was terribly difficult to admit that he might be or was perceptually handicapped, for we didn't know really what that meant. But we agreed that we'd never be able to do anything for him unless everyone we knew was in there working with us. Sometimes I used to think that if only I could climb up on the roof with a great megaphone and shout to the world what our problem was that it would be just that much more support for Gary. He's a great boy—a teenager now—and he's always been a wonderful boy. Why should he be punished because I haven't taken the time to tell my neighbors and friends, and his teachers and his friends, what the problem is? When they know a little about his behavior and the reasons for it they rarely do anything but want to get into the act and cooperate. It's true

that there have been times when even the honest facts about Gary have been misunderstood by someone in whom I had confided. However, these experiences have been very few and relatively unimportant at their worst. For the most part I am sure that it has been better to face the world realistically. I never have had that gnawing feeling which some of my acquaintances have of being afraid my secret will slip out. There is no secret. The whole world can know if in knowing it will help Gary.

There is an important consideration for parents in the earlier mentioned action of the doctor who referred the secretive mother to a friend who also had a learning disabled child. Although in this instance not much change was effected in the behavior of the first mother, the procedure is an important one. Often parents of handicapped children find it of great value to be able to talk with other parents of children who have similar problems.

In one community parents of learning disabled children have selected from within their group several couples who have learned to accept their family problem and who have broad and understanding points of view regarding it. These parents made themselves available to physicians, psychologists, and educators as ones to whom others might be referred to see how the problems of a learning disabled child were handled by at least one family. In this community the new family was accepted almost on a "big brother" basis by the family who had lived with the problem longer. No professional counsel was provided, but the parents who might only recently have learned about the problem of their child could discuss the normal problems of family living and see how they were met. Eating, bathing, playing in the neighborhood, parental attitudes, adjustment to other children in the family, family outings and celebrations—these and many other typical family experiences could be discussed. It could informally be determined by the 'new" parents where the learning disabled child fitted into each activity. New parents report this to be a remarkable help in initially understanding their child. "Without the help of Mr. and Mrs. Green," said a mother, "I don't know where my husband and I would be today. The professional people were wonderful, but they could go only so far. No one of them ever had his own perceptually handicapped child in his family. The Greens had lived with the problem for a good many years by the time we met them, and they were like parents to us. I felt I could call her when I got into hot water and she'd have some suggestion to follow. Later I began to call her when we had won a battle. I never had the feeling I was imposing. It's been a real people-to-people experience, I can assure you."

Another family reported:

> Our family contacts helped us to break out of our shell. We were pretty numb after we learned the facts about Bobby from our clinic staff. For a while we hardly even wanted to talk about it to ourselves. Then the psychologist at the clinic suggested that it might be helpful if we talked to the Johnsons, a couple who had a brain-injured boy a little older than ours. We agreed, I think out of fear mostly—fear of not knowing what else to do. The Johnsons called and suggested that we go on a picnic with them near their home and that we not bring Bobby. Their boy was present, however, and we saw how he behaved and functioned. We suddenly realized that there were at least two children in the world with similar problems, ours and the boy we were watching. We weren't the only ones. Later that evening at the Johnsons' home we had the first of many talks—talks which have grown into a rich friendship. We learned that there was hope if it were coupled with patience, and we learned that to bottle up the problem would do no good. To be able to talk with someone who has experienced the problem is a wonderful thing. It made it possible for us to break out of our emotional bind. Secretiveness is impossible for us now.

The importance of these informal contacts for parents of learning disabled children cannot be overestimated. It is an important service which parent associations can perform. It must be recognized, however, that not all parents should accept the responsibility for assisting new parents. Couples who will perform this important service should be carefully evaluated. They should be parents who have come to a realistic understanding of their own child or children and who also have a realistic expectancy for their learning disabled child. They must be parents who volunteer for or willingly accept the invitation to serve in this important capacity. There should be no compulsion involved. It is also undoubtedly wise that not more than one or two sets of new parents be assigned to a single couple, for the value of the plan will diminish if the "counselor" couple begins to feel imposed upon in terms of time. It must be remembered that these people are also parents whose continuing responsibilities are ever present for their own learning disabled child. If, however, careful matching of families can be effected within reasonable time limitations, then a very valuable service can be established for those whose children more recently have been diagnosed as learning disabled. One plan which utilized the "family counselor" idea provides some guidance regarding the role of the couples agreeing to participate in this program. The orientation may be provided by the psychologist, psychiatrist, or social worker associated with the parent organization. At other times the plan is more informal and full reliance is placed on the quality and adjustment of the couples who are invited to participate. Both concepts have proved their worth.

DO WE SPARE THE ROD AND SPOIL THE CHILD?

I realized that my son's power to reason was much better than I had given him credit for. I promised his sister she might ride in the front seat on the return trip home from the pool as Todd had ridden to the pool in that seat. A very wet little Todd climbed on the front seat to go home. My daughter reminded me that I had promised her the front seat. I told her that Todd had already wet the seat so why not just let him sit there. It was then that Todd said. "I always get my own way." Needless to say, I became more aware from that moment on where learning disabled behavior stopped and a bad little boy began.

A mother said to the author:

If it's a question of giving in to Jim or going through an unpleasant situation to insist that he do something our way, my husband and I usually take the path of giving in. We know that he gets away with murder, but I just don't have the energy to cope with the emotions which would result if we said "no" to him. The problem, though, is that it seems to be getting worse as the days go by.

The situation will continue to worsen as long as the child in his immaturity is the pilot of his ship. Children do need adults and their leadership.

Learning disabled children are no different than are normal children in their need to test limits, to seek the easiest way out of a situation, or to find satisfactions of a sort in maintaining a position of mastery over the adult. Parents should not be confused by their knowledge that their child has a physical disability. As the mother stated, it is necessary to determine where learning disabled behavior" leaves off and the behavior of a "bad little boy begins." In one earlier chapter we discussed the need for parents to establish appropriate limitations for their child and then to accept the child at all times despite his behavior. We stated that even when the child is misbehaving he must be accepted as a child who can be loved and who is wanted. This however, does not mean that the child's *behavior* need be accepted in the same light. If a child oversteps the limitations which have been set up, then he, like all children, must realize the consequence to himself and to others of his actions. It goes without saying that discipline must be appropriate to the behavior—"the punishment must fit the crime." If disciplinary measures are unduly harsh in relationship to what the child may have done, he is aware of and looks upon the adult as an unfair person in this competitive game of growing up. On the other hand, the child will undoubtedly know when the bounds have been overstepped. He will accept fair discipline from the adult and will respect him for insisting upon a recognition of the limitations. As a matter of fact, children appear to enjoy having some limitations established, and, though they cannot verbalize it, they understand the need for maintaining them.

Children who are not held to fair standards of behavior are unhappy. This applies to learning disabled children as well as any other child. A success experience can be achieved by the learning disabled child which is as effective as any other when his parents or teachers can point out to him how well he behaved in a certain situation. "David," said his teacher, "I was surely proud of you yesterday when you said good morning and held the door open for Miss Jones when she came in with her arms filled with packages." David, a perceptually handicapped, nine-year-old boy who is still far from ready to achieve successfully in all things, is complimented on good behavior on an occasion when he had no thought of misbehaving. He has a warm glow of accomplishment for having his correct behavior recognized later by an adult in whom he has confidence. Out of this informal type of teaching comes a success experience as important as any other which makes David begin to realize that he can accomplish his ends with adults in socially satisfying ways almost better than when he misbehaves and calls for their attention through unpleasant actions. David, when he first joined his teacher and seven other boys in a clinical teaching program, was completely antisocial. He had no consideration for anyone, for no one cared for him. He neither read nor understood writing or number concepts and was malicious, threatening, explosive, and unpredictable in his behavior. The home life has changed imperceptibly in the two-year period David has been in a special program. In spite of this, while there is still a way to go. David is much more responsive to people. He is considerate of their feelings. He tries to find ways to help others, sometimes in an ingratiating way, for all of his techniques for working with others are not yet well developed. He enjoys sharing his things, showing others his prized possessions, and *asking for advice.* He now knows that in others he can seek and often find satisfying solutions to his problems. This change in David's behavior, in spite of a completely unstable home situation, is essentially the result of a program of limitation-establishment, acceptance of the child, insistence on maintenance of the limitations of behavior, fair discipline when limitations are exceeded, and praise for things which the boy does appropriately without having been prompted. An alert teacher is a necessity in this situation.

Drs. Fritz Redl and Ruth Newman have developed a concept that parents and teachers will find helpful in their contacts with learning disabled children. This is the concept of the life-space interview. Many children, particularly emotionally disturbed and perceptually handicapped children, find themselves propelled into behavioral situations without understanding how they got there. This is not to indicate that the behavior of these children is preordained but that with a poor background of success feelings, with their entire perspective clouded by tension, with perceptual problems which are fundamental to appropriate action, and with feelings of insecurity in their dealings with adults, learning disabled children will often be triggered to action which normal children would be able to control. On more than one occasion when a child has been asked by the author why he did something, his genuine and honest response was, "I don't know."

Since the learning disabled child may not understand why he has behaved as he has, the life-space interview is a most effective technique to use to build up understanding with him. After the incident is over, the child and the adult sitting together or walking together, literally analyze the incident which has just passed. "What did you do? What did you think about when you were doing it? How did you feel? What do you think he felt about it? What do you think I felt about it? What could you do another time to prevent this from happening again?" These questions are not asked in a scolding manner; no preaching or criticism is involved. The interview instead is a cool and reflective analysis of the elements of the situation which had just occurred. If the child cannot verbalize, the adult may be able to reconstruct the problem for him and as well make an attempt to reconstruct the child's feelings and emotions. The child profits from simply hearing the situation discussed in an objective way. He has a frame of reference provided him upon which he can build a better understanding of himself and his actions. These interviews need not be lengthy. They are never formal, "across-the-desk" arrangements, nor should they take place in the heat of emotion. It is best for the interview to follow problem behavior, and the situation should be warm and accepting. This is a time when both child and adult can analyze their feelings and their behavior. Out of these objective experiences can come better understanding between the child and parent or teacher. The child feels confidently that even when he has done something "bad" the adult will take time to work it through with him so that, as one child said, "There is never any bad taste left for me when I talk with Mr. Roberts." Parents report that the life-space interview, or modifications of it, serves as an important technique of child adjustment in the home as well as in the school. Often it will be the "other" parent who will work with the child in analyzing some incident which took place earlier with the mother or father just as, in the school or clinic setting, it may not be the teacher necessarily who always enters into the interview with the child. It may be the principal, a guidance counselor, a school psychologist, or other adult with whom the child has a reasonably satisfactory relationship.

Sometimes the child with learning disabilities is so "concrete-minded" that even the life-space interview situation is difficult for him to accept. The author has employed a technique frequently with these children which makes the situation concrete and also quickly attracts the attention of the child to the issue at hand. Assume that there are five children involved in an encounter in a classroom. The perceptually handicapped child is the center of the issue, and has been removed from the class temporarily. The counselor removes coins from his pocket—a half dollar, a quarter, a dime, a nickel, and a penny. "Which one of these is you?" asks the counselor. The half dollar is frequently chosen, because it is the largest. Perhaps the counselor is more directive, and states, "This coin is you." "Let's line the coins up, and let's give them each a name like yours has. Place them in any order you wish." The child arranges them in an order. "That's fine, and we'll come back to that arrangement in a moment. Now put them in a line to show me where you are in relation to the other four"—in terms of height, strength, reading ability, ability to get along with others, etc. "Now show me where you were in terms of the problem we are trying to solve. Who was most important in starting the fight?"—the least, and other settings which provide the counselor with an understanding of what really went on. The child's perception of the situation comes to the fore quickly. He can manipulate the coins easily. If verbal communication is a problem, little is required. The coins are a "third party." The child's "self" is not directly affronted as in talking with an adult. Both the child and the adult can "look at" the coins in a detached manner. Yet the situation becomes clear to both, as the child sees it, and interpretation can be forthcoming. Sometimes the child can go so far as to respond appropriately and differently than earlier when the counselor tells him to "place the coins showing how Fred [his opponent in the fist fight] would line them up as he saw it."

Whatever techniques are employed, it must be recognized that the internally unstable life which the perceptually handicapped child has requires an externally secure environment. Structure as it has earlier been defined need not be harsh, emotionally limiting, punitive, or thoughtless. Structure is present for an important and valid reason, namely, to provide the child with those essential things which he himself lacks and to make it possible for him gradually to learn through success experiences socially acceptable ways of living. Intelligent uses of discipline and the intelligent insistence on the recognition and the maintenance of the limitations which have been established will go far to assist the learning disabled child in meeting the goal.

> In many cases I find that it does no good to run into a blank wall of obstinacy. With a little careful handling we can open a side door and find a purring cat, but to storm into the front door produces a roaring lion.
>
> During his early years, he wanted nothing changed from the way it was. This included his bed sheets. After a few terrible scenes where he pulled the clean sheets off his bed when he found me in the act of changing them, I decided that there was an easier way. While he was outside, I would post my mother at a window and change the bed with a frenzy of a Keystone Cop. Maybe this handling would be considered incorrect by the psychologist with the overall view in mind that the world will not handle him with special care. Wrong or right, my experience over the past four years has led me to believe that calmness on my part has encouraged calmness on his part and little by little the need to handle him with special care and go in through a side door has been less necessary. By the time he is ready to face the world on his own, his habit of balking may be at a minimum and he will have had a far more pleasant childhood to remember.

Whether or not one agrees with this mother's procedure for changing bed linen, the procedure is effective in keeping tensions at a minimum without sacrificing behavior standards by the child. The calm approach to this and dozens of similar daily experiences keeps the possibility of parent-child friction at a minimum.

> The handicapped child in the home is always a source of a problem, great or small. The problems differ greatly with the size of the handicap and the size of the family. Can you imagine how difficult it must be to have twins with one normal and one learning disabled? Each one thinks the other has the advantage. As both twins become teenagers, can you imagine how the handicapped one longs for the life of his twin?

In these circumstances parents must not only be wise, they must be diplomats. Nothing that one can say will solve all of the problems inherent in these situations. A policy of absolute honesty and understanding combined with a calm intellectual approach to all problems within the home, and a long history of impeccable fairness in dealing with each child will provide the springboard for children to realize that in all situations over which parents have any control the best decisions can be expected.

CAN I PLAY TOO?

A parent said that it would be so wonderful if someone could find the magic word to tell the world that these children are not always retarded. The fact that they cannot accomplish tasks in some areas has still not affected their ability to reason, to want to be accepted by the neighborhood children, or to receive praise and understanding for the tasks that they do well. The fact that many are not retarded means that such children are even more sensitive when they are ridiculed or ostracized from neighborhood groups.

I know I do not have to explain the heartbreak that the parent feels when her child is set aside because he just does not fit into the group. I watched the neighborhood children playing baseball. My son was sitting off by himself. The children that were playing were the very same children he plays with when they play something he also can play. When they play make-believe, there is no finer make-believer on the whole block! He can supply conversation for all the make-believers. But a ball game eliminates his participation.

But we are some of the fortunate parents. I explained at a very early date, to all who would normally come in contact with my son, the difficulties we had with him and the fact that they might find him difficult at times also. We are blessed with a fine neighborhood and people. On the whole they react with kindness and understanding when you value their friendship and trust them enough to explain. We used the same philosophy with the church and the kindergarten. I thank God for the boy across the street who is the same age as my child. This child accepts my child as he is. Once, after playing with my child for only a short time, he returned to his home. His mother asked if we had sent him home. She said that her child said, "No, Todd sent me home, but I will sit here a few minutes and then go on back and he will have forgotten it." If such understanding can be found in a child of eight, it does not speak well, in some cases, for adults with no understanding who are 28 and 38.

Reasonable actions and attitudes are based on understanding.. The key to the behavior of the child and the neighbors which has just been described is the fact that this parent did not defend her child's behavior selfishly. She took the initiative and time to explain the child's problem to neighbors and particularly to the parents of the children who she hoped would play with her son. She was aggressive in behalf of her child. She was neither secretive nor defensive. She was understanding when problems in neighborhood play occurred as they inevitably will in spite of the best laid plans. Neighborhood play is another aspect of childhood which for the learning disabled boy or girl cannot be left entirely to chance. It is, like all aspects of life planning for these children, one which must be planned for and seriously considered. Todd's passive participation during the baseball game may not really be a defeat for him, since he knows that under other circumstances he will be accepted by the group. Although he may want to play baseball, and some day undoubtedly will have the skills to do so, he feels accepted in watching the game, and he is confident that at other times he will be an active participant. Perceptually handicapped children must recognize that no one individual has all the skills he wishes. No one individual can perform equally well in all things nor, perhaps, achieve all the goals he sets.

WHERE IS THE REPORT CARD?

We fell into divided camps on the matter of report cards. In most cases the parents realized that a report card was only a means of comparing one child to another on different subjects with a group of children at the same age and mental level. They realized that such a report could really tell them nothing. But because Johnny Public School takes a report card home, our children feel that they are being further set apart because they do not have one. It seems that the report card would only serve as a morale builder.

The problem mentioned by these parents is recognized by educators. Most of those who have worked with learning disabled children for any length of time feel that it is better not to use a variation of the traditional report card to inform parents of their children's progress. Whether or not the report card is the best way to report any child's achievement level is an appropriate question. It is certainly not an adequate method in the case of learning disabled children. A report card cannot accurately express the progress of a learning disabled child until such time as, through the processes of education and learning, he has been brought to an achievement level commensurate with his chronological age group, or in the case of a mentally retarded child with his mental age group. Prior to that time it is better to use the conference technique in reporting.

One effective reporting technique involves two steps. First the teacher sends a written report to the parents every six or eight weeks. Most learning disabled children progress too slowly during the initial months of their educational experience to warrant reporting on a more frequent basis. However, it is best not to allow more than two months between reports. Parents are interested in the teacher's judgment of how well their children are doing, and a two-month interval provides a good opportunity for assessing growth.

The written report will contain a subjective evaluation by the teacher regarding the child's progress in those skills which are being emphasized with him. These will be the areas of deficiency which have been indicated by the various diagnosticians who have seen the child together with those noticed by the teacher during his continuous educational evaluation. Thus, in the case of a given child the report to parents may include a paragraph on motor training and the development of gross-and fine-motor skills. In the same report there may be comments on the child's ability to work with puzzles, pegboards, tracing materials—all basic to the abstract skills indicated in Table 2 in an earlier chapter. If the child is beginning to read or to deal with number concepts in a more formal manner, this, too, will be reported upon.

With the report to parents will be found a card indicating a suggested time for a parent conference at which both parents are expected to be present. If both cannot be present, then a different time will be sought when they can both be there. The presence of both parents is desirable so that both will hear the same thing, facilitating agreement regarding plans for the child and approaches to home adjustment. Many misunderstandings and disagreements occur when only one parent attends the educational or the diagnostic staff conferences.

During the parent conference the teacher will elaborate fully on the written report which has been sent home. The child's work will be examined and compared with that of the previous conference. Parents should not come to these meetings seeking compliments for their child. If this can be the outcome, fine. More important, however, is that these meetings should be a time for absolute frankness on the part of three members of the team who are trying to meet the needs of a brain-injured child. In a face-to-face meeting parents and teachers can come to important agreements. They can agree upon a learning schedule for the child in the weeks immediately ahead. On some occasions it will be an agreement to continue the same program currently underway. In other instances the teacher may feel that the child is ready for something new or on a more advanced level. This will be explained to the parents, and suggestions may be made regarding modification of home activities. The decision may be made to retreat to a level of greater simplicity for a period. Joint planning such as is here described can result in a continuously appropriate program for the learning disabled child. The child is compared to himself, not to others of different abilities, mental capacities, or chronological age.

One school with which we are familiar makes no use of the report card concept. Rather the parents are urged and expected to visit the school and the child's classroom at any time. Over the years an informal "drop in" practice has been established, and both mothers and fathers (to a lesser extent) do come to the school with great frequency. The visitations are so frequent that both teacher and the children essentially ignore the presence of the visitors who over time get to know all the children by name. The adults stop to visit with the children, not only their own, join a reading group, take part in a motor activity (usually losing), and in other ways enter into the activity of the class while they are there. The teacher on the other hand provides informal opportunities for the parents to observe their own child, and these observations not only give the parent some idea of the progress being made but serve as the basis for the parent conference which will take place more formally at regularly scheduled intervals when both father and mother can be present together.

The informality of this approach has much to be said for it. Group and individual comparisons within a group are not possible. The child does not carry home a rating which can be ridiculed or criticized by brothers, sisters, or others. The evaluations are continuous, spontaneous, and realistic. The children look forward to the classroom visits and the conversations regarding their progress which accompany them. There is nothing artificial.

SUMMER ARRIVES AND THEN WHAT?

Frequently parents have asked the author for advice regarding summertime activities for their children. Should we send the child to a summer camp or should he continue in school? Should we employ a tutor? The answers will depend upon the individual child's needs. However, for a child who needs the special class and clinical teaching which has been described in this book, the two or three months of summer vacation may prove to be too long a cessation of his needed educational experience. It is advantageous for the child if the school year can be extended to include a major portion of the summer. If the full vacation is taken, a long period of reorientation and relearning will be necessary in the fall.

The question of summer camps, vacation day schools, or other informal recreational activities must definitely be measured in terms of the child's development, skills, and abilities. Camps built around permissive concepts are certainly inappropriate for learning disabled children. There are only a few summer camps established to serve the needs of learning disabled children which have both professionally prepared staff members and an educational concept which will support the school-year program. On the other hand, a summer camp program which takes into consideration the learning disabled child's needs may provide enriching experiences for the child.

PARENT ORGANIZATIONS

Since 1960, many organizations have been formed to provide opportunities for parents to exchange ideas, to participate in both informal and formal educational programs, and to serve as a medium through which efforts could be made to improve or to sponsor the development of educational, diagnostic, and therapeutic services. In the appendix of this book is a list of many national, state, and local organizations of this type to which the reader may refer. Often these organizations have professional advisory committees made up of doctors, psychologists, and educators from the community. It is a nearly ideal situation when parents and professional people can work together toward a mutual goal.

Parents of learning disabled children are encouraged to seek out a parent organization and to become affiliated with it. In the event that no nearby organization exists, parents might find it helpful to contact the national Association for Children with Learning Disabilities, Inc., likewise noted in the Appendix. This organization is concerned with the development of comprehensive programs for learning disabled children. It is also possible through contact with this organization to learn about national conferences related to brain injury and learning problems; parents are always welcome at these meetings. It is possible also to obtain information regarding the creation of chapters of the association in communities where none exist.

Parent organizations provide an excellent forum for exchange of ideas. They permit parents to become acquainted with others who are seriously concerned about mutual problems. In some cases they provide specific services of diagnosis, parent consultation, and education. Usually, however, it is the policy to work through existing professional agencies rather than to establish separate parent-operated programs.

EXPECTANCIES

It is reasonable for parents to ask about the future of their children. Measures of prediction for normal children are relatively crude; for brain-injured children they simply do not exist. One parent made the following remark:

> I think that the ghost of the future haunts us all if we let it. Many parents are concerned about what will become of their children when they are young men and women. To those of us who have younger children, I cannot but think that there is much hope. In another few years something might be done to make the public realize that even though some of these children were not able to complete a full high school program, they may excel in some field even more than a child who has a fully rounded education. If he can do the one thing he can do well, he might be a very desirable employee. But education and the public will have to open these doors.

The concerns expressed by this parent are valid ones, and they are undoubtedly typical of those felt by most parents of learning disabled children. This author is one who also feels that the future holds much promise for learning disabled children as a group. There are several reasons for feeling this way.

First, throughout the United States, Canada, and many other countries of the world there is a deep parental concern about these children. This concern is expressing itself in the development of parent organizations which are bringing the problem to the attention of federal and state legislatures, of the leaders in many professions, and to the public in general. When parents themselves bring the problem to light where it can be viewed objectively, where it can be made apparent for all to see, constructive plans for attack can be created. It is essential that this problem be seen objectively for what it really is, namely, a complex problem of human development which must be challenged on an interdisciplinary basis and for which immense sums of money must be set aside in order that it can be studied and in order that plans for its solution can be projected. Informed parents can assume important leadership roles, and through their efforts national, state, and local action programs appropriate to our understanding of the problem can be initiated. This is being done. Sound programs of action are being developed, and implementation is taking place in an increasing number of communities.

Secondly, simultaneously to the development of informed parent groups, federal agencies and private foundations are allocating large sums of money to broadly based programs of research. The perinatal studies mentioned in an early chapter of this book are examples of this. The National Institute for Neurological Diseases and Blindness, the Bureau for the Education of the Handicapped in the United States Office of Education, and the National Institute of Mental Health, worthwhile federal agencies, have already made significant investments of public money in research and demonstration projects pertaining to learning disabled children. Private organizations have individually and sometimes jointly made significant grants to a variety of research pertaining to learning disabilities in children and young people. Admittedly much more is needed. We are not suggesting that what has been done is enough. What has been done is significant, however, and it is indicative of a basic interest on the part of fund-granting agencies. Epidemiological studies are needed, and these are needed soon in order that adequate community planning can be undertaken. Studies concerned with etiology need further emphasis, and, following these, studies must be undertaken which are concerned with prevention. Research is required regarding the learning process of these children. More information is needed on how these children perceive. Studies are needed in the area of educational technique and method. More important, studies are needed of learning disabled children and youth as they leave special classes, enter high school, and eventually accept jobs; this kind of study will indicate the effectiveness of educational, medical, or psychological regimens. Parents have reason to expect that these research investments will be made. They can be encouraged that the stage is set. Some extensive studies have been completed, and others have been initiated. Much more is required before complete satisfactory answers can be had to the many pressing problems which still exist.

Thirdly, professional personnel with appropriate preparation are becoming more available. It is perfectly obvious that patience is going to be required for some years to come, however. A corps of research personnel interested in the problems of learning disabilities cannot be created over night. College professors competent to prepare teachers of learning disabled children will have to be developed before teacher preparation programs of high quality can be initiated. These do not exist in sufficient number now, not at least in quality. Pediatricians, psychologists, psychiatrists, and the many other professional people who are needed in diagnosis and continuing services have to be sensitized or prepared to assume major roles in this aspect of child development. All this takes time, money, effort, and patience. The brief history of the field cannot be made an excuse for minimal action in starting progams of professional training. The problem is now known to exist, and the community as well as state and federal governments must share fully in its solution.

Let us assume that a full complement of services is available in a community and that children can be properly served with education, medical, and ancilliary services. What then is the expectancy which the parent can reasonably have for his child? Definite answers unfortunately cannot be given which apply to all children. Some generalizations, however, can be made.

First, the earlier the discovery of the problem and the earlier the initiation of appropriate educational and parent counseling services, the greater is the possibility of their being effective with a particular child. It is the author's considered opinion that services which are initiated with children before the chronological age of seven have much greater possibility of resulting in favorable adjustment than when the service if first brought to the child after this age. This statement is made in the full recognition that some children can profit from the program after seven years of age. The author's chief experience with learning disabled children from an educational point of view has indeed been with children older than seven. An inclusive program of education for children with learning disabilities will, of course, provide for children of all ages. The earlier this can be made available to the child, however, the better it is for him and his family and the greater the possibility that he will profit measurably from it.

We have earlier said that delayed recognition of the problem results in situations which are sometimes more than either a good teacher or a willing child can overcome. In the schools of this nations there are children making marginal adjustments to kindergarten who are passed on to the first grade. Here the teacher attempts to extend the preacademic experiences of the earlier year in the hopes that what she believes is immaturity, will be thereby minimized. In the second grade and third grade—an earlier year often having been repeated—these children continue to struggle with decreasing effectiveness. Remedial teaching is ineffective. Mainstreaming as it is presently practiced is of little value and may in many instances be a detriment to the child's progress. Parent conferences result in little understanding of the problem by either teacher or parents. Hope is ever present, but reality convinces the teacher or parents. Hope is ever present, but reality convinces the teacher that in terms of past experience this child will make little progress. A break must be made in the progression toward maladjustment, but no one seem to know where to start. A dramatic modification of the program for the child is indicated, but even now it may be too late to provide for some children what they in truth needed three or four years earlier.

It is the feeling of this author that if early identification of the problem can be made and if early clinical programs are started for the child, the great majority of the children can be helped to achieve acceptable levels of personal adjustment and behavior, permitting them to be re-integrated into an educational program commensurate with their mental age. We do not mean that all of these children will graduate from high school. We mean that the educational placement goal for the learning disabled mentally handicapped child, for example, whose intelligence quotient is below normal irrespective of the brain injury, will be a good special class for mentally retarded children. The educational placement goal for a learning disabled child whose intelligence level is normal or above normal is the regular class in the neighborhood school. Without question, many children when they are given full supportive services can attain these goals. Exact information regarding the number of children who can and do attain these goals will have to wait until longitudinal studies have been initiated and completed. These are the goals, however, and their achievement is dependent in part on the degree of excellence of the program and the early exposure of the child to it.

The keys to the achievement of these goals are early discovery, interdisciplinary assessment, and application of appropriate educational methods. By early discovery we mean *at the latest* utilizing the kindergarten as the identification and assessment year. Initiation of specialized educational methods to those children who need them will take place by the beginning of what for normal children would be the first grade or the sixth chronological year if not earlier. Thereafter the program for the learning disabled child will not be a matter of grade-by-grade progression as with normal children. It will be the continuous expansion of his learning based upon his mental age and his capacity to react with profit to the visuomotor, audiomotor, and tactuomotor training which the teacher provides him. As these skills are acquired the instruction will blend, as we have discussed it, into the beginning of abstract learning involving reading, writing, number concepts, spelling, and related academic emphases. When through this educational process the child demonstrates his achievement at his own rate and in ways that the teacher can interpret professionally, consideration will be given to his gradual reassimilation into the regular track of the school's program. How long this will take will depend upon the child, the nature of his problems, the effectiveness of psychotherapy or parent counseling if they are indicated, and a myriad of other considerations. Some children will respond, as we have stated, in a reasonably short time; others may require four to six years before the return to the regular grades can be considered. Still others, fewer in number, may need the special educational program based on principles described in this book for the duration of their school experience.

Figure 45. This boy, once unable to cope with the most simple group activities, is a contributing member of his Boy Scout Troop and is functioning quite satisfactorily in his neighborhood school sixth grade.

Goals must always be set on an individual basis for the learning disabled child. It is not possible to make predictions for these children as a group. For some few, college and professional life is not an unreasonable expectancy. Until we have careful studies of the achievement of learning disabled children, it must be assumed that this high achieving group constitutes an exceedingly small percentage of the total. For others, and a still larger group, it is not unreasonable to expect that if they possess normal intellectual ability they will be able to complete an adjusted high school program and find satisfactory employment either directly or following some sort of prevocational trade training.

For still others, and probably an increasingly large group, the completion of high school education is undoubtedly impossible. It should not be assumed that these children must be early dropouts. The schools should provide adapted educational and prevocational experiences for learning disabled children for as long as it is legally permitted. These children, however, may not graduate from high school. It is impossible to predict accurately what levels of achievement they may actually attain. The first effort of the schools will be to prepare them for satisfactory personal adjustment and for membership in society at whatever level they are able to function. It is this group of children which the schools in general now fail to serve adequately. It is this large group of adolescents which professional educators must seek ways of serving more appropriately.

We have stated earlier in this volume that some children will need separate and specialized educational programs at the junior and senior high school levels. Children needing such separate facilities often may be those whose enrollment in the special education program came relatively late, too late to prepare them sufficiently to make a satisfactory adjustment in the junior high school. It may be due to the fact that normal growth characteristics of preadolescents when superimposed on the problems of the learning disabled child together results in such a complex situation that the child cannot live happily in the unstructured junior high school. It may be that the child's problem is so deep seated and severe that regardless of early discovery and programming, he needs longer special education planning. As we have said, educators will have to provide for a small number of special classes in both levels of secondary education. Parents have a right to expect the public schools to make as adequate provisions for their children during all the school years as are made for any other type of exceptional child in the community.

This author has always tried to be realistic with parents. It is quite obvious in our present stage of understanding and in the light of the available educational facilities that some learning disabled children who need educational services at the secondary school level will probably also need supervision and extensive community services as young adults. This final group consists of some children with extensive problems who may need the services of a sheltered workshop which provides both prevocational training as well as in the case of some long-term vocational opportunities. As professional understanding of the problems of the learning disabled child becomes greater, as research opens up new avenues of investigation and its results bring solution to problems, as teachers who are highly qualified to provide services to learning disabled children become available and sound educational programs are established, as parents receive and accept appropriate parent counseling—then the number of learning disabled children who must be cared for as adults will become smaller and smaller. Individuals in this group are often characterized by multiple disabilities. The problems we have discussed which are coincident with brain injury may be complicated by severe emotional disturbance, low mental ability, or severe neurological injuries. The sheltered workshop may need to provide them with employment and social opportunities throughout most of their adult lives.

The problem of learning disabled or perceptually handicapped becomes more complicated the lower the intellectual level. In spite of what may be a good educational program, the child may be unable to profit fully from it if he also is characterized by deep-seated emotional disturbances. Some children's learning problems are so extensive as to involve not only the perceptual areas we have discussed in this book, but also by a failure to understand someone or all aspects of communication stimuli. They may also lack the ability to translate these incoming stimuli into appropriate written or spoken responses. These conditions are referred to as types of aphasia, and when they occur in connection with the other learning problems we have described, the prognosis for the child is as of now quite limited.

One thing is certain. Without highly specialized educational programs such as the one which is described in this book, learning disabled children will live unsatisfactory lives as many of them have been doing in the past. With educational programs supported by the many-faceted interdisciplinary services which we have described, the brain-injured child has indeed an opportunity and an expectancy to achieve an adult status which is reasonable in the eyes of society. Without a program specifically geared to his unusual and highly individual needs, the learning disabled (perceptually handicapped or PPD child) child faces an adult future often filled with maladjustment, tension, and rejection. With a program conceived in terms of the nature of the child's problems, he has more than a mere chance of taking his place in adult society as one who is wanted for the contribution he can make to the social and economic world.

While at present there are more unsolved problems than solved ones concerning learning disabled children, this need not always be the case. Many problems have been solved which only three decades ago were looked upon as insurmountable. There are realistic future expectancies for learning disabled children. With continued efforts of parents, professional people, and the financial resources of national agencies in time these expectancies should be reasonably achieved with significant results for many if not all learning disabled children.

Appendix

NATIONAL AND STATE ORGANIZATIONS

T HE FOLLOWING national organization is concerned with the problem of the child with learning disabilities and is a source of information for parents and professional personnel. It maintains a permanent office with an executive director and staff.

> (National) Association for Children with Learning Disabilities
> 5225 Grace Street
> Pittsburgh, Pennsylvania 15236

Parents and teachers may wish to seek information about learning disabled children from sources in their own city or state. Listed below are the names and addresses of organizations which may have available such information. Although an attempt has been made to provide a complete list, in this developing area new organizations make their appearance frequently. Thus there may be unintentional omissions, and addresses, correct at the time of publication, may change. If contact cannot be made through the information here provided, it is suggested that inquiry be made to the Director of Special Education of the State Department of Education of your state. This official always has his headquarters in the state capital, and his address should be easy to obtain.

ACLD STATE AFFILIATES

ALABAMA (Alabama ACLD)
  State Office: P.O. Box 3383-A
                Birmingham, Alabama 35205

ARIZONA (Arizona ACLD)

State Office: P.O. Box 15525
                 Phoenix, Arizona 85060; or
                 Family Services, 1530 E. Flower, Phoenix, Arizona
                 85014
                 Phone: (602) 248-7373

ARKANSAS (Arkansas ACLD)

State Office: P.O. Box 5508
                 Brady Station
                 Little Rock, Arkansas 72205

CALIFORNIA (CANHC)

State Office: P.O. Box 4088
                 Los Angeles, California 90051
                 Phone: (213) 831-8644

COLORADO (Colorado ACLD)

State Office: P.O. Box 955, Loretto Station
                 Denver, Colorado 80236
                 Phone: (303) 934-6956

CONNECTICUT (CACPLD, Inc.)

State Office: 20 Raymond Road
                 W. Hartford, Connecticut 06107
                 Phone: (203) 236-3953

DELAWARE (Diamond State ACLD)

State Office: Hanover Presbyterian Church
                 18th & Baynard Blvd.
                 Wilmington, Delaware 19803
                 Phone: (302) 571-0230

FLORIDA (Florida ACLD)

State Office: P.O. Box 15187
                 Sarasota, Florida 33579
                 Phone: (813) 922-2687

GEORGIA (Georgia ACLD)

State Office: P.O. Box 29492
                 Atlanta, Georgia 30329
                 Phone: (404) 633-1234

HAWAII (Hawaii ACLD)
  State Office: P.O. Box 4203
                Honolulu, Hawaii 96813
                Phone: (808) 949-4941

IDAHO (Idaho ACLD)
  Office of President: 3973 Kilarney
                      Boise, Idaho 83704
                      Phone: (208) 384-3105

ILLINOIS (Illinois ACLD)
  State Office: P.O. Box A 3239
                Chicago, Illinois 60690

INDIANA (Indiana ACLD)
  State Office: 4026 Huth Drive
                Fort Wayne, Indiana 46804

IOWA (Iowa ACLD)
  Office of President: 1948 N.W. 92nd Court
                      Des Moines, Iowa 50322

KANSAS (Kansas ACLD)
  Office of President: P.O. Box 208
                      Colby City, Kansas 67701
                      Phone: (913) 462-6348

KENTUCKY (Kentucky ACLD)
  State Office: Louisville Medical Center, Inc.
                334 E. Broadway, Suite 323
                Louisville, Kentucky 40202
                Phone: (502) 584-6289

LOUISIANA (Louisiana ACLD)
  State Office: P.O. Box 14634 S.E. Station
                Baton Rouge, Louisiana 70808
                Phone: (504) 924-1581

MARYLAND (Maryland ACLD)
  State Office: 320 Maryland National Bank Bldg.
                Baltimore, Maryland 21202

MASSACHUSETTS
  Office of President: 1296 Worcester Road, Box 908
                      Framingham, Mass. 01701

MICHIGAN (Michigan ACLD)

State Office: 2338 N. Woodward
Royal Oak, Michigan 48073
Phone: (313) 548-4455

MINNESOTA (Minnesota ACLD)

State Office: 1821 University Avenue
St. Paul, Minnesota 55104
Phone: (612) 646-6136

MISSISSIPPI (Mississippi ACLD)

State Office: P.O. Box 12083
Jackson, Mississippi 39211
Phone: (601) 982-2812

MISSOURI (Missouri ACLD)

State Office: P.O. Box 3303
Glenstone Station
Springfield, Missouri 65804

MONTANA (Montana ACLD)

State Office: Box 2457
Missoula, Montana 59801
Phone: (406) 549-8687

NEBRASKA (Nebraska ACLD)

State Office: P.O. Box 6464
Omaha, Nebraska 68106
Phone: (402) 391-8622

NEW HAMPSHIRE (New Hampshire ACLD)

State Office: 1 E. Dunstable Rd.
Nashua, New Hampshire 03060
Phone: (603) 888-0474

NEW JERSEY (New Jersey ACLD)

State Office: P.O. Box 249
Convent Station, N.J. 07961
Phone: (201) 539-4644

NEW MEXICO (New Mexico ACLD)

State Office: P.O. Box 1931
Santa Fe, New Mexico 87501
Phone: (505) 662-2200

NEW YORK (New York ABIC)

　　State Office:　Richardson Hall, Room 276
　　　　　　　　SUNY-Albany, Albany, N.Y. 12222
　　　　　　　　Phone: (518) 472-7110

NEVADA (Nevada ACLD)

　　Office of President:　4034 S. Great Plains Way
　　　　　　　　Las Vegas, Nevada 89121
　　　　　　　　Phone: (702) 458-1445; (702) 878-6841

NORTH CAROLINA (North Carolina ACLD)

　　State Office:　Box 1086
　　　　　　　　Kinston, North Carolina 28501
　　　　　　　　Phone: (919) 851-3968

NORTH DAKOTA (North Dakota ACLD)

　　State Office:　P.O. Box 36
　　　　　　　　Christine, North Dakota 58015
　　　　　　　　Phone: (701) 998-2947

OHIO (Ohio ACLD)

　　State Office:　333 W. National Road
　　　　　　　　Englewood, Ohio 45322
　　　　　　　　Phone: (513) 836-0415

OKLAHOMA (Oklahoma ACLD)

　　State Office:　3701 N.W. 62nd Street
　　　　　　　　Oklahoma City, Oklahoma 73112
　　　　　　　　Phone: (405) 943-9434

OREGON (Oregon ACLD)

　　Office of President:　Portland State University Special Education
　　　　　　　　Department, P.O. Box 751
　　　　　　　　Portland, Oregon 97207
　　　　　　　　Phone: (503) 229-4439

PENNSYLVANIA (Pennsylvania ACLD)

　　State Office:　P.O. Box 664
　　　　　　　　Allentown, Pennsylvania 18101
　　　　　　　　Phone: (215) 435-9386

PUERTO RICO (Puerto Rico ACLD)

　　Office of President:　El Monte Hall, Suite 11
　　　　　　　　Hato Rey, Puerto Rico 00918
　　　　　　　　Phone: (809) 765-4912

RHODE ISLAND (Rhode Island ACLD)

State Office: P.O. Box 6685
Providence, Rhode Island 02904

SOUTH CAROLINA (South Carolina ACLD)

Office of President: 115 Greenfield Drive
Greenville, South Carolina 29607
Phone: (803) 268-7573

SOUTH DAKOTA (South Dakota ACLD)

Office of President: 704 Valley View
Vermillion, South Dakota 57069
Phone: (605) 624-9139

TENNESSEE (Tennessee ACLD)

Office of President: 3911 Mallard Pt.
Memphis, Tennessee 38128
Phone: (901) 386-8556

TEXAS (Texas ACLD)

State Office: 7986 Fallmeadow Lane
Dallas, Texas 75240
Phone: (214) 239-4362

UTAH (Utah ACLD)

Office of President: 2327 Bryan Avenue
Salt Lake City, Utah 84108
Phone: (801) 582-6295

VERMONT (Vermont ACLD)

Office of President: 28 Crescent Street
Rutland, Vermont 05701
Phone: (802) 775-3042

VIRGIN ISLANDS (Virgin Islands ACLD)

Office of President: P.O. Box 3668
St. Thomas, Virgin Islands 00801

VIRGINIA (Virginia ACLD)

Office of President: 26 Langhorne Road
Newport News, Virginia 23606
Phone: (804) 596-5738

WASHINGTON (Washington ACLD)
  State Office: 217 9th North
                    Seattle, Washington 98109
                    Phone: (206) 682-2433

WEST VIRGINIA (West Virginia ACLD)
  Office of President: 1931 Seventh Ave.
                          St. Albans, West Virginia 25177
                          Phone: (304) 722-2254

WISCONSIN (Wisconsin ACLD)
  Office of President: P.O. Box 446
                          Stevens Point, Wisconsin 54481
                          Phone: (715) 369-3636

Index

Learning Disabilities in Home, School, and Community

was composed in 10-point Datapoint Times Roman, leaded two-points,
with display type in Univers Medium Condensed,
and printed on 55-pound White Bookmark Offset
by Science Press;
Smyth-sewn and bound over boards in Columbia Riverside Chambray
by Vail-Ballou Press, Inc.;
and published by

SYRACUSE UNIVERSITY PRESS
SYRACUSE, NEW YORK 13210